The New Sabin

The New Sabin;
Books Described by Joseph Sabin and His
Successors, Now Described Again on the
Basis of Examination of Originals,
and Fully Indexed by Title, Subject,
Joint Authors, and Institutions and Agencies

by

Lawrence S. Thompson

Entries 5803-8443

Volume III

The Whitston Publishing Company
Troy, New York
1976

To Harry Miller Lydenberg,

1874-1960

PREFACE

The New Sabin describes and indexes fully titles which are in the original work or which would have been eligible for the original work by its standards for inclusion and which are today in print in microform. The first two volumes recorded titles which are available on microfiche from the Lost Cause Press in Louisville. The third volume records titles available on 35 mm microfilm from the General Microfilm Company of Cambridge, Massachusetts. In addition to being on 35 mm microfilm, these titles are also available in eye-legible electrostatic copy.

This volume describes several groups of material which represent cornerstone collections in their areas. All are growing constantly, and future volumes of The New Sabin will record them. The cumulative indexes of The New Sabin (the first tentatively scheduled to go with the fifth volume) will ultimately reflect quite extensive collections in a number of different fields of Americana.

The Lincolniana (some 600 titles) includes a group of books, pamphlets, periodicals, and broadsides that are from one of the largest collections on Lincoln and his era in existence, that of Lincoln Memorial University in Harrogate, Tennessee. Few are in general research libraries which do not have special Lincoln collections, and many are absent evenin those libraries which have made a strong effort to collect Civil War materials. Some two decades ago the catalog of the LMU collection was checked against that of the University of Kentucky Library, which held most of the generally available Lincoln items, few of the rariora and less well known pieces. All titles not in Lexington were filmed, and thus it may reasonably be assumed that this collection will supplement effectively the average research library collection which has simply aimed at adequacy for reference purposes, not depth.

The Latin American periodicals recorded in this volume were selected from Sturgis E. Leavitt's Revistas hispanoamericanas; indice bibliográfico, 1843-1935 (1960), which indexes comprehensively the individual articles, reviews, and belletristic material in the most important journals of the Spanish American countries in the nineteenth and early twentieth centuries. About half of the journals indexed by Leavitt are recorded here, and future volumes of The New Sabin will record the others as they become available on film from the General Microfilm Company. At the same time, however, General Microfilm has made available many titles not indexed by Leavitt, and some are recorded here.

General Microfilm has also embarked on the ambitious project of filming systematically the titles recorded by José Toribio Medina in his Biblioteca hispano-americana as well as in his national and local bibliographies and titles which Medina would have recorded had he known them. This project is moving ahead rapidly, and at present some 500 titles from Medina are on film and are in this volume. No separate listing of the Medina titles has been made, since General Microfilm has short-title lists showing items on each roll and also issues catalog cards for all Medina titles available to date. The same is true of General Microfilm's other series.

Very substantial and rapidly growing collections of Canadiana and of Latin American travel and history issued by General Microfilm are in this volume. Many very rare titles are included, but also there are contemporary titles of importance. Many sets that are almost impossible to secure complete in the original are in this volume. A noteworthy example is the Voyage de Humboldt et Bonpland (23 v., 1805-1834), of which no truly complete set has appeared in the antiquarian book market for almost three decades. The microfilm edition had to be put together from the sets in two American and one European research library. Further, the microfilm edition of works such as the seventy-three volumes of Thwaites' Jesuit Relations and many basic nineteenth-century editions of works relating to the period of exploration and discovery are from the best copies of works that are often imperfect, mutilated, or on friable paper in the originals.

A final group is the microfilm edition of "Americana Not in Sabin" issued by General Microfilm. This group includes only some of the more obvious titles missed by Sabin and his successors. Ultimately it will include some tens of thousands of such titles.

As in the previous volumes, the entries in the present one often show inconsistent forms of capitalization, abbreviation, and punctuation, due to the fact that the cards copied for the microfilm editions from different libraries reflect varying policies over the years. But to paraphrase one distinguished bibliographer, form, however attractive and desirable, is secondary to the compiler's intentions, which must be perfectly clear at all times.

Lawrence S. Thompson
Lexington, Kentucky

5803 [Abad, Diego José] 1727-1779.
Breve descripcion de la fabrica, y adornos del
Templo de la Compañia de Jesus de Zacatecas; con
una succinta relacion de las fiestas con que se
solemnizò su dedicacion: sacanla a luz, y la
consagran al ss. patriarcha señor s. Joseph los
seis ilustres caballeros, patronos de la solemnidad, y lucimientos de la dedicacion. Mexico, Por
la viuda de d. Joseph Bernardo de Hogal, 1750.
15 p.l., 26 p., 1 l. 24 p., 1 l., 25-61, [1]
p., 1 l., 63-95, [22] p. 24 cm.
Error in pagination (1st group of paging):
p. 23-24 misnumbered 13-14.
Authorship of the "Breve descripcion" and
"Rasgo epico" attributed to Abad by Sommervogel,
Bibliothèque de la Compagnie de Jesus.

5804 Abad, Diego José, 1727-1779.
De Dios, y sus atributos. Poema dispuesto en
verso español... Barcelona, Francisco Suriá y
Burgada, 1788.
2 v. 24 cm.

5805 Abad, Diego José, 1727-1779.
Jacobi Josephi Labbe Selenopolitani De Deo
Deoque homine heroica. Editio altera, dimidio
auctior... Ferrariae, Apud Josephum Rinaldi,
1775.
xxxii, 237, [1] p. 23 cm.

5806 Abarca y Valda, José Mariano de, b. 1720.
Loa, y explicacion del arco, que la santa
Iglesia metropolitana de Mexico, para desempeno
de su amor, erigiò en la entrada que hizo a su
govierno el excelentissimo señor don Augustin de
Ahumada, y Villalon, marques de las Amarillas...
Escribiola don Joseph Mariano de Abarca, Valda,
y Velasquez... [Mexico] Con licencia en la im-

parenta nueva de la Bibliotheca mexicana, enfrente
de San Augustin, 1756.
8 p.   20 cm.

5807   Abarca y Valda, José Mariano de, b. 1720.
Ojo politico, idea cabal, y ajustada copia de
principes, que dió a luz la santa Iglesia metropolitana de Mexico, en el Magnifico arco, que
dedicó amorosa en la entrada que hizo a su govierno
el excelentissimo señor don Augustin de Ahumada,
y Villalon, marquès de las Amarillas... Escribiola
don Joseph Mariano de Abarca, Valda, y Velasquez...
[Mexico] Con licencia en la imprenta nueva de la
Bibliotheca mexicana, enfrente de S. Augustin,
1756.
[56] p.   22 cm.
Privileges signed: Ignacio Fernando Matheos y
Herrera; dr. d. Juan Miguel de Carballido, y
Cabuenas; señor dr. d. Francisco Xavier Gomez de
Cervantes.
Poetry, including verses by Pedro Joaquín
Medrano, Manuel Urrutia de Vergara y Estrada &
Josè Ignacio de Abarca y Valda: on p. [13]-[14].

5808   Abascal, Valentin.
Santiago de los Caballeros de Goathemala.
Guatemala, Centro Editorial del Ministerio de
Educación Pública, "José de Pineda Ibarra", 1961.
237 p.   illus.   21 cm.

5809   Abbeville, Claude d', fl. 1614.
Histoire de la mission des pères capvcins en
l'Isle de Maragnan et terres circonvoysines...
Paris, François Hvby, 1614.
[423] p.   18 1/2 cm.

5810   Abbot, Abiel, 1770-1828.
Cartas, escritas en el interior de Cuba, entre
las montañas de Arcana, en el este, y las de Cusco,
al oeste, en los meses de Febrero, Marzo, Abril y
Mayo de 1828. Traducción de José Vander Gucht.
La Habana, Consejo Nacional de Cultura, 1965.
378 p.   11 cm.

5811   Abbot, Willis John, 1863-1934.

Panama and the canal in picture and prose...
by Willis J. Abbot ... Water-colors by E. J.
Read and Gordon Grant; profusely illustrated by
over 600 unique and attractive photographs taken
expressly for this book by our special staff.
London, New York [etc.] Pub. in English and Spanish by Syndicate publishing company, 1913.
1 p.l., 412 p. front. (fold. map), illus.,
col. plates. 29 1/2 cm.

5812 Aborigines' Protection Society, London.
Canada west and Hudson's-Bay company; a political and humane question of vital importance to
the prosperity of Canada, and to the existence
of the native tribes; being an address to the
Right Honorable Henry Labouchere... presented
by the Aborigines' Protection Society... London,
Printed for the Society by William Tweedie, 1856.
19 p. 22 cm.

5813 Aborigines' Protection Society, London.
The Red River insurrection: three letters and
a narrative of events. London, Aborigines' Protection Society, 1870.
28 p. 18 cm.

5814 Abraham Lincoln: a study... Liverpool, McKowen
& Finglass, 1865.
32 p. 18 cm.

5815 Abraham Lincoln Association, Springfield, Ill.
... Bulletin, no. 1-58. December 20, 1923-
December, 1939. Springfield, 1923-1939.
58 nos. 19-30 cm.
Indices follow nos. 50 & 58.
Continued by Abraham Lincoln quarterly.

5816 Abraham Lincoln Association, Springfield, Ill.
Lincoln in Springfield, a guide to the places
in Springfield which were associated with the
life of Abraham Lincoln. Pub. by the Lincoln
Centennial Association; sketches by Virginia Stuart
Brown. [Springfield, c1925]
[30] p. map. 19 cm.

5817　Abraham Lincoln Centre and All Souls Church,
　　　　Chicago.
　　　　　The Abraham Lincoln Centre and All Souls
　　　　Church annual reports of 1908, with an account
　　　　of the Lincoln centennial, February 7-13, 1909.
　　　　Chicago, Abraham Lincoln Centre, 1909.
　　　　105 p.　illus.　22 cm.

5818　Abraham Lincoln Foundation, New York.
　　　　　Statement of the purpose and plans of the
　　　　Abraham Lincoln Foundation and the Abraham
　　　　Lincoln university.　New York, Abraham Lincoln
　　　　Foundation [c1929]
　　　　37 p.　20 cm.

5819　Abraham Lincoln Memorial Garden, Springfield, Ill.
　　　　　The prilgrimage tour:　tour of Lincoln shrines,
　　　　Springfield, Ill., May 4-5, 1954.　Springfield,
　　　　Abraham Lincoln Memorial Garden Foundation [1954?]
　　　　[8] p.　illus.　22 cm.

5820　Abraham Lincoln Memorial Highway Association.
　　　　　Historic proofs and data in support of the
　　　　Lincoln Way, being the route traveled by the
　　　　Thomas Lincoln family in coming from Indiana to
　　　　Illinois in the year 1830, for submission to the
　　　　Governor of the State of Illinois and the Depart-
　　　　ment of Public Works and Buildings of the State
　　　　of Illinois.　Greenup, Ill., 1929.
　　　　57 p.　illus., ports., fold. map.　21 cm.

5821　Abraham Lincoln quarterly.　v. 1-7; Mar. 1940-
　　　　Dec. 1952 [Springfield, Ill.]　Abraham Lincoln
　　　　Association, 1940-1952.
　　　　7 v.　plates, ports., facsims.　24 cm.

5822　Abraham Lincoln University (proposed)
　　　　　Abraham Lincoln University, Springfield, Ill.
　　　　[Springfield?, n.d.]
　　　　32 p.　illus.　21 cm.

5823　Abraham Lincoln's last case in Chicago.　[n.p.]
　　　　Barnard and Miller [1933]
　　　　11p.　illus.　20 cm.

5824 Abramo Lincoln: com ei visse, qual opera compie,
      qual fu la sua morte. Firenze, Tipografia
      Claudiana, 1866.
         68 p.   21 cm.

5825 Acereto, Albino.
         Evolución histórica de la relaciones políticas
      entre Mexico y Yucatán por Albino Acereto.
      Mexico, Imprenta Müller hnos., 1907.
         xxii, 124 p., 2 l.   20 cm.

5826 The Acme Haversack's Lincoln memoranda... Sum-
      mary of the inspiration he has bequeathed; con-
      densed history of his life, with due details of
      his lowly days in poverty; and forty quotations
      from his immortal eloquence... Syracuse, N. Y.,
      Acme Haversack [n.d.]
         50-63 p.   port.

5827 Acosta, José de, 1539 (ca.)-1600.
         Historia natural y moral de las Indias, escrita
      por el p. Joseph de Acosta, de la Compañia de
      Jesus. Publicada en Sevilla en 1590. Y ahora
      fielmente reimpresa de la primera edición. Ma-
      drid [R. Anglés, impr.] 1894.
         2 v. in l.   19 cm.

5828 Acta in Commitijs Provincialibus Angelopolitanae
      Sancti Michaelis, et Sanctorum Angelorum Pro-
      vinciae Ordinis Praedicatorum... die vigesima
      Mensis Maij Anno Domini M.DCC. LXXV... Puebla,
      Herederos Viuda Miguel de Ortega Bonilla [1775]
         22 p.   21 cm.

5829 Acta Provincialis, S. Michaelis Archāg and SS.
      Angelorum Provinciae Ordinis Praedicatorum, in
      Commitijs habltis [?] in Convento S.P.N.
      Dominici Angelopolitano, die 20 Maij anni 1724
      ... [Puebla, 1724]
         40 p.   22 cm.

5830 Adam y Arriaga, José, d. 1698.
         Imperialis Mexicana vniversitas illvstrata
      ipsius per constitvtionvm scholia, academico
      generali commentario, theorico practico, fvnda-

tionis, patronatvs, institvti, privilegiorvm,
exemptionum consvetvdinv, pontificij, ac caesarej
vniversi ivris stvdia concernentis, et rervm eivis
insignivm. Avthore d. Iosepho Adame et Arriaga...
Cvm geminato elencho eorum, quae in constitutionum
textibus, & quae in elucidario eorum continentur,
Hispali, Ex typographia haeredvm Thomae Lopez de
Haro, 1698.
    16 p.l., 907 (i.e. 887), 108 p.   26 cm.
    Errors in pagination: p. 865-887 misnumbered
885-907; in second group of paging, no. 52-53 repeated, no. 55-58 omitted. Several other pages
are incorrectly numbered.
    Privileges signed in Mexico by J. de Olachea, F.
de Aguilar, L. Mendes, J. de Miranda, J. de Torres.

5831 Adams, Charles Francis, 1835-1915.
        Richard Henry Dana, a biography, by Charles
      Francis Adams ... Boston and New York, Houghton
      Mifflin and company, 1890.
        2 v. fronts. (ports.)   20 1/2 cm.

5832 Adams, George Everett, 1840-
        Lincoln; address delivered at Quincy, Ill.,
      Tuesday, October 13, 1908, before the State His-
      torical Society of Illinois... Peterboro, N. H.,
      Transcript co., 1908.
        12 p.   22 cm.

5833 Adams, George Everett, 1840-
        Lincoln: address delivered in Chicago, Feb.
      9, 1909, before Columbus post, G.A.R. ...
      [Chicago? 1909?]
        11 p.   22 cm.

5834 Adams, Horace.
        ... Thaddeus H. Caraway in the United States
      Senate... Nashville, Tenn., George Peabody Col-
      lege for Teachers, 1935.
        7 p.   23 1/2 cm. (Abstracts of Contributions
      to education, No. 166)

5835 Adams, John Merriman, 1834-
        A history of the Adams and Evarts families...
      Chatham, N. Y., The Courier printing house, 1894.

1 p.l., [5]-81, [1] p., 1 1.   22 cm.

5836 Adams, Randolph Greenfield, 1892-
       Hudibrastic aspects of some editions of the
      Emancipation Proclamation [by] Randolph G.
      Adams ... Philadelphia, 1946.
       1 p.l., 11-17 p.   23 cm.

5837 Adams, W   L
       Lecture on Oregon and the Pacific coast...
      Boston, Isaac W. May, 1869.
       39 p.   22 cm.

5838 Address to the people of the United States, recom-
      mending the re-election of Abraham Lincoln to
      the presidency. New York, Sanford, Harroun &
      co., printers, 1864.
       cover-title, 7 p.   21 1/2 cm.

5839 Addresses and memorials, together with articles,
      reports, &c., &c. from the public journals,
      upon the occasion of the retirement of Sir James
      Douglas, K.C.B., from the governorship of the
      colonies of Vancouver's Island and British Columbia.
      Deal, Edward Hayward, Victoria printing office,
      1864.
       74 p.   21 cm.

5840 Adelman, David C
       Life and times of Judah Touro. Tercentenary
      address... delivered before the officers and
      members of the Touro Fraternal Association.
      [Providence, R.I.?] Published by the Touro
      Fraternal Association, 1936.
       13 p. front. (port.), illus., facsims.

5841 Adet, Pierre-Auguste, 1763-1834.
       The gros mousqueton diplomatique, or, diplomatic
      blunderbuss, containing Citizen Adet's notes to
      the secretary of state, as also his cockade pro-
      clamation, with a preface by Peter Porcupine
      [pseud.] Philadelphia, W. Cobbett, 1796.
       vi, 5-72 p.   21 1/2 cm.

5842 After Dinner Club, Moline, Ill.

The After Dinner Club, Moline, Ill.: thirty-
first dinner, Moline Club, Monday, February 12,
1912... [Moline, 1912]
[7] p.   17 1/2 x 14 cm.

5843   After Dinner Club, Moline, Ill.
The After Dinner Club, Moline, Ill.: eighty-
seventh dinner, Moline Commercial Club, Monday,
February 10, 1919... [Moline, 1919]
[9] p.   20 cm.

5844   Agresti, Antonio, 1866-1927.
... Abramo Lincoln nel primo centenario della
sua nascita. Roma, 1909.
15 p. illus. (ports.)   30 cm.

5845   Aguas termales de Cartago, Costa-Rica. Fuente
mineral caliente 55⁰ c.ó sea 131⁰ far. Obsequio
á los accionistas, fundadores de esta humanitaria
institución. San José, Costa-Rica, America Central, Imprenta de J. Canalías, 1886.
1 p.l., 15, xiv, 16, [7], [17]-36, [8], [35]-
114, [16] p.   20 cm.

5846   Aguero y Sota, Baltasar de.
Conclusiones in repetitione agitandae...
Defendentvr in Regali ac Pontificio S. Caroli
Mvsaeo a Lic. D. Balthasare de Agvero et Sota
Limanae ac huius Regalis Chancellariae Causidico
... Die Mensis Ianuarij anno 1690. Goaotemalae,
Apud Antonium de Pineda, & Ybarra Typographum
[1690]
1 l. illus.   28 cm.

5847   Aguilar, Federico Cornelio, 1834-1887.
Ultimo año de residencia en México, por el
presbítero doctor Federico C. Aguilar. Bogotá,
Impr. de I. Borda, 1885.
263 p.   23 cm.

5848   Aguirre, José M
Uncle Sam in pontifical robes, John Bull destitute
of attire, and other conspicuous figures in native
costumes. An open letter to the great American
statesman and illustrious Republican leader, James

G. Blaine, on national and international politics,
and the grand idea of a continental confederation
of peace. With views on England and her historic
relations toward other countries. By J. M. Aguirre.
New York. G. W. Dillingham, successor to G. W.
Carleton & co., 1888.
2 p.l., iii-xxiv, [25]-235 p. 19 1/2 cm.

5849 Aguirre, Juan Francisco, d. 1811.
Diario de Aguirre...
(In Buenos Aires. Biblioteca nacional. Anales.
Buenos Aires, 1900- 27 cm. t. 4 (1905)
p. [ix]-xi, 1-271; t. 7 [1911])

5850 Aked, Charles Frederic, 1864-
Abraham Lincoln, man of God; a sermon preached
... February 12, 1939, All Souls Church, Los
Angeles, California. Los Angeles, 1939.
14 p. 20 cm.

5851 Album mexicano, colección de paisajes, monumentos,
costumbres y ciudades principales de la república,
litografiadas por C. Castro, A. Gallice, M. Mohar
[y otros] ... Mexico, Antigua litografia Debray
suc., C. Montauriol [18]
v. plates (part col.) 24 x 34 1/2 cm.

5852 Alcalá Galiano, Dionisio de, 1760-1805.
Memoria sobre las observaciones de latitud y
longitud en el mar... [Madrid] Viuda de D.
Joachim Ibarra, 1796.
87 p. tables. 23 cm.

5853 Alcazar y Zúñiga, Andres del, conde de la Marquina.
El Benjamin de la ss.ma trinidad, y niñas de
sus ojos, la gracia; y la descripcion del hombre
... Sevilla, Francisco de Leesdel, 1721.
unpaged. 20 cm.

5854 Alcazar y Zúñiga, Andres del, conde de la Marquina.
Satisfacion, y descargos, qve el maestro de
campo D. Andres del Alcazar y Zúñiga... dio a los
cargos, qve se le formaron en Madrid... en la
confianca, y privativa disposicion... las seis
fragatas de guerra de Francia, qve con nombre de

flota fueron a la Nueva España con la capitana de
Barlovento, a cargo del almirante general, D.
Andres de Pez, el año passado de 1708. [Sevilla?
1709?]
   58 p.   22 cm.

5855 Alcedo y Herrera, Dionisio de, 1690-1777.
      Memorial informativo que pusieron en las reales
   manos... el Tribunal del consulado de la ciudad
   de Los Reyes y la Junta general de comercio de
   las provincias del Perú... [n.p., ca. 1730?]
      157 p.   24 cm.

5856 Alcocer y Sasinana, Baltasar De.
      Exequias a la translacion de los huessos de
   los... obispos de la santa yglesia de Oaxaca.
   [n.p.] 1702.
      10 p.l., 10 numb. 1 illus.   20 cm.

5857 Alcover y Beltrán, Antonio Miguel, 1875-
      Historia de la villa de Sagua la Grande y su
   jurisdicción; documentos - apuntes - reseñas -
   monografías - consideraciones, por Antonio Miguel
   Alcover y Betrán.   Obra subvencionada por el
   Ayuntamiento de Sagua y llevada a cabo por suscrip-
   ción popular.   Sagua la Grande, Imprentas unidas
   "La Historia" y "El Correo español," 1905.
      592, [14] p.   front., illus., plates, ports.,
   plans.   25 cm.

5858 Aldao, Carlos A   , 1860-
      ... Miranda y los origenes de la independencia
   americana, seguido de la traducción de The history of Don Francisco de Miranda's attempt to
   effect a rovolution [!] in South America, by a
   gentleman who was an officer under that general.
   Por Carlos A. Aldao.   Buenos Aires, Talleres
   gráficos argentinos de L. J. Rosso, 1928.
      129 p., 1 l. illus. (facsim.)   19 1/2 cm.

5859 Aldrich, Julia Carter.
      A memory of eighteen hundred sixty-five; a
   tribute to Abraham Lincoln.   Wauseon, O., Kenyon
   & Weir, 1914.
      [3] p.   26 cm.

5860 Aldrich, Lewis Cass.
History of Franklin and Grand Isle counties,
Vermont... Syracuse, N.Y., D. Mason & co.,
1891.
821 p. pl., port. 25 1/2 cm.

5861 Alemán, Mateo, 1547-1614?
Primera, y segunda parte de la vida, y hechos
del picaro Guzman de Alfarache, escrita por
Matheo Aleman ... Dedicado al señor don Joseph
Bermudez ... Corr. y enmendado en esta impresion.
Año 1750. En Madrid: En la imprenta de Lorenzo
Francisco Mojados, impreso a su costa.
4 p.l., 476 p. 25 cm.

5862 Alemán, Mateo, 1547-1614?
Vida, y hechos del picaro Guzman de Alfarache.
Atalaya de la vida humana. Por Mateo Aleman.
Parte primera [-segunda] En Valencia: Por
Joseph, y Thomas de Orga. M.DCC.LXXIII. Con
las licencias necessarias. Se hallara en la
librería de Diego Mallén.
v. 1: 10 p.l., 452, [4] p. front.; v. 2: 8 p.l.,
596, [4] p. 25 cm.

5863 Alexander, Sir James Edward, 1803-1885.
The burning of the St. Louis theatre, Quebec.
A record of the eminent services of the military.
By Sir J. E. Alexander... [Quebec, 1846]
8 p. illus. 20 cm.

5864 Alfaro, Francisco de, 16th cent.
... Tractatus de officio fiscalis, deque
fiscalibus priuilegiis... Vallesoleti, apud
Ludouicum Sanchez [1606]
[8], 362, 65 p. 25 cm.

5865 Allan, Dorothy Carter, 1896-
A birthday present for Lincoln; a play in one
act. Boston, Walter H. Baker co., 1932.
16 p. 18 cm.

5866 Allen, Ethan, 1796-1879.
A discourse prepared for the national fast day,
June 1st, 1865, on account of the murder of our

11

late president, and preached at St. Thomas'
church, Homestead, Baltimore County, Md.
Baltimore, Wm. K. Boyle, 1865.
12 p.   19 cm.

5867   Allen, Lyman Whitney, 1854-1930.
Abraham Lincoln; a poem. 2d ed. New York,
Putnam, 1896.
vi, 122 p.   19 cm.

5868   Allen, Lyman Whitney, 1854-1930.
An epic trilogy... by Lyman Whitney Allen...
New York, Thornton W. Allen company, 1929.
3 v.   fronts., ports.   19 1/2 cm.

5869   Allen, Lyman Whitney, 1854-1930.
The Lincoln pew. [President Lincoln's pew is
in the New York Avenue Presbyterian church of
Washington, D.C.] [n.p., n.d.]
4 p.   20 cm.

5870   Alloza, Juan de, 1598-1666.
Flores svmmarvm, sev Alphabetvm morale, omnium
serè casuum qui confessoribus contingere possunt,
ex selectioribvs doctoribvs praecipuè Societatis
Iesv, ex vtroque iure, ac manuscriptis peruanis.
Opus sedulo labore per annos triginta conquisitum, ex
legibus imperatorum, decretis pontificum, vsu
parachorum, & praetorum huius Peruani regni.
Authore r. p. Ioanne de Alloza... Lvgdvni, sumpt.
H. Boissat, & G. Remevs, 1666.
7 p.l., 781 p.   25 cm.

5871   [Allston, Robert Francis Withers] 1801-1864.
Rules and history of the Hot and Hot Fish Club
and All Saints Parish, South Carolina. Lexington, Ky., Erasmus Press, 1973.
15 p.   22 cm.
Reprint of 1860 edition.

5872   Almanacs. Nova Scotia.
The Nova-Scotia calendar, or an almanack for
the year of the Christian aera, 1770... By A.
Lilius. Halifax, Anthony Henry [1768]
25 p.   16 mo.

5873 Almanacs.   Nova Scotia.
The Nova-Scotia calendar, or an almanack for
the year of the Christian aera, 1771... By A.
Lilius.   Halifax, Anthony Henry [1769]
32 p.   16 mo.

5874 [Alonso de San Juan] supposed author.
Relacion breve y verdadera de algunas cosas de
las muchas que sucedieron al padre fray Alonso
Ponce en las provincias de la Nueva España, siendo
comisario general de aquellas partes.   Trátanse
algunas particularidades de aquella tierra, y
dícese su ida á ella y vuelta á España, con algo
de lo que en el viaje le aconteció hasta volver á
su provincia de Castilla.   Escrita por dos religiosos,
sus compañeros, el uno de los cuales le acompaño
desde España á México, y el otro en todos los demás
caminos que hizo y trabajos que pasó.   Madrid,
Impr. de la Viuda de Calero, 1873.
2 v.   plate.   23 cm.
Indice de la crónica de fray Alonso Ponce [por]
Grace Metcalfe.   México, 1946.
56-84 p.   24 cm.
Indice clasificado [por] Raúl Guerrero.   México,
Vargas Bea [i.e. Rea] 1949.
86 p.   20 cm.

5875 Alpizar Caire, Ramón.
México arqueológico.   [México] Petróleos Mexicanos
[1948]
76 p.   illus.   22 cm.

5876 Altamira, Juan Rodríguez de Albuerne, marqués de.
Puntos de parecer que el sr. marques de Altamira
expusiera al excelentísimo señor virrey conde de
Fuenclara el 4 de julio de 1744, con motivo de su
viaje a las provincias internas.   [México, Vargas
Rea] 1943.
[33] p.   fold. map.   24 cm.

5877 Altamirano, Diego.
Por don Carlos Colón de Córdoua Bocanegra y
Pacheco... contra don Alvaro Colón de Portugal
... y don Luis Colón de Toledo.   [n.p., 165]
[9] l.   20 cm.

13

5878   Alva y Astorga, Pedro de, d. 1667.
        Militia immaculatae conceptionis Virginis
     Mariae, contra malitiam originalis infectionis
     peccati. In qua ordine alphabetico recensentur
     auctores antiqui & moderni, saneti & alij, eccle-
     siastici & saeculares, ex omni statu ac natione,
     que clare & expresse, aut insinuative & obscure
     locuti sunt in individuo de ipsa praeservatione,
     vel formali conceptionis atque animationis instanti;
     aut universaliter de incontaminata ab omni macula,
     naevo, labe, & defectu, vel aliquid singulare in
     honerem virginalis immunitatis molitici fuerunt.
     Compilata ac disposita a r.a.p.f. Petro de Alva et
     Astorga... Cum permissu superiorum. In typographia
     immaculatae conceptionis Lovanij, sub signo Gratiae,
     anno 1663.
        28 p.l., 1534 (i.e. 1536) col. illus. (coat of
     arms)   26 cm.

5879   Alva y Astorga, Pedro de, d. 1667.
        Sol veritatis, cvm ventilabro seraphico, pro
     candida Aurora Maria in suo conceptionis ortu
     saneta, pura, immaculata, & a peccato originali
     praeseruata. Tritvrando auctores opinionis
     aduersae sexaginta antiquos atque modernos,
     opuscula omnia, libros, tractatus, sermones, atque
     quaestiones. Ventilando opera allegata trecentorvm
     qvindecim ecclesiae doctorum stylo positiuo,
     scholastico, historico, necnon apologetico.
     Separat ab ipsorum sexcentis qvadraginta auctor-
     itatibus lucem à tenebris, granum à paleis, &
     triticum a zizaniis, &c. Studio, ac labore.
     r.p.f. Petri de Alva & Astorga... [Colophon:
     Impresso Matriti ex typhographia Pauli de Val,
     anno M.DC.LX]
        18 p.l., 888, 12 p. front.   26 cm.
        Errors in pagination: nos. 105-106 omitted,
     nos. 144-145 repeated; several other pages mis-
     numbered.

5880   Alvarado Pinto, Carlos Román.
        Rapsodia de recuerdos. Guatemala [Editorial de
     Ejército] 1967.
        103 p. illus.   22 cm.

5881   Alvarado Tezozomoc, Fernando, fl. 1598.
        Crónica mexicana, escrita por d. Hernando
        Alvarado Tezozomoc hácia el año de MDCXCVIII.
        Anotada por el. sr. lic. d. Manuel Orozco y Berra,
        y precedida del Códice Ramirez, manuscrito del
        siglo XVI intitulado: Relación del origen de
        los Indios que habitan esta Nueva España según sus
        historias. Y de un examen de ambas obras, al cual
        va anexo un estudio de cronología mexicana por el
        mismo sr. Orozco y Berra. José M. Vigil, editor.
        México, Impr. y litog. de I. Paz, 1878.
        viii, [9]-712 p. 16 pl. 29 cm.

5882   Alvarez de Velasco, Gabriel, fl. 1650.
        D. d. Gabrielis de Velasco, Vallesoletani, Novi
        Regni Granatensis senatoris; De privilegiis
        pauperum et miserabilium personarum ad legem
        unicam eod. quando imperator inter pupillos &
        viduas, aliasque miserabiles personas cognoscat.
        Tractatus in duas partes divisus. Editie tertia.
        Accedunt Joannis Mariae Novarii jurisconsulti
        Lucani, De privilegiis miserabilium personarum
        item de incertorum et male ablatorum privilegiis
        tractatus duo. Opera juris studiosis et in fo o ver-
        santibus omnino necessaria, ac bonarum literarum
        sectatoribus accomadatissima. Tomus primus [-se-
        cundus] Lausonii & coloniae Allobroqum, samptibus
        Marci-Michaelis Bousqet et sociorum, 1739.
        2 v.   27 cm.

5883   Alvarez de Velasco, Gabriel, fl. 1650.
        Epitoma de legis hvmane, mvndiqve fictione,
        veritatis divinae, aeterni, temporalisque dif-
        ferentia, nunc primum prodit. Lvgdvni, sumptibus
        Horatii Boissat & Georgii Remevs, 1662.
        416, [72] p.   25 cm.

5884   Alvarez, José Justo, 1821-1897.
        Itinerarios y derroteros de la República Mexicana,
        publicados por los ayudantes del Estado mayor del
        ejército, José J. Alvarez y Rafael Durán. México,
        Impr. de J. A. Godoy, 1856.
        480, [4] p.   22 cm.

5885   Alvin, Juan.

Memorial regvlar, y veridico, qve pone en las
reales manos de V. Magestad el ministro general
de toda la Orden de s. Francisco fray Jvan Alvin,
en qve representa la svprema, y ordinaria autoridad, que tiene vniuersalmente sobre todos los
frayles de esta orden, y la especial, que tiene
sobre los comissarios generales de la familia,
y de Indias, y sus gouiernos; sobre los procuradores,
y agentes de la Curia romana, y cortes de los
reyes, y sobre el vice-comissario de Indias de
Sevilla. Y manifiesta las irregvlares preten-
siones contenidas en vn memorial de el comissario
general de Indias fray Julian Chumillas. [n.p.,
169-?]
   1 p.l., 28 numb. l. 22 cm.

5886 Amat y Junient, Manuel de, viceroy of Peru, 18th
    cent.
    Don Manuel de Amat y Junient... Por quanto el
rey nuestro señor, por su real orden, de S.
Ildefonso à 24. de agosto de 1765. me manda
aplicar el mayor zelo á la instruccion, y arreglo
de los cuerpos de milicias del reyno... [Lima,
1766]
   7 p. 22 cm.

5887 American Autograph Shop, Merion Station, Pa.
    Lincoln: a good son... Merion Station, Pa.,
American Autograph Shop, 1940.
   [4] p. 20 cm.

5888 American Institute of Mining, Metallurgical, and
    Petroleum Engineers.
    In Mexico with the special trains, November,
1901. [n.p., 1902?]
   cover-title, 59 p. illus., port., map. 26 cm.

5889 American notes & queries; a journal for the cur-
    ious. v. 1-8, Apr. 1941-Mar. 1950. [New York,
1941-1950]
   8 v. 24 cm.

5890 Ames, Fisher, 1758-1808.
    Speeches of Fisher Ames in Congress, 1789-1796.
Ed. by Pelham W. Ames. Boston, Little, Brown,

and company, 1871.
166 p.   24 1/2 cm.

5891   Ampère, Jean Jacques Antoine, 1800-1864.
Promenade en Amériqve; Etats-Unis - Cuba -
Mexique...   Nouv. éd., entièrement rév. ...
Paris, Michel Lévy Frères, 1856.
2 v.   22 cm.

5892   Amunátegui, Miguel Luis, 1828-1888.
... La dictadura de O'Higgins.   Madrid, Editorial-América [1917?]
400 p.   23 cm.

5893   Amunátegui, Miguel Luis, 1828-1888.
... La reconquista española de Chile en 1814.
Madrid, Editorial-América [1922]
449 p., 1 1.   22 cm.

5894   [Anburey, Thomas]
Journal d'un voyage fait dans l'intérieur de
l'Amérique Septentrionale.   Ouvrage dans lequel
on donne des détails précieux sur l'insurrection
des Anglo-Américains, et sur la chute désastreuse
de leur papier-monnoie.   Tr. de l'anglois et
enrichi de notes par M. Noël ...   Paris, La
Villette, 1793.
2 v.   2 pl. (1 fold.), fold. map, fold. plan.
22 1/2 cm.

5895   [Anburey, Thomas]
Voyages dans les parties intérieures de l'Amérique, pendant le cours de la dernière guerre, par un
officier de l'armée royale.   Tr. de l'anglois, par
M. Lebas ...   Paris, Briand, 1792.
2 v.   fold. map.   19 1/2 cm.

5896   Anderson, Alexander Caulfield.
A brief account of the province of British
Columbia, its climate and resources.   An appendix
to the British Columbia directory, 1882-82...
Victoria, B.C., Published by B. T. Williams, 1883.
33 p.   illus., fold. map.   20 cm.

5897   Anderson, Alexander Caulfield.

The dominion at the west. A brief description of the province of British Columbia, its
climate and resources... Victoria, B.C.,
Printed by Richard Wolfenden, government printer,
1872.
iv, 112, xlii p. 20 cm.

5898 Anderson, Alexander Caulfield.
Hand-book and map of the gold region of Frazer's
and Thompson's rivers, with table of distances...
to which is appended Chinook jargon - language used
etc., etc. San Francisco, Published by J. J. Le
Count [1858]
31 p. 17 cm.

5899 Anderson, Alexander Caulfield.
Notes on north-western America, by Alexander
Caulfield Anderson... Montreal, Mitchell &
Wilson, printers, 1876.
cover-title, 22 p. 22 cm.

5900 Anderson, Alexander Caulfield.
... Notes on the Indian tribes of British
North America, and the northwest coast. Communi-
cated to Geo. Gibbs, esq. by Alex. C. Anderson,
esq., late of the hon. H. B. Co., and read before
the New York historical society. November, 1862.
[New York, 1863]
[73]-81 p. 24 x 18 1/2 cm.
Reprinted from the Historical magazine...
V.7, no. 3.

5901 Anderson, Barbara.
Farmington's chapter in the Lincoln story.
Louisville, Ky., Historic Homes Foundation,
1959.
16 p. illus. 20 cm.

5902 Anderson, Charles Palmerston, bp., 1863-1930.
The Grand Army Hall and Memorial Association
of Illinois; Nineteenth Lincoln birthday service,
Memorial Hall, Chicago... February 12th, 1918;
address by Rt. Rev. Charles P. Anderson. [Chicago?
G.A.R., 1918]
29 p. 21 cm.

5903   Anderson, David.
        A charge delivered to the clergy of the diocese
of Rupert's Land at his primary visitation.
London, T. Hatchard, 1851.
      48, 12 p.

5904   [Anderson, David]
        Notes of the flood at the Red River, 1852. By
the bishop of Rupert's Land. London, Hatchard,
1851.
      124 p.   22 cm.

5905   Anderson, Homer.
        Where I saw Lincoln: address of the sixth
annual Lincoln banquet, February 12, 1909. By
Homer Anderson, first vice president of Lincoln
society, Peekskill, N. Y. (Corporal, Co. I, 90
Reg. O.V.I.) Peekskill, N. Y., 1909.
      cover-title, [12] p. port.   17 1/2 cm.
      Portrait on p. [2] of cover.

5906   Anderson, John T
        Address of the democratic members of the leg-
islature to the people of Virginia. [Richmond?
1836?]
      24 p.   21 cm.

5907   Andrade, Alonso de, 1590-1672.
        Varones ilvstres en santidad, letras, y zelo de
las almas. De la Compañia de Iesvs. Tomo qvinto,
a los qvatro qve saco a lvz el venerable, y erudito
padre Iuan Eusebio Nieremberg ... Por el padre
Alonso de Andrade ... Dedicale al ilvstrissimo
señor don Andres Brauo ... Madrid, Por Ioseph
Fernandez de Buendia, 1666.
      6 p.l., 863 (i.e. 867) p.   28 cm.

5908   Andrews, George.
        Genealogy of the Andrews of Taunton and Stoughton,
Mass.; descendants of John and Hannah Andrews of
Boston, Mass., 1656-1886. Rochester, N. Y., E. R.
Andrews, printer, 1887.
      86 p.   22 cm.

5909   Anghiera, Pietro Martire d', 1455-1526.

Décadas del Nuevo Mundo, vertidas del latín
a la lengua castellana por el Dr. D. Joaquín
Torres Asensio... Buenos Aires, Editorial
Bajel, 1944.
lii, 675 p.   24 cm.

5910   Angle, Paul McClelland, 1900-
Dedication of Abraham Lincoln's post office, New
Salem state park, February 12, 1940. [n.p.,
1940]
[4] p.   22 cm.

5911   Angle, Paul McClelland, 1900-
The foundations of Lincoln's fame; an address
delivered at Carleton College, February 15,
1939. [Northfield, Minn.? Carleton College
1939]
15 p.   20 cm.

5912   Ann Rutledge: heart story of the early Lincoln.
Philadelphia, Pa. [n.d.]
112 p.   21 cm.

5913   Anti-Jackson Convention, Richmond, Va., 8 January
1828.
Proceedings of the Anti-Jackson convention,
held at the capitol, in the city of Richmond
with their address to the people of Virginia
(accompanied by documents) Richmond, Printed by
Samuel Shepherd and co., 1828.
38 p.   21 cm.

5914   Anti-Van Buren members of the General Assembly of
Virginia.
Address of the Anti-Van Buren members of the
general Assembly... to the people of Virginia...
[Richmond, Va.? 1836?]
15 p.   21 cm.

5915   Apolla, Arnaldo, 1879-
Nell'America del Nord. Impressioni di viaggio
in Alaska, State Uniti e Canada. Con illustra-
zioni fuori testo e carta geografica. Torino,
G. B. Paravia, 1926.
344 p. illus., fold. col. map.   20 cm.

5916 Appleton's hand-book of American travel. Containing a full description of the principal
cities, towns, and places of interest: together
with the routes of travel, and leading hotels
throughout the United States and British provinces. By Edward H. Hall ... 9th annual ed.
New York, London, D. Appleton & company, 1869.
xvi, 467, [1], 51 p. 17 fold. maps (incl.
front.) 19 cm.

5917 Appleton's hand-book of American travel. Northern
and eastern tour. Including New York, New Jersey,
Pennsylvania, Connecticut, Rhode Island, Massachusetts, Maine, New Hampshire, Vermont, and the
British dominions ... Revised for summer of
1873, with appendix. New York, D. Appleton and
company; [etc., etc.] 1873.
x, 294 p. front. (fold. map), fold. plans.
19 1/2 cm.

5918 Appleton's illustrated hand-book of American travel:
a full and reliable guide ... to ... the United
States and the British provinces. By T. Addison
Richards. With careful maps of all parts of the
country, and pictures of famous places and scenes,
from original drawings by the author and other
artists ... New York, D. Appleton & co.; [etc.,
etc.] 1857.
420 p. fold. front., illus., fold. maps, fold.
plans. 20 cm.

5919 Araoz de la Madrid, Gregorio, 1795-1857.
... Memorias del general Gregorio Araoz de la
Madrid. Madrid, Editorial-América [1921?]
2 p.l., [7]-415, [1] p. 22 1/2 cm.

5920 Arber, Edward, 1836-1912, ed.
The first three English books on America
[?1511]-1555A.D. Being chiefly translations,
compilations, &c. by Richard Eden, from the
writings, maps, &c., of Pietro Martire, of
Anghiera... Sebastian Münster... Sebastion Cabot...
Birmingham, 1885.
xlviii, 408 p. 29 x 23 cm.

5921 Arce, Francisco de.
        ... Impresiones sobre Guatemala. Apuntes de
    viaje. Guatemala, Tipografía nacional, 1907.
    [3], ii, 40 p. plates, port. 18 1/2 cm.

5922 Argow, Wendelin Waldermar Wieland, 1891-
        "Was Abraham Lincoln a Christian?" being an
    address delivered in the People's church, Cedar
    Rapids, Iowa... February 12, 1922. [Cedar
    Rapids, Torch press, 1922]
        7 p. 19 cm.

5923 Arguedas, Alcides, 1879-1946.
        ... Historia de Bolivia; la fundación de la
    república. Madrid, Editorial-América [1920]
        3 p.l., [9]-386 p. 23 cm.

5924 [Argyll, John George Edward Henry Douglas Suther-
        land Campbell, 9th duke of] 1845-1914.
        ... Canadian life and scenery, with hints to
    intending emigrants and settlers. By the marquis
    of Lorne, K. T. With six illustrations. [London]
    The Religious tract society, 1891.
        191, [1] p. incl. front., illus. 14 1/2 cm.
    (The R. T. S. library--illustrated. [1])

5925 Argyll, John George Edward Henry Douglas Suther-
        land Campbell, 9th duke of, 1845-1914.
        ... The Canadian North-west. Speech delivered
    at Winnipeg by His Excellency the Marquis of
    Lorne, governor general of Canada, after his tour
    through Manitoba and the Northwest, during the
    summer of 1881... Ottawa, 1881.
        22 p. front (fold. map.) 21 1/2 cm.

5926 [Argyll, John George Edward Henry Douglas Suther-
        land Campbell, 9th duke of] 1845-1914.
        Canadian pictures, drawn with pen and pencil.
    By the Marquis of Lorne, K. T. With numerous
    illustrations from objects and photographs in the
    possession of and sketches by the Marquis of
    Lorne, Sydney Hall, etc. Engr. by E. Whymper.
    London, The Religious tract society [1884]
        viii, 224 p. incl. front., illus., plates,
    port., map. fold map. 28 1/2 cm.

5927 [Argyll, John George Edward Henry Douglas Sutherland Campbell, 9th duke of] 1845-1914.
Memories of Canada and Scotland; speeches and
verses by the Right Hon. the Marquis of Lorne...
London, S. Low, Marston, Searle & Rivington, 1883.
xi, 360 p. 19 cm.

5928 [Argyll, John George Edward Henry Douglas Sutherland Campbell, 9th duke of] 1845-1914.
A trip to the tropics and home through America.
By the Marquis of Lorne. 2d ed. London, Hurst
and Blackett, 1867.
xii, 355 p. front. 23 cm.

5929 Argyll, John George Edward Henry Douglas Sutherland Campbell, 9th duke of, 1845-1914.
Yesterday & to-day in Canada; by the Duke of
Argyll... London, G. Allen & sons, 1910.
xv, [1], 429 p. fold. map. 20 cm.

5930 Armes, Elizabeth Marie.
The Washington Manor House, England's gift to
the World... New York, Published by the American
branch of the Sulgrave Institution [1922]
38 p. illus., geneal. table. 21 1/2 cm.

5931 Armstrong, Mrs. Louise (Van Voorhis) 1889-
The old history book; an Americanization pageant.
New York, Longmans, Green, 1928.
34 p. 18 cm.

5932 Arnold, Channing.
The American Egypt; a record of travel in
Yucatán by Channing Arnold and Frederick J.
Tabor Frost. London, Hutchinson, 1909.
391 p. plates, fold. map. 24 cm.

5933 Arnold, Isaac Newton, 1815-1884.
Abraham Lincoln: a paper read before the
Royal Historical Society, London, June 16th,
1881, by Hon. Isaac N. Arnold, F.R.H.S. Stephen
A. Douglas: an eulogy delivered before the Chi-
cago university, July 3d, 1861, by Hon. James W.
Sheahan. Chicago, Fergus printing company, 1881.
1 p.l., [165]-194, [194ª]-194ᵈ, [195]-212,

[49]-52 p.   20 cm.   (Fergus' historical
series, no. 15)

5934   Arnold, Isaac Newton, 1815-1884.
       In memoriam, Orville H. Browning.   Chicago,
       Beach, Barnard, & co., 1882.
       14 p.   20 cm.

5935   Arnold, Isaac Newton, 1815-1884.
       Reminiscences of the Illinois bar forty years
       ago: Lincoln and Douglas as orators and lawyers.
       By Hon. Isaac N. Arnold...   Chicago, Fergus
       printing company, 1881.
       29 p.   23 1/2 cm.

5936   Arriaga, Miguel.
       El Distrito Federal y territorios de la Re-
       pública Mexicana, por Miguel Arriaga (geógrafo)
       México, R. de S. N. Araluce, 1900.
       107 p.   incl. 4 col. fold. maps.   fold. pl.,
       col. fold. map, col. fold. plan.   21 1/2 x 11 cm.

5937   Arriaga, Pablo José de, 1564-
       ... La extirpación de la idolatría en el Perú...
       Anotaciones y concordancias con las crónicas
       de Indias por Horacio H. Urteaga.   Biografía
       del Padre Arriaga por Carlos A. Romero.   Lima,
       Imprenta y librería Sanmarti y ca., 1920.
       xxxii, 214 p.   19 1/2 cm.

5938   Arriola, Juan de, b. 1698.
       Canción famosa a un desengaño por el P. Juan
       de Arriola, ingenio mexicano.   Puebla, Herederos
       Viuda Miguel de Ortega Bonilla, 1776.
       16 p.   22 cm.

5939   Arthur, Richard.
       Ten thousand miles in a yacht round the West
       Indies and up the Amazon; introd. by William M.
       Ivins.   New York, R. Arthur, 1906.
       253 p.   illus., port., maps.   21 cm.

5940   Arthur, Samuel John.
       Lincoln's legacy; a tribute to the world's
       great commoner by Samuel J. Arthur...   Boston,

R. G. Badger [c1923]
45 p. incl. front. (port.), plates. 21 cm.

5941 Artigue, Jean d'.
Six years in the Canadian north-west...
Toronto, Hunter, Rose and company, 1882.
205 p. 22 cm.

5942 Artrip, Louise.
Memoirs of Daniel Fore (Jim) Chisholm and the
Chisholm Trail, by Louise and Fullen Artrip.
[n.p., 1949]
89 p. front. (port.), illus. 19 1/2 cm.

5943 Ashe, Samuel A'Court, 1840-1938.
A southern view of the invasion of the
Southern states and the war of 1861-65...
Raleigh, N. C. [1935?]
75 p. 23 cm.

5944 Ashley, James Monroe, 1824-1896.
Abraham Lincoln: address delivered in Memorial
hall, Toledo, Ohio, February 12, 1918. [Toledo,
1918]
6 p. 23 cm.

5945 Ashley, James Monroe, 1824-1896.
Address of Hon. J. M. Ashley, at the fourth
annual banquet of the Ohio Republican League,
held at Memorial hall, Toledo, Ohio, February
12, 1891; pub. by request. New York, Evening
Post print [1891]
23 p. 23 cm.

5946 Ashley, James Monroe, 1824-1896.
Reminiscences of the Great rebellion: Calhoun,
Seward and Lincoln; address of Hon. J. M. Ashley
... Toledo, Ohio, June 2, 1890; published by re-
quest. New York, Evening Post Job Press [1890]
4 p. 23 cm.

5947 Ashmead, A   S
Russia to Abraham Lincoln: "God bless you;"
Compliments of A. S. Ashmead, M. D., late foreign
director, Tokio Hospital, Japan [n.p., n.d.]

12 p.   20 cm.

5948   Asociación mexicana de turismo.
    Mexico, the faraway land nearby. [México]
    Asociación mexicana de turismo [1939?]
    48 p. illus.   22 cm.

5949   Asociación mexicana de turismo.
    ... Viajes de vacaciones. México, 1939.
    cover-title, 17, [1] p. illus., tables (1
    fold.)   19 cm.

5950   Aspinall, Sir Algernon Edward, 1871-
    The pocket guide to the West Indies, by
    Algernon E. Aspinall. London, E. Stanford,
    1907.
    xii, 316 p. 8 pl. (incl. front.), 8 double
    maps, 3 fold. tab.   17 cm.

5951   Aspinall, Sir Algernon Edward, 1871-
    The pocket guide to the West Indies, British
    Guiana, British Honduras, the Bermudas, the
    Spanish Main, and the Panama canal, by Algernon
    E. Aspinall ... [New and rev. ed.] Chicago,
    New York, Rand, McNally & company [1914]
    viii, 488 p., 2 l. front., illus., plates,
    double maps, double plans, facsim.   17 1/2 cm.

5952   L'Assemblée des noirs, asiégée hier au soir par le
    peuple, rue Royale. [Paris, De l'impr. de L. L.
    Girard, 1790]
    7 p.   20 cm.

5953   At the end of the trail: the story of the journey
    of Thomas Lincoln and his family through Hardin
    and Breckinridge counties, Ky., to Indiana in
    1816. Breckinridge-Perry County Lincoln Highway
    Association, [1938]
    24 p. illus.   20 cm.

5954   Ateneo de Costa Rica, San José.
    Anales. San José, 1912-1916.
    5 v.   22 cm.

5955   Ateneo de Honduras; revista mensual, órgano del

centro del mismo nombre. [Tegucigalpa, Honduras,
C. A.] Tipografía nacional, 1913-1923.
    5 v. illus., ports. 28 cm.

5956 El Ateneo de Lima. Publicación mensual. Lima,
      Peru, 1886-1889.
          4 v. 23 cm.
      Supersedes Club literario de Lima.

5957 Athenaeum association, New York.
          Commemorative proceedings of the Athenaeum
      Club on the death of Abraham Lincoln, president
      of the United States: April, 1865. [New York,
      C. S. Westcott, 1865]
          36 p. front. 26 cm.

5958 Atkins, Smith Dykins, 1836-1913.
          Abraham Lincoln. Smith D. Atkins, Opera
      house, Streator, Ill., February 12, 1909, at in-
      vitation of G. A. R., Woman's relief corps,
      Spanish-American veterans, and the Daughters of
      the American revolution. [Freeport, Ill., Journal
      ptg. co., 1909]
          [16] p. 22 cm.

5959 Atkinson, Mrs. Eleanor (Stackhouse) 1863-
          The boyhood of Lincoln. New York, McClure,
      1908.
          57 p. illus. 21 cm.

5960 Atkinson, Mrs. Eleanor (Stackhouse) 1863-
          Lincoln's love story. New York, Doubleday,
      Page, 1909.
          60 p. front. 19 cm.

5961 ... Atlántida. [Ciencias, letras, arte, historia
      americana, administración] Buenos Aires, Coni
      hermanos, 1911-14.
          13 v. illus. (incl. facsims.), plates. 25
      1/2 cm.

5962 Au Mexique. Où? Quand? Comment? Aide-mémoire
      pour touristes, par I.E.S. México, D. F., Cen-
      tral de publicaciones, s.a. [1936]
          4 p.l., [7]-110 p. 19 1/2 cm.

5963   Au pilori; la trahison des chefs conservateurs
       demontrée par les témoignages recueilliṣ devant
       le Comité du Nord-ouest (extraits de L'Événement)
       Quebec, Imprimerie de L'Événement, 1874.
        22 p.   22 cm.

5964   Aubert, Georges.
        ... Les nouvelles Amériques; notes sociales et
       économiques: États-Unis, Mexique, Cuba. Colombie,
       Guatemala, etc. ... Paris, E. Flammarion [1901]
        4 p.l., 438 p. incl. illus., plates, port.,
       double map. 18 1/2 cm.

5965   Aubertin, John James, 1818-1900.
       A flight to Mexico, by J. J. Aubertin ...
       London, K. Paul, Trench & co., 1882.
        4 p.l., 325 p. front., plates, fold. map.
       19 1/2 cm.

5966   Audubon, John Woodhouse, 1812-1862.
       Illustrated notes of an expedition through
       Mexico and California, by J. W. Audubon. New-
       York, J. W. Audubon, 1852. Tarrytown, N. Y.,
       Reprinted, W. Abbatt, 1915.
        83 p. 4 col. pl. (incl. front.) 26 1/2 cm.

5967   Aurora de Chile... reimpresión paleográfica a plana
       y renglón; con una introducción por Julio Vicuña
       Cifuentes. Santiago de Chile, Impr. Cervantes, 1903.
        2 v. in 1.   35 1/2 cm.
       Originally published weekly.

5968   Austin, Stephen Fuller, 1793-1836.
       ... The "Prison journal" of Stephen F. Austin.
       (In Texas state historical association. The
       quarterly. Austin, Tex., 1899.)
        v. 2, [183]-210 p. 26 1/2 cm.

5969   Avalos Guzmán, Gustavo.
       ... Don Antonio de Mendoza, comendador de
       Socuellamos y caballero de la Orden de Santiago,
       primer virrey de la Nueva España. Portado e
       ilustraciones de Julio Prieto. Morelia, Publica-
       ciones de la Universidad Michoacana, 1941.
        149 p., 6 l. incl. illus., port. 24 1/2 cm.

5970 Avery, Ralph Emmett.
The greatest engineering feat in the world at
Panama... with a graphic description of the
Panama-Pacific International Exposition, the
official celebration of the completion of America's
triumph at Panama... under the supervision of
Col. George W. Goethals, U.S.A. [Special rev. and
enl. ed.] Edited by William C. Haskins. New
York, Leslie-Judge Co. [1915]
384 p. illus., ports.   28 cm.

5971 Avila, Esteban de, 1549-1601.
De censvris ecclesiastics tractatvs. Per
Stephanvm de Avila... Nuno denuò in lucem
emissus, & multis mendis expurgatus. Ad excel-
lentissimvm d.d. Lvdovicvm Velasco... Cvm privilegio regis. Lvgdvni, Apud Horatium Cardon,
M.D.C.VIIII.
12 p.l., 422, [68] p.   25 cm.

5972 Ayala, Manuel José de, 1726-1805.
Notas a la Recopilación de Indias, origen e
historia ilustrada de las Leyes de Indias, por
Manuel Josef de Ayala... Obra inédita. Trans-
cripción y estudio preliminar de Juan Manzano
Manzano... Madrid, Ediciones cultura hispánica,
1945-46.
2 v. facsims.   27 1/2 cm.

5973 Ayeta, Francisco de.
Manifestacion breve, radical, y fvndamental de
la persecucion que ha padecido, y padece la Religion Seráfica en las Provincias de Nueva-España
... [n.p., co. 1669]
69 p.   24 cm.

B

5974 Babcock, Mrs. Bernie (Smade) 1868-
The soul of Ann Rutledge; the dramatized love
story of Abraham Lincoln, in six acts, a prologue,
and an epilogue, adapted... from her novel of the

same name... Rock Island, Ill., Frederick B.
Ingram productions, inc. [1934]
95 p.   19 cm.

5975   Bacon, George Washington, 1830-1921, comp.
The life and administration of Abraham Lincoln:
presenting his early history, political career,
speeches, messages, proclamations, letters, etc.,
with a general view of his policy as president
of the United States... Also the European press
on his death. Comp. by G. W. Bacon. London,
S. Low, son, and Marston [etc.] 1865.
vi, [2], 183 p.   front. (port.), fold. map.
20 1/2 cm.

5976   Badger, Henry Clay, 1832-1894.
The humble conqueror: a discourse commemorative
of the life and services of Abraham Lincoln,
preached to the Cambridgeport parish, April 23,
1865.   Boston, W. V. Spencer, 1865.
18 p.   22 cm.

5977   Badillo, Luisa Bernardi de.
Catecismo de geografía de la República Mexicana
para uso de los niños escrito por Luisa Bernardi
de Badillo. México, Castañeda y Rodriguez, 1373
[i.e. 1873]
59 p.   15 1/2 cm.

5978   Baedeker, Karl, firm, publishers, Leipzig.
The Dominion of Canada, with Newfoundland, and
and excursion to Alaska; handbook for travellers,
by Karl Baedeker ... 2d rev. ed.   Leipsic, K.
Baedeker [etc., etc.] 1900.
lxii, 268 p.   10 maps (incl. front.), 7 plans.
16 cm.

5979   Baedeker, Karl, firm, publishers, Leipzig.
The dominion of Canada with Newfoundland and an
excursion to Alaska.   Handbook for travellers.
With 14 maps and 12 plans.   4th rev. and augmented
ed.   Leipzig, K. Baedeker; New York, C. Scribner's
sons [etc., etc.] 1922.
lxx, 420 p.   14 maps (incl. fold. front.), 12
plans (part. fold.)   16 cm.

5980 Baedeker, Karl, firm, publishers, Leipzig.
Nordamerika, die Vereinigten Staaten nebst
einem Ausflug nach Mexiko, Handbuch für
Reisende. 2. Aufl. Leipzig, 1904.
lxiv, 591 p. maps (part col., part fold.),
plans. 16 cm.

5981 Baedeker, Karl, firm, publishers, Leipzig.
The United States, with an excursion into
Mexico; handbook for travellers, by Karl Baedeker;
with 25 maps and 35 plans. 3d rev. ed. Leipzig,
K. Baedeker; New York, C. Scribner's sons;
[etc., etc.] 1904.
ciii, 660 p. fold. front., maps (partly fold.),
plans (partly fold.) 16 cm.

---The Louisiana purchase exposition at St. Louis,
1904; gratis supplement to the 3rd ed. of Baedeker's
United States; with a plan of the exposition.
Leipzig, K. Baedeker, 1904.
cover-title, 9 p. double plans. 15 1/2 cm.

5982 Bailey, Wilfred Ormrod.
... Supposed speech of Abraham Lincoln, on the
occasion of his second election to the presidency
of the United States (in the style of Thucydides)
Oxford, B. H. Blackwell, 1893.
14 p. 20 cm.

5983 Baillie-Grohman, William Adolph, 1851-
Fifteen years' sport and life in the hunting
grounds of western America and British Colombia,
by W. A. Baillie-Grohman. With a chapter by
Mrs. Baillie-Gorhman. Illustrated by seventy-
seven photographs, including the best trophies
of North America big game killed by English and
American sportsmen, with table of measurements and
notes. With three specially prepared maps of
the northwest coast of the United States, British
Colombia and the Kootenay district. London,
H. Cox, 1900.
xii, 403 p. front. (port.), illus., plates,
fold. maps. 24 1/2 cm.

5984 Baker, Charles T

Hints and helps for writers in the Lincoln play writing contest, featuring Abraham Lincoln's Hoosier years, sponsored by the Southwestern Indiana civic association; skeleton material... from the historical collections of Charles T. Baker. Grandview, Ind., The Monitor [c1938]
20 p.   21 cm.

5985   Baker, David Charles.
Lincoln vs. liquor. St. Louis, Mo., Baker pub. co. [c1908]
35 p.   port.   19 cm.

5986   Baker, Frank Collins, 1867-
A naturalist in Mexico: being a visit to Cuba, northern Yucatan and Mexico ... By Frank Collins Baker ... Chicago, D. Oliphant, 1895.
4 p.l., 145 p.   front., illus., plates, map. 20 cm.

5987   Baker, Ray Stannard, 1870-1946.
The capture, death and burial of J. Wilkes Booth. By Ray Stannard Baker. Reproduced from McClure's magazine, May, 1897. Chicago, The Poor Richard press, 1940.
13 l.   incl. ports., map.   25 1/2 cm.

5988   Baldwin, Frank.
A Virginia raid in 1906.   [n.p., 1906?]
49 p.   23 cm.

5989   Bale, Ida L
New Salem as I knew it, by Ida L. Bale. [Petersburgh, Ill., printed by the Petersburgh observer co., c1939]
32 p.   illus.   23 cm.

5990   Ballantyne, Robert Michael, 1825-1894.
Hudson's Bay; or, Every-day life in the wilds of North America, during six years' residence in the territories of the Hon. Hudson's bay company. By Robert Michael Ballantyne ... Boston, Phillips, Sampson and company, 1859.
vii, 293 p.   incl. 3 pl.   front.   18 cm.

5991 Ballou, Maturin M[urray] 1820-1895.
    Aztec land by Maturin M. Ballou ... Boston
and New York, Houghton, Mifflin & co., 1890.
    x, 355 p. 20 1/2 cm.

5992 Ballou, Maturin Murray, 1820-1895.
    Due south; or, Cuba past and present, by Maturin
M. Ballou... 6th ed. Boston and New York,
Houghton, Mifflin and co., 1891.
    ix, 316 p. 20 1/2 cm.

5993 Baltimore and Ohio Railroad.
    In this temple, as in the hearts of the people
for whom he saved the union, the memory of Abraham
Lincoln is enshrined forever... [n.p.] Baltimore
and Ohio Railroad, 1922.
    [4] p. illus. 22 cm.

5994 Banco Nacional de México.
    Examen de la situación económica de México.
[México] 1925-1929.
    46 v. in 26. illus., maps (part. fold.)
22 cm.

5995 Bancroft, George, 1800-1891.
    Memorial address on the life and character
of Abraham Lincoln, delivered at the request
of both houses of Congress of the United States
before them in the hall of the House of representatives by the Honorable George Bancroft on February
twelfth, 1866; with an introduction by John
Drinkwater. San Francisco, Printed for the Book
Club of California by J. H. Nash, 1929.
    xi, 35, a-d p. 2 port. (incl. front.)
mounted facsims. (4 p.) 20 cm.

5996 Bancroft, Hubert Howe, 1832-1918.
    The native races of the Pacific states of North
America. By Hubert Howe Bancroft... New York,
D. Appleton and company, 1874-76.
    5 v. illus., fold. maps. fold. tab. 24 cm.

5997 Bar Association of the City of Boston.
    Tributes of the bar and of the Supreme judicial
court to the memory of Solomon Lincoln. [Boston?

1908?]
    2 p.l., 35, [1] p.   22 cm.

5998   Barba, Alvaro Alonso, b. 1569.
    Arte de los metales, en que se enseña el
verdadero beneficio de los de oro, y plata por
azogue. El modo de fundirlos todos, y como se
han de refinar, y apartar unos de otros. Compuesto por el licenciado Alvaro Alonso Barba...
Nuevamente aora añadido. Con el tratado de las
antiguas minas de España, que escribio don Alonso
Carrillo y Laso... Madrid, Bernardo Peralta,
[1729]
    5 p.l., 224 p., [3] p.   illus.   28 cm.

5999   Barba de Coronado, Juan.
    Señor. El capitan don Iuan Barba de Coronado.
Dize; es hijo legitimo, y el mayor, del licenciado
don Alōso de Coronado Maldonado. [Madrid, 1630]
    4 numb. l.   20 cm.

6000   Barbee, David Rankin, 1874-
    An excursion in southern history, briefly set
forth in the correspondence between Senator A. J.
Beveridge and David Rankin Barbee... Republished
by Langbourne M. Williams of Richmond, Va.
[Asheville, Service Printing Co.] 1928.
    64 p.   22 cm.

6001   Barbosa, Joseph.
    El México que yo he visto. Obstáculos para su
industrialización. El comunismo, en crisis.
Madrid, Editora Nactional, 1950.
    213 p.   22 cm.

6002   Barbour, James, 1775-1842.
    Eulogium upon the life and character of James
Madison. Washington, Printed by Gales & Seaton,
1836.
    29 p.   22 cm.

6003   Barère de Vieuzac, Bertrand, 1755-1841.
    ... Rapport fait au nom du Comité de salut
public, par Barère, sur les colonies françaises
Isles du Vent, dans la séance du 19 thermidor, l'an

2... [Paris, Impr. nat., 1794]
       3 p.   22 cm.

6004 Barker, Harry Ellsworth, 1862–
       Abraham Lincoln, his life in Illinois; being
year by year incidents from 1830 to 1865, written
and compiled by H. E. Barker ... New York, M.
Barrows and company, inc. [c1940]
       vi p., 2 l., 11-64 p. front., plates.   23 1/2 cm.

6005 Barlow, Jöel, 1774-1812.
       Avis aux ordres privilégiés, dans les divers
états de l'Europe, tiré de la nécessité, dans le
sens proprement dit, d'une révolution générale
dans le principe du gouvernement. Londres, J.
Johnson, 1794.
       136 p.   19 1/2 cm.

6006 Barondess, Benjamin, 1891–
       The adventure of the missing briefs. New York,
Civil War Round Table of N. Y., 1955.
       [12] p. facsims.   24 cm.

6007 Barreda, Francisco de.
       El marinero instruido en el arte de navegar,
especulativo y practico, que para la enseñanza
de los colegiales del Real Seminario de San Telmo
dispuso Don Francisco de Barreda... Segunda
impresión. Sevilla, 1786.
       8, 336, 97 p. front., maps (part fold.)   25 cm.

6008 Barrenechea, Juan de.
       Relox astronomico de temblores de la tierra,
secreto maravilloso de la natvraleza, descubierto,
y hallado por d. Juan de Barrenechea... A la
Serenissima Emperatriz de los Cielos Madre de
Dios, y S.ª Nuestra de el Camino, que con reverente
culto se venera en el antiquissimo, y sumptuoso
templo de la cuidad de Pamplona, corte novilissima
del esclarecido reyno de Navarra. Con licencia
de los svperiores. Lima, En la Imprenta antuer-
pinana, 1725.
       16 p.   21 cm.

6009 Barrett, Frank William Zelotes, 1867–

Mourning for Lincoln, by Frank W. Z. Barrett.
Philadelphia, The J. C. Winston company, 1909.
2 p.l., 7-91 p.   20 cm.

6010   Barrette, J   E   T
Récit d'aventures dans le nord-ouest, etc.
... Montréal, W. F. Daniel, 1881.
26 p.   21 cm.

6011   Barrientos, Felipe Santiago.
... Por parte de don Fernando Carrillo de
Cordova y Roldán, posseedor de el mayorasgo,
que fundaron el general Hernan Carrillo de Cordova,
y doña Leonor de Carabajal, marido, y muger: en
los autos de el concurso de acreedores à las casas
de el real Colegio de San Martin: paraque [:] U.
Señoria se sirva de graduar en la sentencia de
preferidos, que se pronunciare, el principal de
el censo perteneciente al expressado mayorasgo,
con mas sus corridos, en el lugar que le corresponde
conforme à derecho, segun la fecha de la escritura
de imposicion. [Lima, 1735]
[29] p.   illus. (coat of arms)   24 cm.

6012   Barrios, Juan de, fl. 1590-1610.
Verdadera medicina, cirurgia, y astrologia...
Mexico, Balli, 1607.
3 pts. in 1 v.   25 cm.

6013   Barry, Charles.
Report of Colonel Charles Barry, on the preliminary survey, cost of construction, and es-
timated revenue of a branch of the Central Pacific
railroad...   Salem, Oregon, Statesman power press,
1864.
66 p.   22 cm.

6014   Bartholow, Otho F
The spiritual life of Abraham Lincoln; a sermon
preached in the First Methodist Episcopal Church,
Mount Vernon, N. Y. ... [Feb. 7, 1909]...   New
York, Lafetra press, 1909.
15 p.   20 cm.

6015   Bartholow, Otho F

The symmetry of Lincoln's character: a sermon
preached in the First Methodist Episcopal Church,
Mount Vernon, N. Y. ... [Feb. 13, 1910] ... New
York, Lafetra press, 1910.
17 p.   20 cm.

6016 Barton, Mary.
Impressions of Mexico with brush and pen, by
Mary Barton ... London, Methuen & co. ltd. [1911]
xi, 163, [1] p.   front., mounted col. plates.
23 cm.

6017 Barton, Robert S
How many "Lincoln Bibles"?   [n.p.] 1951.
12 p.   illus.   20 cm.

6018 Barton, Robert S
Lincoln and the "Effie Afton" case...   Foxboro,
Mass., Foxboro Recorder, 1951.
[4] p.   illus.   20 cm.

6019 Barton, Robert S
Lincoln and the McCormick reaper case...
[n.p.] Privately published, 1952.
[5] p.   illus.   20 cm.

6020 Barton, William Eleazar, 1861-1930.
Additional information. The Lincoln cabin on
Boston Common. [Peoria, Ill., Printed by E. J.
Jacob] 1929.
20 p.   illus.   23 cm.

6021 Barton, William Eleazar, 1861-1930.
Lincoln and Douglas in Charleston: an address
... delivered at the sixty-fourth anniversary
celebration, Charleston, Ill., September 18,
1922. Charleston, Ill., Charleston daily courier,
1922.
8 p.   23 cm.

6022 Barton, William Eleazar, 1861-1930.
The Lincolns in their old Kentucky homes: an
address delivered before the Filson Club, Louisville, Kentucky, December 4, 1922, by William E.
Barton... Berea, Ky., Berea College press, 1923.

24 p.   29 x 23 1/2 cm.

6023   Barton, William Eleazar, 1861-1930.
        "Old theories upset," being the brief re-
        port of an address on Abraham Lincoln's lost grand-
        mother, by William E. Barton... This address
        was delivered before... the Chicago Historical
        Society. [Chicago, 1923]
        [4] p.   21 1/2 cm.

6024   Bateman, Newton, 1822-1897.
        Abraham Lincoln; an address by Hon. Newton
        Bateman, LL.D. Galesburg, Illinois, The
        Cadmus Club, 1899.
        46 p.   19 cm.

6025   Bates, David Homer, 1843-1926.
        Lincoln stories told by him in the Military
        office in the War department during the Civil
        war; recorded by one of the listeners... New
        York, W. E. Rudge, 1926.
        64 p.   front.   23 cm.

6026   Bates, Finis Langdon.
        The escape and suicide of John Wilkes Booth;
        or, The first true account of Lincoln's assassina-
        tion; containing a complete confession by Booth
        many years after the crime, giving in full detail
        the plans... of the conspirators, and the treachery
        of Andrew Johnson... written for the correction of
        history... Memphis, Historical pub. co. [n.d.]
        309 p.   22 cm.

6027   Bates, James Hale, 1826-1901.
        Notes of a tour in Mexico and California. By
        J. H. Bates... printed for private distribution.
        New York, Burr Printing House, 1887.
        viii, 167 p.   18 cm.

6028   Bates, Lindon Wallace, Jr., 1883-
        The path of the conquistadores, Trinidad and
        Venezuelan Guiana; by Lindon Bates, jr. ...
        With twenty-four illustrations and a map. London,
        Methuen & co. ltd. [1912]
        vii, 307, [1] p.   front. (port.), 24 pl., map.

23 cm.

6029 Bathurst, Henry Bathurst, 3rd earl of.
       Correspondence in the years 1817, 1818 and
       1819 between Earl Bathurst and J. Halkett on the
       subject of Lord Selkirk's settlement at the Red
       River, North America. [London, 1819]
          180 p.   22 cm.

6030 Baxter, James Phinney, 1831-
       Christopher Levett, of York, the pioneer colonist
       in Casco Bay. By James Phinney Baxter, A.M. ...
       Portland, Me., Printed for the Gorges society,
       1893.
          xii, 166 p. incl. facsim. pl., maps, fold.
       geneal tab.   22 x 18 cm.

6031 Baxter, Perceval P
       James Phinney Baxter, historian. Portland,
       Maine, 1831-1921. A short biography written for
       the Maine Writers' Research Club. A lifelong
       opponent of vivisection, written for the Christian
       Science Monitor. [Augusta, Me.] Published for
       the Maine State Library [1921?]
          [12] p. front. (port.)   23 cm.

6032 Baxter, Sylvester, 1850-
       The cruise of a land yacht, by Sylvester Baxter.
       Illustrated by L. J. Bridgman. Boston, The
       Authors' publishing co., 1891.
          iv, 263 p. incl. illus., pl. front.   23 1/2 x
       19 1/2 cm.

6033 [Baylor, Orval W   ]
       Lincoln in his parent's home country; a souvenir
       of the Lincoln country of Washington county, Ken-
       tucky. [n.p.] 1936.
          23 p.   21 cm.

6034 [Baylor, Orval W   ]
       Now! Visit Kentucky's newest historical shrine,
       Lincoln Homestead Park, in the "original Lincoln
       country": Lincoln homestead cabin... 1935. [n.p.]
       1935.
          [6] p. illus.   20 cm.

6035 [Baylor, Orval W   ]
       Visit the original Lincoln country and Lincoln
       homestead... [n.p., n.d.]
       [6] p. illus.   21 cm.

6036 Baz, Gustavo Adolfo, 1852-1904.
       ... Un año en México. México, Imprenta de E.
       Dublan y comp., 1887.
       3 p.l., [v]-vi, [9]-230, ii p. illus. (incl.
       ports.), plates (part col)   21 cm.

6037 Baz, Gustavo Adolfo, 1852-1904.
       History of the Mexican railway; wealth of Mexico,
       in the region extending from the Gulf to the capital
       of the republic, considered in its geological,
       agricultural, manufacturing and commercial aspect:
       with scientific, historical and statistical notes,
       by Gustavo Baz & E. L. Gallo. Translated into
       English by George F. Henderson. Mexico, Gallo &
       cº, 1876.
       3 p.l., 9-211 p. 32 pl. (incl. ports.), fold.
       map.   39 cm.

6038 [Beach, Thomas Miller] 1841-1894.
       Twenty-five years in the secret service; the
       recollections of a spy, by Major Henri Le Caron
       [pseud.] ... 6th ed. London, W. Heinemann,
       1892.
       vi p., 1 l., 311 p. front., ports., facsims.
       21 1/2 cm.

6039 Beaugrand, Honoré.
       De Montréal à Victoria par le transcontinental
       canadien... Conférence devant la Chambre de
       commerce du district de Montréal. Montreal, 23
       mars, 1887.
       52 p. illus.   21 cm.

6040 Beaumont, Pablo de la Purisima Concepción, fray.
       Tratado de la agua mineral caliente de San
       Bartholome; a solicitud de el exemo. illmo. sr. d.
       Francisco Antonio Lorenzana ... Su autor el r. p.
       fr. Pablo de la Purissima Concepcion Beaumont ...
       en el siglo, don Juan Blas Beaumont ... [Mexico]
       Con licencia: en la imprenta del br. d. Joseph

Antonio de Hogal, calle de Tiburcio, 1772.
6 p.l., 111 p.   23 cm.

6041   Beauregard, George.
Le 9me bataillon au nord-ouest (journal d'un
militaire)... Quebec, Imprimerie de Jos. - G.
Gingras & c^{ie}, 1886.
100 p.   21 cm.

6042   Becerra, Ricardo, 1836-1905.
... Vida de don Francisco de Miranda, general
de los ejércitos de la primera República francesa
y generalíssimo de los de Venezuela... Madrid,
Editorial-América [1918?]
2 v.   23 cm.

6043   Becher, Carl Christian.
Cartas sobre México; la República Mexicana durante
los años decisivos de 1832 y 1833. Traducción del
alemán, notas y prólogo por Juan A. Ortega y Medina.
[1. ed. española] México, Facultad de Filosofía y
Letras,   Universidad Nacional Autónoma de México,
1959.
240 p.   fold. map.   23 cm.

6044   Becher, Carl Christian.
Mexico in den ereignissvollen Jahren von 1832
und 1833 und die reise hin und zurück... Hamburg,
In Komission bei Perthes & Besser, 1831.
269 p.   illus., fold. map.   20 cm.

6045   Becher, Carl Christian.
Mexico in den ereignissvollen jahren 1832 und
1833 und die reise hin und zurück ... nebst
mercantilischen und statistischen notizen, von
C. C. Becher... Hamburg, Perthes & Besser, 1834.
xii, p., 1 l., 269 p.   front., fold. map.
21 1/2 cm.

6046   Becher, Henry C   R
A trip to Mexico, being notes of a journey from
Lake Erie to Lake Tezcuco and back, with an appendix, containing and being a paper about the ancient
nations and races who inhabited Mexico before and
at the time of the Spanish conquest, and the ancient

stone and other structures and ruins of ancient
cities found there. By H. C. R. Becher...
Toronto, Willing and Williamson, 1880.
    vii, 183 p. front., pl., photos., port., plan,
map.   22 1/2 cm.

6047 Beecher, Henry Ward, 1813-1887.
      Oration at the raising of "The old flag" at
      Sumter; and Sermon on the death of Abraham Lincoln
      ... Manchester [England] A. Ireland & co., 1865.
      55, [3] p.   19 cm.

6048 Beechey, Frederick William
      Narrative of a voyage to the Pacific and Beering's
      Strait, to co-operate with the polar expedition:
      performed in His Majesty's ship Blossom... in the
      years 1825, 26, 27, 28... London, Henry Colburn
      2nd, Richard Bentley, 1831.
      2 v. illus., maps.   20 cm.

6049 Begg, Alexander, 1839-1897.
      The creation of Manitoba; or, A history of the
      Red River troubles... Toronto, A. H. Hovey [etc.,
      etc.] 1871.
      v, 408 p. front. (4 port.)   19 cm.

6050 Begg, Alexander, 1839-1897.
      The great Canadian north west: its past his-
      tory, present condition and glorious prospects
      ... Montreal, Printed by John Lovell & son, 1881.
      135 p.   22 cm.

6051 Begg, Alexander, 1839-1897.
      History of British Columbia from its earliest
      discovery to the present time. Toronto, William
      Briggs, 1894.
      xvii, 568 p. ports., fold. map.   23 cm.

6052 Begg, Alexander, 1839-1897.
      History of the North-West. By Alexander Begg
      ... Toronto, Hunter, Rose & co., 1894-95.
      3v. fronts., ports.   22 1/2 cm.
      "Reference books on the Northwest":   v. 3, p.
      [xxi]-xxvii.

6053   Begg, Alexander, 1839-1897.
      Report relative to the Alaskan boundary question,
    submitted by Alexander Begg, C. C. [Victoria,
    B. C., Printed by R. Wolfenden, 1896]
      caption-title, 17 p.   27 cm.

6054   Begg, Alexander, 1839-1897.
      Review of the Alaskan boundary question. By
    Alexander Begg... Victoria, B. C., T. R. Cusack,
    printer [1900?]
      cover-title, 32 p.   22 cm.

6055   Begg, Alexander, 1839-1897.
      Seventeen years in the Canadian northwest. A
    paper read on April 8, 1884, at the Royal Colonial
    Institute. Reprinted from The colonies and India.
    Published by authority of the Council. London,
    Spottiswoode & co., 1884.
      35 p.   20 cm.

6056   Begg, Alexander, 1839-1897.
      Ten years in Winnipeg. A narration of the prin-
    cipal events in the history of the city of Winnipeg
    from the year A. D. 1870 to the year A. D. 1879,
    inclusive, by Alexander Begg, and Walter R. Nursey.
    Winnipeg, Manitoba, Printed at the "Times printing
    and publishing house," 1879.
      3 p.l., [3]-226 p. illus. (plan)   22 1/2 cm.

6057   Beker, Ana.
      Woman on a horse. [Translated from the Spanish
    by James Cleugh] London, W. Kimber [1956]
      204 p. illus., maps (on lining papers)   22 cm.

6058   Belcher, Edward.
      The last of the Arctic voyages; being a narra-
    tive of the expedition in H.M.S. Assistance... in
    search of Sir John Franklin, during the years 1852-
    53-54. With notes on the natural history by Sir
    John Richardson, Professor Owen, Thomas Bell,
    J. W. Salter, and Lovell Reeve... London, Lovell
    Reeve, 1855.
      2 v. illus., maps.   26 cm.

6059   Belcher, Edward.

Narrative of a voyage around the world, performed by Her Majesty's ship Sulphur, during the
years 1836-1842... London, Henry Colburn, 1843.
2 v. illus., fold maps. 21 cm.

6060 Belden, David, 1832-
Obsequies of President Lincoln: an oration
delivered in Nevada City in 1865... Marysville,
Calif., Marysville herald press, [18-?]
8 p. 23 cm.

6061 Belew, Pascal Perry, 1894-
My old Kentucky home, or Experiences from life
... Kansas City, Mo., Printed for Rev. P. P.
Belew by the Nazarene Publishing House [n.d.]
48 p. front. (port.) 19 cm.

6062 Bell, Charles Napier.
Our northern waters; a report presented to the
Winnipeg board of trade regarding the Hudson's
Bay and Straits... Winnipeg, Printed by Authority
of the Winnipeg board of trade [1894]
78 p. fold. maps. 22 cm.

6063 Bell, Landon C
An address at Johnson's Island in memory of the
Confederate soldiers who while prisoners there died,
and are buried on the island. [n.p., 1929?]
22 p. 23 cm.

6064 Bellegarde, Dantes, 1877-
... La nation haitienne. Paris, J. de Gigord,
1938.
2 p.l., [vii]-x, 361, [1] p. illus. (incl.
ports., maps (1 double)) 25 cm.
"Bibliographie": p. [354]-359.

6065 [Bellemare, Louis] i.e. Eugène Louis Gabriel de,
1809-1852.
Impressions de voyages et aventures dans le
Mexique, la haute Californie et les régions de
l'or; par Gabriel Ferry [pseud.] Bruxelles, En
vente chez tous les libraires de la ville et du
royaume, 1851.
410 p. 21 1/2 cm.

44

6066 Belmar, Francisco, 1859-
    Lenguas indígenas de Mexico. Familia mixteco-
zapoteca y sus relaciones con el otomí. - Familia
zoguemixe. - Chontal. - Huave y mexicano. Por el
Lic. Francisco Belmar... Mexico, Imprenta particular, 1905.
    2 p.l., [3]-374, [4] p.   22 cm.

6067 Below, Ernst, 1845-1910.
    Mexiko. Skizzen und typen aus dem Italien der
Neuen welt von Ernst Below. Mit sechs illustrationen. 2. aufl. Berlin, Allgemeiner verein für
deutsche litteratur, 1899.
    xvii, 362 p. front., plates.   21 cm.

6068 Beltrami, Giacomo Costantino, 1779-1855.
    Le Mexique, par J.-C. Beltrami ... Paris,
Crevot [etc.] 1830.
    2 v.   20 cm.

6069 Benavides y de la Cueva, Diego de.
    Horae svccisivae: sive elucvbrationes D.
Didaci Benavidii, & de la cveva comitis S. Stephani,
& concentaniae marchionis Solerae & c. In praecentia
peruanae proregis alias Nauarrae & Galleciae
moderatoris... Lvgdvni, Sampt. Ioannis de Argaray,
bibliopolae pampelonensis, 1664.
    19 p.l., 388 p. port.   17 cm.

6070 Benítez, José R
    Como me lo contaron te lo cuento por la Calle
de Juarez. Guadalajara, Jal., Ediciones del Banco
industrial de Jalisco [1963]
    150 p.   23 cm.

6071 Bera Cerxcada, Antonio.
    El patronato disputado...   [n.p.] 1741.
    118 p.   22 cm.

6072 Bianconi, F   , 1840-
    Le Mexique à la portée des industriels, des
capitalistes, des négociants importateurs et ex-
portateurs et des travailleurs... par F. Bianconi
... Octobre, 1889. Paris, Imprimerie Chaix, 1889.
    144 p. fold. map.   18 1/2 cm.

6073   Biart, Lucien, 1828-1897.
       A travers l'Amérique, nouvelles et récits par
       Lucien Biart; vingt-huit dessins hors texte par F.
       Lix, gravures de Gérard, Hotelin, Langeval, A.
       Leray, F. Méaulle et Ravenel. Paris, Bibliothéque
       de Magasin des demoiselles [1876]
       4 p.l., 383, [1] p. front. (port.), plates.
       27 cm.

6074   Biart, Lucien, 1828-1897.
       Amerikanisches wanderbuch. Land- und leben-
       sbilder aus Nord- und Mittel-Amerika. Preisge-
       krönt von der Franz. Akademie. Nach Lucian Biart
       frei bearbeitet von Philipp Laicus [pseud.] Mit
       55 illustrationen. Einsiedeln, New-York [etc.]
       Gebr. K. und N. Benziger, 1880.
       316 p. incl. front. (port.), illus.   29 cm.

6075   The Bibliophile Society.
       Lincoln letters [facsimiles of original Lincoln
       letters, the property of William K. Bixby] [n.p.,
       Bibliphile Society] 1913.
       [12] p. facsims.   22 cm.

6076   Bibliothèque linguistique américaine.
       Paris, Maisonneuve, 1871-1903.
       25 v.   24 cm.

6077   Biempica y Sotomayor, Salvador, bp., 1730-1802.
       D. Salvador Biempica y Sotomayor,... por la
       Divina Gracia... Obispo de la Puebla de los Angeles,
       ... A nuestros muy amados Hermanos los venerables
       Párrocos ... [Puebla, 1790]
       16 p.   22 cm.

6078   Biempica y Sotomayor, Salvador, bp., 1730-1802.
       Nos, D. Salvador Biempica y Sotomayor, del Orden
       de Calatrava, Obispo de la Puebla de los Angeles,
       ... La grave decadencia, diminucion y deterioro á
       que se hallon reducidos, asi los fondos de Capel-
       lanias, [Puebla, 1790]
       9 p.   20 cm.

6079   Biempica y Sotomayor, Salvador, bp., 1730-1802.
       Nos, D. Salvador Biempica y Sotomayor,... Obispo

de la Puebla de los Angeles,... a nuestro Ven.
Cabildo y á todos los Párrocos de esta Ciudad y
Obispado... [Puebla, 1791]
   30 p.   22 cm.

6080 Bigelow, Burton.
      Abraham Lincoln; "drumbeats of his re-echoing
      doom." [n.p.] 1940.
      [8] p.   27 cm.

6081 Bigelow, John, 1817-1911.
      Some recollections of the late Édouard Laboulaye.
      [New York, Putnam, 1889?]
      81 p.   18 cm.

6082 Binney, Horace, 1780-1875.
      The privilege of the writ of habeas corpus under
      the Constitution. Philadelphia, T. B. Pugh, 1862.
      52 p.   19 cm.

6083 Bird, Mark Baker, 1807-1880.
      The victorious: a small poem on the assassina-
      tion of President Lincoln. Kingston, Jamaica, M.
      de Cordova, McDougall & co., 1866.
      xvii, 57 p.   18 cm.

6084 Birkinbine, John, 1844-
      ... Industrial progress of Mexico. [By] John
      Birkinbine ... Read June 15, 1909 ... [Philadel-
      phia, 1909?]
      38 p. illus.   25 1/2 cm.

6085 Bishop, Mrs. Anna (Rivière) 1814-1884.
      Travels of Anna Bishop in Mexico. Philadelphia,
      C. Deal [c1852]
      1 p.l., v-xii, 13-317 p. front. (port.), pl.
      19 cm.

6086 Bishop, Isabella Lucy (Bird) "Mrs. J. F. Bishop,"
      1831-1904.
      A lady's life in the Rocky Mountains. G. P.
      Putnam's sons, New York, 1879.
      316 p.   23 cm.

6087 Bishop, William Henry.

Mexico, California and Arizona; being a new
and revised edition of Old Mexico and her lost
provinces; by William Henry Bishop ... New
York, Harper & brothers, 1889.
    xii pp., 1 l., 569 pp. incl. front., illus.,
pl., port., maps. 20 1/2 cm.

6088 Bishop, William Henry.
    Old Mexico and her lost provinces; a journey
in Mexico, southern California, and Arizona, by
way of Cuba. By William Henry Bishop... New
York, Harper & brothers, 1883.
    x p., 1 l., 509 p. incl. front., illus., plates,
ports., maps. 20 1/2 cm.

6089 [Black, Robert]
    A memoir of Abraham Lincoln, president elect
of the United States of America, his opinion on
secession, extracts from the United States Constitution, & c.; to which is appended an historical sketch on slavery reprinted by permission
from "The Times". London, S. Low, son & co.,
1861.
    126 p. front. (port) 17 1/2 cm.

6090 Black, William, Harman, 1868-
    The real North America pocket guide book (from
official sources) (number 11 of the pocket guides
known as "Black's blue books") covering 1243 cities,
two routes across Canada and four routes across
the United States, and 268 other routes in the
United States, Canada, Alaska, Newfoundland,
Mexico, Cuba and Hawaii ... with outline maps and
a simple index; every question answered, by Harman
Black ... New York City, Real book company [etc.,
etc.] 1926.
    xxxvii, 409 p. fold. maps. 16 1/2 cm.

6091 Black, William Harman, 1868-
    The real United States and Canada pocket guide-
book (number 3 of the Nutshell travel series known
as "Black's blue-books") describing two routes
across Canada and four routes across the United
States, and 175 other routes north, south, east
and west, covering 350 cities ... Actual diary and

48

expense account of a trip from New York to San
Francisco; with maps and a simple index; list of
towns and map of Lincoln Highway. Every question
answered. New York, Printed by the Association
for New York, 1915.
xlii, 305 p. maps. 17 cm.

6092 Blacknall, O   W
Lincoln as the South should know him... 3d ed.
Raleigh, N. C., Reprinted by Manly's Battery
chapter, Children of the Confederacy [1915]
23 p. 21 cm.

6093 Blackwell, Robert.
Original acrostics on all the states and presidents of the United States, and various other subjects, religious, political, and personal... by
Robert Blackwell. Nashville, Tenn., Pub. for the
author, 1861.
x, [11]-224 p. incl. front., illus., ports.
20 1/2 cm.

6094 Blackwell, Sarah Ellen, 1828-
A military genius: life of Anna Ella Carroll,
of Maryland ("the great unrecognized member of
Lincoln's cabinet")... Washington, D. C., Judd &
Detweiler, 1891-1895.
2 v. illus. 17 cm.

6095 Blair, Francis Preston, 1791-1876.
... Letter of Francis P. Blair, esq., to the
Republican association of Washington, D. C.
[Washington, Buell & Blanchard, printers, 1856]
caption title, 7 p. 22 1/2 cm.

6096 Blair, Montgomery, 1813-1883.
Speech of the Hon. Montgomery Blair, on the
causes of the rebellion and in support of the
president's plan of pacification, delivered
before the legislature of Maryland at Annapolis,
on the 22d of January, 1864. Baltimore, Sherwood
& co., 1864.
22 p. 23 cm.

6097 Blair, Montgomery, 1813-1883.

Speech of the Hon. Montgomery Blair (postmaster
general) on the revolutionary schemes of the ultra
abolitionists... delivered at... Rockville...
Maryland... October 3, 1863. [New York, D. W.
Lee] 1863.
20 p.   23 cm.

6098   Blake, Harrison, Gray, 1818-1876.
Equality of rights in the territories; speech
of Harrison G. Blake, of Ohio, made in the House
of Representatives... June 12, 1860. [n.p.]
1860.
8 p.   20 cm.

6099   Blake, Mrs. Mary Elizabeth, 1840-1907.
Mexico: picturesque, political, progressive, by
Mary Elizabeth Blake... and Margaret F. Sullivan
... Boston, Lee & Shepard; New York, C. T. Dilling-
ham, 1888.
228 p.   18 1/2 cm.

6100   Blauvelt, Charles Clare.
Accepted appearance of the log cabin birthplace,
February 12, 1809, of Abraham Lincoln, Big South
Fork, Nolin Creek, Kentucky. Souvenir of the
February 11, 1950, meeting of the Lincoln Group
of Boston, at the Parker House... Boston, 1950.
[4] p. illus.   20 cm.

6101   Bledsoe, A   J
Indian wars of the northwest... San Francisco,
Bacon & compnay, book and job printers, 1885.
505 p.   22 cm.

6102   Blichfeldt, Emil Harry, 1874-
A Mexican journey, by E. H. Blichfeldt ... New
York, Thomas Y. Crowell company [1912]
viii, 280 p. front., plates, ports., fold. map.
21 1/2 cm.

6103   The Blue guide to Cuba ... Season of 1935-1936-
Havana, Cuba, R. Le Febure, c1936-
v. illus., maps (1 fold.)   18 cm.

6104   Boardman, James.

America and the Americans... By a citizen of
the world. London, Longman, Rees, Orme, Brown,
Green and Longman, 1833.
xi, xii, xvi, 430 p. 23 cm.

6105 Boban, Eugène.
... Documents pour servir à l'histoire du
Mexique; catalogue raisonné de la collection de
m. E.-Eugéne Goupil (ancienne collection J.-M.-
A. Aubin); manuscrits figuratifs, et autres sur
papier indigéne d'agave mexicana et sur papier
européen antérieurs et postérieurs à la conquête
de Mexique (xvie siecle)... avec une introduction
de m. E.-Eugène) Goupil et une lettre-préface de m.
Auguste Génin... Paris, E. Leroux, 1891.
2 v. 2 port. 36 cm. and atlas of 80 pl.
37 x 46 cm.

6106 Bolduc, Jean-Baptiste-Zacharie.
Mission de la Colombie. Deuxiéme lettre et
journal... Québec, J. B. Fréchette, 1845.
28 p. 20 cm.

6107 Boletín histórico de Puerto Rico.
San Juan, Puerto Rico, Tip, Cantero, Fernández
& Co., 1914-27.
14 v. 25 cm.

6108 Bolívar, Simón, 1783-1830.
Cartas de Bolívar, 1823-1824-1825. (Con un apéndice que contiene cartas de 1801 a 1822). Notas
de R. Blanco-Fombona. Madrid, Editorial-América,
1921.
xv, 427 p. port., facsims. 23 cm.

6109 Bolívar, Simón, 1783-1830.
Cartas de Bolívar, 1825-1826-1827. Notas de R.
Blanco-Fombona ... [Madrid, Editorial-América,
1922?]
1 p.l., vi, 510, xi p. 22 cm.

6110 Bolívar, Simón, 1783-1830.
... Papeles de Bolívar, publicados por Vicente
Lecuna ... Madrid, Editorial-América, 1920.
2 v. facsims. 22 cm.

6111   Bolles, Frank, 1856-1894.
        From Blomidon to Smoky, and other papers, by
        Frank Bolles, Boston and New York, Houghton, Mif-
        flin and company, 1894.
        3 p.l., 278 p.   18 cm.

6112   Bonar, Lewis J
        The Lincoln I voted for.   [n.p.] Richland
        County Lincoln Association, 1931.
        14 p.   port.   20 cm.

6113   Bond, Christiana.
        Memories of General Robert E. Lee...   Baltimore,
        The Norman Remington Company, 1926.
        52 p.   illus.   18 1/2 cm.

6114   Book of anecdotes, and joker's knapsack; including
        witticisms of the late President Lincoln, and hu-
        mors, incidents and absurdities of the war...
        Philadelphia, J. E. Potter & co., [1866]
        350 p.   18 1/2 cm.

6115   Book of the prophet, Stephen, son of Douglas;
        wherein marvellous things are foretold of the
        reign of Abraham.   New York, Feeks & Bancker
        [c1863-64]
        2 v.   18 cm.

6116   Booth, John Wilkes, 1838-1865.
        Confession de John Wilkes Booth, assassin du
        president Abraham Lincoln; pub. d'après le manu-
        scrit original; traduit de l'anglais.   Paris
        [Poupart-Davyl et cie.] 1865.
        266 p.   19 cm.

6117   Bordeaux, Albert François Joseph, 1865-
        ... Le Mexique et ses mines d'argent, avec une
        carte et 16 gravures hors texte.   Paris, Plon-
        Nourrit et cie, 1910.
        2 p.l., ii, 295 p., 2 l.   plates, fold. map.
        19 cm.

6118   Borja, Francisco de, principe de Esquilache, 1582-
        1658.
        Napoles recvperada por el rey don Alonso; poema

heroico de don Francisco de Borja, principe de
Esquilache ... En Ambers, En la emprenta plantin-
iana de Baltasar Moreto, M.DC.LVIII.
xxiiij, 398 p., 1 l.   26 cm.

6119   Borja, Francisco de, príncipe de Esquilache, 1582-
        1658.
            Las obras en verso de don Francisco de Borja,
        principe de Esquilache ... dedicadas al rey nvestro
        señor don Philipe IV. Edicion segunda, reuista y
        muy añadida. Amberes, En la emprenta plantiniana
        de Balthasar Moreto, 1654.
            8 p.l., 692, [18] p., 1 l., 3 p.   22 cm.
            Title-page engraved by Th. Galleus, from a
        painting by Rubens.
            Half-title: Obras en verso del principe de
        Esqvilache.

6120   Borja, Francisco de, príncipe de Esquilache, 1582-
        1658.
            Las obras en verso de don Francisco de Borja,
        principe de Esquilache... Dedicadas al rey nvestro
        señor don Philipe IV. Edicion postrera, reuista y
        muy añadida. Amberes, En la Emprenta plantiniana de
        Balthasar Moreto. 1663.
            8 p.l., 736, [21] p.   23 cm.

6121   Borragán, María Teresa.
            ... Doce mil kilómetros a través de los sistemas
        de riego en México; impresiones de viaje. México,
        1937.
            117 p., 3 l.   illus.   23 1/2 cm.

6122   Borragán, María Teresa.
            ... Presas y paisajes del agro mexicano. México,
        D. F. [A. Mijares y hno., impresores] 1938.
            1 p.l., 5-180 p.   illus.   23 cm.

6123   Boston, City Council.
            A memorial of Abraham Lincoln... Boston, printed
        by order of the City Council, 1865.
            153 p.   21 cm.

6124   Boston. City Council.
            Proceedings of the city council of Boston,

April 17, 1865, on occasion of the death of
Abraham Lincoln... Boston, Pub. by order of the
City Council, 1865.
35 p. 27 cm.

6125 Botero, Giovanni, 1540-1617.
Descripcion de todas las provincias y reynos
del mvndo... Gerona, Caspar Gorrich, 1622.
[8], 360 l. 25 cm.

6126 [Boucher, Pierre, sieur de Boucherville] 1620?-1717.
Histoire véritable et natvrelle des moevrs et
prodvctions dv pays de la Novvelle France, vvl-
gairement dite le Canada. Paris, chez Florentin
Lambert, 1674.
1 p.l., [22], 168 p. 13 cm.

6127 Bouchette, Joseph, 1774-1841.
The British dominions in North America; or, A
topographical and statistical description of the
provinces of Lower and Upper Canada, New Brunswick,
Nova Scotia, the islands of Newfoundland, Prince
Edward, and Cape Breton. Including considerations
on land granting and emigration. To which are
annexed, statistical tables and tables of distances, &c. By Joseph Bouchette ... London,
Longman, Rees, Orme, Brown, Green, and Longman,
1832.
2 v. front. (port.), pl., maps, plans. 28 x 23
cm.

6128 Bouchette, Joseph, 1774-1841.
A topographical description of the province
of Lower Canada, with remarks upon Upper Canada,
and on the relative connexion of both provinces
with the United States of America. By Joseph
Bouchette... Embellished by several views, plans
of harbours, battles, &c. London, Printed for
the author and pub. by W. Faden, 1815.
xv, 640, lxxxvi, [2] p. front. (port.), plates,
plans (part fold.), 2 tab. (1 fold.) 24 1/2 cm.

6129 Boulton, Charles Arkoll, b. 1841.
Reminiscences of the North-west rebellions, with
a record of the raising of Her Majesty's 100th

regiment in Canada, and a chapter on Canadian
social & political life, by Major Boulton, commanding
Boulton's scouts... Toronto, Grip printing and
publishing co., 1886.
   5 p.l., [7]-531 p. front. (port.), illus.,
pl., map. 3 plans. 18 cm.

6130 Bourinot, Sir John George, 1837-1902.
    Canada... London, T. Fisher Unwin; New York,
G. P. Putnam's sons, 1897.
   xx, 436 p. incl. illus., port., plans, front.,
fold maps. 19 1/2 cm.

6131 Bourinot, Sir John George, 1837-1902.
    Canada. New York, G. P. Putnam, 1902.
   463 p. illus., ports., fold. maps.   20 cm.

6132 Bourinot, Sir John George, 1837-1902.
    Canada as a home. By John George Bourinot...
Reprinted from the Westminster review for July,
1882. London, Trübner & co., 1882.
   30 p.   22 cm.

6133 Bourinot, Sir John George, 1837-1902.
   ... Our intellectual strength and weakness; a
short historical and critical review of literature,
art and education in Canada... Montreal, F. Brown
& co. [etc., etc.] 1893.
   xii, 99 p.   27 x 20 1/2 cm.

6134 Boutwell, George Sewall, 1818-1905.
    Why I am a Republican: a history of the Re-
publican party, a defense of its policy, and the
reasons which justify its continuance in power, with
biographical sketches of the Republican candidates.
Hartford, Conn., W. J. Betts & co., 1884.
   195 p. illus. 18 cm.

6135 Bowditch, Charles Pickering, 1842-1921.
    The numeration, calender systems and astronomical
knowledge of the Mayas, by Charles P. Bowditch.
Priv. print. Cambridge, The University press, 1910.
   xvi p., 1 l., 346 p., 19 l. illus., plates
(part fold.), tables (part fold.)   26 1/2 cm.

6136 Bowdoin college.
Obituary record of the graduates of Bowdoin College
and the Medical school of Maine for the decade
ending 1 June 1909. Brunswick, Me., Bowdoin College
Library, 1911.
viii, 527 p.   22 1/2 cm.

6137 Bowers, Claude Gernade, 1878-1958.
John Tyler. Address... at the unveiling of the
bust of President Tyler in the State Capitol,
Richmond, Virginia, June 16, 1931. Richmond,
Va., Richmond press, inc., 1932.
30 p. front.   23 cm.

6138 [Box, Henry W   ] ed.
In memoriam: Abraham Lincoln, assassinated at
Washington, April 14, 1865... Buffalo, N. Y.,
Matthews & Warren, 1865.
66 p.   20 cm.

6139 Box, Michael James.
Capt. James Box's adventures and explorations in
new and old Mexico. Being the record of ten years
of travel and research, and a guide to the mineral
treasures of Durango, Chihuahua, the Sierra Nevada
... and the southern part of Arizona. By Capt.
Michael James Box, of the Texan rangers. New
York, J. Miller, 1869.
344 p.   18 1/2 cm.

6140 Boyce, J   R
Facts about the Montana territory and the way to
get there... [Helena, Mont.] Contributed to the
Rocky Mountain Gazette [1872]
24 p.   22 cm.

6141 Boyce, William Dickson, 1848-1929.
Illustrated South America; a Chicago publisher's
travels and investigations in the republics of South
America, with 500 photographs of people and scenes
from the Isthmus of Panama to the Straits of
Magellan, by W. D. Boyce ... Chicago, New York,
Rand, McNally & company [c1912]
1 p.l., vii-xv, 638 p. front., illus., double
maps.   22 1/2 cm.

56

6142 Boyd, Andrew.
Abraham Lincoln foully assassinated, April 14,
1865: a poem with an illustration from the
London Punch for May 6, 1865; republished with
an introd. by Andrew Boyd. Albany, N. Y., Joel
Munsell, 1868.
13 p. 20 cm.

6143 Brabant, Augustin Joseph, 1845-1912.
Vancouver Island... and its mission 1874-1900.
Reminiscences of the Rev. A. J. Brabant. [n.p.,
1899]
89 p. illus. 20 cm.

6144 Brackett, Albert G[allatin] 1829-1896.
General Lane's brigade in central Mexico. By
Albert G. Brackett ... Cincinnati, H. W. Derby
& co.; New York, J. C. Derby, 1854.
ix, [10]-336 p. front. (port.) 19 1/2 cm.

6145 Bradford, Mary F
Side trips in Jamaica, by Mary F. Bradford.
3d ed. Boston and New York, Sherwood Publishing
Co., 1902.
100 p. illus. fold. map, plans. 18 cm.

6146 Bradley, Arthur Granville, 1850-1943.
Canada... New York, H. Holt and company [etc.,
etc., 1912]
256 p. 17 cm.

6147 Bradley, Arthur Granville, 1850-1943.
Canada in the twentieth century, by A. G. Bradley
... Westminster, A. Constable & co., ltd., 1903.
xii, 428 p. 50 pl. (incl. front.), fold. map.
23 cm.

6148 Bradley, Arthur Granville, 1850-1943.
The fight with France for North America. 2d
ed. rev. Westminster, A. Constable, 1902.
xiii, 399 p. plates, ports., maps. 22 cm.

6149 Bradley, Arthur Granville, 1850-1943.
The making of Canada, by A. G. Bradley... New
York, E. P. Dutton and company, 1908.

viii, 396 p.   2 fold. maps.   22 1/2 cm.

6150   Bradley, John C
        Brief sketches of a few American Bradleys, with
        reference to their English progenitors. [Hoosick
        Falls, N. Y.] Press of Hoosick Valley Democrat,
        1889.
        46 p.   22 cm.

6151   Bradley, Thomas H
        O'Toole's mallet; or the resurrection of the
        second national city of the United States of
        America.   Second edition.   [n.p.] 1894.
        65 p.   20 cm.

6152   Brainerd, David, 1718-1747.
        Extracts from the Journal of David Brainerd,
        missionary to the Indians.   Selected by Wm. R.
        Newell...   Chicago, The Moody Bible Institute,
        1900.
        76 p.   15 cm.

6153   Brasseur de Bourbourg, Charles Étienne, 1814-1874.
        Quatres lettres sur le Mexique, exposition
        absolue du système hiéroglyphique mexicain.   La
        fin de l'âge de pierre.   Époque glaciaire temp-
        oraire.   Commencement de l'âge de bronze.   Origi-
        nes de la civilisation et des religions de l'anti-
        quité; d'après le Teo-Amoxtli et autres documents
        mexicains, etc.   Par M. Brasseur de Bourbourg...
        Paris, Maisonneuve et c^{ie} [etc., etc.] 1868.
        xx, 463, [1] p.   illus.   24 1/2 cm.

6154   Brassey, Annie (Allnutt) baroness, 1839-1887.
        In the trades, the tropics, & the roaring
        forties.   By Lady Brassey.   With 292 illustra-
        tions engraved on wood by G. Pearson and J. Cooper
        after drawings by R. T. Pritchett.   New York, H.
        Holt and company, 1885.
        xiv p., 1 l., 532 p.   illus., 9 maps (2 fold.)
        22 cm.

6155   Brehme, Hugo.
        Das malerische Mexiko, herausgegeben von Hugo
        Brehme ...   Mexico [Lichtbildwerkstätte (Fotografïa

artística) H. Brehme, c1923]
xxvii, 197 p. illus. 31 1/2 cm.

6156 Brehme, Hugo.
México pintoresco, publicado por Hugo Brehme...
Mexico [Fotografía artística H. Brehme, c1923]
xii, 197 p. illus. 31 1/2 cm.

6157 Bremer, Fredrika, 1801-1865.
The homes of the New world; impressions of
America. By Fredrika Bremer. Translated by Mary
Howitt... New York, Harper & brothers, 1854.
2 v. 20 cm.

6158 Breve descripcion de los sucesos festivos con que
la ciudad de la Puebla de los Angeles celebró el
decreto de Su Santidad de 12. de septiembre del
año pasado de 1767, de la fama de santidad,
virtudes, y milagros en general del v. señor d.
Juan de Palafox y Mendoza. Con licencia. En
Madrid: En la imprenta de d. Manuel Martin, calle
de la Cruz. frente de la del Pozo, donde se
hallará. Puebla, Impresa en el Colegio real de
San Ignacio de la Puebla de Los Angeles, 1767.
48 p. front. (port.) 23 cm.

6159 Breve descripcion de los sucesos festivos con que
la ciudad de la Puebla de los Angeles celebro el
decreto de Su Santidad de 12 de Septiembre del ano
pasado de 1767 ... Barcelona, Joseph Altés, [1768]
Madrid, Manuel Martin, 1768.
48 p. 23 cm.

6160 Breve noticia de las fiestas, en que la muy ilustre
ciudad de Zacatecas explicó su agradecimiento en
la confirmacion del patronato de Nrâ. Srâ. de
Guadalupe, el mes de septiembre del año de 1758,
por n. ss. p. el señor Benedicto XIV. & sermones
predicados en dicha funcion. Siendo sus comissarios
diputados los señores d. Joseph de Joaristi... y d.
Francisco Xavier de Aristoarena, y Lanz... Por un
apassionado de dicha ciudad de Zacatecas. Impressa
con las licencias necessarias en Mexico, En la
imprenta de los herederos de doña Maria de Rivera,
1759.

20 p.l., 64, 150 p.   illus. (coat of arms)
24 cm.

6161 Breve relacion de lo dispvesto en distintas reales
cedulas sobre el modo, forma y cantidad permiso
de comercio entre las Islas Filipinas, y Nueva
España... Cadiz, Gerónymo de Peralta [ca. 1720]
34 p.   24 cm.

6162 [Brewer, Charles]
Reminiscences. [n.p., 1884?]
67 p.   20 cm.

6163 Brewster, Lewis Waterbury, 1830-
Elder William Brewster and the Brewster family
of Portsmouth, New Hampshire, collated by Lewis
W. Brewster. Portsmouth, Press of A. G. Brewster,
1908.
18 p.   18 cm.

6164 Bridwell, N   W
The life and adventures of Robert McKinnie,
alias "Little Reddy," from Texas. The dare-devil
desperado of the Black Hills region, chief of the
murderous gang of treasure coach robbers. Also
a full account of the robberies committed by him
and his gang in Highland, Pike and Ross counties;
with full particulars of Detective Norris' adventures while effecting the capture of members of
the gang... Hillsboro, O., Printed and published
at the Hillsboro Gazette office, 1878.
60 p.   illus.   22 cm.

6165 Briggs, Lloyd Vernon, 1863-
Arizona and New Mexico, 1882, California, 1886,
Mexico, 1891, by L. Vernon Briggs ... Boston,
Priv. print., 1932.
x, 282 p. front., illus. (incl. facsims.),
plates, ports.   23 1/2 cm.

6166 Brigham, William Tufts, 1841-1926.
Guatemala: the land of the quetzal; a sketch
by William T. Brigham, A. M. New York, C. Scribner's
sons, 1887.
xv, 453 p. front., illus., pl., port., maps.

22 1/2 cm.

6167 Brine, Lindesay, 1834-1906.
Travels amongst American Indians, their ancient earthworks and temples; including a journey in Guatemala, Mexico, and Yucatan, and a visit to the ruins of Pantinamit, Utatlan, Palenque, and Uxmal. By Vice-Admiral Lindesay Brine... London, S. Low, Marston & company, limited, 1894.
xvi, 429 p. double front., illus. (incl. plans), plates, maps. (part fold.) 23 1/2 cm.

6168 Brink, McCormick, & co., publishers.
Illustrated atlas map of Sangamon county, Ill.; carefully compiled from personal examinations and surveys. Chicago, Brink, McCormick, & co., 1874.
108 p. illus. maps. 45 cm.

6169 Brink, (W. R.) and company.
Illustrated atlas map of Menard county, Ill.; carefully compiled from personal examinations and surveys. [Edwardsville?] Ill., W. R. Brink & co., 1874.
2 p.l., 7-117 p. incl. 19 col. maps (part fold.) illus. 45 cm.

6170 Brinson, Lessie Brannen.
A study of the life and works of Richard Malcolm Johnston. Nashville, Tenn., George Peabody College for Teachers, 1937.
11 p. 24 cm.

6171 Brissot [de Warville] Anacharsis.
Voyage au Guazacoalcos aux Antilles et aux États-Unis, par M. A. Brissot. Paris, A. Bertrand, 1837.
2 p.l., iv, 390 p. front., pl., map.

6172 Brissot, Jean-Pierre, called Brissot de Warville; 1754-1793.
Mémoire sur les noirs de l'Amérique septentrionale, lu à l'assemblée de la Société des amis des noirs, le 9 février 1789. Paris, Au bureau du Patriote français; Chez Bailly [&] de Senne [De l'imp. de Cailleau] 20 décembre 1789.

56 p.   20 cm.

6173   British Columbia and Vancouver's Island. A complete
hand-book, replete with the latest information concerning the newly discovered gold fields, with a
map. [London? 1858?]
67 p. map.   20 cm.

6174   British Columbia. Bureau of Mines.
Report on the iron ores of the coast of British
Columbia, by the provincial mineralogist. [Victoria,
B. C., Printed by R. Wolfenden, 1903]
30 p. illus., plates.   26 cm.

6175   British Columbia. Bureau of provincial information.
... Population of British Columbia, according to
proposed electoral districts. [Victoria, B. C.,
Printed by R. Wolfenden, 1902]
10 p.   25 1/2 x 18 1/2 cm.

6176   British Columbia, Canada's most westerly province;
its position, advantages, resources and climate; new
fields for mining, farming and ranching along the
lines of the Canadian Pacific railway; information
for prospectors, miners and intending settlers.
[n.p.] 1899.
63 p. illus., fold. map.   21 1/2 cm.

6177   British Columbia. Dept. of Agriculture.
British Columbia and its agricultural capabilities.
A brief descriptive pamphlet issued by the Depart-
ment of Agriculture, British Columbia. Victoria,
B. C., Printed by R. Wolfenden, 1902.
29 p. plates.   26 cm.

6178   British Columbia, its present resources and future
possibilities. A brief attempt to demonstrate the
value of the province. Published by direction of
the provincial government. Victoria, B. C., "The
Colonist" printing and publishing co., 1893.
109, [3] p. front. illus., fold. map.   22 1/2 cm.

6179   British Columbia. Lands and Works Dept.
... Columbia river exploration, 1865-66. Instructions, reports & journals relating to the government

exploration of the country lying between the
Shuswap and Okanagan lakes and the Rocky mountains.
Victoria, B. C., Printed at the Government printing
office [1866?]
　　36, 28 p.　　20 cm.
　　Title-page repeated and new pagination begins
after p. 36.

6180　British Columbia.　Lands Dept.
　　... Peace River land recording division.　Issued
by the Department of lands.　Honourable William R.
Ross, K. C., minister of lands.　Printed by
authority of the Legislative assembly.　[Victoria,
Printed by W. H. Cullin, 1914]
　　cover-title, 48 p.　illus.　25 1/2 cm.

6181　British Columbia.　Porcupine district commission.
　　Porcupine - Chiltat districts.　Report under the
Porcupine district commission act, 1900, by the
Honourable Archer Martin, special commissioner,
with observations on the P. and C. districts.
Victoria, B. C., Printed by R. Wolfenden, 1901.
　　13 p.　26 1/2 cm.

6182　British Columbia.　Royal commission of inquiry on
　　　timber and forestry.
　　Final report of the Royal commission of inquiry
on timber and forestry 1909-10...　Victoria, Printed
by R. Wolfenden, printer to the king's most excellent
Majesty, 1910.
　　116 p.　front. (fold. map), illus., plates
(partly col.)　27 cm.

6183　British Columbia.　Royal commission on acquisition
　　　of Texas Island.
　　Papers relating to the appointment and proceedings
of the Royal commission for instituting enquires
into the acquisition of Texada Island. Presented to
the Legislative assembly by command of His Excellency
the lieutenant-governor.　Victoria, Printed by
Richard Wolfenden, government printer, at the Government printing office, James Bay, 1874.
　　cover-title, 66 p.　25 1/2 cm.

6184　Britten, Mrs. Emma (Hardinge) d. 1899.

The great funeral oration on Abraham Lincoln,
delivered... April 16, 1865, at Cooper Institute,
New York... New York, American News Co. [1865]
28 p. 23 cm.

6185 Brocklehurst, Thomas Unett.
Mexico today: a country with a great future,
and a glance at the prehistoric remains and antiquities of the Montezumas. By Thomas Unett
Brocklehurst. With coloured plates and illustrations from sketches by the author, London, J.
Murray, 1883.
xv, 259 p. LVI pl. (part. col; incl. front.,
maps, facsim.) 22 cm.

6186 Bromme, Traugott, 1802-1866.
Traugott Bromme's Hand- und reisebuch für aus-
wanderer und reisende nach Nord-, Mittel- und Süd-
Amerika (den gesammten Vereinigten Staaten, Texas,
Canada, Brasilien, Mejiko, u.s.w.). 8., sehr verm.
und verb. aufl. von Gustav Struve. Mit einem
rathgeber in amerikanischen rechtsangelegenheiten
und einer spezial-karte der Vereinigten Staaten von
Nord-Amerika in stahlstich. Bamberg, Buchner;
New-York, B. Westermann u.co., 1866.
xii, 740 p. 19 cm.

6187 Brooke, Rupert, 1887-1915.
Letters from America, by Rupert Brooke. With a
preface by Henry James. New York, C. Scribner's
sons, 1916.
xiii, 180 p. front. (port.) 19 1/2 cm.

6188 Brooks, Geraldine, 1875-
Dames and daughters of the young republic...
illustrated by H. A. Ogden. New York, T. Y. Crowell
and co. [1901]
vii, 287 p. front., pl. 20 1/2 cm.

6189 Brooks, James, 1810-1873.
... Speech of the Hon. James Brooks, at 932
Broadway... December 30, 1862. [New York, 1863]
16 p. 23 cm.

6190 Brooks, Noah, 1830-1903.

The character and religion of President Lincoln:
a letter ... May 10, 1865. Champlain, Privately
printed, 1919.
11 p.   25 cm.

6191   Brooks, Noah, 1830-1903.
Lincoln, by friend and foe... Democratic manual of
1864; ed. by Robert J. Cole. London, N. Y., [etc.]
Gold medal library, [c1922]
96 p. illus.   12 cm.

6192   Broughton, William Robert.
A voyage of discovery to the North Pacific
coast... performed in His Majesty's sloop Providence,
and her tender, in the years 1795, 1796, 1797, 1798.
London, Printed for T. Cadell and W. Davies in the
Strand, 1804.
394 p. fold. maps, pl. (part.fold.) 22 cm.

6193   Browder, Earl Russell, 1891-
Lincoln and the Communists. [New York, Workers
Library Publishers, 1936]
14 p. port.   19 cm.

6194   Brown, George Stayley.
Yarmouth, Nova Scotia: a sequel to Campbell's
history. Boston, Rand Avery Company, 1888.
524 p.   24 cm.

6195   Brown, John, fl. 1858.
The Northwest passage and the plans for the search
for Sir John Franklin... London, Published by E.
Stanford, 1858.
xii, 463 p. illus., fold. maps.   22 cm.

Bound at end is John Brown, A sequel to the
Northwest passage and the search for Sir John
Franklin. A review... London, Published by E.
Stanford, 1860.
64 p.   22 cm.

6196   Brown, Marcus Monroe,° 1854-
A study of John D. Rockefeller, the wealthiest man
in the world; with his name left out, the history
of education and religion could not be written. By

65

Marcus M. Brown. Cleveland, O., 1905.
150 p. front., double pl., ports. 20 cm.

6197 Brown, Mary Edwards, 1866-1858.
Mrs. Mary Edwards Brown tells story of Lincoln's
Wedding, edited by Wayne C. Temple... Limited
edition published for members of the National
Lincoln-Civilian Council. Harrogate, Tenn.,
Lincoln Memorial University Press, 1960.
6 p. 22 1/2 cm.

6198 Brown, R   C   Lundon.
British Columbia. An essay... New Westminster,
Printed at the Royal Engineer Press, 1863.
64, xxxiii p. 20 cm.

6199 Brown, Sarah Poseg, 1859-
Down memory's lane. (Shelbyville, Ky.? Shelby
News? n.d.]
[15] p. 30 cm.

6200 Brown, William, of Leeds.
America: a four years' residence in the United
States and Canada; giving a full and fair description of the country, as it really is, with manners,
customs, & character of the inhabitants, anecdotes
of persons and institutions, prices of land and
produce, state of agriculture and manufactures.
By William Brown... Leeds, Printed for the author
by Kemplay and Bolland, 1849.
iv, 108 p. 20 1/2 cm.

6201 [Browne, Charles Farrar] 1834-1867.
Artemus Ward on his visit to Abe Lincoln:
Letter III. Reprinted from Vanity fair, December
8, 1860. Chicago, The Home of Books, Inc., 1939.
[12] p. front. 17 cm.

6202 Browne, Edith A   , 1874-
... Panama, by Edith A. Browne ... with sixteen
full-page illustrations, eight of them in colour.
London, A. and C. Black, 1913.
vii, [1], 87, [1] p. incl. maps. 15 pl. (part
col., incl. col. front.) 20 cm.

6203   Browning, Charles Henry.
          Americans of royal descent... Comp., ed., and
       copyrighted by Charles H. Browning. Philadelphia,
       Porter & Coates, 1883.
          2 p.l., [9]-319 p.   27 cm.

6204   Browning, Charles Henry.
          Americans of royal descent. A collection of
       genealogies of American families whose lineage is
       traced to the legitimate issue of kings. Reproduced
       ... by Charles H. Browning... 2d ed. ...   Philadel-
       phia, Porter & Coastes, 1891.
          732 p.   26 1/2 cm.

6205   Browning, Charles Henry.
          Americans of royal descent. Collection of
       genealogies showing the lineal descent from kings
       of some American families. Reproduced from recognized
       authoritative genealogical works, from printed
       family histories, and verified information supplied
       in manuscript pedigrees. Pub. by Charles H. Brown-
       ing... 7th ed. Philadelphia, 1911.
          546, [23], 547-549 p.   geneal. tables.   26 1/2 cm.

6206   Bruce, George A
          The capture and occupation of Richmond.   [n.p.,
       n.d.]
          46 p.   illus., maps.   24 cm.

6207   Bruchesi, Jean, 1901-
          Le Canada.   [Paris] F. Nathan [c1952]
          189 p. (p. 49-176 illus.)   24 cm.

6208   Bruges, Roger, graf von.
          Reiseskizzen aus West-Indien, Mexico und Nord-
       Amerika, gesammelt im jahre 1872.   Von Roger, graf
       von Bruges. Leipzig, Duncker & Humblot, 1873.
          x, 405, [1] p.   19 1/2 cm.

6209   [Brundle, John] 1882-
          The girl who died of a broken heart; from the pen
       of John, a Suffolk herd boy...   [Roche's Point,
       Ontario, c1941]
          1 p.l., 33 p.   20 cm.

6210 [Brundle, John] 1882-
        The woman of the unbeaten trail [Nancy Hanks]
      [Roche's Point, Ontario, John Brundle, 1940]
        8 p.   20 cm.

6211 Bryan, William Jennings, 1860-1925.
        Speeches of William Jennings Bryan, rev. and
      arranged by himself, with a biographical introduction
      by Mary Baird Bryan, his wife... New York and Lon-
      don, Funk & Wagnalls company, 1911.
        2 v.   fronts. (ports.)   17 1/2 cm.

6212 Bryant, Wilbur Franklin.
        The blood of Abel...   Hastings, Neb., Gazette-
      Journal co., 1887.
        169 p.   illus.   20 cm.

6213 Bryant, William Cullen, 1794-1878.
        Letters of a traveller; or, Notes of things seen
      in Europe and America. By William Cullen Bryant.
      2d ed.   New York, G. P. Putnam; [etc., etc.] 1850.
        442 p.   20 1/2 cm.

6214 [Bryant, William Cullen] 1794-1878, ed.
        Picturesque America; or, The land we live in,
      A delineation by pen and pencil of the mountains,
      rivers, lakes, forests, water-falls, shores,
      canons, valleys, cities, and other picturesque
      features of our country. With illustrations on
      steel and wood by eminent American artists...   New
      York, D. Appleton and company [c1872-74]
        2 v.   front., illus., plates.   32 1/2 cm.

6215 Bryce, George, 1844-1931.
        ... Among the mound builders' remains, by George
      Bryce... [Winnipeg, Manitoba free press company,
      1904]
        cover-title, 47, [1] p.   illus. (incl. maps)
      22 cm.   (The Historical and scientific society of
      Manitoba. Transaction, no. 66)

6216 Bryce, George, 1844-1931.
        ... Early days in Winnipeg. By George Bryce ...
      Winnipeg, Manitoba free press print, 1894.
        cover-title, 1 p.l., 8 p.   illus., port., plan.

22 1/2 cm.   (The Historical and scientific society of
Manitoba. Transaction no. 46)

6217   Bryce, George, 1844-1931.
        Educational reminiscences of one-third of a
    century in Winnipeg, 1871 to 1904, by Rev. Prof.
    George Bryce... president Manitoba college literary
    society; inaugural address delivered in convocation
    hall, Manitoba college, Winnipeg, November 18,
    1904. [Winnipeg? 1904?]
        cover-title, 12 p. illus.   23 cm.   (His
    Canadian pamphlets, 1871-1913, no. 29)

6218   Bryce, George, 1844-1931.
        Everyman's geology of the three prairie provinces
    of the Canadian west, by George Bryce... Winnipeg,
    1907.
        68 p. maps (1 fold.), diag.   21 1/2 cm.   (His
    Canadian pamphlets, 1871-1913. no. 34)

6219   Bryce, George, 1844-1931.
        ... Intrusive ethnological types in Rupert's
    Land, by Rev. Dr. G. Bryce. Ottawa, For sale by J.
    Hope & sons [etc., etc.] 1903.
        cover-title, 135-144 p.   23 cm.   (His Canadian
    pamphlets, 1871-1913, no. 26)

6220   Bryce, George, 1844-1931.
        ... The Lake of the Woods; its history, geology,
    mining and manufacturing. By George Bryce...
    Winnipeg, The Manitoba free press company, 1897.
        cover-title, 17, [1] p. illus., fold. map.
    22 cm.   (The Historical and scientific society of
    Manitoba, Transaction no. 49)

6221   Bryce, George, 1844-1931.
        ... Mackenzie, Selkirk, Simpson, by Rev. George
    Bryce, D. D. Ed. de luxe. Toronto, Morang & co.,
    limited, 1905.
        6 p.l., 305 p. 3 port. (incl. front.)   24 cm.

6222   Bryce, George, 1844-1931.
        Manitoba: its infancy, growth, and present con-
    dition. With maps and illustrations. London,
    Sampson Low, Marston, Searle & Rivington, 1882.

viii, 367 p. illus., maps, ports. 20 cm.

6223 Bryce, George, 1844-1931.
      ... Notes and comments on Harmon's journal,
      1800-1820, by Rev. Professor Bryce... Winnipeg,
      Manitoba daily free press, 1883.
          cover-title, 7 p. 22 cm. (The Historical and
      scientific society of Manitoba, Transaction no. 3)

6224 Bryce, George, 1844-1931.
      ... The old settlers of Red River, by George
      Bryce... A paper read before the society on the
      evening of 26th November, 1885... Winnipeg, Mani-
      toba daily free press, 1885.
          cover-title, 9 no. 22 1/2 cm. (The Historical
      and scientific society of Manitoba, Transaction
      no. 19)

6225 Bryce, George, 1844-1931.
      ... Original letters and other documents relating
      to the Selkirk settlement, read before the society
      January 17th, 1889, by Rev. Dr. Bryce and C. N.
      Bell. Winnipeg, Manitoba free press print, 1889.
          cover-title, [3]-10 p. 22 1/2 cm. (The His-
      torical and scientific society of Manitoba, Trans-
      action no. 33)

6226 Bryce, George, 1844-1931.
      ... Our Canadian mountain provinces, by Rev.
      Prof. George Bryce... honorary president of Manitoba
      college literary society; inaugural address delivered
      in Convocation hall, Manitoba college, Winnipeg,
      November 3rd, 1905. [Winnipeg? 1905?]
          cover-title, 8 p. 23 cm. (His Canadian pamphlets
      1871-1913. no. 31)

6227 Bryce, George, 1844-1931.
      ... A poet's message: being a discourse given
      by Rev. George Bryce... during the visit of the
      British association for the advancement of science,
      delivered... August 29th, 1909, in Knox church,
      Winnipeg. [Winnipeg? 1909?]
          cover-title, 15 p. 21 1/2 cm. (His Canadian
      pamphlets, 1871-1913. no. 43)

6228   Bryce, George, 1844-1931.
        The remarkable history of the Hudson's bay company,
        including that of the French traders of north-western
        Canada and of the North-west, XY, and Astor fur
        companies, by George Bryce... London, S. Low,
        Marston & company, 1900.
        xx p., 1 1., 501, [1] p. front. plates, ports.,
        maps, facsim., coat of arms.   21 cm.

6229   Bryce, George, 1844-1931.
        The romantic settlement of Lord Selkirk's
        colonists (the pioneers of Manitoba) By George
        Bryce...   Toronto, The Musson book company limited,
        1909.
        328 p.   front., illus., plates, ports.   22 1/2 cm.

6230   [Bryce, George] 1844-1931.
        "Seven Oaks"; an account of the affair of Seven
        Oaks; the circumstances which led up to it; a
        description of the contestants; The events of the
        conflict, including death of Governor Semple and
        his followers; and a report of the proceedings of
        the gathering for the unveiling of the "Seven Oaks
        monument," June 19th, 1891... Winnipeg, Manitoba,
        Manitoba free press co. [1891?]
        cover-title, 38 p. incl. 1 pl. map (facsim.)
        22 cm.   (The Historical and scientific society of
        Manitoba. Transaction no. 43)

6231   Bryce, George, 1844-1931.
        A short history of the Canadian people, by George
        Bryce...   London, S. Low, Marston, Searle & Riving-
        ton, 1887.
        vii, 528 p. fold. map.   19 1/2 cm.

6232   Bryce, George, 1844-1931.
        ... Sketch of the life and discoveries of Robert
        Campbell, chief factor of the Hon. Hudson's Bay
        company, by George Bryce... Winnipeg, Manitoba
        free press company, 1898.
        cover-title, 18 p. incl. illus., 1 port.   22 cm.
        (The Historical and scientific society of Manitoba,
        Transaction no. 52)

6233   Bryce, George, 1844-1931.

... Sketch of the life of John Tanner, a famous
Manitoba scout. A border type... by George Bryce
... Winnipeg, Manitoba free press print, 1888.
cover-title, 4 p. 22 cm. (The Historical and
scientific society of Manitoba, Transaction no. 30)

6234 Bryce, George, 1844-1931.
... The Souris country, its monuments, mounds,
forts and rivers, by George Bryce... Winnipeg,
Manitoba free press print, 1887.
cover-title, 7 p. 22 cm. (The Historical and
scientific society of Manitoba, Transaction no. 24)

6235 Bryce, George, 1844-1931.
... Winnipeg country. Its discovery and the
great consequences resulting. [by] Rev. Professor
Bryce... [Winnipeg, 1883]
cover-title, 9 p. 23 cm. (The Historical and
scientific society of Manitoba, Transaction no. 4)

6236 Bryce, George, 1844-1931.
... Worthies of old Red river, by George Bryce...
Winnipeg, Manitoba free press print, 1896.
cover-title, 12 p. illus. (incl. ports., map)
22 cm. (The Historical and scientific society of
Manitoba, Transaction no. 48)

6237 Buache, J   N
Mémoires sur les pays de l'Asie et de l'Amérique,
situés au nord de la mer du sud. Accompagnés d'une
carte de comparaison des plans de MM. Engel & de
Vaugondy avec de plan des cartes modernes...
Paris, Chez l'auteur, 1775.
21 p. map. 20 cm.

6238 Buache, Philippe.
Considérations géographiques et physiques sur les
nouvelles découvertes au nord de la grande mer,
appellée vulgairement la mer de sud. Paris, avec
l'approbation & sous le privilège de l'Académie
royale des sciences, 1753.
158, [6] p. fold. pl., fold. maps. 20 cm.

6239 Buchan, Susan (Grosvenor) 1882-
Canada [by] Lady Tweedsmuir; with twelve plates

in colour and thirty-two illustrations in black
and white. London, Pub. for Penns in the rocks
press by W. Collins, 1941.
    47, [1] p. illus. (incl. ports., maps), col.
plates.   22 1/2 cm.

6240   Buckingham, John Edward, 1828-1909.
    Reminiscences and souvenirs of the assassination
of Abraham Lincoln. Washington, D. C., R. H.
Darby, 1894.
    89 p. illus.   23 cm.

6241   Buckley, Michael Bernard, 1831-1872.
    Diary of a tour in America ... by Rev. M. B.
Buckley, of Cork, Ireland, a special missionary in
North America and Canada in 1870 and 1871. Ed. by
his sister, Kate Buckley ... Dublin, Sealy, Bryers
& Walker, 1886.
    4 p.l., 384 p. front. (port.)   19 cm.

6242   Buckley, Michael Bernard, 1831-1872.
    Diary of a tour in America ... By Rev. M. B.
Buckley, of Cork, Ireland. A special missionary in
North America and Canada in 1870 and 1871. Edited
by his sister Kate Buckley... Dublin, Sealy,
Bryers & Walker, 1889.
    2 p.l., ii p., 1 l., 384 p. front. (port.)   19 cm.

6243   [Buel, Oliver Prince] 1838-1899.
    The Abraham Lincoln myth: an essay in "higher
criticism" by Bocardo Bramantip [pseud.], Huxleyan
professor of dialectics in the University of Conco.
From the Thirty-seventh century magazine of April
A. D. 3663. New York, Mascot pub. co., 1894.
    88 p.   19 cm.

6244   Buenos Aires. Universidade.
    Anales. Buenos Aires, 1888-1900.
    15 v.   25 cm.

6245   Bullock, Alexander Hamilton, 1816-1882.
    Abraham Lincoln: the just magistrate, the
representative statesman, the practical phil-
anthropist: address... before the City Council
and citizens of Worcester, June 1, 1865. Worcester,

C. Hamilton [1865]
49 p.   24 cm.

6246   Bullock, William, fl. 1808-1828.
Mexiko in 1823; of, Beschrijving eener reis door
Nieuw-Spanje ... door M. Beulloch ... voorafgegaan
door eene inleiding van Sir John Byerley, en
verrijkt met historische bescheiden en aanteekeningen
zoo van den vertaler, als van den schrijver ...
Delft, Weduwe J. Allart, 1825.
2 v. in 1.   fronts.   22 cm.

6247   Bullock, William, fl. 1808-1828.
Le Mexique en 1823, ou Relation d'un voyage
dans la Nouvelle-Espagne, contenant des notions
exactes et peu connues sur la situation physique,
morale et politique de ce pays; accompagné d'un
atlas de vingt planches; par m. Beulloch ... ouvrage
traduit de l'anglais par M***.   Précédé d'une
introduction, et enrichi de pièces justificatives
et de notes; par Sir John Byerley ...   Paris,
Alexis-Eymery, 1824.
2 v.   20 1/2 cm.

6248   Bullock, William, fl. 1808-1828.
Six months' residence and travels in Mexico;
containing remarks on the present state of New
Spain, its natural productions, state of society,
manufactures, trade, agriculture, and antiquities,
etc...   By W. Bullock...   London, J. Murray, 1824.
1 p.l., [v]-xii, 532 p.   fold. front., plates
(part col.), 2 fold. maps, fold. tab.   22 cm.

6249   Bulnes, Francisco, 1848-
... Las grandes mentiras de nuestra historia; la
nación y el ejército en las guerras extranjeras
por Francisco Bulnes.   Paris, México, la v^{da} de C.
Bouret, 1904.
3 p.l., 924 p.   22 cm.

6250   Búlnes, Gonzalo, 1851-
... Bolívar en el Perú; ultimas campañas de la
independencia del Peru ...   Madrid, Editorial-
América, 1919.
2 v.   22 1/2 cm.

6251 Bungener, Laurence Louis Felix, 1814-1874.
      Lincoln: sa vie, son oeuvre, et sa mort, par F.
Bungener. Lausanne, G. Bridel, 1865.
    160 p.   18 cm.

6252 Burbank, Addison, 1895-
      Guatemala profile, written and illustrated by
Addison Burbank. New York, Coward-McCann, inc.,
1939.
    x, 296 p. illus.   22 1/2 cm.

6253 Burch, George W
      Ancestry and descendants of John Russell Haynes.
Hartford, Conn., 1924.
    140 p.   22 cm.

6254 Burkart, Josef, 1798-1874.
      Aufenthalt und reisen in Mexico in den jahren
1825 bis 1834. Bemerkungen über land, produkte,
leben und sitten der einwohner und beobachtungen aus
dem gebiete der mineralogie, geognosie, bergbaukunde,
meteorologie, geographie etc. Von Joseph Burkart
... Mit einem vorworte von dr. J. Nöggerath ...
Stuttgart, E. Schweizerbart, 1836.
    2 v. in 1. xi fold. pl. (part col.; incl.
maps)   22 cm.

6255 Burke, Arthur Meredyth.
      The prominent families of the United States of
America, edited by Arthur Meredyth Burke ...
Volume one. London, The Sackville press, ltd.
[1908]
    510 p. illus. (coats of arms)   20 cm.

6256 Burney, James, 1750-1821.
      A chronological history of the discoveries in
the South sea or Pacific ocean... By James Burney
... London, Printed by L. Hansard, 1803-17.
    5 v. fronts., plates maps.   30 cm.

6257 [Burham, Benjamin Franklin] 1830-1898.
      ... The prayer of the presidents: being Washington's
"New year aspiration" with Jefferson's plural
pronouns, etc., and Adams and Lincoln's accretions;
from the manuscript of a minister of Lincoln's ad-

ministration. Boston, The Antique book-store, 1887.
16 p. 26 1/2 cm.

6258 Burriss, Charles Walker, 1860–
From New York to San Francisco by way of Panama
Canal Zone and all Central American ports of the
Pacific Ocean, by Chas. W. Burris... [Kansas
City? Mo., 1911]
cover-title, 1 p.l., 5-96 p. 18 1/2 x 15 cm.

6259 Bury, Viscount.
Balance sheet of the Washington treaty of 1872,
in account with the people of Great Britain and her
colonies... London, Edward Stanford, 1873.
27 p. map. 20 cm.

6260 [Butel-Dumont, Georges Marie] 1725-1788.
Der engländischen pflanzstädte in Nord-America,
geschichte und handlung nebst einer zuverlässigen
nachricht von der gegenwärtigen anzahl der dasigen
einwohner, und einer umständlichen beschreibung der
landesverfassung, absonderlich was Neu-England,
Pennsylvanien, Carolina und Georgien betrifft, Aus
dem französischen übersetzt. Stuttgart, J. B.
Metzler, 1755.
8 p.l., 216 p. 17 cm.

6261 [Butel-Dumont, Georges Marie] 1725-1788.
Geographische und historisch-politische nachrichten
von demjenigen theil des Nördlichen Amerika, um
dessen gränzen, zwischen den Franzosen und Engländern
gegenwartig krieg geführet wird. Nebst einen
beschreibung der dasigen notheithaften handlung und
beschaffenheit des landes, besonders was Neuland
oder Terreneuve, Akadien oder Neuschottland, Neuengla
Pensilvanien, Philadelfia, Carolina, Georgien, u.s.w.
betrift. Aus dem französischen übersetzt, und mit de
nordamerikanischen kriegsgeschichte, von englischer
seite herausgegeben, begleitet... Frankfurt and
Leipzig, 1756.
12 p.l., 238, xviii, 121 p. 2 pl. (1 fold.)
fold. map. 17 1/2 cm.

6262 Butler, Edward C
Our little Mexican cousin... Boston, L. C. Page

& company, 1905.
100 p. illus.   20 1/2 cm.

6263 Butler, Sir William Francis, 1838-1910.
       The great lone land: a narrative of travel
and adventure in the North-west of America. By
Major W. F. Butler... 5th ed. London. S. Low,
Marston, Low & Searle, 1873.
       x p., 1 1., 386 p. front. (fold. map) plates.
19 1/2 cm.

6264 Butler, Sir William Francis, 1838-1910.
       The wild north land: being the story of a winter
journey, with dogs, across northern North America.
By Captain W. F. Butler... 4th ed. London, S. Low,
Marston, Low & Searle, 1874.
       x p., 1 1., 358 p. front. (port.), 15 pl., fold.
map.   22 cm.

6265 Butler, Sir William Francis, 1838-1910.
       The wild northland, being the story of a winter
journey, with dog, across northern North America, by
Gen. Sir William Francis Butler... New York, A. S.
Barnes and company, 1904.
       1 p.l., vii-xxii, 360 p. front. (fold. map)
17 1/2 cm.

6266 Byxbee, O   F
       Establishing a newspaper. A handbook for the
prospective publishers, including suggestions for
the financial of existing daily and weekly journals.
By O. F. Byxbee. Chicago, Ill., The Inland printer
company, 1901.
       113 p.   20 cm.

                              C

6267 Cabot, James Elliot, 1821-1903.
       A memoir of Ralph Waldo Emerson, by James Elliot

Cabot... Boston and New York, Houghton, Mifflin and
company, 1887.
2 v. front. (port.) 20 cm.

6268 [Cabrera, Luis]
... La herencia de Carranza, por el Lic. Blas
Urrea [pseud.] Mexico [Imprenta nacional, s.a.]
1920.
131 p., 1 l., [2] p. 22 1/2 cm.

6269 [Cabrera y Quintero, Cayetano] d. 1775.
El patronato disputado, dissertacion apologetica,
por el voto, eleccion, y juramento de patrona, a
Maria Santissima, venerada en su imagen de Guadalupe
de rezo Mexico, e invalidado para negarle el del
comun, (que à titulo de patrona electa y jurada,
segun el decreto de la sagrada Congregacion de
ritos) se le ha dado en esta metropoli, por el
b^r. d. Jvan Pablo Zetina Infante, mrō. de ceremonias
en la cathedral de la Puebla, en el singularissimo
dictamen, y parecer, que sin pedirselo, diò en
aquella, y quiso extender â esta ciudad, à corregir
el que le pareciò arrojo de esta metropolitana.
Dedicase al ill^{mo}. v. señor dean, y Cabildo sede-
vacante de la santa iglesia de los Angeles. Por
mano del d^r. d. Joseph Fernandez Mendez... Con
licencia, en Mexico, En la Imprenta real del superior
gobierno, y del nuevo rezado de doña Maria de Rivera,
en el Empedradillo, 1741.
5 p.l., 106 p. illus. 24 cm.

6270 Cadiz, Diego José de, 1743-1801.
Carte del M.R.P. Fr. Diego de Cadiz, á una
Señora en respuesta á la consulta que le hizo sobre
si son licitos los Bayles... Puebla, reimpresa, R.
Seminario Palafoxiano, 1793.
15 p. 21 cm.

6271 Caird, Sir James, 1816-1892.
Prairie farming in America. With notes by the
way on Canada and the United States. By James
Caird ... London, Longman, Brown, Green, Longmans,
& Roberts, 1859.
viii, 128 p. front. (fold. map) 18 cm.

6272 [Calderon de la Barca, Frances Erskine (Inglis)]
1804-1882.
Life in Mexico during a residence of two years
in that country. By Mme. C - de la B -... Boston,
C. C. Little and J. Brown, 1843.
2 v. fronts. 18 1/2 cm.

6273 Calderón de la Barca, Frances Erskine (Inglis) 1804-
1882.
... La vida en México; prólogo y selección de
Antonio Acevedo Escobedo. México, Secretaría de educación pública, 1944.
ix, [11]-04, [2] p. 20 cm.

6274 Calderón de la Barca, Pedro, 1600-1681.
Comedia famosa. La aurora en Copacabana. De
don Pedro Calderon de la Barca. [n.p., 17-]
52 p. 21 cm.

6275 Calderon, Fray Francisco Santiago, bp., d. 1736.
Avissos pastorales, que... Don Fr. Francisco
Santiago Calderon... dá a todos los Mynistros de
Almas de su Obispado ... Puebla, Viuda Miguel de
Ortega Bonilla, 1751.
30 p. 21 cm.

6276 Calderón, Jacinto.
Relacion del el grave aparato con qve la re-
ligiosissma Prouincia de Oaxaca de el Orden de
predicadores celebró la solemnidad de su capitulo
prouincial del ano de 1646. Con el svperior
patrocinio, y soberano amparo del illustriss. y rr.
señor doctor don Bartholome de Venauides y de la
Cerdaio. Y concorde eleccion de prouincial en el
muy r.p.m.fr. Martin de Regvena... Hizola el p.
presentado fr. Iacintho Calderon... Mexico,
Iuan Ruyz, 1646.
13 l. 21 cm.

6277 Calderón, Juan Alonso.
Memorial, y discurso historico-ivridico-politico
qve dio a la magestad Catolica... Don Philipe
qvarto... Madrid, Diego Diaz de la Carrera, 1651.
26 l. 22 cm.

6278　California. State library, Sacramento. Sutro
　　　　branch, San Francisco.
　　　　... An account of early settlements in upper
　　　　Canada. With an introduction by Carey McWilliams
　　　　... Prepared by the personnel of the Works progress
　　　　administration, Project no. 665-08-3-236. A. Yedidi₤
　　　　supervisor. P. Radin, editor ... Sponsored by the
　　　　California state library. San Francisco, 1940.
　　　　7 p.l., 5-95 numb. l. incl. illus., map, plans,
　　　　tables, forms. 27 1/2 cm.

6279　Callcott, Maria (Dundas) Graham, lady, 1785-1842.
　　　　... Diario de su residencia en Chile (1822) y
　　　　de su viaje al Brasil (1823). San Martin.--
　　　　Cochrane.--O'Higgins. Prólogo de don Juan Concha.
　　　　Madrid, Editorial-América [1916]
　　　　451 p., 1 l. 23 cm.

6280　Calvo, Joaquín Bernardo, 1857-1915.
　　　　The Republic of Costa Rica, by Joaquin Bernardo
　　　　Calvo. Translated from the Spanish and edited by
　　　　L. de T. with introduction, additions, and exten-
　　　　sions by the editor... Chicago and New York, Rand,
　　　　McNally & co., 1890.
　　　　292 p. incl. front., plates, ports., 2 fold.
　　　　maps. 20 cm.

6281　Camacho Roldán, Salvador, 1827-1900.
　　　　Abraham Lincoln; translated from La Opinión,
　　　　Bogotá, Colombia, June 7, 1865. [Tarrytown, N. Y.,
　　　　Reprinted by W. Abbott, 1925]
　　　　9 p. 20 cm.

6282　Camargo, Jerónimo de.
　　　　... Por el real fisco, y en sv nombre el licenciad₤
　　　　don Geronimo de Camargo, fiscal del Consejo real
　　　　de las Indias. Con Andres Martinez de Amileta,
　　　　vezino de la Ciudad de los Reyes, en los reynos del
　　　　Perù. Sobre la confirmacion de la sentencia de
　　　　vista del cosejo de 22. de enero del año passado
　　　　de 43 por la qual se absoluiò al real fisco de los
　　　　treinta y seis mil pesos del prometido que pretendi₤
　　　　auer ganado por el crecimiento q auia hecho en el
　　　　cabezon de las alcaualas de dicha ciudad. y lo
　　　　acordado. [n.p., 1644?]

8 numb. l.   21 cm.

6283   Cameron, Agnes Deans.
The new north; being some account of a woman's
journey through Canada to the Arctic. With many
illustrations from photographs by the author.
New York and London, D. Appleton and company, 1910.
    xix, 398 p. front., illus. (incl. ports.), map.
23 1/2 cm.

6284   Cameron, Mrs. Charlotte (Wales-Almy)
Mexico in revolution, an account of an English
woman's experiences & adventures in the land of
revolution, with a description of the people, the
beauties of the country & the highly interesting
remains of Aztec civilisation, by Charlotte Cameron
... London, Seeley, Service & co. limited, 1925.
    4 p.l., 13-278 p. front., plates.   22 cm.

6285   Cameron, Edward Robert, 1857-
Memories of Ralph Vansittart, a member of the
Parliament of Canada, 1861-1867. Toronto, Musson
Book Co. [c.1902]
    229 p.   19 cm.

6286   Cameron, Kenneth Walter, 1908-
The Presbury family of Maryland and the Ohio
Valley; materials for the writing of a family
history, with data on the following related lines:
Hall, Stansbury, Colegate, Phillips, White, Lytle
(Little), Patterson, Beall, Bayless, Kaminsky,
Parry, Shockley, Foster, Hyndman, Rodgers, Foor,
Fell, Barker, Cameron, Jones, James, and Rossoff.
Hartford, 1950.
    2 v. (398 l.)   illus., ports., geneal. tables.
27 cm.

6287   Camison, Rosendo.
Carta instructiva de d. Rosendo Camison, maestro
de primeras letras en el Cuzco, y opositor a
escuelas vacantes de esta corte a los autores del
Diario, en la qual les hace algunas amistosas
adventencias sobre faltas de excititud; y con éste
motivo se trata del verdadero arte de escribir. Con
licencia. Madrid, En la Imprenta real, 1786.

32 p.   21 cm.

6288   The campaign of 1860, comprising the speeches of
       Abraham Lincoln, William H. Seward, Henry Wilson,
       Benjamin F. Wade, Carl Schurz, Charles Sumner,
       William M. Evarts, & c.   Albany, Weed, Parsons &
       company, 1860.
       18 (i.e. 16) no. in 1 v.   23 1/2 cm.

6289   Campbell, John Kerr.
       Through the United States of America and Canada,
       being a record of holiday rambles and experiences.
       London, Partridge [1886]
       xii, 260 p.   20 cm.

6290   Campbell, Patrick.
       Travels in the interior inhabited parts of North
       America in the years 1791 and 1792, by P. Campbell;
       edited, with an introduction, by H. H. Langton, and
       with notes by H. H. Langton and W. F. Ganong.
       Toronto, The Champlain society, 1937.
       xxi, 326, xii p.   front., ports., 2 pl. (1 fold.)
       25 cm.

6291   Campbell, Reau.
       Campbell's new revised complete guide and descrip-
       tive book of Mexico; by Reau Campbell.   Mexico,
       Sonora news company, 1899.
       351 p.   front. (port.), illus., fold. map.
       19 x 14 1/2 cm.

6292   Campbell, Reau.
       Mexico and the Mexicans, the material matters
       and mysterious myths of that country and its people.
       By Reau Campbell ...   Mexico, Sonora news company,
       1892.
       1 p.l., 5-131 p.   front., illus.   17 cm.

6293   Campbell, W   P
       ... The escape and wanderings of J. Wilkes
       Booth, until ending of the trail by suicide in
       Oklahoma...   Oklahoma City, Privately printed,
       1922.
       144 p.   illus.   21 cm.

6294 Campillo, Gines.
  Compendio curioso del atlas abreviado, el que
con mucha claridad dá noticia de todo el mundo, y
cosas inventadas... Pamplona, En la oficina de
los Herederos de Martinez, 1769.
  5 p.l., 274 p. 15 cm.

6295 Canada.
  Manitoba and the North-west territories Assiniboia,
Alberta, Saskatchewan, in which are included the
newly discovered gold fields of the Yukon; information as to the resources and climates of these
countries for intending farmers, ranchers, and
miners, 1897. Ottawa, Government printing bureau,
1898.
  48 p. incl. front., illus. 1 pl., fold. map.
24 cm.

6296 Canada. Archives.
  ... Catalogue of maps, plans and charts in the
Map room of the Dominion archives, classified and
indexed by H. R. Holmden, in charge of the Map
division, Pub. by authority of the secretary of
state under the direction of the archivist. Ottawa,
Government printing bureau, 1912.
  xii, 685 p. 25 cm.

6297 Canada. Archives.
  Papers from the Canadian archives...
  (In Wisconsin. State Historical Society.
Collections. Madison, 1888-92. 23 cm. v. 11,
p. [97]-212; v. 12, p. [23]-132)

6298 Canada. Auditor-general's office.
  Expenditure arising out of trouble in the North-
west Territories from 1st July 1885, to 15th
March, 1886. Also subsidiary statement of the
Hudson Bay company's supplies... Ottawa, Printed
by Maclean, Roger & co., 1886.
  cover-title, 60 p. 24 1/2 cm.

6299 Canada. Dept. of Agriculture.
  Province of Manitoba and north west territory
of the Dominion of Canada... Ottawa, 1876.
  79 p. 22 cm.

6300   Canada. Dept. of Justice.
        In the case of Louis Riel, convicted of treason,
        and executed therefore. Memorandum of Sir
        Alexander Campbell. Ottawa, Printed by Maclean,
        Roger & co., 1881.
        10 p.   23 cm.

6301   Canada. Dept. of Justice.
        Trials in connection with the north-west rebel-
        lion, 1885. Ottawa, Printed by Maclean, Roger &
        co., 1886.
        cover-title, 408 p.   22 cm.

6302   Canada. Dept. of Marine and Fisheries.
        Report on the Dominion government expedition
        to Hudson Bay and the Arctic islands on board the
        D. G. S. Neptune, 1903-1904, by A. P. Low. ...
        officer in charge. Ottawa, Government printing
        bureau, 1906.
        xvii, 355 p., incl. front., illus., plates,
        fold. map (in pocket)   23 1/2 cm.

6303   Canada. Dept. of Marine and Fisheries.
        Report on the Dominion government expedition to
        the northern waters and Arctic archipelago of the
        D. G. S. "Arctic" in 1910, under command of J. E.
        Bernier. [Ottawa? 1911?]
        161 p.   illus., fold. maps (1 in pocket)   25 cm.

6304   Canada. Dept. of Militia and Defence.
        Report of Lieutenant-Colonel W. H. Jackson
        ... on matters in connection with the suppression
        of the rebellion in the north-west territories in
        1885. Presented to Parliament. Ottawa, Maclean,
        Roger & co., 1887.
        44 p.   22 cm.

6305   Canada. Dept. of the Interior.
        Facts for the people. The Northwest rebellion.
        The question of the half-breeds and the government's
        treatment of them. [Ottawa? 1887?]
        18 p.   21 cm.

6306   Canada. Dept. of the Interior, Natural resources
        intelligence branch.

The Peace river country, Canada: its resources
and opportunities, by H. F. Kitto... (3d ed., rev.)
... Ottawa, F. A. Acland, printer to the king, 1930.
115, [1] p. incl. illus., maps, tables.   23 cm.

6307 Le Canada français; revue publiée sous la direction
      d'un comité de professeurs de l'Université Laval.
      Religion, philosophie, histoire, beaux-arts, sciences
      et lettres, v. 1-4; année 1888-91. Québec, Impr.
      de L.-J. Demers, 1888-91.
      4 v.   26 cm.

6308 Canada. Geological survey.
      Guide-book[s] no. 1-10. Ottawa, 1913.
      10 no. illus., maps.   21 cm.

6309 Canada. Parliament. House of commons. Select
      standing committee on banking and commerce.
      ... Revision of the act respecting banks and
      banking. Minutes of proceedings, evidence, &c.,
      Committee on banking and commerce during parlia-
      mentary session of 1912-1913. Appendix no. 2 to
      Journals of the House of commons. Ottawa, C. H.
      Parmelee, printer to the King's most excellent
      Majesty, 1913.
      vii, 725 p. tables.   25 1/2 cm.

6310 Canada. Parliament. Senate. Select committee on
      resources of territory between Labrador and the Rocky
      Mountains.
      Canada's fertile northland; a glimpse of the
      enormous resources of part of the unexplored regions
      of the Dominion: Evidence heard before a select
      committee of the Senate of Canada during the par-
      liamentary session of 1906-7, and the report based
      thereon; ed. by Captain Ernest J. Chambers... Pub.
      under direction of R. E. Young, D.L.S., supt.,
      railway lands, Dept. interior... Ottawa, Government
      printing bureau, 1907.
      3 p.l., 139 p. 16 pl. and atlas of 5 fold. maps.
      25 1/2 cm.

6311 Canada. Parliament. Senate. Select committee on
      Rupert's Land, Red River, and North-west territory.
      Report... together with minutes of evidence.

Ottawa, 1870.
38 p.   fold. map.   25 cm.

6312   Canada.   Provincial secretary's office.
Papers relative to the exploration of the
country between Lake Superior and the Red River
settlement.   Presented to both houses of Parliament
by command of Her Majesty.   London, Eyre and Spottis
woode, 1859.
163 p.   fold. maps.   27 cm.

6313   Canada.   Provincial secretary's office.
Report on the exploration of the country between
Lake Superior and the Red River settlement ...
Toronto, John Lovell, 1858.
425 p.   22 cm.

6314   Canada.   Secretary of State.
Return.   Instructions to surveyors sent to
the North-West territory...   Ottawa, Printed by
J. H. Taylor, 1870.
cover-title, 21 p.   tables.   22 cm.

6315   Canada.   Secretary of State.
Return.   Instructions to the Honorable A. Archi-
bald, lieutenant-governor of Manitoba and of the
North-west territory, & c., & c.   ...   Ottawa,
Printed by L. B. Taylor, 1871.
135 p.   22 cm.

6316   Canada.   Secretary of State.
Statement of claims made on the Dominion government upon the insurrection in the north-west territories...   Ottawa, Printed by L. B. Taylor, 1871.
57 p.   23 cm.

6317   Canadian Alpine journal...   v. 1-   ; 1907-
[Banff, Can.]   The Alpine club of Canada, 1907-
v.   fronts., illus., plates (part fold.),
ports., maps (part fold.)   23 cm.

6318   The Canadian guide-book ...   A guide to eastern
Canada and Newfoundland ... by Charles G. D. Roberts
... and western Canada to Vancouver's island...
New York. D. Appleton & company, 1891-19--.

v.   illus., plates, maps (part fold.)
fold. plans.   28 cm.

6319   The Canadian Pacific Railway Company.
        The Canadian Pacific, the new highway to the
east across the mountains, prairies & rivers of
Canada.   [Montreal? 1887]
        45 p.   illus., map.   27 cm.

6320   Canadian Pacific Railway Company.
        The Canadian Pacific, the new highway to the
orient, across the mountains, prairies, and
rivers of Canada.   [Montreal? 1893?]
        cover-title, 48 p.   illus., map.   26 cm.

6321   Canadian Pacific Railway Company.
        Description of the country between Lake Superior
and the Pacific Ocean, on the line of the Canadian
Pacific railway.   Compiled from the last authorities,
and published by order of the Canadian government.
Ottawa, November, 1876.
        143 p.   20 cm.

6322   Canadian Pacific Railway Company.
        Summer tours.   Montreal, Passenger Dept.,
Canadian Pacific Railway, 1887.
        138 p.   illus., fold. map.   17 cm.

6323   Canadian Pacific Railway Company.   Colonization
        Dept., Calgary.
        Irrigation farming in the kingdom of alfalfa Bow
River Valley in Southern Alberta, Canada.   Alberta,
Canada, 1910.
        63 p.   illus., tables.   20 cm.

6324   The Canadian Pacific Rockies: a series of twenty-
        four hand colored photogravues.   Banff, Canada,
        Published by Byron Harmon [n.d.]
        [25] p.   illus.   23 x 34 cm.

6325   A Canadian tour: a reprint of letters from the
        special correspondent of the Times ...   London,
        Printed by G. E. Wright, 1886.
        cover-title, 58 p.   double map.   29 cm.

6326 Canigonet, merchant in Haiti.
Très-humbles et trés-respectueuses représenta-
tions adressées à messieurs du Comité colonial
résident à Paris, sur leur arrêté du 30 Octobre
1788. [n.p., 1788]
32 p.   20 cm.

6327 Canisius, Theodor.
Abraham Lincoln. Zweite Ausgabe. Berlin,
Abenheimsche Verlagsbuchhandlung, 1878.
340 p. front.   16 cm.

6328 Cañizares, José de, 1676-1750.
... Comedia famosa. El pleyto de Hernan Cortés
con Panfilo de Narvaez, de don Joseph de Cañizares.
[Colophon: Con licencia: En Valencia, En la
imprenta de la viuda de Joseph de Orga, calle de la
Cruz Nueva, en donde se hallará esta, y otras de
diferentes títulos. Año 1762]
32 p.   24 cm.
At head of caption title: N. 27. Pag. I.

6329 Cano, Juan.
Reformacion moral, politica, y christiana del
comercio, en doze estatvtos, qve restavran treinta
millones de reales de a ocho de renta cada año a
la monarqvia española. Colegida en diez y seis
años de experiencias continvas por todas las
placas comerciales del vniuerso, y puesta à las
plantas del mayor monarca de sus quatro partes,
don Carlos II. rey de España, por Ivan Cano,
natvral de la villa de San Clavdio, en el condado
de Borgoña. Impresso en Madrid. Año de 1675.
18 p.l., 12, 21, 9, 15, 30, 9, 13, 9, 11, 8, 8,
11, 1., [4] p.   23 cm.

6330 Carbutt, Mary (Rhodes) Lady, "Mrs. E. H. Carbutt."
Five months' fine weather in Canada, western
U. S., and Mexico, by Mrs. E. H. Carbutt. London,
S. Low, Marston, Searle & Rivington, limited, 1889.
2 p.l., 243, [1] p.   19 cm.

6331 Cardona, Adalberto de.
De México á Chicago y Nueva York. Guía para
el viajero ... por S. Adalberto de Cardona. 3. ed.,

aumentada y corregida hasta la fecha, y con un
apéndice descriptivo de la vida y viajes de
Cristóbal Colón ... Nueva York, Imprenta de Moss
engraving co., 1893.
   3 p.l., 799 p. illus. (incl. maps), port.
21 cm.

6332   Cardona, Adalberto de.
   México y sus capitales; reseña histórica del país
desde los tiempos más remotos hasta el presente;
en la cual también se trata de sus riquezas
naturales, escrita por S. Adalberto de Cardona,
con la cooperación del sr. d. Trinidad Sánchez
Santos y otros distinguidos escritores... México,
Tip. de J. Aguilar Vera y y comp. (s. en c.) 1900.
   3 p.l., 864 p. illus. (incl. maps), plates, ports.
21 cm.

6333 Caribbean Commission.
   Caribbean tourist trade, a regiónal approach.
Washington [1945]
   171 p. illus., map.   24 cm.

6334   Carles, Rubén Darío.
   La ciudad de Colón y la Costa de Oro. 4 ed.
[Panamá, 1955]
   152 p. illus., map.   23 cm.

6335   Carleton, James Henry, 1814-1873.
   ... Mountain meadow massacre... Special report
of the Mountain Meadow Massacre... [Washington,
Government printing office, 1902]
   17 p.   23 cm.

6336   Carman, Louis Dale, 1860-
   Abraham Lincoln, freemason: an address
delivered before Harmony lodge No. 17, F.A.A.M.,
Washington, D. C., January 28, 1918; with an appendix containing the actions taken by the Masonic
grand lodges of the United States on Lincoln's
death. [Washington?] Printed for private dis-
tribution, 1914.
   26 p.   23 cm.

6337   Carmon, Louis Dale, 1860-

Dr. Abraham Lincoln. [Newark?] 1922.
7 p.   17 cm.

6338   Carman, Louis Dale, 1860-
Some account of John Summerfield Staples, the
representative recruit of Abraham Lincoln in the
civil war. [Washington] 1927.
16 p.   illus.   23 cm.

6339   Carmichael, Mrs. A   C
Domestic manners and social condition of the
white, coloured, and negro population of the West
Indies.   By Mrs. Carmichael ...   London, Whittaker,
Treacher, and co., 1833.
2 v.   21 cm.

6340   Carmichael, Sarah E
Poems; by Sarah E. Carmichael.   A brief selec-
tion, published by permission of the authoress, for
private circulation.   San Francisco, Towne and
Bacon, 1866.
vi, 7-72 p.   19 cm.

6341   Carnahan, David Todd, 1820-1901.
Oration on the death of Abraham Lincoln... delivered...   Gettysburg, Pa., June 1, 1865. Gettysburg, Aughinbaugh & Wible, 1865.
24 p.   23 cm.

6342   Carnegie, James, 1827-1905, Earl of Southesk.
Saskatchewan and the Rocky Mountains, a diary
...   Edinburgh, Edmonston and Douglas, 1875.
447 p.   illus., maps.   23 cm.

6343   Carpenter, Francis Bicknell, 1830-1900.
Six months at the White House with Abraham
Lincoln: the story of a picture.   By F. B. Carpenter, New York, Hurd and Houghton, 1866.
vii, [9]-359 p.   18 cm.

6344   Carpenter, William W
Travels and adventures in Mexico: in the course
of journeys of upward of 2500 miles, performed
on foot.   Giving an account of the manners and
customs of the people, and the agricultural and

mineral resources of that country. By William
W. Carpenter ... New York, Harper & brothers,
1851.
    xi, [13]-300 p.   19 1/2 cm.

6345 Carr, Clark Ezra, 1836-1919.
      Lincoln at Gettysburg: an address. Chicago,
      A. C. McClurg, 1906.
      92 p. illus. map.   19 cm.

6346 Carr, Clark Ezra, 1836-1919.
      The Lincoln-Douglas debates: an address delivered
      before the Illinois State Bar Association, at
      Galesburg, Illinois, July 11, 1907. [n.p.] 1907.
      28 p.   19 cm.

6347 Carr, Julian Shakespeare, 1845-1924.
      The Hampton Roads conference: a refutation of
      the statement that Mr. Lincoln said if union was
      written at the top the southern commissioners might
      fill in the balance. [Durham, N. C., 1917?]
      36 p. illus.   20 cm.

6348 Carrillo, Alonso.
      Señor. El capitan Matheo Rodriquez de Almogabar,
      que assiste en esta corte à la defensa de Gaspar de
      Salcedo, preso en la ciudad de Lima, y puerto del
      Callao, y de Ioseph de Salcedo, su hermano difunto.
      Dize, que cumpliendo con la obligacion... [n.p.,
      16-]
      7 numb. 1.   21 cm.

6349 Carrillo, José.
      Del Gran Cairo al Grijalva; impresiones de un
      viaje por el sureste de México. Carátula y
      viñetas del pintor Eduardo Monroy. Ed. de la
      "Sociedad de Amigos del Libro Mexicano." México,
      1956.
      179 p. illus.   17 x 24 cm.

6350 Carrillo, Mariano.
      Por parte de d. Joseph Manuel Gutierres de
      Quintanilla se hacen presentes á V. S. los funda-
      mentos de derecho que manifiestan haber succedido
      en el mayorazgo que fundaron d. Melchor Malo de

Molina, y doña Mariana Ponze de Leon su legitima
muger. [Lima, 1781]
104, [6] p.   25 cm.

6351   Carroll, Anna Ella, 1815-1894.
Reply to the speech of Hon. J. C. Breckinridge,
delivered in the U. S. Senate, July 16th, 1861.
Washington, H. Polkinhorn, 1861.
15 p.   24 cm.

6352   Carta misiva de de [!] lo acaecido al navio San
Martin [Lima, 1760]
[12] p.   22 cm.

6353   Carver, William F   , 1840-
Life of Dr. William F. Carver, of California,
champion rifle-shot of the world... truthful
story of his capture by the Indians when a child
and romantic life among the savages for a period
of sixteen years. To which is appended, record of
his remarkable exhibitions of skill with a rifle
... Pub. by the author. Boston, Press of Rockwell and Churchill, 1878.
iv, [5]-177 p.   18 1/2 cm.

6354   Casanate, Luis de.
Por don Felix Fernandez de Guzman, vezino de la
Ciudad de los Reyes, con Alonso de Carrion, escriuanc
publico, y del Cabildo de la dicha ciudad. Sobre
si ay grado de segunda suplicacion, en la que el
dicho don Felix tiene interpuesta de las sentencias
dadas por el Audiencia de aquella ciudad. [n.p.,
16--]
7 numb. 1.   20 cm.

6355   Casas, Bartolomé de las, bp. 1474-1566.
Aqui se contiene vna disputa o controuersia entre
el Obispo Dō Fray Bartholome delas Casas o Casaus
... y el Doctor Gines de Sepulveda coronista del
emperado nuestro señor... [Sevilla, Sebastian
Trujillo, 1552]
[124] p.   22 cm.

6356   Casas, Bartolomé de las, bp., 1474-1566.
Aqui se cōtiene treynta proposiciones muy

jurídicas... Colijo las dichas treynta proposiciones
el Obispo Dō Fray Bartholome de las Casas / o Casaus
... [Sevilla, Sebastian Trugillo, 1552]
10 1.   22 cm.

6357   Casas, Bartolomé de las, bp., 1474-1566.
Aqui se cōtienē vnos auisos y reglas para los
confessores q̄ oyeren confessiones delos españoles
que son o han sido en cargo a los indios delas
Indias del mar oceano... [Sevilla, Sebastian
Trugillo, 1552]
15 1.   22 cm.

6358   Casas, Bartolomé de las, bp., 1474-1566.
Breuíssima relación de la destruyción de las
Indias: colegida por el Obispo Dō Fray Bartolomé
de la Casas, o Casaus de la Orden de Sācto
Domingo. Año 1552. [Sevilla, Sebastian Trugillo,
1552]
[100] p.   22 cm.

6359   Casas, Bartolomé de las, bp., 1474-1566.
Entre los remedios q̄ Dō Fray Bartolome delas
Casas: obispo dla ciudad real de Chiapa: refirio
por mandado del Emperado Rey ñro Señor... par
reformaciō delas Yndias... [Sevilla, Jacome Cromberger, 1552]
[56] p.   22 cm.

6360   Casas, Bartolomé de las, bp., 1474-1566.
Este es vn tratado q̄ el obispo dela ciudad real
de Chiapa Dō Fray Bartholome de las Casas / o
Casaus compuso por comission del Consejo Real
delas Indias: sobre la materia delos yndios que
se han hecho en ellas esclauos... [Sevilla,
Sebastian Trugillo, 1552]
[36] 1.   22 cm.

6361   [Casas, Bartolomé de las, bp.] 1474-1566.
Lo que sigue es vn pedaço de vna carta y relacion
que escriuio cierto hombre: delos mismos que
andauā en estas estaciones... [Sevilla? 1552?]
4 1.   22 cm.

6362   Casas, Bartolomé de las, bp., 1474-1566.

Principia quedā ex quibus procedendum est in
disputatione ad manifestandam et defendendam
iusticiam Yndorum... [Sevilla, Sebastian
Trujillo, 1552]
10 l.   22 cm.

6363   Casas, Bartolomé de las, bp., 1474-1566.
Tratado cōprobatorio del imperio soberano y
principado vniuersal que los reyes de Castilla y
Leon tienen sobre las Indias... [Sevilla,
Sebastian Trugillo, 1553]
81 l.   22 cm.

6364   Casas Mota y Flores, Lucas de las.
Accion gratulatoria, que el dr.d. Lucas de las
Casas, Mota, y Flores... embia de officio al
r.p.fr. Pedro Antonio Buzeta... insigne, y memorable
descubridor, traductor, y conductor de las aguas
â la ciudad de Guadalaxara, en la Nueva Galicia,
&c. on 15. de henero de 1742.   Con licencia de los
superiores.   Mexico, Por la viuda de d. Joseph
Bernardo de Hogal, impressora del real, y apostolico
Tribunal de la santa cruzada en toda esta Nueva-Españ
[1742?]
7 p.l., 41, [3] p.   21 cm.

6365   Castaneyra, Isidro Alphonso de.
Manval summa de las ceremonias de la provincia
de el santo evangelio de Mexico.   Sgvn el orden
del capitvlo general de Roma, el año de 1700...
Mexico, M. de Ribera Calderón, 1703.
4 p.l., 81 p.   20 cm.

6366   Castelfuerte, José de Armendáriz, marqués de,
viceroy of Peru.
Don Ioseph de Armendaris [!] marqves de Castel-
fverte... Por quanto en el aviso, que de España à
llegado à esta ciudad el dia 31. del passado se à
recibido la sensible noticia de la muerte del
serenissimo señor, el señor duque de Parma...
[Lima, 1728]
4 p.   22 cm.

6367   Castelfuerte, José de Armendáriz, marqués de,
viceroy of Peru.

Don Ioseph de Armendaris [!] marqves de Castel-
fverte... Por quanto està prohibido por diferentes
vandos, que se han publicado que no vsen de armas
ofensivas, ni defensivas los indios, mestisos,
mulatos, sambos, ni negros, assi esclavos como
libres vajo de diferentes penas... [Lima, 1725]
2 p.   22 cm.

6368   Castelfuerte, José de Armendáriz, marqués de,
viceroy of Peru.
Por Ioseph de Armendaris [!] marqves de Castelfuerte... Por quanto el señor doct. d. Pedro
Antonio de Echave, y Roxas de la Orden de Alcantara
oydor de esta Real audiencia me hizo vna consulta,
que su tenor respuesta del señor fiscal a la vista
que se le dió lo proveydo, y de la ley real, que
trata de la materia es como se sigue. [Lima, 1726]
7 p.   22 cm.

6369   Castellanos García, Gerardo, 1879–
... Paseo de la Habana a Acapulco; mi conquista
del Pacífico. Habana, Cuba [Se imprimió en la
casa editora Ucar, García y compañia] 1938.
235 p., 1 l.   incl. illus., fold. map.   20 cm.

6370   Castillo de Herrera, Alonso de.
Señor. El licenciado don Alonso de Castillo
de Herrera, oydor, y alcalde de corte de la Real
audiencia y chancilleria que reside en la ciudad
de san Francisco del Quito. Digo, que abrà catorce
años V. Magestad fue seruido hazerme merced de esta
placa... [n.p., 1633?]
9 numb. 1., [2] p.   23 cm.

6371   Castillo, F
De México a Veracruz por la línea más pintoresca de
América; guía histórico descriptiva, por F. Castillo,
con setenta y cinco ilustraciones. 8. ed. en español.
[México, Cía. impr. pap., s.a.] 1935.
101, [1] p.   incl. illus., pl., fold. map, tables
(1 fold.)   17 cm.

6372   Castillo, F
From Mexico city to the port of Veracruz over the
picturesque standard gauge electrified line of

Mexico; historical descriptive hand book compiled
by F. Castillo ... 6th ed., rev. [México, Cía.
impr. pap., s.a.] 1935.
99 [1] p. incl. illus., plates. fold. map,
tables (1 fold.)   16 1/2 cm.

6373   Castillo, Martín del, d. 1680.
Grammatikee têes glóosees helleenikees en têe
dialectoo iberikeê.   Grammatica de la lengua griega,
en idioma español.   Por el r.p.f. Martin del Castillo...   Con tódo lo necessario, pára podèr por si
solo qualquièr aflicionádo, leèr, escrebir, pro-
nunciár, y savèr la generàl y muy noble lengua
griega.   Leon de Francia, A costa de Florian Anisson,
mercader de libros en Madrid, 1678.
16 p.l., 557 p.   23 cm.

6374   Castillo, Martín del, d. 1680.
Relacion apologetica en defensoria satisfacion a
la Carta pastoral del m.r.p.fr.   Hernando de la
Rva... Por el p. fr. Martin de Castillo... A n[s]
reverendissimos padres prelados generalissimo de
toda la religion, y commissario general de todas
las Indias, residente en la corte de nuestro rey
catolico.   Año de 1669.   [Mexico, 167-?]
74 numb. l.   23 cm.

6375   Castillo y Piña, José.
... Los oasis del camino.   Méjico, Imprenta Efrén
Rebollar, 1936.
vii, 486, [2], xxviii p.   illus., port.   19 cm.

6376   Castrillo, Hernando, 1586-1667.
Historia y magia natural, o Ciencia de la filosofia
ocvlta...   Madrid, Juan Garcia Infanzon, 1692.
[16], 342, 16 p.   24 cm.

6377   Castro, Lorenzo.
The republic of Mexico in 1882; with revised
and corrected map, by Lorenzo Castro.   New York,
Thompson & Moreau, printers, 1882.
iv, 271 p.   fold. map.   20 1/2 cm.

6378   Castro, Luis de.
Declamacion, funebre en las sepulchrales honras,

que las muy reverendas madres senoras religiosas
capuchinas, de esta ciudad de Queretaro; celebraron
en su iglesia, el dia 1. de diciembre de. este ano
de 1732. como afectuosas, y agradecidas hijas. A
su muy amado padre, y pastor peregrino. El b. d.
Phelipe de las Cassas ... Dixolo el r.^{do}p.fr. Luiz
de Castro... Sacanlo a luz a sus expensas: los
sobrinos albaceas de el prelado difunto. Quienes
en concurrencia de dichas muy reverendas madres,
lo dedican, y consagran por mano de el orador. A
nuestro seraphico padre s'.s Francisco, Por los
herederos de la viuda de Francisco Rodriguez
Lupercio, en la puente de Palacio, 1733.
8 p.l., 15 p. illus. 22 cm.

6379 Catherwood, Mary (Hartwell) 1847-1902.
The romance of Dollard, by Mary Hartwell Catherwood... New York, The Century co., 1906.
3 p.l., 206 p. front., plates. 20 cm.

6380 Catholic church. Congregatio sacrorum rituum.
Sacra rituum congregatione corum sanctissimo
domino nostro Clemente pp. xiv, oxomen, beatïfica-
tionis, & canonizationis ven. servi Dei Johannis
de Palafox et Mendoza episcopi angelopolitani,
postea oxomen. In supremo Indiarum, & Aragoniae
consiliarii, pro-regis, ac ducis generalis Nove
Hispaniae, archiepiscopi Mexici electi &c. Re-
strictus responsionis ad animadversiones r.p.d.s.
fidei promotoris vna cvm summario additionali super
dubio an constet de virtutibus theologicis fide,
spe, & charitate erga Deum, & proximos, ac de
cardinalibus prudentia, justitia, fortitudine, ac
temperantia, earum que adnexis in gradu heroico in
casu, & ad effectum &c. Romae, MDCCLXXI, Ex
typographia reverendae camerae apostolicae.
1 p.l., 45, 55, 142, 175 p. 20 cm.

6381 Catholic church. Liturgy and ritual. Ritual.
Manval para administrar los santos sacramentos
conforme al reformado de Paulo v.p.m. Mandado sacar
dêl por el illvstrissimo y reverendissimo señor
maestro don fray Payo de Ribera ... obispo de
Guatemala, y de la Vera-Paz ... Sacado, y trasvmp-
tadas las rubricas y notas de latin en romance, y

añadidas algunas cosas y ceremonias tocantes
á la administracion de los santos sacramentos, por
el bachiller don Nicolas Alvarez de Vega ... Con
licencia en Guatemala, Por Ioseph de Pineda Ybarra.
Año de 1665.
    10 p.l., 122 numb. l.   27 cm.

6382   Catholic Church, Mexico. Archbishop.
    Descripción del Arzobispado de México...
    Mexico, José Joaquin Terrazas y hijas, 1877.
    463 p.   20 cm.

6383   Catholic Church, Pope, 1644-1655.
    Breve de nvestro mvy santo Padre Innocencio X
    ... [Puebla, 1649]
    12 p.   22 cm.

6384   Catholic Church. Sacra Rituum Congregatio.
    Sacra ritvvm congregatione eminentiss. et
    reverendiss. d. card. de Carpineo mexicana beatifi-
    cationis, & canonizationis ven. servi Dei fr.
    Sebastiani de Aparitio... Rome, 1692.
    12, 84, 4, 10 p.   21 cm.

6385   Catholic Church. Sacra Rituum Congregatio.
    Sacra Ritvvm Congregatione eminentissimo, &
    reverendissimo domino card. Coloredo limana
    beatificationis, & canonizationis ven. Servi Dei
    Nicolai Aillon... Roma, 1697.
    1 p.l., 26, 292, 16, 19 p.   27 cm.

6386   Caudevilla y Escudero, Joaquín.
    ... Memorial ajustado, hecho con citacion de las
partes de mandato del consejo, del pleyto que en
grado de revista se controvierte en el entre los
apoderados de las casas de don Francisco de Mendin-
ueta, y don Joseph Aguirre Acharán, socios que fueron
juntos con el marqués de Murillo, de la compañia que
los tres formaron para el asiento de negros de
Guinea, y comercio de Buenos Ayres. Con don Joachîn
de Zuloaga, vecino, y del comercio de la ciudad de
Cádiz, como factor que fue de la citada compañia.
Sobre que éste satisfaga y reintegre al fondo de la
compañía 1.97⩾ 435 rs. y 15 mrs. de plata, que de
los caudales de ella entregó al marqués de Murillo

de cuenta particular. [Madrid, 1790]
1 p.l., 90 numb. l.   22 cm.

6387 Cedarholm, Rev. A   , 1822-1867.
Autobiography of Rev. A. Cedarholm, with a
sketch of his labors among the Scandinavian population of the United States, and as first missionary of the M. E. Church in Sweden... Translated
from the Swedish and published by Mrs. Caroline
Cedarholm... Piqua, O., Helmet steam print., 1879.
84 p.   19 cm.

6388 Cervantes de Salazar, Francisco, ca. 1514-1575.
México en 1554. Tres diálogos latinos que
Francisco Cervantes Salazar escribió é imprimió
en México en dicho año. Los reimprime, con traducción castellanea y notas, J. García Icabalceta...
México, Andrade y Morales, 1875.
344 p.   facsim.   22 1/2 cm.

6389 Cervantes de Salazar, Francisco, ca. 1514-ca. 1575.
... México en 1554; tres diálogos latinos traducidos
por Joaquín García Icazbalceta; notas preliminares
de Julio Jiménez Rueda. México, Universidad
nacional autónoma, 1939.
v, [1], 189, [1] p., 2 l.   20 1/2 cm.

6390 Chabrand, Émile.
... De Barcelonnette au Mexique. Inde - Birmanie
- Chine - Japon - États-Unis. Quarante illustrations par G. Profit d'après les photographies de
l'auteur. Paris, E. Plon, Nourrit et c^{ie}, 1892.
4 p.l., 472 p.   incl. illus., plates.   19 cm.

6391 Chafee, George D
To commemorate the debate of Abraham Lincoln and
Anthony Thornton on freedom of territories, June
15, 1856, in old court house, Shelbyville, Illinois.
Shelbyville, Shelby County Leader Print, 1923.
23 p.   illus.   20 cm.

6392 Chamberlain, Leander Trowbridge, 1837-1913.
An address of the early history of old Brookfield,
Mass... and remarks by his brother, the Hon. D. H.
Chamberlain... [Brooklyn, N. Y., Press of Larkin &

co., 1895?]
36 p.   22 1/2 cm.

6393   Chamberlain, Mellen, 1821-1900.
       John Adams, the statesman of the American
       revolution; with other essays and addresses,
       historical and literary... Boston and New York,
       Houghton, Mifflin and company, 1898.
       vi p., 1 l., 476 p., 1 l.   21 cm.

6394   Chamberlain, Nathan Henry.
       The assassination of President Lincoln. A
       sermon preached at James Church, Birmingham,
       Ct., April 9th, 1865. New York, G. W. Carleton,
       1865.
       22 p.   18 cm.

6395   Chambon, Ludovic.
       ... Un Gascon au Mexique. Paris, Imprimerie P.
       Dupont, 1892.
       2 p.l., 341 p.   18 1/2 cm.

6396   Champlain, Samuel de, 1567-1635.
       Oeuvres de Champlain, pub. sous le patronage de
       l'Université Laval par l'abbé C.-Il. Laverdière
       ... 2. éd. ... Québec, Imprimé au Séminaire par
       G.-E. Desbarats, 1870.
       5 v. in 2 front. (port.) plates (part col., part
       fold.) maps (part fold.) plans (part fold.)
       26 1/2 x 20 cm.

6397   Chapais, Thomas, 1858-1946.
       Le marquis de Montcalm (1712-1759) Québec,
       J. P. Garneau, 1911.
       xii, 695 p. port., plans.   24 cm.

6398   Chapleau, Joseph Adolphe.
       La question Riel; lettres...   [Ottawa, 1885]
       cover-title, 14 p.   20 cm.

6399   Chapleau, Joseph Adolphe.
       Speech of Hon. Mr. Chapleau, M. P., on the execu-
       tion of Louis Riel. (From the official debates).
       House of Commons, March 24th, 1886. Ottawa, Printed
       by Maclean, Roger & co., 1886.

50 p.   22 cm.

6400   Chappe d'Auteroche, Jean, 1728-1769.
        Voyage en Californie pour l'observation du passage
        de Vénus sur le disque du soleil, le 3 juin 1769;
        contenant les observations de ce phénomène, & la
        description historique de la route de l'auteur à
        travers le Mexique. Par feu m. Chappe d'Auteroche
        ... Rédigé & publié par m. de Cassini fils... Paris,
        C.-A. Jombert, 1772.
        2 p.l., 170 [2] p. II pl., tables (1 fold.), diagrs.
        26 1/2 x 21 cm.

6401   Chappe d'Auteroche, Jean, 1728-1769.
        A voyage to California, to observe the transit
        of Venus. By Mons. Chappe d'Auteroche. With an
        historical description of the author's route through
        Mexico, and the natural history of that province.
        Also, a voyage to Newfoundland and Sallee, to make
        experiments on Mr. Le Roy's timekeepers. By
        Monsieur de Cassini. London, Printed for E. &
        C. Dilly, 1778.
        4 p.l., 215 p. front. (fold. plan)   22 1/2 cm.

6402   Charles, Cecil.
        Honduras: the land of great depths ... By
        Cecil Charles ... Chicago, New York, Rand,
        McNally & co., 1890.
        216 p. 2 port. (incl. front.), fold. map.
        19 1/2 cm.

6403   Charlevoix, Pierre François Xavier de, 1682-1761.
        Journal of a voyage to North-America. Under-
        taken by order of the French king. Containing the
        geographical description and natural history of
        that country, particularly Canada. Together with
        an account of the customs, characters, religion,
        manners and traditions of the original inhabitants.
        In a series of letters to the Duchess of Lesdi-
        guières. Translated from the French of P. de
        Charlevoix ... London, Printed for R. and J.
        Dodsley, 1761.
        2 v. fold. map.   21 cm.

6404   Charlevoix, Pierre François Xavier de, 1682-1761.

A voyage to North-America: undertaken by command
of the present king of France. Containing the
geographical description and natural history of
Canada and Louisiana. With the customs, manners,
trade and religion of the inhabitants ... By Father
Charlevoix. Also, a description and natural
history of the islands in the West Indies belonging
to the different powers of Europe ... Dublin,
Printed for J. Exshaw, and J. Potts, 1766.
2 v. fronts. (1 port.) 8 fold. maps. 20 cm.

6405 Charnay, Désiré, 1828-1915.
À travers les forêts vierges; aventures d'une
famille en voyage ... Paris, Hachette & cie., 1890.
3 p.l., 391 p. 22 cm.

6406 Charnay, Désiré, 1828-1915.
Les anciennes villes du Nouveau monde; voyages
d'explorations au Mexique et dan l'Amérique Centrale,
par Désiré Charnay, 1857-1882. Ouvrage contenant
214 gravures et 19 cartes ou plans. Paris,
Hachette et c^{ie}, 1885.
xii, 469 p., 1 l. incl. illus., plates, maps,
front. (port.), fold. map. 35 1/2 cm.

6407 Charnay, Désiré, 1828-1915.
The ancient cities of the new world. Being
travels and explorations in Mexico and Central
America, from 1857-1882. By Désiré Charnay ...
Translated from the French by J. Gonino and Helen
S. Conant. London, Chapman and Hall, limited,
1887.
xxxii, 514 p. incl. front. (port.), illus.,
plates. fold. map. 27 cm.

6408 Charnay, Désiré, 1828-1915.
Cités et ruines américaines, Mitla, Palenqué,
Izamal, Chichen-Itza, Uxmal; recueillies et photo-
graphiées par Désiré Charnay; avec un texte par M.
Viollet-le-Duc ... suivi du voyage et des documents
de l'auteur ... Paris, Gide [etc.] 1863.
3 p.l., ix, 543 p. illus. 25 cm. and atlas
of 49 phot. 73 1/2 cm.

6409 Charnay, Désiré, 1828-1915.

... Le Mexique; souvenirs et impressions de voyage.
Paris, E. Dentu [etc.] 1863.
2 p.l., 439 p.   19 cm.

6410   Charpenne, Pierre.
Mon voyage au Mexique, ou Le colon du Guazacoalco
... Paris, Roux, 1836.
2 v. front.   18 cm.

6411   Charrney, Theodore S
As we think of him: a series of illustrations of
young Abraham Lincoln. Chicago, Privately printed,
1956.
[20] p. illus.   26 cm.

6412   Chase, Thomas, 1827-1892.
An address on the character and example of
President Abraham Lincoln, delivered before the
Athenaeum and Everett societies of Haverford college, on Fifth day evening, Seventh month 6th,
1865. Philadelphia, Sherman & co., 1865.
35 p.   29 cm.

6413   Chatterjee, Sudhananda, 1912-
পৃথিবী পরিক্রমা. [লেখক] সুধানন্দ চট্টোপাধ্যায়. কলিকাতা,
আনন্দ পাবলিশার্স [1967-
v.   23 cm.

6414   [Chauveau, Pierre Joseph Olivier] 1820-1890.
The visit of His Royal Highness the Prince of
Wales to America, reprinted from the Lower Canada
Journal of Education, with an appendix containing
poems, addresses, letters, &c. Montreal, Printed
by Eusebee Senecal, 1860 [i.e. 1861]
113 p., 1 l., xxvi p., 1 l. port., illus.,
plates.   22 cm.

6415   Chicago bar association.
... Chicago bar association lectures. Part
one ... [Chicago, Fergus printing company, 1882]
cover-title, [7]-106 p. port.   20 cm.

6416   The Chicago Copperhead Convention: the treasonable
and revolutionary utterances of the men who composed
it: Extracts from all the notable speeches de-

103

livered in and out of the "Democratic" convention
... Washington, D. C., Pub. by the Congressional
union committee, 1864.
16 p.   20 cm.

6417 Chicago Tribune.
The Logan emancipation cabinet of letters and
relics of John Brown and Abraham Lincoln; being an
article prepared specially for the Chicago Tribune.
Chicago, 1892.
40 p.   illus.   20 cm.

6418 Chiniquy, Charles Paschal Telesphore, 1809-1899.
Die Ermordung des Präsidenten Abraham Lincoln
eine That der Jesuiten, von Pater Chinique (Se-
paratabdruck aus dessen Werk: "Fünfzig jahre in
der römischen Kirche") Barmen, D. B. Wiemann
[1890]
32 p.   19 cm.

6419 Christmas greetings, 1864: General William
Tecumseh Sherman to President Abraham Lincoln.
Chicago, Ralph G. Newman, The Home of Books,
Christmas, 1940.
[4] p.   folder.

6420 Churchill, Winston, 1871-1947.
The man of sorrows: winning declamations, No.
20. Ripon, Wisconsin, Pi Kappa Delta, Ripon College [n.d.]
10 p.   20 cm.

6421 [Cifuentes, Domingo de] fl. 1673.
Señora. Cavsas ay que obligan à romper el
silencio, y à bolver por la razon, y la verdad de
tal suerte, q̃ el no hazerlo sea falter à las pro-
prias obligaciones... [n.p., 16-]
14 numb. l.   28 cm.

6422 Cipolla, Arnaldo, 1879-
... Norte América y los norte americanos; viaje
por Alaska, Canadá y Estados Unidos; traducción
del italiano de Ramón Mondría. Santiago, Concepción, Chile, Nascimento, 1929.
264 p.   19 cm.

6423   A circuit rider in early Indiana. Fort Wayne, Ind.,
       Public Library of Fort Wayne and Allen County, 1954.
       [8] p. illus.   19 cm.

6424   Clark, Charles Eugene.
       Abraham Lincoln: an address... [n.p., 1909?]
       8 p.   21 cm.

6425   Clark, Daniel, 1809-1891.
       Eulogy on the life and character of Abraham
       Lincoln, before the city government of Manchester,
       N. H., June 1st, 1865. Manchester, Mirror steam
       job printing establishment, 1865.
       36 p.   23 cm.

6426   Clark, William Jared, 1854?-1922.
       Commercial Cuba; a book for business men, by
       William J. Clark, with an introduction by E.
       Sherman Gould... New York, C. Scribner's sons,
       1898.
       xvii, 514 p. front., plates, fold. maps,
       fold. plans.   24 cm.

6427   Clavijero, Francisco Javier, 1731-1787.
       Storia antica del Messico cavata da' migliori
       storici spagnuoli, e da' manoscritti, e dalle
       pitture antiche degl'indiani: divisa in dieci
       libri... e dissertazioni sulla terra, sugli animali,
       e sugli abitatori del Messico... Cesena, Gregorio
       Biasimi, 1780-81.
       4 v. illus., map.   22 cm.

6428   Clay, Henry, 1777-1852.
       Reply to John Randolph. Address to Lafayette.
       Lexington, Ky., Erasmus Press, 1973.
       [4] p.   22 cm.

6429   Clay, Henry, 1777-1852.
       Speech of the Hon. Henry Clay, before the American
       representatives, January 20, 1827. With an appendix,
       containing the documents therein referred to. Washing-
       ton, Printed at the Columbian office, 1827.
       12, 8 p.   23 cm.

6430   Clemente, Claudio, 1594?-1642 or 3.

Tabla chronologica de los descvbrimientos,
conqvistas, fvndaciones, poblaciones; y otras
cosas ilvstres, assi eclesiasticas como secvlares
de las Indias occidentales islas, y Tierra-Firme
del mar oceano, desde el año de 1492, hasta el
presente de 1642. Escriviola el padre Clavdio
Clemente... Dedicada al mvy ilvstre señor don
Bartholomé de Ocampo y Matta... [Colophon: En
Zaragoça: Por los herederos de Diego Dormer,
impressores de la ciudad. Año 1676]
caption-title, 2 l. 20 cm.

6431 Clemente, Claudio, 1594?-1642 or 3.
Tabla chronologica de los descvbrimientos,
conqvistas, y otras memorias ilvstres; assi
eclesiasticas como secvlares, en la Africa oriental,
India, y Brasil, desde el año de 1410. hasta el
de 1640. Escriviola el padre Clavdio Clemente...
Dedicada al mvy ilvstre señor d. Ivan Francisco
Fernandez de Heredia... [Colophon: En Zaragoça:
Por los herederos de Diego Dormer, impressores de
la ciudad, año 1676]
2 l. 23 cm.

6432 Clemente, Claudio, 1594?-1642 or 3.
Tabla chronologica del govierno secvlar, y
eclesiastico de las Indias occidentales, islas y
Tierra Firme del mar oceano, desde sv primero
descvbrimiento año de 1492, hasta el presente de
1642. Escriviola el padre Clavdio Clemente...
Dedicada al ilvstrissimo, y reverendissimo señor
don Diego del Castrillo... [Colophon: En Zaragoza:
Por los herederos de Diego Dormer, impressores de
la ciudad. Año de 1676]
caption-title, 2 l. 21 cm.

6433 Cleveland, Grover, pres. U. S., 1837-
Principles and purposes of our form of govern-
ment as set forth in public papers of Grover
Cleveland. Comp. by Francis Gottsberger. New
York, G. G. Peck, 1892.
3 p.l., [3]-187 p. 21 cm.

6434 Cluny, Alexander.
The American traveller: containing observations

on the present state, culture and commerce of the British colonies in America, and the further improvements of which they are capable; with an account of the exports, imports and returns of each colony respectively,--and of the numbers of British ships and seamen, merchants, traders and manufacturers employed by all collectively: together with the amount of the revenue arising to Great-Britain therefrom. In a series of letters, written originally to the Right Honourable the Earl of********* By an old and experienced trader (Alexander Cluny) ... London, 1770, Tarryton, N. Y., Reprinted, W. Abbatt, 1930.

(In the Magazine of history with notes and queries. Tarrytown, N. Y., 1930. 26 cm.. Extra number. no. 162 (v. 41, no. 2) p. [5]-77)

6435 [Cluny, Alexander]
Le voyageur américain; ou, Observations sur l'état actuel: la culture, le commerce des colonies britanniques en Amérique les exportations & importations respectives entre elles & 1 Grande Bretagne, avec un état des revenus que cette dernièr en retire &c. Addressées par un négociant expérimenté, e forme de lettres, au très-honorable comte de ... Tr. de l'anglois. Augm. d'un Précis sur l'Amérique Septentrional & la république des treize-Etats-Unis. Par m. Jh. M. Amsterdam, J. Schuring, 1783.
viii, 264 p. fold. map, fold. tables. 22 cm.

6436 Cobbett, Griffith Owen.
Notes on Rupert's America, its history and resources, enclosed with a letter to His Grace, the Duke of Buckingham, secretary of state for the colonies... [Dulwich] 1868.
88 p. 21 cm.

6437 Coddington, David Smith, 1823-1865.
The crisis and the man: address... on the presidential crisis, delivered before the Union war democracy, at the Cooper institute, New York, Nov. 1, 1864. New York, W. C. Bourne, 1865.
16 p. 23 cm.

6438 Codex Fejerváry-Mayer.

Codex Fejerváry-Mayer; a manuscrit mexicain
précolombien des Free Public Museums de Liverpool
(M 12014) publié en chromophotographie par le duc
de Loubat... Paris [Imprimé par P. Renouard] 1901.
27, [2] p. col. front., 44 facsim. 18 1/2 x
18 cm.

6439 Cody, Sherwin, 1868–
Lincoln: life, speeches and anecdotes. Chicago,
The Old Greek press [c1907]
112 p. port. 21 cm.

6440 Coe, Fanny E
Our American neighbors. By Fanny E. Coe. Ed.
by Larkin Dunton ... New York, Boston [etc.]
Silver, Burdett & co., 1899.
328 p. illus. 19 cm.

6441 Coffin, Alfred Oscar.
Land without chimneys; or, The Byways of Mexico.
Cincinnati, Ohio, The Editor pub. co., 1898.
352 p. illus. pl. 20 cm.

6442 Coggins, James Caswell, 1865–
Abraham Lincoln, a North Carolinian; with proof,
by J. C. Coggins... 2d ed., rev. Gastonia, N. C.,
Carolina printing co. [c1927]
7 p.l., 194 p. illus., pl., port. 18 1/2 cm.

6443 Colby, Charles William, 1867–
The founder of New France; a chronicle of Champlain
Toronto, Glasgow, Brook, 1915.
vii, 158 p. 3 plates, 2 ports., 2 maps. 19 cm.

6444 Colección Chimalistac de libros y documentos acerca
de la Nueva España. Madrid, J. Porrua Turangas,
1958-1973.
35 v. 24 cm.

6445 Coleman, John Winston, 1898–
John Bradford, Esq., pioneer Kentucky printer and
historian... Lexington, Ky., Winburn Press, 1950.
24 p. 23 cm.

6446 Coleman, John Winston, 1898–

John Filson, esq., Kentucky's first historian
and cartographer... Lexington, Ky., Winburn press,
1954.
16 p. 23 cm.

6447 [Coleman, William Macon] 1838-
... The evidence that Abraham Lincoln was not
born in lawful wedlock; or, The sad story of
Nancy Hanks... [Dallas? Tex., 1899?]
caption-title, [3]-18 p. 24 cm.

6448 Collins, Clarissa W
Mexican vignettes, by Clarissa W. Collins ...
New York, Snellgrove publications, 1938.
6 p.l., 95, [1] p. incl. col. front., illus.
(part col.) 23 1/2 cm.

6449 Collinson, Richard.
Journal of H. M. S. Enterprise in search of
Sir John Franklin's ships by Behring Strait.
1850-55... Edited by his brother, Major-General
T. B. Collinson... London, Sampson Low, Marston,
Searle & Rivington, 1889.
532, 32 p. fold. map. 25 cm.

6450 Comfort, Benjamin Freeman.
Lewis Cass and the Indian treaties, a monograph
on the Indian relations of the Northwest Territory
from 1813 to 1831... Detroit, Printed by the
Chas. F. May co., 1923.
62 p. 23 cm.

6451 Conde y Oquendo, Francisco Xavier, 1733-1799.
Elogio de Felipe V., rey de España... Madrid,
Joachin Ibarra, 1779.
30 p. 22 cm.

6452 Conder, Josiah, 1789-1855.
A popular description, geographical, historical and topographical of Mexico and Guatemala.
Boston, Wells & Lilly; Philadelphia, T. Wardle,
1830.
2 v. 6 pl. (incl. front., v. 2) fold. map
(front., v. 1) 16 1/2 cm.

6453　Congreso nacional de geografía.　3d. Guadalajara,
　　　　Mexico, 1942.
　　　　　... Memoria del III Congreso nacional de geografía,
　　　　verificado del 5 al 10 de febrero de 1942 en la ciuda
　　　　de Guadalajara, Jal. Guadalajara, Jal., 1943.
　　　　117 p.　23 cm.

6454　Conkling, Alfred Ronald, 1850-1917.
　　　　　Appletons' guide to Mexico, including a chapter
　　　　on Guatemala, and an English-Mexican vocabulary.
　　　　By Alfred R. Conkling ...　New York, D. Appleton
　　　　& co., 1884.
　　　　xv, 378 p.　front. (map)　19 cm.

6455　Conkling, Alfred Ronald, 1850-1917.
　　　　　Appletons' guide to Mexico, including a chapter
　　　　on Guatemala and an English-Spanish vocabulary.
　　　　By Alfred R. Conkling ...　With a railway map and
　　　　illustrations.　4th ed. rev.　New York, D. Apple-
　　　　ton and company, 1891.
　　　　xviii, 390 (i.e. 396) p.　incl. illus., tables.
　　　　front (fold. map), facsim.　19 cm.

6456　Conkling, Howard.
　　　　　Mexico and the Mexicans; or, Notes of travel
　　　　in the winter and spring of 1883.　By Howard Conk-
　　　　ling.　New York, Taintor brothers, Merrill & co.,
　　　　1883.
　　　　x, [1], 298 p.　front., pl.　19 1/2 cm.

6457　Connor, Charlotte Reeve.
　　　　　A memoir with letters of Mrs. Horatio G. Phillips,
　　　　"Kitty" Patterson, a pioneer woman...　Dayton,
　　　　Ohio, Press of the N.C.R. Co., 1914.
　　　　48 p.　front. (port.), illus.　22 1/2 cm.

6458　Connor, Selden, 1839-
　　　　　An address by General Selden Connor, May 5,
　　　　1909, at a meeting of the Maine commandery of the
　　　　Military Order of the Loyal Legion of the United
　　　　States at Riverton Park casino, Portland, Maine,
　　　　to commemorate the one hundredth anniversary of the
　　　　birth of Hannibal Hamlin, in Paris, Maine, August
　　　　27, 1809.　Bangor, Me., Press of the T. W. Burr
　　　　printing co. [1909]

31 p.   incl. port.   23 cm.

6459   Conover, Charlotte Reeve.
The Patterson log cabin.   [Dayton, Ohio, Press
of the N.C.R., May 1906]
44 p.   illus., map,   24 1/2 cm.

6460   Conrotte, Manuel.
... Notas mejicanas.   Madrid, Romo y Füssel,
1899.
391, [2] p.   18 1/2 cm.

6461   Conroy, Kitty.
... George Calvin, Kentucky statesman and educa-
tor...   Lexington, University of Kentucky, 1944.
60 p.   front. (port.)   23 cm.   (Bulletin of
the Bureau of School Service, College of Education,
University of Kentucky, vol. XVI, March, 1944,
number 3)

6462   Contemporáneos.
México, 1928-31.
11 v.   illus.   22 1/2 cm.

6463   Cook, Joel, 1842-1910.
... The Anglo-Saxons' historic and romantic
America, by Joel Cook ...   New York, London,
Merrill and Baker 1900?
6 v.   col. fronts. (3 mounted), plates.   22 cm.

6464   Cooke, John, fl. 1794.
Diary of Captain John Cooke, 1794.   Fort Wayne,
Ind., prepared by the staff of the Public Library
of Fort Wayne and Allen County, 1953.
[18] p.   illus.   21 1/2 cm.

6465   Cooper, Myers Young, 1873-
Address of Myers Y. Cooper... twentieth annual
banquet, Lincoln Protective Club, Brown Hotel,
Louisville, Ky., February 12, 1934.   [Louisville,
1934]
15 p.   20 cm.

6466   Corbella y Fondebila, Antonio.
Tratado de las enfermendades mas principales,

agudas y cronicas del pecho, en el qual, para que
mejor se comprendan, se hace una descripcion
anatómica de sus partes continentes y contenidas
por d. Antonio Corbella y Fondebila... Dedicada al
sr. d. Francisco Martinez Sobral... Madrid, En
la imprenta de la viuda de Hilario Santos, 1785.
8 p.l., 359, 1 p. 27 cm.

6467 Corbett, Griffith Owen.
The Red River rebellion: the causes of it. In
a series of letters to the British government on
the importance of opening an overland route
through Rupert's America to British Columbia...
London, printed for the author by Cassell, Petter,
& Balpin, 1870.
36 p. 22 cm.

6468 Córdoba y Salinas, Diego de.
Coronica de la religiosissima provincia de los
doze apostoles del Perv, de la orden de n.p.s.
Francisco de la regvlar observancia. Dispvesta en
seys libros, con relacion de las provincias qve
della han salido, y son sus hijas. Representa la
piedad y zelo con qve los reyes de Castilla, y
de Leon goviernan el Nvevo Mvndo, dilatando la fe
catolica, y conocimiento del verdadero Dios por
innvmerables reynos y naciones de indios. Y lo
mvcho qve para esto han servido y sirven las religion
sagradas. Con las acciones mas memorables de los
predicadores evangelicos, qve con zelo apostolico
acabaron svs vidas en tan gloriosa empressa.
Hazese vna breve descripcion de todas las tierras
del Perv, la entrada en ellas de nvestros españoles.
La riqueza, poder, culto, y politica de los reyes
inquas. Compvesta por el r.p.fr. Diego de Cordova
Salinas... Dirigida a la catolica magestad de don
Felipe III ... Lima, Por Iorge Lopez de Herrera,
1651.
19 p.l., 214 (i.e. 216), 695 (i.e. 707), [2] p.
24 cm.

6469 Córdoba y Salinas, Diego de.
Vida, virtvdes, y milagros del apostol del Peru
el venerable p, fray Francisco Solano ... Sacada de
las declaraciones de quinientos testigos, que

juraron ante los illustrisimos arçobispos y
obispos de Seuilla, Granada, Lima, Cordoua, y
Malaga, y de otras muchas informaciones, que por
authoridad apostolica se an actuado en diferentes
villas y ciudades. Por el padre fray Diego de
Cordoua ... Y en esta segunda edicion añadida por
el p,* fray Alonso de Mendieta... Al rey nro senor
d Felipe IIII rey de las Espanas y ambas Indias.
Madrid, En la Emprenta real, 1643.
   31 p.l., 686 (i.e. 692), [12] p. port.   22 cm.

6470 Córdoba y Salinas, Diego de.
   Vida, virtvdes, y milagros del apostol del
Perv el b.p.fr. Francisco Solano ... Sacada de
las declarationes de qvinientos testigos, que
juraron ante los ilustrissimos arçobispos, y
obispos de Seuilla, Granada, Lima, Cordoua, y
Malaga, y de otras muchas informaciones que por
autoridad apostolica se han actuado en diferentes
villas, y ciudades. Por el p.fr. Diego de Cordova
... Tercera impression, qve saca a lvz el m.r.p.
fr. Pedro de Mena... Y dedica al excmo. señor d.
Pedro Portocarrero Folch de Aragon y Cordoua,
conde de Medellin, &c. Madrid, En la Imprenta
real, 1676.
   10 p.l., 544, [8] p.   26 cm.

6471 Corlett, William Thomas, 1854-
   The American tropics; notes from the log of a
midwinter cruise ... by William Thomas Corlett.
Cleveland, The Burrows brothers co., 1908.
   221 p. incl. front. 26 pl.   19 1/2 cm.

6472 Corn, James Franklin.
   Jim Witherspoon, a soldier of the South, 1862-
1865. [Cleveland, Tenn., 1962]
   36 p. illus., ports., facsim.   25 cm.

6473 Cornejo Franco, José.
   La calle de San Francisco. [Guadalajara, Jal.,
Ediciones del Banco industrial de Jalisco] 1945.
   218 p., 50 pl., [4] l.   23 1/2 cm.

6474 Cornish, Louis Craig.
   The settlement of Hingham, Massachusetts, by

Louis C. Cornish. Boston, The Rockwell & Churchill
press, 1911.
cover-title, 23 p. plates. 22 cm.

6475 Corrêa, Virgilio, 1887-
Viagem ao México. Rio de Janeiro, Instituto
Brasileiro de Geografia e Estatística, Conselho
Nacional de Geografia, 1949.
38 p. 23 cm.

6476 Correo del Orinoco, Angostura (Venezuela) 1818-1821.
Paris, Desclée, De Brouwer & c^{ie}, 1939.
2 p.l., xv p. facsim: [522] p. 37 1/2 cm.

6477 Correspondance secrète des députés de Saint-Domingue
avec les comités de cette isle. Paris, 1792.
iv, [5]-53 p. 19 1/2 cm.

6478 Cortés, Hernando, 1485-1547.
Cartas y relaciones con otros documentos rela-
tivos a la vida y a las empresas del conquistador.
Buenos Aires, Emecé editores [n.d.]
690 p. 17 cm.

6479 Cortés, José Domingo, 1839-1884.
La república de Méjico. Apuntes jeográficos,
estadísticos, administrativos, históricos i de
costumbres. Publicados por José Domingo Cortés.
Santiago, Impr. de "El Independiente," 1872.
3 p.l., [3]-233, [1] p. 22 cm.

6480 Cortijo Herraiz, Tomás.
Discurso apologetico, medico astronomico:
pruebase la real influencia de los cuerpos celestes
en estos sublunares, y la necesidad de la observanic
de sus aspectos, para el mas recto uso, y exercicio
de la medicina: con un examen sobre el uso de el
chocolate en las enfermedades... [Salamanca]
Eugenio Garcia de Honorato, 1729.
[48], 120 p. 22 cm.

6481 Cosio, Pedro Antonio De.
Condiciones comunes de las contratas celebradas
con los cosecheros de tabaco, de las villas de
Cordova y Orizavo, por el tiempo que dentro se

expressa. Mexico, En la imprenta del br. d.
Joseph Antonio de Hogal, impresor del Superior
govierno, Calle de Tiburcio [1780?]
    1 p.l., 13 p.   20 cm.

6482 Cosio, Pedro Antonio De.
        Reglamento... sobre estableces una casa, y hos-
        pital de convalecencia para la tropa, extramuros
        de Veracruz. [Mexico, 1781]
        caption-title, 7 p.   19 cm.

6483 Coulter, Ellis Merton, 1890-
        The attempt of William Howard Taft to break
        the solid south.   Savannah, Georgia Historical
        Quarterly, 1935.
        11 p.   23 cm.

6484 Coumand, Antoine de, abbé, 1747-1814.
        Réponse aux observations d'un habitant des
        colonies, sur le mémoire en faveur des gens de
        couleur... par M. Grégoire. [n.p., 1789]
        37 p.   20 cm.

6485 Cowen, Benjamin Rush, 1831-1908.
        Abraham Lincoln: an appreciation, by one who
        knew him. Cincinnati, R. Clarke co., 1909.
        63 p.   20 cm.

6486 Cox, Earnest Sevier.
        Lincoln's Negro policy, by Earnest Sevier Cox.
        Richmond, Va., The William Byrd press, 1938.
        36 p.   illus. (ports)   19 cm.

6487 Cozzens, Frederick Swartwout, 1818-1869.
        Acadia; or, A month with the blue noses...
        New York, Derby & Jackson, 1859.
        xi, 13-329 p. front., pl.   18 1/2 cm.

6488 Craig, Wheelock, 1824-1868.
        Two sermons of April, 1865... A key to our joy
        ... [and] ... The fruits of our bereavement...
        delivered in the Trinitarian Church... New Bed-
        ford, Mass., E. Anthony & sons, 1865.
        24, 14 p.   20 cm.

6489   Crane, Cephas Bennett, 1833–
         Sermon on the occasion of the death of
         President Lincoln, preached in the South Baptist
         church, Hartford, Conn. ... April 16, 1865.
         Hartford, Press of Case, Lockwood & co., 1865.
         29 p.   23 cm.

6490   Crawford, Cora Hayward.
         The land of the Montezumas, by Cora Hayward
         Crawford ... New York, J. B. Alden, 1889.
         xiii, 311 p. front., pl.   20 1/2 cm.

6491   Crawford, Francis Marion, 1854–1909.
         An American politician, a novel. Boston, New
         York, Houghton, Mifflin and Company, 1885.
         2 p.l., [7]–356 p.   18 1/2 cm.

6492   Crawford, Francis Marion, 1854–1909.
         Casa Braccio, with illustrations by A. Castaigne.
         New York and London, Macmillan and co., 1895.
         2 v. plates.   18 cm.

6493   Crawford, Francis Marion, 1854–1909.
         The children of the king; a tale of southern
         Italy. New York, Macmillan, 1893.
         320 p.   19 cm.

6494   Crawford, Francis Marion, 1854–1909.
         Don Orsino, by F. Marion Crawford ...   New
         York, The Macmillan company; London, Macmillan
         & co., ltd., 1896.
         2 p.l., 448 p.   19 cm.

6495   Crawford, Francis Marion, 1854–1909.
         Greifenstein.   London and New York, Macmillan
         and co., 1889.
         3 p.l., 357 p.   19 cm.

6496   Crawford, Francis Marion, 1854–1909.
         Katharine Lauderdale.   With illustrations by
         Alfred Brennan.   New York and London, Macmillan
         and Co., 1894.
         2 v. plates, port.   18 cm.

6497   Crawford, Francis Marion, 1854–1909.

Khaled, a tale of Arabia. London and New
York, Macmillan and Co., 1891.
2 p.l., 258 p.   19 1/2 cm.

6498   Crawford, Francis Marion, 1854-1909.
Marion Darche. A story without comment.
New York, Macmillan, 1893.
309 p.   19 cm.

6499   Crawford, Francis Marion, 1854-1909.
Marzio's crucifix. London and New York, Macmillan, 1887.
250 p.   19 1/2 cm.

6500   Crawford, Francis Marion, 1854-1909.
Paul Patoff, by F. Marion Crawford ...   New
York, The Macmillan company; London, Macmillan &
co., ltd., 1911.
2 p.l., 456 p.   20 cm.

6501   Crawford, Francis Marion, 1854-1909.
Pietro Ghisleri. New York, Macmillan, 1893.
429 p.   20 cm.

6502   Crawford, Francis Marion, 1854-1909.
The Ralstons, by F. Marion Crawford...   New
York and London, Macmillan and co., 1895.
2 v.   18 1/2 cm.

6503   Crawford, Francis Marion, 1854-1909.
A Roman singer. London, New York, Macmillan,
1889.
305 p.   20 cm.

6504   Crawford, Francis Marion, 1854-1909.
Sant' Ilario. Authorized ed. Leipzig, B.
Tauchnitz, 1889.
2 v.   17 cm.

6505   Crawford, Francis Marion, 1854-1909.
Saracinesca, by F. Marion Crawford...   New York,
Macmillan and co., 1894.
3 p.l., 450 p.   20 cm.

6506   Crawford, Francis Marion, 1854-1909.

A tale of a lonely parish. London and New York,
Macmillan, 1886.
380 p.   20 cm.

6507 Crawford, Francis Marion, 1854-1909.
The three fates, by F. Marion Crawford...
London and New York, Macmillan and co., 1892.
3 p.l., 412 p.   19 1/2 cm.

6508 Crawford, Francis Marion, 1854-1909.
The witch of Prague; a fantastic tale. Illustrated by W. J. Hennessey. London and New York,
Macmillan and co., 1891.
2 p.l., 435 p. illus.   20 cm.

6509 Crawford, Francis Marion, 1854-1909.
Zoroaster. London, Macmillan and co., 1885.
2 v.   19 cm.

6510 Cresap, Bernarr.
The career of General Edward O. C. Ord to 1864
... Nashville, Tenn., 1951.
29 p.   24 cm.

6511 Crespel, Emmanuel.
Travels in North America, by M. Crespel. With
a narrative of his shipwreck, and extraordinary
hardships and sufferings on the island of Anti-
costi; and an account of that island ... London,
Printed by and for S. Low, 1797.
xxviii, 187 p.   16 1/2 cm.

6512 Crespel, Emmanuel.
Voyages du r. p. Emanuel Crespel, dans le Canada
et son naufrage en revenant en France. Mis au jour
par le sr. Louis Crespel son frére. A Francfort
sur le Meyn, H. L. Broenner, 1752.
4 p.l., 135 p.   16 cm.

6513 Crespo y Martinez, Gilberto, 1853-
En México y Cuba; datos para varios estudios, de
Gilberto Crespo y Martinez. Habana, Imprenta
Avisador comercial, 1905.
2 p.l., [7]-224 p., 1 l.   19 cm.

6514   Crew, Harvey W   , ed.
       Centennial history of the city of Washington,
       D. C. With full outline of the natural advantages,
       accounts of the Indian tribes, selection of the
       site, founding of the city... to the present time
       ... Dayton, O., Pub. for H. W. Crew by the United
       Brethren publishing house, 1892.
       xvi, 17-770 p., 1 1. ports. 25 cm.

6515   Crisfield, John Woodland, 1808-1897.
       The rebellion and the proclamation; speech...
       delivered in the House of Representatives, Dec.
       19, 1862.
       15 p.   20 cm.

6516   Crocker, Samuel Leonard, 1804-1883.
       Eulogy upon the character and services of Abraham
       Lincoln... delivered... Taunton... June 1, 1865.
       Boston, Prtd. by J. Wilson & son, 1865.
       28 p.   23 cm.

6517   Croffut, W[illiam] A[ugustus] 1835-
       Folks next door; the log book of a rambler, by
       W. A. Croffut ... 3d ed. Washington, D. C., The
       Eastside publishing company [1904]
       xv, [1] 371 (i.e. 389), [2] p. incl. front.,
       illus.   20 1/2 cm.

6518   Croix, Carlos Francisco de Croix, marqués de, 1699-
       1786.
       Varias cartas del marqués de Croix, XLV virey
       de la Nueva España; publicados por A. Nuñez Ortega.
       Bruselas, G. Mayolez, 1884.
       25 p.   26 1/2 cm.

6519   Croix, Teodoro de, 1730-1791.
       Don Teodoro de Croix... Por quanto (a pesar de la
       publicacion oportuna de repetidos bandos... con el
       interesante objecto de corregir el detestable lujo
       ... en los lutos, entierros, exêquias, y cabos de año
       por los difuntos...) se acredita por una experiencía
       dolorosa... [Lima, 1786]
       [10] p.   23 cm.

6520   Crowley, Mary Catherine, d. 1920.

119

A daughter of New France; with some account of the gallant Sieur Cadillac and his colony on the Detroit; by Mary Catherine Crowley... illustrated by Clyde O. De Land. Boston, Little, Brown, and company, 1901.

xii p., 1 l., 409 p. front., 5 pl. 20 cm.

6521 Crozer, Hiram P
The nation's loss: a discourse upon the life and death of Abraham Lincoln... delivered at Huntington, L. I., April 19th, 1865. 2d ed. New York, J. A. Gray & Green, 1866.

32 p. 23 cm.

6522 Cuba contemporánea; revista mensual. Havana, 1913-27.

44 v. in 36. 26 cm.

6523 Cuba contemporánea; revista mensual.
Indice de Cuba contemporánea. [Havana] Municipio de La Habana, 1940.

143 p. incl. port. 23 cm.

6524 Cuba. Oficina del censo.
Cuba: population, history and resources 1907. Comp. by Victor H. Olmsted, director, and Henry Gannett, assistant director: census of Cuba, taken in the year 1907. Washington, United States bureau of the census, 1909.

275 p. front. (port.), plates. 23 1/2 cm.

6525 Cubero Sebastián, Pedro, 1640-ca. 1696.
Descripcion general del mvndo, y notables sucessos del. Compuesto por el doctor don Pedro Cvbero Sebastian... Dedicalo a la serenissima reyna de los angeles Maria Señora Nvestra, del Pilar de Zaragoza, vnica protectora del reyno de Aragon. Napoles, Por Saluador Castaldo regio impressor, 1584.

5 p.l., 446 (i.e. 444), [8] p. pl., port. 23 c
Errors in pagination: no. 386-387 omitted; p. 200, 243 incorrectly numbered 300, 233.

6526 Cubero Sebastían, Pedro, 1640 - ca. 1696.
Descripcion general del Mvndo y notables svcessos

qve han svcedido en el. Con la armonia de sus
tiempos, ritos, ceremonias, costumbres, y trages de
sus naciones, y varones ilustres que en el ha avido.
Escrita por el dotor Don Pedro Cvbero Sebastian...
Valencia, V. Cabrena, 1697.
    7 p.l., 342 p.   pl.   19 1/2 cm.

6527 Cubero Sebastian, Pedro, 1640-ca. 1696.
    Peregrinacion que ha hecho de la mayor parte del
    mundo. Zaragoza. 1688.
    8 p.l., 288 p.   illus.   20 1/2 cm.

6528 Cudworth, Warren Handel, d. 1883.
    Eulogy on the life, character, and public
    services of the late President, Abraham Lincoln,
    delivered... East Boston, May 8, 1865... Boston,
    Wright & Potter, 1865.
    27 p.   23 cm.

6529 Cumings, Samuel.
    The western navigator; containing directions for
    the navigation of the Ohio and Mississippi, and
    ... information concerning the towns, &c. on their
    banks... Accompanied by charts of the Ohio river,
    in its whole extent; and of the Mississippi river,
    from the mouth of the Missouri to the Gulf of
    Mexico... Philadelphia, E. Littell, 1822.
    v.   20 cm.

6530 Cunningham, J   O
    Some recollections of Abraham Lincoln... de-
    livered before the Firelands Pioneer Association,
    at Norwalk, Ohio, July 4, 1907, and reprinted
    from the Pioneer of Dec. 1909. Norwalk, Ohio,
    American Publishing Co., 1909.
    20 p.   20 cm.

6531 [Currie, David]
    The letters of Rusticus [pseud.]; investiga-
    tions in Manitoba and the north-west, for the
    benefit of the intending emigrant... Montreal,
    John Dougall & son, 1880.
    82 p.   fold. maps.   23 cm.

6532 Currie, Mrs. Emma Augusta (Harvey) 1829-1913.

The story of Laura Secord and Canadian reminiscences, by Emma A. Currie, with portraits and engravings. St. Catharines [Ont.] 1913.
3 p.l., 254 p. front., illus. (plan, facsims.),
plates, ports.   20 cm.

6533 Curt, Louis, chevalier de, 1722-1804.
Motion... au nom des colonies réunies. [Paris,
le 27 novembre 1789] Paris, Chez Baudouin, 1789.
15 p.   20 cm.

6534 Cutter, Edward Francis.
Eulogy on Abraham Lincoln, delivered at Rock-
ford, Maine, April 19, 1865... Boston, D. C.
Colesworthy, 1865.
16 p.   23 cm.

6535 Cuyas y Armongol, Arturo, 1845-1925.
Desde México; cartas dirigidas al "Diario de la
marina" de la Habana, por Arturo Cuyas ("K. Landas")
México, I. Escalante, 1895.
95 p.   15 cm.

6536 Cventa de lo qve se ha pagado, por gastos generales.
Satisfechos, por la plata, frvtos, y mas efectos,
que se sacaron de todos los navios de la flota,
del cargo del señor gefe de esquadra don Rodrigo
de Torres, qve vararon en los cayos de boca de
canal de Bahama, en 15. de julio de 1733. Havana,
años de 1733. y 1734. Contadvria del comercio de
España. A cargo de don Joseph Diaz de Gvytian.
[n.p., 1734]
12 p.   21 cm.

D

6537 Daggett, Oliver Ellsworth, 1810-1880.
A sermon on the death of Abraham Lincoln, April
15th, 1865, preached in the First Congregational

church, Canandaigua, N. Y. ... April 16th, 1865...
Canadaigua, N. Y., N. J. Milliken, 1865.
16 p.   20 cm.

6538 Dale, E   I
History and genealogy of the Kent family.
Descendants of Richard Kent, Son., who came to
America in 1633, by E. I. Dale and Edward E. Kent.
Spencer, Mass., E. E. Dickerman, 1899.
143 p.   22 cm.

6539 Dana, Charles Anderson, 1819-1897.
Lincoln and his cabinet: a lecture delivered
... March 10, 1896, before the New Haven Colony
historical society... Cleveland and New York,
DeVinne press, 1896.
70 p.   illus.   17 cm.

6540 Dana, Richard Henry, 1815-1882.
To Cuba and back, a vacation voyage. By
Richard Henry Dana, jr. ... Boston, Ticknor and
Fields, 1859.
viii, [9]-288 p.   18 1/2 cm.

6541 Danielson, J   A
Lincoln's attitude toward prohibition... [New
York, Barnes press, 1927]
26 p.   23 cm.

6542 Daoust, Charles R
Cent-vingt jours de service actif. Recit
historique très complète de la campagne du 65me
au Nord-ouest... Montréal, Eugène Sénécal &
fils, 1886.
242 p.   illus.   22 cm.

6543 D'Arusmont, William E   Guthrie.
Oration on the death of Abraham Lincoln.
Philadelphia, J. Pennington & sons, 1865.
9 p.   14 cm.

6544 Dávila, Vicente, 1874-
Rincones mexicanos. México, 1947.
458 p.   illus., port.   24 cm.

123

6545 Davis, Richard Harding, 1864-1916.
Three gringos in Venezuela and Central America,
by Richard Harding Davis... New York, Harper &
brothers, 1896.
xi, 282 p. incl. front., illus., plates (1
double), ports., map. 19 cm.

6546 Davis, William Watts Hart, 1820-1910.
Life of John Davis, by W. W. H. Davis...
Doylestown, Pa. [Press of "Democrat" job dept.]
1886.
3 p.l., [3]-195, xvii p. 2 pl., 3 port. (incl.
front.) facsim. 24 cm.

6547 [Davison, Gideon Miner] 1791?-1869.
The traveller's guide through the middle and northe
states, and the provinces of Canada. 6th ed. enl. an
improved. Saratoga Springs, G. M. Davison; New-
York, G. & C. & H. Carvill, 1834.
xviii, [19]-452 p. incl. front. 3 pl. 15 1/2 cm.

6548 Davison, Gideon Miner, 1791?-1869.
The traveller's guide through the middle and
northern states, and the provinces of Canada. By
G. M. Davison. 8th ed. Saratoga Springs, G. M.
Davison; New-York, S. S. & W. Wood, 1840.
xiv p., 1 l., [19]-395 p. 15 1/2 cm.

6549 Dawson, Aeneas MacDonell, 1810-1894.
Our strength and their strength. The North
West Territory, and other papers chiefly relating
to the Dominion of Canada. By the Rev. Aeneas
MacDonell Dawson. Ottawa, Printed at the Times
Office, 1870.
viii, 326, 7 p. pl., port. 22 cm.

6550 Dawson, Samuel Edward, 1833-1916.
... Canada and Newfoundland, by Samuel Edward
Dawson ... Maps and illustrations. London, E.
Stanford, 1897.
xxiv, 719 p. incl. front., illus. maps (part
fold.) 20 cm.

6551 Dawson, Samuel Edward, 1833-1916.
Hand-book for the Dominion of Canada. Prepared

for the meeting of the British association for the
advancement of science, at Montreal, 1884. By
S. E. Dawson ... Montreal, Dawson brothers, 1884.
xii, 335 p. 4 maps (part fold.) 17 1/2 cm.

6552 Dawson, Simon James.
... Report on the line of route between Lake
Superior and the Red River settlement... Printed
by order of the House of Commons. Ottawa, Printed
by Hunter, Rose & co., 1868.
44 p. fold. map. 24 cm.

6553 Dean, Sidney, 1818-1901.
Eulogy pronounced in the City Hall, Providence,
April 19, 1865, on the occasion of the funeral
solemnities of Abraham Lincoln... Providence,
H. H. Thomas & co., 1865.
23 p. 23 cm.

6554 Death of President Lincoln as illustrated and described
in Harper's weekly, a journal of civilization: and
Frank Leslie's illustrated newspaper. New York,
1865.
30 no. in v. 1. illus. 41 cm.
Harper's weekly Apr. 29, May 6, 13, 20, 27, June
3, 10, 17, July 1, 8, 22, Aug. 26: Frank Leslie's
illustrated newspaper: Apr. 29, May 6, 13, 20, 27,
June 3, 17, July 22.

6555 Deaville, Alfred Stanley.
The colonial postal systems and postage stamps
of Vancouver Island and British Columbia 1849-
1871. A sketch of the origin and early development
of the postal service on the Pacific seaboard of
British North America... Victoria, B. C., Printed
by Charles F. Banfield, 1928.
210 p. illus. 24 1/2 cm.

6556 Deckert, Emil, 1848-1916.
Cuba, von dr. E. Deckert ... Bielefeld und
Leipzig, Velhagen & Klasing, 1899.
2 p.l., 116 p. incl. illus., plates. map.
26 cm.

6557 Deckert, Emil, 1848-1916.

Die neue welt. Reiseskizzen aus dem norden und
süden der Vereinigten Staaten sowie aus Kanada und
Mexiko. Von Emil Deckert. Berlin, Gebrüder
Paetel, 1892.
xi, 488 p. 24 cm.

6558 Decretum Oxomen beatificationis, et canonizationis
servi Dei Joannis de Palafox et Mendoza Episcopi
Angelopolitani et postea Oxomen. Madrid, Andres
Ortega, 1761.
7 p. 22 cm.

6559 DeLand, Charles Victor, 1826-
DeLand's history of Jackson County, Michigan;
embracing a concise review of its early settlement, industrial development and present conditions,
together with interesting reminiscences, comp. by
Colonel Charles V. DeLand... [Logansport, Ind.]
B. F. Bowen, 1903.
3 p.l., [13]-1123 p. ports. 28 cm.

6560 Delaplaine, Edward Schley, 1893-
Lincoln's companions on the trip to Antietam.
Harrogate, Tenn., Lincoln Memorial University press,
1954.
10 p. illus. 20 cm.

6561 Delgado, José María.
... Por las tres Américas; crónicas de viaje.
Montevideo, Palacio del libro, 1928.
268 p., 2 l. 19 cm.

6562 Delluc, Louis, 1890-1924.
Charlie Chaplin, by Louis Delluc; translated
by Hamish Miles. London, John Lane; New York,
John Lane company, 1922.
96 p. plates, ports. 23 1/2 cm.

6563 Demagny, René, 1930-
Cuba; l'exil et la ferveur. Paris, Buchet/
Chastel [1962]
222 p. 19 cm.

6564 Deming, Henry Champion, 1815-1872.
Eulogy of Abraham Lincoln... before the General

Assembly of Connecticut, at... Hartford... June
8th, 1865. Hartford, A. N. Clarke, 1865.
58 p. 22 cm.

6565 Democratic party. National committee, 1860-1864.
... The great issue to be decided in November
next! Shall the Constitution and the Union stand
or fall, shall sectionalism triumph? Lincoln and
his supporters: behold the record! [n.p.,
Democratic National Committee, 1860]
24 p. 20 cm.

6566 Democratic party. National committee, 1864-1868.
... Address of the National Democratic committee.
The perils of the nation. Usurpations of the administration in Maryland and Tennessee. The remedy
to be used. [Washington? 1864]
8 p. 24 cm.

6567 Democratic party. National committee, 1864-1868.
George P. Hambrecht. Corruptions and frauds of
Lincoln's administration. [n.p.] Democratic
national committee, 1864.
8 p. 22 cm.

6568 Democratic party. National committee, 1864-1868.
The Harrison's Bar letter of Gen. McClellan;
opinions of James Guthrie, John Van Buren,
Reverdy Johnson, etc. ... Democratic national
committee, 1864.
4 p. 22 cm.

6569 Democratic party. National committee, 1864-1868.
... Lincoln's treatment of General Grant...
Democratic national committee, 1864.
8 p. 22 cm.

6570 Democratic party. National committee, 1864-1868.
... Miscegenation endorsed by the Republican
party. [n.p.] Democratic national committee,
1864.
8 p. 22 cm.

6571 Democratic party. National committee, 1864-1868.
... Mr. Lincoln's arbitrary arrests: the acts

which the Baltimore platform approves. [n.p.]
Democratic national committee, 1864.
   24 p.   22 cm.

6572 Democratic party. National committee, 1864-1868.
      Republican opinions about Lincoln. [n.p.]
      Democratic national committee, 1864.
         16 p.   22 cm.

6573 De Normandie, James, 1836-1924.
      The Lord reigneth; a few words on... April
      16th, 1865, after the assassination of Abraham
      Lincoln. [Portsmouth, N. H.? 1865]
         8 p.   17 cm.

6574 Dent, John Charles, 1841-1888.
      The last forty years; Canada since the union of
      1841. Toronto, G. Virtue [1881]
         2 v.   col. fronts., pl. port.   26 x 20 cm.

6575 Denys, Nicolas, 1598-1688.
      The description and natural history of the
      coasts of North America (Acadia) by Nicolas Denys;
      tr. and ed., with a memoir of the author, col-
      lateral documents, and a reprint of the original,
      by William F. Ganong...   Toronto, The Champlain
      society, 1908.
         xvi, 625 p.   illus., plates, fold. maps.   25 cm.

6576 De Ros, John Frederick Fitzgerald, 1804-1861.
      Personal narrative of travels in the United
      States and Canada in 1826. With remarks on the
      present state of the American Navy... 3d ed.   Lon-
      don, W. H. Ainsworth, 1827.
         xii, 235 p.   plates (1 fold.), maps.   22 cm.

6577 De Ros, John Frederick Fitzgerald, 1804-1861.
      ... Travels in the United States and Canada in
      1826. By Lieut. the Hon. F. Fitzgerald de Roos,
      Royal navy. Prepared by the personnel of the
      Works progress administration, Project no. 665-
      08-3-236. A. Yedidia, supervisor. P. Radin,
      editor. ... Sponsored by the California state
      library. San Francisco, 1939.
         4 p.l., 72 numb. l.   27 cm.

6578 Desaché, Gaétan.
Souvenir de mon voyage aux États-Unis et au
Canada. Tours, Impr. P. Bouserez [1878]
192 p.   12 cm.

6579 Desengaños sobre las preocupaciones del dia.
Discursos polemicos entre un Español, sobre la
libertad, gobiernos, revoluciones, y religion.
Dispuestos P.D.S.H.P.   Roma, 1796.
2 v. in 1.   15 cm.

6580 DeVere, Paul.
The flight of J. Wilkes Booth.   New York, [19-?]
8 p.   22 cm.

6581 Dewey, John, 1859-1952.
John Dewey on Henry George and what some others
say. New York, Robert Schalkenbach Foundation
[n.d.]
8 p.   15 cm.

6582 Dexter, Henry Martyn, 1821-1890.
What ought to be done with the freedmen and with
the rebels? A sermon preached in... Boston...
April 23, 1865.   Boston, Nichols & Noyes, 1865.
36 p.   24 cm.

6583 Dhormoys, Paul, 1829-
... Une visite chez Soulouque: souvenirs d'un
voyage dans l'île d'Haïti.   Paris, L. Hachette et
cie., 1864.
2 p.l., 256 p.   front. (port.)   18 cm.

6584 Diálogo político. La verdad, y la justicia.
[Colophon: Impresso en Lima. A principios de
marco del año de 1724]
caption-title, [19] p.   22 cm.

6585 El Diario, Mexico.
Mexico en su primer siglo de independencia;
publicacion de la compañia editorial "El Diario,"
s.a., Mexico, septiembre de 1910. Dirección
artística y literaria de Don Gonzalo G. Travesi.
[Mexico, Talleres de "El Diario," 1910]
2 p.l., 189 p., 1 l.   illus. (part col., incl.

ports.)   35 1/2 cm.

6586   The diary of a public man: an intimate view of the
national administration, December 28, 1860 to
March 15, 1861; and A page of political correspondence, Stanton to Buchanan; prefatory notes by F.
Lauriston Bullard; foreword by Carl Sandburg.
Chicago, Ill., Priv. print. for Abraham Lincoln
bookshop, 1945.
        3 p.l., ix-xi, 117, [1] p. ports. facsim.
24 cm.

6587   Díaz y Díaz, Jesús.
        Itinerario que manifesta varios puntos de la
República Mexicana formado por el c. comandante de
escuadrón Jesús Díaz y Díaz en la última campaña
contra los franceses... Mexico, Impr. de M.
Villanueva, 1869.
        v, 67, [1] p. port.   20 cm.

6588   Dickens, Charles, 1812-1870.
        American notes and Pictures from Italy, by
Charles Dickens; a reprint of the first editions,
with the illustrations, and an introduction, biographical and bibliographical, by Charles Dickens
the younger. London and New York, Macmillan and
co., 1903.
        xvii p., [1] l., 379, [1] p. illus., facsim.
19 1/2 cm.

6589   Dickens, Charles, 1812-1870.
        ... Christmas stories. Pictures from Italy and
American notes ... Boston, Houghton, Osgood and
company; Cambridge, The Riverside press, 1880.
        4 v. in 1. fronts. (port., v. 3)   17 1/2 cm.

6590   Dickens, Charles, 1812-1870.
        Pictures from Italy. American notes. By
Charles Dickens ... London, Chapman and Hall,
limited [n.d.]
        vii p., 1 l., 437 p. front. plates.   21 cm.

6591   Dickens, Charles, 1812-1870.
        Pictures from Italy, Sketches by Boz, and American
notes. By Charles Dickens. Illustrated by Thomas

Nast and Arthur B. Frost. New York, Harper &
brothers, 1877.
    383 p. incl. front., illus., 2 pl.   25 1/2 cm.

6592 Dickinson, Daniel Stevens, 1800-1866.
    Speeches, correspondence, etc., of the late Daniel
S. Dickinson, of New York. Including: addresses
on important public topics; speeches in the state
and United States Senate, and in support of the
government during the rebellion; correspondence,
private and political (collected and arranged by
Mrs. Dickinson), poems (collected and arranged by
Mrs. Mygatt), etc. Ed., with a biography, by his
brother, John R. Dickinson ... New York, G. P.
Putnam & sons, 1867.
    2 v.   24 1/2 cm.

6593 Diener, Frau Mietze (Glanz)
    Reise in das moderne Mexiko. Erinnerungen an den
x. Internationalen geologen-kongress in Mexiko.
Von Mietze Diener. Mit 30 illustrationen (nach
originalaufnahmen) und einer karte. Wien und
Leipzig, A. Hartleben, 1908.
    4 p.l., 112 p. illus., fold. map.   22 1/2 cm.

6594 Diez De La Calle, Juan, fl. 1646.
    Memorial y compendio breve del libro intitvlado
Noticias sacras y reales de los imperios de la
Nueva España, el Perú y sus islas de las Indias
Occidentales. [n.p., 1648?]
    32 p.   24 cm.

6595 Dinwiddie, William, 1867-1934.
    Puerto Rico; its conditions and possibilities,
by William Dinwiddie; with illustrations and photographs by the author. New York and London, Harper
& bros., 1899.
    vii, [1], 293, [1] p. front., plates.   21 cm.

6596 Disney, Daniel, defendant.
    The trial of Daniel Disney, esq; captain of a
company in His Majesty's 44th regiment of foot,
and town-major of the garrison of Montreal... on
... the 28th day of February... 1767... Quebec,
printed by Brown & Gilmore, 1767.

46 p.   22 cm.

6597 Dittenhoefer, Abram Jesse, 1836-
    How we elected Lincoln: personal recollections
    of Lincoln and men of his time... New York,
    Harper [1916]
    94 p. illus.   19 cm.

6598 Dix ans sur la côte du Pacifique par un missionnaire
    canadien... Québec, Imprimerie de Léger Brousseau,
    1873.
    100 p.   20 cm.

6599 Dix, Edwin Asa, 1860-1911.
    Champlain, the founder of New France, by Edwin
    Asa Dix... New York, D. Appleton and company,
    1903.
    4 p.l., 246 p.   6 pl., 2 port. (incl. front.)
    map.   19 1/2 cm.

6600 Dixon, George.
    A voyage round the world; but more particularly
    of the north-west coast of America: performed in
    1785, 1786, 1787, and 1788, in the King George and
    Queen Charlotte, Captains Portlock and Dixon...
    London, Published by George Goulding, 1789.
    552, [55] p. pl. (part fold.), fold. maps.
    22 cm.

6601 Dobbs, Arthur, 1689-1765.
    A reply to Capt. Middleton's answer to the remarks
    on his vindication of his conduct, in a late
    voyage made by him in the Furnace sloop... to find
    out a passage from the northwest of Hudson's Bay,
    to the western and southern ocean of America...
    London, Printed and sold by J. Robinson, 1745.
    128 p.   22 cm.

6602 Dobrizhoffer, Martin, 1717-1791.
    An account of the Abipones, an equestrian people
    of Paraguay. From the Latin of Martin Dobrizhoffer,
    eighteen years a missionary in that country.
    London, John Murray, 1822.
    3 v.   21 1/2 cm.

6603 [Dock, Herman]
A descriptive reading on picturesque Mexico.
Illustrated by fifty lantern slides. Philadelphia,
W. H. Rau, 1889.
38 p. 19 cm.

6604 Documentos para la historia de Méjico... Méjico,
Impr. de J. R. Navarro, 1853-57.
21 v. in 19. 20 cm.

6605 Dodds, James.
The Hudson's Bay company, its position and
prospects. The substance of an address, delivered
at a meeting of the shareholders, in the London
tavern, on the 24th January, 1866... London,
Edward Stanford and A. H. Baily & co., 1866.

6606 Dollero, Adolfo.
... México al día (impresiones y notas de viaje)
... Paris [etc.] V^{da} de C. Bouret, 1911.
972 p. illus. 23 cm.

6607 Domenech, Emmanuel Henri Dieudonné, 1825 or 6-1886.
Journal d'un missionaire au Texas et au Mexique,
par l'abbé E. Domenech, 1846-1852. 2. éd. Paris,
Gaume frères et J. Duprey, 1872.
xii, 417 p. 18 cm.

6608 Domenech, Emmanuel Henri Dieudonné, 1825 or 6-1886.
Le Mexique tel qu'il est; la vérité sur son
climat, ses habitants et son gouvernement, par
Emmanuel Domenech ... 2. éd. Paris, E. Dentu, 1867.
2 p.l., iv, 350 p., 1 l. 18 1/2 cm.

6609 Domenech, Emmanuel Henri Dieudonné, 1825 or 6-1886.
Souvenirs d'outre-mer. Mes missions au crépuscule
de la vie, par l'abbé Domenech. Paris, Gaume et c^{ie},
1884.
viii, 392 p. 18 1/2 cm.

6610 Domingo, Marcelino, 1884-
... Alas y garras. Madrid, Editorial "Mundo
latino" [1922?]
235, [2] p. 18 1/2 cm.

6611   Domínguez, Josefina.
       Geografía de la República mexicana, por la
       señorita Josefina Domínguez. México, D. F., 1933.
       221 p.   19 1/2 cm.

6612   Don Bullebulle; periódico burlesco y de extravagancias,
       redactado por una sociedad de bulliciosos. Mérida
       de Yucatán, 1847.
       2 v.   25 cm.

6613   [Donaldson, Sir Stuart Alexander] 1812-1867.
       Mexico thirty years ago, as described in a
       series of private letters, by a youth ... London,
       Printed by W. R. Gray, 1865.
       vi, [2], 236 p., 1 l. front. (fold. map)   19 cm.

6614   Donnavan, Corydon.
       Abenteuer in Mexiko, während siebenmonatlicher
       gefangenschaft. Enthaltend eine erzählung, wie der
       verfasser durch Canales guerillabande gefangen
       genommen, nach Valladolid transportirt und in die
       sclaverei verkauft worden; nebst vielen romantischen
       abenteuern, und einer beschreibung des landes,
       bodens, klimas und der produkte ... &c. Von C.
       Donnavan. Kutztaun, Pa., Gedruckt in Hawrecht's
       "Geist der zeit" druckerei, 1848.
       144 p.   22 1/2 cm.

6615   Donnavan, Corydon.
       Adventures in Mexico: experienced during a cap-
       tivity of seven months in the interior-having been
       captured at Camargo, by Canales' band of guerrillas
       ... and sold into slavery... final escape, and
       perilious journey to the United States with a view
       of the present war... By C. Donnavan. Cincinnati,
       Robinson & Jones, 1487 [i.e. 1847]
       v, [ix]-xi, [13]-112 p.   23 cm.

6616   Doolittle, James Rood, 1815-1897.
       Speech... on the Lincoln-Johnson policy of
       restoration; delivered in the Senate of the United
       States, January 17, 1866. Washington, Congressional
       globe office, 1866.
       22 p.   24 cm.

6617   Dougall, Allan H
      The death of Captain Wells. Fort Wayne, Ind.,
      Public Library of Fort Wayne and Allen County,
      1954.
      [12] p. front. (port.), illus. 20 1/2 cm.

6618   Douglass, Frederick, 1817-1895.
      Oration by Frederick Douglass delivered on the
      occasion of the unveiling of the Freedman's monu-
      ment in memory of Abraham Lincoln park, Washington,
      D. C., April 14, 1876. With an appendix. New
      York, N. Y., Pub. for the Frederick Douglass his-
      torical and cultural league by the Pathway press,
      1940.
      34 p. incl. front. 17 cm.

6619   Downey, Edgar.
      Schuylkill county and some of its people when
      Abraham Lincoln was assassinated: a paper...
      written for the Historical society of Schuylkill
      county, Pennsylvania... Pottsville, Pa., 1952.
      20 p. 20 cm.

6620   Downey, Edgar.
      There were kinsmen of Abraham Lincoln in
      Schuylkill county: a paper... written for the
      Historical society of Schuylkill county, Pennsylvania.
      Pottsville, Pa., 1952.
      22 p. 20 cm.

6621   [Dowse, Thomas]
      Manitoba and the Canadian north-west, from the
      Chicago Commerical advertiser, August 30th, 1877.
      31 p. illus., fold. map. 25 cm.

6622   Doyle, Sir Arthur Conan, 1859-1930.
      The refugees; a tale of two continents, by A.
      Conan Doyle... illustrated by T. De Thulstrup.
      New York, Harper & brothers, 1893.
      5 p.l., 366 p. front., plates. 19 cm.

6623   Doyle, William.
      Some account of the British dominions beyond the
      Atlantic, containing chiefly what is most interesting
      and least known with respect to those parts: par-

ticularly the important question about the Northwest
Passage is satisfactorily discussed: with a large
map... London, Printed for the author by J. Browne,
1770.
87 p., 1 l. fold. map. 22 cm.

6624 [Drage, Theodore Swaine]
An account of a voyage for the discovery of a
northwest passage by Hudson's Streights, to the
Western and Southern ocean of America, performed
in the year 1746 and 1747, in the ship California,
Capt. Francis Smith, commander. By the clerk of the
California. Adorned with cuts and maps. London,
Printed; and sold by Mr. Jolliffe, in St. James
street; Mr. Corbett, in Fleet street; and Mr.
Clarke, under the Royal Exchange.
2 v. illus., maps. 34.7 x 22 cm.

6625 Drascomb, Alfred Brooks, 1837-1894.
A discourse preached... at Watsfield, Vt., in
honor of our late chief magistrate, on Sunday,
April 23, 1865... Montpelier, Vt., Walton's steam
printing establishment, 1865.
23 p. 23 cm.

6626 Drees, Charles William.
Thirteen years in Mexico (from letters of Charles
W. Drees) ed. by Ada M. C. Drees. New York, Printed
for the author by the Abingdon press [c1915]
3 p.l., 5-276 p. front., ports. 21 cm.

6627 Drummond, Josiah H
Genealogy of Isaac Dean of Grafton, N. H., fourth
in descent from John Dean of Taunton. Portland,
Me., Smith & Sale, printers, 1902.
35 p. 22 cm.

6628 Duane, Richard Bache, 1824?-1875.
A sermon preached at St. John's church, Providence,
on... April 19, 1865... for the funeral obsequies
of President Lincoln. Providence, H. H. Thomas &
co., 1865.
15 p. 22 cm.

6629 Duarte Level, Lino.

... Cuadros de la historia militar y civil de
Venezuela, desde el descubrimiento y conquista de
Guayana hasta la batalla de Carabobo ... Madrid,
Editorial-América [1917]
 2 p.l., [7]-460 p.   23 cm.

6630 Duclós-Salinas, Adolfo.
... The riches of Mexico and its institutions.
By Adolfo Duclós Salinas. St. Louis, Nixon-Jones
printing co., 1893.
 509 p. front., illus., plates, ports.   25 cm.

6631 Dudley, John Langdon, 1812-1894.
Discourse preached in the South Congregational
Church, Middletown, Ct. ... after the assassination
of President Lincoln. Middletown, D. Barnes, 1865.
 28 p.   22 cm.

6632 Dudley, Thomas Underwood.
Sermon in memory of the Reverend Stephen
Elliott Barnwell, late rector of St. John's Church,
Louisville, Ky. ... Louisville, John P. Morton and
company, 1891.
 22 p. front. (port.)   24 cm.

6633 Dueñas Bolante, Fernando de.
Manifesto, qve don Fernando de Dueñas Bolante
... medioracionero de la santa Iglesia catedral
metropolitana de la ciudad de Lima, y su procurador
general en la corte del rey de España nuestro señor,
haze al mvndo... Y mas en particular, a todos los
vezinos de la dicha ciudad de Lima, de qualquier
estado, calidad, y condition que sean. De treze
cargos, que por diferentes personas, vnas a cara
descubierta, y otras con mas dissimulo le hazen,
en que le acusan de lo que en ellos se contiene, y
adelante se verà. Y assimismo de la respuesta que
a todos, y a cada yno dellos da, para que assi se
reconozca, la verdad desnuda que le assiste, y cō
ella se quiten los velosque la embidia, ò malos, y
muy apassionados informes pusieren los ojos del
entendimiento, y voluntad de los que assi le acusan.
[Madrid, 1671]
 18 numbered l.   22 cm.

6634 Dufferin and Ava, Hariot Georgina (Hamilton)
      Hamilton-Temple-Blackwood, marchioness of.
        My Canadian journal, 1872-'78; extracts from My
      letters home, written while Lord Dufferin was
      governor-general; by the Marchioness of Dufferin
      and Ava... With illustrations from sketches by
      Lord Dufferin, portrait and map. New York, D.
      Appleton and company, 1891.
        xvip., 1 l., 456 p. illus., plates, 2 port.
      (incl. front.), fold. map. 19 1/2 cm.

6635 Dugas, George, 1833-
        Histoire véridique des faits qui ont préparé
      le mouvement des métis à la Rivière Rouge en 1869,
      par l'abbé J. Dugas. Montréal, Librairie Beauchemin
      [à resp. limitée] 1905.
        ix, 288 p. 20 cm.

6636 Dunbar, Edward E
        ... The Mexican papers... [1st series, no. 1-5]
      New York, J. A. H. Hasbrouck & co., printers,
      1860-61.
        1 p.l., 175, iii, [i], 177-279 p. 24 cm.

6637 Dunbar, M
        Genealogy of the Dunbar family... Boston,
      Stanley and Usher, 1886.
        35 p. 22 cm.

6638 Dunbar, Seymour.
        A history of travel in America, being an
      outline of the development in modes of travel
      from archaic vehicles of colonial times to the
      completion of the first transcontinental railroad;
      the influence of the Indians on the free movement
      and territorial unity of the white race: the part
      played by travel methods in the economic conquest
      of the continent: and those related human exper-
      iences, changing social conditions and governmental
      attitudes which accompanied the growth of a national
      travel system... With two maps, twelve colored
      plates and four hundred illustrations. Indianapolis,
      Bobbs-Merrill co. [1915]
        4 v. col. fronts., illus. (incl. facsims.)
      col. plates, maps (2 double) 23 cm.

6639　Duncan, John Morison.
　　　　Travels through part of the United States and
　　　Canada in 1818 and 1819.　New York, W. B. Gilley;
　　　New Haven, Howe & Spalding, 1823.
　　　　2 v.　maps.　18 cm.

6640　Dundonald, Thomas Cochrane, 10th earl of, 1775-1860.
　　　　... Memorias de lord Cochrane.　Madrid, Edi-
　　　torial-América [1917?]
　　　　301 p.　23 cm.

6641　Dunraven, Windham Thomas Wyndham-Quin, 4th earl of,
　　　1841-1926.
　　　　Canadian nights; being sketches and reminiscences of
　　　life and sport in the Rockies, the prairies, and
　　　the Canadian woods.　London, Smith, Elder, 1914.
　　　　296 p.　21 cm.

6642　Dupin de Sainte-André, 1840-1921.
　　　　Le Mexique aujourd'hui:　impressions et souvenirs
　　　de voyage, par A. Dupin de Sainte-André...　Paris,
　　　E. Plon, Nourrit et cie., 1884.
　　　　2 p.l., iv, 284 p.　19 cm.

6643　Dupré, Joseph, 1742-1823.
　　　　Mémoire sur le commerce en général et celui du
　　　Languedoc, dans ses rapports avec les échelles
　　　du Levant, la compagnie des Indes, les colonies &
　　　la traite des noirs.　Paris, Impr. nat., 1790.
　　　　35 p.　20 cm.

6644　Durán, Diego, d. 1588?
　　　　Historia de las Indias de Nueva-España y islas de
　　　Tierre Firme, por el padre Fray Diego Durán...
　　　México, Impr. de J. M. Andrade y F. Escalante,
　　　1867-80.
　　　　2 v. and atlas of facsims. on 66 pl. (63 col.)
　　　30 1/2 cm.

6645　Durand, John, 1822-1908.
　　　　John Trumbull, by John Durand (Reprinted from
　　　"The American art review") Boston, Estes and Lauriat,
　　　1881.
　　　　1 p.l., 24 p.　front., illus., plates, facsim.
　　　34 1/2 cm.

6646   Durand, Luz María.
          ... Poemas de México. México, 1943.
          3 p.l., 9-108 p., 2 l. illus.   20 1/2 cm.

6647   Durham, John George Lambton, 1st earl of, 1792-1840.
          Lord Durham's report on the affairs of British
       North America; ed. with an introduction by Sir
       C. P. Lucas. Oxford, Clarendon Press, 1912.
          3 v.   23 cm.

6648   Durham, John George Lambton, 1st earl of, 1792-1840.
          Report on the affairs of British North America
       from the Earl of Durham, Her Majesty's high
       commissioner, etc., etc., etc. Presented by Her
       Majesty's command. [n.p.] Ordered by the House
       of Commons to be printed, 1839.
          1v. (various pagings)   33 cm.

6649   Dussieux, Louis Étienne, 1815-1894.
          Le Canada sous la domination française, d'après
       les archives de la marine et de la guerre, par L.
       Dussieux... 2. éd. Paris, J. Lecoffre, 1862.
          2 p.l., 471 p. fold. map.   18 cm.

6650   Dutrône la Couture, Jacques-Francois.
          Vues générales sur l'importance du commerce des
       colonies, sur le caractère du peuple qui les cultive,
       & sur les moyens de faire la constitution qui leur
       convient. [n.p.] 1790.
          26 p.   20 cm.

6651   Dyer, John Percy.
          The Civil War career of General Joseph Wheeler
       ... Nashville, Tenn., 1935.
          32 p.   24 cm.

6652   Dyson, Howard F
          Lincoln in Rushville. Rushville, Illinois,
       reprinted from the Rushville Times, Feb. 12, 1903.
       Rushville, Ill., 1903.
          37 p.   22 cm.

6653 East, Ernest Edward, 1885-
Abraham Lincoln sees Peoria: an historical and
pictorial record of seventeen visits from 1832 to
1858. Peoria, Ill. [Record publishing co.] 1939.
1 p.l., [1], 37 p. illus. (incl. ports.,
facsims.) 27 1/2 cm.

6654 Eastman, Mary F
The biography of Dio Lewis... Prepared at the
desire and with the co-operation of Mrs. Dio Lewis,
by Mary F. Eastman... New York, Fowler and Wells
co., 1891.
398 p. front. (port.) 19 1/2 cm.

6655 Eaton, Thomas Treadwell, 1845-1907.
The cruise of the Kaiserin. With poetical narrative by Martin Luther Berger. Louisville, Ky.,
Baptist Book Concern, 1903.
125 p. illus., map. 20 cm.

6656 Eaves, Catherine, pseud.
... How I twice eloped; an Indiana idyll, sug-
gested by Abraham Lincoln, elaborated by Catherine
Eaves... Chicago, Oak printing & pub., co., [c1901]
88 p. illus. 22 cm.

6657 Echezárraga, Juan de.
... Manifiesto legal de la ineluctable justicia
del conde de Fuente Gonzalez, vecino de la ciudad
de Lima, y sus tres hijos legitimos d. Juan, d.
Josef y doña Francisca Gonzalez de la Fuente,
habidos en su matrimonio con doña Rosa de la
Fuente, condesa del mismo titulo, y del Villar,
en el pleyto suscitado por d. Antonio Estebez y
Pombal... y d. Vicente Quiroga Mendez de Sotomayor

... sobre ideada sucesion al vinculo, que del tercio de sus bienes apeteció se fundase d. Josef del Villar y Andrade, del mismo domicilio de Lima. [Madrid? 1796?]
1 p.l., 22 numbered. l. fold. geneal. tab. 23 cm.

6658 Eckman, James.
A day in the life of a country newspaper: the assassination of Abraham Lincoln, reprinted from the Mantonville Express, April 21, 1865. Rochester, Minnesota, Doomsday press, 1955.
19 p.

6659 Eddy, Richard, 1828-1906.
"The martyr to liberty:" three sermons preached in the First Universalist Church, Philadelphia... Philadelphia, H. G. Leisenring's steampower printing house, 1865.
27 p.   23 cm.

6660 Edgar County Historical Society, Paris, Illinois.
Memoirs of Abraham Lincoln in Edgar County, Illinois. [Paris, Ill., Edgar county historical society, 1925]
31 p.   illus.   23 cm.

6661 Edwards, William Seymour, 1856-
On the Mexican highlands, with a passing glimpse of Cuba, by William Seymour Edwards ... Cincinnati, Press of Jennings and Graham [c1906]
283 p.   99 pl., double map.   20 1/2 cm.

6662 Ehrmann, Bess Virginia (Hicks)
Historic Rockport & Spencer county, Indiana. [n.p., 1942]
[24] p.   illus.   20 cm.

6663 Ehrmann, Bess Virginia (Hicks)
Lincoln and his neighbors. Prepared for the Spencer County Historical Society. Rockport, Ind., Democrat Pub. Co., 1948.
[46] p.   illus., ports.   23 cm.

6664 Ehrmann, Bess Virginia (Hicks)

The Lincoln Pioneer Village: a Lincoln memorial;
Rockport, Indiana. [Rockport] Democrat Pub. Co.,
1949.
[8] p. illus. 21 cm.

6665 Ehrmann, Bess Virginia (Hicks)
The missing chapter in the life of Abraham
Lincoln; a number of articles, episodes, photographs, pen and ink sketches concerning the life
of Abraham Lincoln in Spencer county, Indiana,
between 1816-1830 and 1844, by Bess V. Ehrmann;
pen and ink sketches by Mary Lee Gabbert. Chicago,
Ill., W. M. Hill [c1938]
4 p.l., [vii]-xiv p., 1 l., 150 p. illus., 28
pl. (incl. ports., map, facsims.) on 20 l.   24
1/2 cm.

6666 Eighty years' progress of British North America;
showing the wonderful development of its natural
resources... giving, in a historical form, the
vast improvements made in agriculture, commerce,
and trade, modes of travel and transportation,
mining, and educational interests, etc., etc., with
a large amount of statistical information, from
the best and latest authorities. By H. Y. Hind...
T. C. Keefer... J. S. Hodgins... Charles Robb...
M. H. Perley... Rev. Wm. Murray. Fully illustrated
with steel and electrotype plate engravings...
(Furnished to subscribers only) Toronto, L.
Stebbins, 1863.
766 p. incl. illus., pl. front., plates.   23 cm.

6667 Eisenschiml, Otto, 1880-
The case of A. Lincoln, aged 56: some curious
medical aspects of Lincoln's death and other
studies, by Otto Eisenschiml. Chicago, Ill.,
Priv. print. for the Abraham Lincoln bookshop,
1943.
55 [1] p. incl. front., 1 illus. facsim.
23 1/2 cm.

6668 [Ellice, Edward]
The communications of Mercator [pseud.] upon the
contest between the Earl of Selkirk and the Hudson's
Bay company, on the one hand, and the Northwest

company on the other. Republished from the
Montreal Herald. Montreal, Published by W. Gray,
1817.
99, 12 p., 1 l.   20 cm.

6669 [Ellis, Charles Mayo] 1818-1878.
The power of the commander-in-chief to declare
martial law, and decree emancipation; as shown
from B. R. Curtis; by Libertas [pseud.] Boston,
A. Williams & co., 1862.
24 p.   13 cm.

6670 Ellis, Henry.
A voyage to Hudson's Bay, by Dobbs Galley and
California, in the years 1746 and 1747, for dis-
covering a North west passage; with an accurate
survey of the coast and a short natural history
of the country... Dublin, Printed for George and
Alexander Ewing, 1749.
152 p.   fold. map.   23 cm.

6671 Ellis, Mina (Benson) Hubbard.
A woman's way through unknown Labrador; an account
of the exploration of the Nascaupee and George
Rivers, by Mrs. Leonidas Hubbard, Jr.   New York,
McClure, 1908.
305 p.   plates, ports., fold. map.   21 cm.

6672 Emmerich-Högen, Ferdinand, 1858-
... In mexikanischen urwäldern.   Leipzig, Ernst
Staneck verlag, g.m.b.h. [1936]
248 p.   incl. plates.   19 cm.

6673 [Empresa editora, s.a.]
Mexico. Fourth regional convention of the World
press congress held in Mexico city in August, 1931.
[Mexico city, 1931]
[140] p.   illus. (incl. ports., facsims.), col.
plates.   23 1/2 x 32 cm.

6674 [Enciso, Martín Fernández de]
Suma de geographia q̄ trata de todas las partidas
7 prouincias del mundo: en especial delas Indias.
7 trata larga mente del arte del marear juntamente
con la espera en romance: con el regimieto del

144

sol y del norte: agora nueuamente emendada de
algunos defectos q̃ tenia enla impressiõ passada.
[Sevilla, J. Cromberger, 1530]
   lx, xiix, lviii, numb. l.   25 cm.

6675 The Englishman's guide book to the United States
   and Canada. Illustrated; with an appendix of the
   shooting and fishing resorts of North America.
   Edition of 1884. London, E. Stanford; New York,
   G. P. Putnam's sons [1884]
      ix p., 1 1., 276, 68 p. front., plates, maps
   (part fold., part col.), fold. col. plans.   17 cm.

6676 Enox, Zimri A
   The early surveyors and surveying in Illinois
   ... Springfield., Ill., Springfield prtg. co.,
   1891.
      7 p.   23 cm.

6677 Ercilla y Zúñiga, Alonso de, 1533-1594.
   La Aravcana de don Alonso de Ercilla y Çuñiga.
   Dirigida a la sacra catholica reál magestad del
   rey don Philippe nuestro señor. Salamanca, En
   casa de Domingo de Portonarijs, impressor de Su
   Catholica Magestad, 1574.
      11 p.l., 392, [8] p. port.   25 cm.
   Errors in pagination: p. 10-11, 49, 194, 224
   misnumbered 8-9, 29, 149 and 204.

6678 Ercilla y Zúñiga, Alonso de, 1533-1594.
   La Aravcana de don Alonso de Erzilla y Çvñiga
   ... Dirigida a la s.c.r.m. del rey don Phelippe
   nuestro señor. Anvers, En casa de Pedro Bellero,
   1575.
      6 p.l., 333, [12] p.   23 cm.
   Errors in pagination: p. 2, 74, 122, 148 misnumbered 4, 47, 22 and 48.

6679 Ercilla y Zúñiga, Alonso de, 1533-1594.
   La Aravcana de don Alonso de Erzilla y Çvñiga
   ... Dirigida a la s.c.r.m. del rey don Phelippe
   nuestro señor. Çaragoça, En casa de Iuan Soler,
   1577.
      8 p.l., 328 (i.e. 330), [6] p.   21 cm.
   Errors in paging: no. 127 repeated, and an extra

145

page numbered 187 inserted before no. 128; numerous
other errors in paging.

6680   Ercilla y Zúñiga, Alonso de, 1533-1594.
        La Aravcana. Primera y segvnda parte. Madrid,
        P. Cosin, 1578.
        724 p.   26 cm.

6681   Ercilla y Zúñiga, Alonso de, 1533-1594.
        La Araucana... Su autor don Alonso de Ercilla y
        Zuñiga ... Madrid, A. de Sancha, 1776.
        3 v. in 2. front. (port.) plates, fold. map.
        18 cm.

6682   Ercilla y Zúñiga, Alonso de, 1533-1594.
        Primera, segvnda, y tercera partes de la
        Araucana de don Alonso de Ercilla y Çuñiga ...
        Dirigidas al rey don Felippe nuestro señor.
        Barcelona, En casa Sebastiã de Cormellas, 1592.
        17 p.l., 330 (i.e. 331) numb. 1.   25 cm.

6683   Ercilla y Zúñiga, Alonso de, 1533-1594.
        Primera, segvnda, y tercera parte de la Araucana
        de dō Alonso de Ercilla y Cuñiga ... Dirigida al
        rey don Felipe nuestro señor. Con licencia.
        Perpiñian, En casa de Sanson Arbus, 1596.
        17 p.l., 323 numb. 1., [4] p.   24 cm.
        Errors in foliation: no. 19 omitted, no. 307
        repeated: leaves 29, 120, 155 misnumbered 39, 130
        and 153.

6684   Ercilla y Zúñiga, Alonso de, 1533-1594.
        Primera, sgvnda, y tercera partes de la Araucana
        de don Alonso de Ercilla y Çuñiga ... Dirigidas
        al rey don Felipe nuestro señor. Madrid, En casa
        del licēciado Castro, 1597.
        32 p.l., 445 (i.e. 457) numb. 1., [23] p.   23 cm.
        Errors in foliation: nos. 420-421 repeated (3
        leaves marked Gggō, catchwords do not match); leaf
        455 misnumbered 445; many other errors in foliation.

6685   Ercilla y Zúñiga, Alonso de, 1533-1594.
        Primera, segvnda, y tercera parte de la Araucana
        de d. Alonso de Ercilla y Zuñiga, cauallero de la
        orden de Santiago, gentilhombre de la camara de la

146

magestad del emperador. Dirigidas al rey nuestro
señor. Madrid, En casa de Iuan de la Cuesta, 1610.
16 p.l., 457 numb. l., 14 l. 25 cm.

6686 Ercilla y Zúñiga, Alonso de, 1533-1594.
Primera, segvnda, y tercera partes de la Aravcana
de don Alonso de Ercilla y Zuñiga, cavallero de la
orden de Santiago, gentilhombre de la camara de la
magestad del emperador. Dirigida al rey don Felipe
nuestro señor. Cadiz, En casa de Gaspar Vezino,
mercader de libros, y a su costa, 1626.
6 p.l., 398 (i.e. 394) numb. l., 8 l. 26 cm.
Errors in foliation: nos. 297-298, 323-324
omitted; leaves 2, 180, 207, 209, 301, 379 misnumbered 6, 18, 107, 206, 30, 376 respectively.

6687 Ercilla y Zúñiga, Alonso de, 1533-1594.
Segvnda parte de la Aravcana de don Alonso de
Erzilla y Çuñiga, que trata la porfiada guerra entre
los españoles, y araucanos, cō algunas cosas notables que en aquel tiempo sucedieron. Çaragoça,
Impresso con licencia, en casa de Iuan Soler, 1578.
3 p.l., 2-335 (i.e., 2 p.l., 335), [5] p. 21 cm.
Errors in paging: no. 83 repeated, no. 92 omitted;
several other pages misnumbered.

6688 Ercilla y Zúñiga, Alonso de, 1533-1594.
Tercera parte de la Araucana de don Alonso de
Ercilla y Çuñiga ... Dirigida al rey don Felipe
nuestro señor. Con priuilegio. En Madrid, En
casa de Pedro Madrigal, año de 1589.
18 p.l., 365-434 (i.e. 435) numb. l., [4] p. incl.
port. 24 cm.

6689 Escalera, Evaristo.
Méjico histórico-descriptivo, seguido de la
crónica militar de la espedición española. Por
Evaristo Escalera y Manuel Gonzalez Llana.
Madrid, Impr. de M. Minuesa, 1862.
3 p.l., iv, 336, 2 p. 24 cm.

6690 Escobar, Manuel de.
Verdad reflexa, platica doctrinal sobre los varios
sucessos que intervinieron en la ciudad de San
Luis Potosi desde el dia 10. de mayor de 1767.

147

hasta el dia 6. de octubre del mismo año, en que
se ejecutaron los ultimos suplicios de los tumul-
tuarios. Dijola en su Plaza mayor el r. p. fr.
Manuel de Escobar... Dedicala al excelentissimo
señor d. Carlos Francisco de Croix, marqués de
Croix... Mexico, Impressa con las licencias
necessarias en la Imprenta real del superior
gobierno: por el br. d. Joseph Antonio de Nogal,
calle de Tiburcio, 1768.
 28 p.l., 57 p. illus. (coat of arms) 26 cm.
Page 43 incorrectly numbered 45.

6691 [Espino Barros, Eugenio]
 Album gráfico de la República Mexicana, 1910.
México, D. F. Müller hnos. [1910]
 411, [3] p. incl. front., illus., ports.
31 x 40 cm.

6692 Esteva, Adalberto A
 Antología nacional; libro de lectura arreglado
por el Lic. Adalberto A. Esteva. Paris, México,
V^da de C. Bouret, 1912.
 428 p. illus. (incl. ports.) 18 cm.

6693 Esteva, Adalberto A
 México pintoresco; antología de artículos
descriptivos del pais, arreglada por Adalberto A.
Esteva. México, Tip. y lit. "La Europea" de J.
Aguilar Vera y compañía, s en c, 1905.
 vii, 253 p., 1 l. fold. pl. 21 cm.

6694 Esteyneffer, Juan de, 1664-1716.
 Florilegio medicinal de todas las enfermedades,
sacado de varios, y clasicos authores, para bien de
los pobres, y de los que tiene falta de medicos,
en particular para las provincias remotas, en donde
administran los rr.pp. missioneros de la Compañia
de Jesvs. Reduçido â tres libros: El primero de
medicina: el segundo de syruxia, con vn apendix,
que pertenece al modo de sangrar, abrir, y curar
fuentes, aplicar ventosas, y sanguixuelas. El
tercero contiene vn cathalogo de los medicamentos
vssuales, que se hazen en la botica, con el modo
de componerlos. Escrito por el hermano Jvan de
Esteyneffer ... Mexico, Por los herederos de Juan

Joseph Guillena Carrascoso, en el Empedradillo, 1712.
17 p.l., 522 (i.e. 520) p.   24 cm.
Errors in pagination: nos. 204 and 433 omitted.

6695   Esteyneffer, Juan de, 1664-1716.
Florilegio medicinal de todas las enfermedades,
sacado de varios, y classicos autores, para bien
de los pobres, y de los que tienen falta de medicos,
en particular para las provincias remotas, en donde
administran los rr. pp. missioneros de la Compañia
de Jesus. Reduçido a tres libros. El primero de
medicina: el segundo de cirugia, con un appendix,
que pertenece al modo de sangrar, abrir y curar
fuentes, aplicar ventosas, y sanguijuelas: el
tercero contiene un catalogo de los medicamentos
usuales, que se hacen en la botica, con el modo
de componerlos. Escrito por el hermano Juan de
Esteyneffer. ... Dedicado a Maria Santissima de
Valvanera. Con licencia. Madrid, En la imprenta
de Joachin Ibarra, calle de las Urosas, a costa
de doña Juana Corrèa. mercadera de libros, frente
de las gradas de San Phelipe el Real, donde se hallarà
[1755?]
16 p.l., 535 p.   24 cm.
Errors in pagination: p. 459 and 474 misnumbered
419 and 274 respectively.

6696   Ethridge, Willie Snow.
An aristocracy of achievement. Hancock county
Negro's twelve children filling many prominent
places in various activities. Benjamin F. Hubert,
President of Georgia State Industrial College, guide
of progressive Georgia Negroes. [Macon, Ga.? 1929?]
19 p. illus.   25 cm.

6697   Evans, Albert S
Our sister republic: a gala trip through tropical
Mexico in 1869-70. Adventure and sight-seeing in
the land of the Aztecs, with picturesque descriptions of the country and the people, and reminiscences
of the empire and its downfall. By Col. Albert S.
Evans... Hartford, Columbian book co.; Toledo, O.,
W. E. Bliss [etc., etc.] 1870.
518 p. front., illus., pl., port.   22 1/2 cm.

149

6698   Evarts, William Maxwell, 1818-1901.
Eulogy on Chief-Justice Chase, delivered by
William M. Evarts, before the alumni of Dartmouth
college, at Hanover, June 24, 1874.   New York,
D. Appleton and company, 1874.
30 p.   23 cm.

6699   Ewart, Frank Carman.
Cuba y las costumbres cubanas, by Frank C.
Ewart...   Boston, New York [etc.] Ginnand company
[c1919]
xiv, 157 p.   incl. front., illus., map, music.
18 cm.

6700   Ewing, Thomas, 1829-1896.
Address delivered, by General Thomas Ewing before
the society of the Sons of the American revolution.
December 4th, 1897.   [New York? 1897?]
[6] p.   25 cm.

6701   Ewing, Thomas, 1829-1896.
Argument of Thomas Ewing, jr., on the jurisdiction
and on the law and the evidence in the case of Dr.
Samuel A. Mudd, tried before a military commission,
of which Maj.-Gen. David Hunter is president, on a
charge of conspiracy to assassinate the President
and other chief officers of the nation.   May and
June, 1865.   Washington, H. Polkinhorn & son,
printers, 1865.
36 p.   22 cm.

F

6702   Fagoaga, Francisco de, 1679-1736.
Tablas de las cuentas del valor liquido de la
plata del diezmo, y del intrinseco, y natural de
la que se llama quintada, y de la reduccion de
sus leyes a la de 12. dineros. Segun las novissimas
ordenanzas de Su Magestad, y de los derechos, que

de la plata, y oro se le pagan en estos reynos, en
conformidad de sus leyes reales, y cedulas. Por
don Francisco de Fagoaga... Quien las dedica al
exmo. senor d. Juan de Acuña, marqués de Casa-
Fuerte... Con licencia de los superiores. Mexico,
Por Joseph Bernardo de Hogal, Calle de la Monterilla,
1729.
    7 p.l., 68 p. illus. (coat of arms)   21 cm.

6703 [Faillon, Etienne Michel] 1800?-1870.
    Histoire de la colonie française en Canada...
Villemarie [Montréal] Bibliothèque paroissiale.
[Paris, Impr. Poupart-Davyl et c^{ie}] 1865-66.
    3 v. front. (port., v. 1) maps (part fold.)
plans (part fold.)   27 cm.

6704 Farming and ranching in the Canadian North-West.
General account of Manitoba and the North-west
Territories. Superior advantages for agricultural
settlers. Unrivalled ranching districts. Free
grants and cheap lands, and how to get them.
Climate and health. How to go, and what to do at the
start. Testimony of actual settlers. [Montreal?
1888?]
    56 p. fold. map.   22 cm.

6705 Farquhar, John.
    The claims of God to recognition in the
assassination of President Lincoln: a sermon
preached... in the Chanceford Presbyterian church,
Lower Chanceford, York co., Pa. ... Lancaster, Pa.,
Pearsol & Geist, 1865.
    23 p.   21 cm.

6706 Farrington, Frank, 1872-
    The nomination of Abraham Lincoln. Delhi, N. Y.,
Greenlawn publications, 1945.
    25 p. illus.   18 cm.

6707 Farrington, Frank, 1872-
    The party of Abraham Lincoln, by Frank Farrington.
Delhi, N. Y., Greenlawn publications, 1946.
    52 p.   18 cm.

6708 Farrington, Oliver Cummings, 1864-

... Observations on the geology and geography of
western Mexico, including an account of the Cerro
Mercado. By Oliver Cummings Farrington ... Chicago,
1904.
1 p.l., 197-228 p. illus., lv-lxx pl., map.
24 1/2 cm.

6709 Faucher de Saint-Maurice, Narcisse Henri Édouard,
1844-1897.
... De Québec à Mexico; souvenirs de voyage, de
garnison, de combat et de bivouac ... Éd. complète.
Montréal, Duvernay, Frères & Dansereau, 1874.
2 v. 18 1/2 cm.

6710 Faucher de Saint-Maurice, [Narcisse Henri Édouard]
1844-1897.
... Deux ans au Mexique, avec une notice par M.
Coquille ... 5. éd. Montréal, Cadieux & Derome
[1875?]
189 p., 1 l. 23 cm.

6711 Faulkner, Charles James, 1806-1884.
Speech of Hon. C. J. Faulkner, of Virginia, on
the compromise--the presidency--political parties.
Delivered in the House of representatives. August
2, 1852. Washington, Printed at the Congressional
globe office, 1852.
16 p. 24 cm.

6712 Fauquier, Francis, 1747-1768.
... Francis Fauquier on An essay on ways and
means, 1756. [Baltimore, Md.] The Lord Baltimore
press, 1915.
40 p. 25 cm.

6713 Faust, Albert Bernhardt.
Francis Daniel Pastorius and the 250th anniversary
of the founding of Germantown... Philadelphia,
Carl Schurz Memorial Foundation, 1934.
21 p. 21 cm.

6714 Faust, Albert Bernhardt.
Inspector General Frederick William von Steuben,
a sketch of his career and personality... [n.p.]
Privately printed by The Steuben Society of America,

1927.
   39 p. front. (port.)   23 cm.

6715 Fay, George Emory, 1927–
    A guide to archaeological sites in Mexico.
Magnolia, Ark., Dept. of Sociology and Anthro-
pology, Southern State College, 1960.
   14 l. illus. 28 cm.

6716 Fay, Herbert Wells.
    The Moultrie County Lincolns; privately published
by Herbert Wells Fay, custodian, Lincoln's tomb.
[Springfield, Ill.] 1933.
   4 p. 20 cm.

6717 Félix de Jesús María, father, 1706–1772.
    Vida, virtudes, y dones sobrenaturales de la ven.
sierva de Dios sor María de Jesus, religiosa professa en el v. monasterio de la Inmaculada concepcion
de la Pueblo de los Angeles en las Indias occidentales,
sacada de los procesos formados para la causa de su
beatificacion, y canonizacion. Su autor, el p. fr.
Felix de Jesus Maria ... Roma, Impr. de J. y P.
de Rossi, MDCCLVI.
   61 p.l., 384 p., 1 l. port.   27 cm.

6718 Ferguson, Adam, 1782–1862.
    Practical notes made during a tour in Canada,
and a portion of the United States, in MDCCCXXXI
... 2d ed., to which are now added notes made
during a second visit to Canada in MDCCCXXXIII.
Edinburgh, W. Blackwood; London, T. Cadell, 1834.
   xvi, 426 p. fold. map. 18 cm.

6719 Ferguson's anecdotical guide to Mexico, with a map
of the railways. Historical, geological, archaeological and critical... Philadelphia, Claxton,
Remsen & Haffelfinger [c1876]
    iv p., 1 l., [7]–128 p. front. (fold. map)
19 cm.

6720 Fernández Cabrera, Manuel.
    ... Mi viaje a México a propósito de la revolución;
prólogo de conde Kostia [pseud.] epílogo de Felix F.
Palaviccini. Habana, Imp. del "Avisador comercial,"

1915.
    xiii, [15]-281, [3] p., 1 l.   21 cm.

6721   Fernandez de Medrano, Sebastian, 1646-1705.
    Breve descripcion del mundo, y sus partes, ò
Guia geographica, y hydrographica, dividida en tres
libros... Dirigido al ex^{mo}. señor don Francisco
Antonio de Agvrto, marques de Gastañaga... por el
capitan d. Sebastian Fernandez de Medrano... En
Brusselas, En casa de los herederos de Francisco
Foppens, 1686.
    15 p.l., 412 (i.e. 414) p. 4 fold. diagr.   24 cm.
    Errors in pagination: no. 63-64 repeated: p. 403
incorrectly numbered 304.

6722   Fernández de Medrano, Sebastian, 1646-1705.
    Geographia; o, Moderna descripcion del mundo, y
sus partes, dividida en dos tomos, y compuesta por
don Sebastian Fernandez de Medrano... Enriquezida
de cartes geographicas y otras estampas, Tomo
primero [-segundo] Amberes, Por Henrico y Cornelio
Verdussen, mercaderes de libros, 1709.
    2 v. pl., maps.   20 cm.

6723   Fernández Guardia, Ricardo.
    ... Cartilla histórica de Costa Rica.   San José,
Costa Rica, Impr. Lehmann, 1933.
    132 p. illus. (incl. ports., maps), map.   19 cm.

6724   Fernández Guardia, Ricardo, 1867-
    Cuentos ticos; short stories of Costa Rica; the
translation and introductory sketch by Gray
Casement. [1st ed.] Cleveland, Burrows Bros. Co.,
1905 [1904]
    293 p. illus., map.   20 cm.

6725   Fernández, José, 1617-1674.
    Apostólica, y penitente vida de el v.p. Pedro
Claver, de la Compañia de Iesvs. Sacada principal-
mente de informaciones juridicas hechas ante el
ordinario de la ciudad de Cartagena de Indias.
A sv religiosisima provincia de el Nuevo Reyno de
Granada. Por el padre Iosef Fernandez... Zaragoça,
Diego Dormer, 1666.
    6 p.l., 680 p. port.   26 cm.

6726 Fernández Mato, Ramón.
Trujillo; o, La transfiguración Dominicana.
Epílogo do Pedro González Blanco. Mexico, 1945.
2 v. plates (poart col.), port. 23 cm.

6727 Fernon, Thomas Sargent.
No dynasty in North America. The west between
salt waters. Hudson Bay a free basin like the
Gulf of Mexico... New York, For sale at Brentano's
literary emporium [1828]
88 p. 22 cm.

6728 Ferrer, Leonardo, 1623-1695.
Astronomica cvriosa, y descripcion del mvndo
svperior, y inferior. Contiene la especvlacion de
los orbes, y globos de entrambas esferas, con
admirable artificio: obra hecha de la poderosa mano
de Dios, provechosa, para qualquier estudioso
curioso. Escriviola el m.fr. Leonardo Ferrer...
Presentala, a la mvy ilvstre, noble, leal, y
coronada ciudad de Valencia, patrona de la Vniversidad
... Valencia, Por los herederos de Geronimo Vilagrasa,
junto al molino de Rovella, año 1677.
5 p.l., 224 p. incl. illus., diagrs. 24 cm.

6729 Ferro Machado, Juan.
Señor. El doctor Juan Ferro Machado, canonigo
de la santa iglesia de Valladolid, en el reyno de
Nueva-España, à los pies de V. Magestad, dize:
que ha mas tiempo de treinta años que continuada-
mente se ha empleado en el servicio de Dios, y
de V. Mag. ... [n.p., 1707?]
[2] p. 19 cm.

6730 Ferrocarriles nacionales de México.
Mexico from border to capital: a brief description of the many interesting places to be seen en
route to Mexico City via the Laredo, the Eagle pass
and the El Paso gateways. Issued by the General
passenger department, National railways of Mexico.
[Chicago, Corbitt railway printing company, 191-?]
48 p. illus. (incl. map) 21 1/2 cm.

6731 A few words on Hudson's Bay company; with a statement
of grievances of the native and halfcaste Indians.

[London, 1847?]
caption-title, 24 p.   22 cm.

6732   Feyjos De Sosa, Miguel.
Formulario para el ajustamiento, y liquidacion
de las cuentas de la Factoria de Chachapoyas.
Lima, 1764.
10 p.   23 cm.

6733   Figueroa Domenech, J
Guía general descriptiva de la República Mexicana;
história, geografía, estadística, etc., etc., con
triple directorio del comercio y la industria,
autoridades, oficinas públicadas, abogados, médicos,
hacendados, correos, telégrafos y ferrocarriles,
etc. ... dirigida y redactada en presencia de datos
oficiales por J. Figueroa Doménech, con la colaborac
de distinguidos escritores... 1 ed...   Mexico and
Barcelona, R. de S. N. Araluce, 1899.
2 v.   front., illus., ports., 2 fold. maps, fold.
plan.   27 1/2 cm.

6734   Figueroa, Pedro Pablo, 1857-1909.
Vida del jeneral don Juan O'Brien, héroe de
la independencia sud-americana, irlandes de nascimen
chileno de adopción...   Santiago de Chile, Impr.
Mejía, de A. Poblete Garin, 1904.
130, [2] p.   port.   25 1/2 cm.

6735   Filteau, Gérard.
... La naissance d'une nation; tableau du Canada
en 1755...   Montréal, Editions de l'A. C.-F.
[1937]
2 v.   illus. (double map)   20 1/2 cm.

6736   Financial reform association, Liverpool.
The Hudson's Bay company versus Magna Charta and
the British people...   Liverpool, The Association;
London, P. S. King, 1857.
36 p.   fold. map.   23 cm.

6737   Finley, John Huston, 1863-
The French in the heart of America, by John
Finley...   New York, C. Scribner's sons, 1915.
x, [2], 431 p.   21 1/2 cm.

6738   Fish, Daniel, 1848-1924.
       Legal phases of the Lincoln and Douglas debates:
annual address before the State Bar Association of
Minnesota at Minneapolis, July 14, 1909, by Daniel
Fish. [n.p.] 1909.
       15 p.   18 cm.

6739   Fiske, Amos Kidder, 1842-1921.
       ... The West Indies; a history of the islands of
the West Indian archipelago, together with an account of their physical characteristics, natural
resources, and present condition, by Amos Kidder
Fiske... New York, G. P. Putnam's sons; [etc.,
etc.] 1902.
       2 p.l., iii-xii p., 1 l., 414 p.   front., plates,
port., fold. maps.   20 cm.

6740   Fiske, John, 1842-1901.
       Edward Livingston Youmans, interpreter of science
for the people; a sketch of his life, with selections from his published writings and extracts from
his correspondence with Spencer, Huxley, Tyndall and
others, by John Fiske.   New York, D. Appleton and
company, 1894.
       vi p., 1 l., 597 p.   illus. (facsim), 2 port.
(incl. front.)   20 1/2 cm.

6741   Fiske, John, 1842-1901.
       ... The historical writings of John Fiske.
Illustrated with many photogravures, maps, charts,
facsimiles, etc.   [Standard library ed. Boston and
New York, Houghton, Mifflin and company, 1902]
       12 v.   fronts., plates, ports., maps, plans,
facsims.   23 cm.

6742   Fitzgerald, James Edward.
       An examination of the charter and proceedings of
the Hudson's Bay company, with reference to the
reference to the grant of Vancouver's Island.   London, Trelawney Saunders, 1849.
       xv, 293 p.   fold. map.   18 cm.

6743   Fitzgibbon, Mary Agnes, 1851-1915.
       A trip to Manitoba.   London, R. Bentley and Son,
1880.

xi, 248 p.   21 cm.

6744 Fitzhugh, Robert H
      R. E. Lee. From an address delivered before the
      Lexington chapter of the United Daughters of the
      Confederacy on the occasion of the centennial
      anniversary of General Lee's birthday, January 19th,
      1907... Lexington, Ky., Press of J. L. Richardson
      & co., 1910.
      21 p.   15 cm.

6745 Fiury, Ed K
      Corresponsal en La Habana [por] Ed K. Fiury. 1.
      ed. México, Servicios Interamericanos de Prensa,
      1970.
      220 p.   22 cm.

6746 Flandrau, Charles Macomb, 1871-1938.
      Viva Mexico! by Charles Macomb Flandrau... New
      York and London, D. Appleton and company, 1910.
      4 p.l., 293, [1] p.   18 cm.

6747 Fleming, Sir Sandford, 1827-1915.
      The Intercolonial. A historical sketch of the
      inception, location, construction and completion of
      the line of railway uniting the inland and Atlantic
      provinces of the Dominion, with maps and numerous
      illustrations. Montreal, Dawson Bros., 1876.
      ix, 268 p.   illus., plates (part fold.), maps
      (part fold.)   24 cm.

6748 Fleming, Sir Sandford, 1827-1915.
      ... Report of progress on the explorations and
      surveys up to January, 1874. Ottawa, Printed by
      MacLean, Roger & co., 1874.
      xi p., 2 l., 286 (i.e. 294) p.   16 fold. pl.
      (incl. maps)   25 cm.

6749 Fleming, Sir Sandford, 1827-1915.
      Report on surveys and preliminary operations on
      the Canadian Pacific railway - up to January 1877.
      By Sandford Fleming, engineer in chief. Ottawa,
      Printed by MacLean, Rogers & co., 1877.
      xvi, 431 p.   3 fold. maps, 4 fold. plans.
      26 1/2 cm.

6750   Fling, Grover, 1867-1909.
        A war correspondent's field notebook kept during
four months with the Cuban Army... illustrated by
the author, with an historical introduction   by
John Fiske. Boston, New York [etc.] Lamson,
Wolffe and company, 1898.
        xxix, 290 p. incl. front. (map), illus., pl.,
port.   20 1/2 cm.

6751   Flint, Thomas, 1824-1904.
        Diary of Dr. Thomas Flint, California to Maine
and return, 1851-1855... Los Angeles, Cal.
[1924]
        cover-title, 78 p. 3 port. on 1 pl., fold. map.
23 cm.

6752   Flippin, John R
        Sketches from the mountains of Mexico, by J. R.
Flippin. Cincinnati, Standard publishing company,
1889.
        xiv, 423 p.   19 1/2 cm.

6753   Florencia, Francisco de, 1619-1695.
        La milagrosa invencion de vn tesoro escondido
en vn campo, que halló vn venturoso cazique, y
escondió en su casa, para gozarlo á sus solas.
Patente ya enel santvario de los Remedios en su
admirable imagen de N. Señora; señalada en milagros;
invocada por patrona de las lluvias, y temporales;
defensora de los espantos, abogada de los indios,
conquistadora de Mexico, erario vniversal de los
indios, conquistadora de Mexico, erario vniversal
de las misericordias de Dios, ciudad de refugio
para todos los que á ella se acogen. Noticias de
sv origen, y vendias á Mexico; maravillas, que ha
obrado con los que la invocan; descripcion de su
casa, y meditaciones para sus Novenas. Por el p.
Francisco de Florencia... Dalas a la estampa el
br. d. Lorenzo de Mendoza... Dedicalas al señor d.
Gonzalo Suarez de San Martin... Con licencia de los
superiores: [Mexico] Por doña Maria de Benavides,
viuda de Juan de Ribera, 1685.
        9 p.l., 80 numb. l., 2 l. illus.   22 cm.

6754 Florencia, Francisco de, 1619-1695.

Origen de los dos celebres santvarios de la Nueva-
Galicia obispado de Guadalaxara en la America
septentrional... Mexico, Juan Joseph Guillena
Carrascoso, 1694.
10 p.l., 154 (i.e. 155), [8] p. front. 2 p.l.
25 cm.

6755 Fodere, M
Les chercheurs d'or au Mexique... Limoges,
Librairie du XXe siécle [19-?]
319 p. 31 cm.

6756 Fonseca, Fabian de, d. 1813.
Historia general de real hacienda, escrita por
d. Fabian de Fonseca y d. Carlos de Urrutia, por
orden del virrey, conde de Revillagigedo. Obra
hasta ahora inédita... Mexico, Impresa por Vicente
G. Torres, 1845-53.
6 v. 20 cm.

6757 [Forbes,   ]
A trip to Mexico; or, Recollections of a ten-
months' ramble in 1849-1850. By a barrister, London, Smith, Elder, and co., 1851.
2 p.l., vii-xii, 256 p. 17 1/2 cm.

6758 Forbes-Lindsay, Charles Harcourt Ainslie, 1860-
Panama and the canal today; an historical account
of the canal project from the earliest times with
special reference to the enterprises of the French
company and the United States, with a detailed
description of the waterway as it will be ultimately
constructed: together with a brief history of the
country and the first comprehensive account of its
physical features and natural resources. By Forbes
Lindsay. With fifty-three illustrations from recent photographs, and five maps. New rev. ed.
Boston, L. C. Page, 1912.
474 p. illus. 21 cm.

6759 Forbes-Lindsay, Charles Harcourt Ainslie, 1860-
The story of Panama and the canal; a complete
history of the isthmus and the canal from the
earliest explorations to the present time... and
a detailed description of the American enterprise.

With official illus. and maps. [n.p., 1913?]
384 p. illus. 21 cm.

6760 Ford, Isaac N[elson] 1848-
Tropical America, by Isaac N. Ford ... New
York, C. Scribner's sons, 1893.
x p., 2 l., 409 p. front., plates, fold. map.
21 cm.

6761 Ford, Worthington Chauncey, 1858-1941, ed.
The controversy between Lieutenant-Governor
Spotswood, and his Council and the House of
Burgesses, on the reappointment of judges on com-
missions of oyer and terminer. Brooklyn, N. Y.,
Historical Printing Club, 1891.
61 p. 17 cm.

6762 Ford, Worthington Chauncey, 1858-1941.
George Washington, by Worthington Chauncey Ford.
Boston, Small, Maynard & company, 1910.
5 p.l., [ix]-xvii p., 1 l., 169 p. front.
(port.) 14 1/2 cm.

6763 Fortenbaugh, Robert, 1892-
Lincoln and Gettysburg [the story of Abraham
Lincoln's immortal address at Gettysburg] Gettysburg, Bookmart, 1949.
53 p. illus., ports., facsims. 23 cm.

6764 Fossey, Mathieu de, comte, 1805-
Le Mexique, par Mathieu de Fossey... Paris,
H. Plon, 1857.
vii, 581 p. 23 cm.

6765 Fossey, Mathieu de, comte, b. 1805.
Viage a Mejico, por Mathieu de Fossey; traducido
del francés. Mejico, Impr. de I. Cumplido, 1844.
363 p. plates. 19 1/2 cm.

6766 Foster, John Watson, 1836-1917.
Diplomatic memoirs, by John W. Foster ...
Boston and New York, Houghton Mifflin company,
1909.
2 v. fronts., plates, ports., facsims.
22 1/2 cm.

6767   Foster, John Watson, 1836-1917.
        ... Las memorias diplomáticas de Mr. Foster sobre
        México, con un prólogo de Genaro Estrada ...
        México, Publicaciones de la Secretaría de relaciones
        exteriores, 1929.
        xxii, 143 p., 1 l.   23 cm.

6768   Fountain, Paul.
        The great North-west and the great lake region
        of North America, by Paul Fountain ...   London,
        New York [etc.] Longmans, Green, and co., 1904.
        viii, 355 p.   23 cm.

6769   Foursin, Pierre.
        La colonisation française au Canada.   Manitoba
        - Territoires du Nord-ouest - Colombie anglaise
        ... Ottawa, Brown Chamberlin, 1891.
        45 p.   illus.   23 cm.

6770   France. Colonies. Citoyens de couleur.
        A l'Assemblée nationale, supplique et pétition
        des citoyens de couleur des isles & colonies
        françoises, sur la motion faite le 27 novembre
        1789, par M. de Curt, député de la Guadeloupe, au
        nom des colonies réunies [du 2 décembre 1789]
        [n.p., 1789]
        21 p.   20 cm.

6771   France. Conseil général du commerce.
        Réplique des députés des manufactures & du com-
        merce de France à MM. les députés de S. Domingue,
        concernant l'approvisionnement de cette colonie.
        [Versailles, De l'impr. de Ph.-D. Pierres, 1789]
        20 p.   20 cm.

6772   France. Laws, statutes, etc., 1774-1792 (Louis XVI)
        The King's proclamation concerning the decree
        of the National assembly, relative to the colonies,
        March 10th, 1790. Tobago [Printed by G. Burnett,
        King's printer, 1790]
        46 p.   22 cm.

6773   France. Treaties, etc., 1799-1804 (Consulate)
        Convention between the French republic and the
        United States of America. [n.p., 1801]

xviii p.   20 1/2 cm.

6774   France.   Tribunat.
   ... Rapport fait par P. A. Adet, sur la convention
   conclue entre la République française et les États-
   Unis d'Amérique, séance du 12 frimaire an 10.
   [Paris, Impr. nationale, an 10, 1801]
      22 p.   22 cm.

6775   Franciscans.
      Informes, que hacen al rey N. S. (que Dios
   guarde) y a su Consejo real de Indias, el virrey
   de Lima, las reales audiencias, y a los dos
   reverendissimos prelados generales, los cabildos
   eclesiasticos (en sedes vacantes) de las ciudades
   de Lima, La Plata, Buenos-Ayres, el señor obispo
   del Tucumàn, y de otras ciudades, y villas mas
   populosas, del fruto que los missioneros apostolicos
   de la religion seraphica y colegio de Santa Rosa
   de Ocopa, han hecho con sus missiones en las
   provincias de catholicos, y gentiles del reyno
   del Perù, y de los missioneros apostolicos, que
   han muerto flechados por la fé.   [n.p., 1751?]
      25 numbered l., [10] p.   23 cm.

6776   Franck, Harry Alverson, 1881-
   ... Mexico and Central America; a geographical
   reader, by Harry A. Franck, with numerous
   illustrations, many from photographs by the author.
   Dansville, N. Y., F. A. Owen publishing company,
   [c1927]
      288 p.   illus.   19 cm.

6777   Franck, Harry Alverson, 1881-
      Tramping through Mexico, Guatemala and Honduras;
   being the random notes of an incurable vagabond,
   by Harry A. Franck... illustrated with photographs
   by the author.   New York, The Century co., 1921.
      9 p.l., 3-378 p.   incl. front., plates. fold.
   map.   21 1/2 cm.

6778   Franklin, Benjamin, 1706-1790.
      Avis aux faiseurs de constitutions.   Tr. André
   Morellet.   [Extrait de la Federal Gazette et
   Philadelphia Evening Post du vendredi, 15 octobre

1788] [n.p., 1789]
12 p.   20 cm.

6779 Franklin, John Hope, 1915–
        Lincoln and public morality; an address delivered
        at the Chicago historical society on February 12,
        1959. [Chicago] Chicago Historical Society, 1959.
        24 p.   21 cm.

6780 Fraser, John Foster, 1868–1936.
        Canada as it is, by John Foster Fraser ... With
        an introduction by the Right Hon. Lord Strathcona.
        Four plates in colour and over fifty black-and-white
        illustrations. London, New York [etc.] Cassell and
        company, limited, 1911.
        xii, 303, [1] p. incl. col. front. plates.
        21 cm.

6781 Fraser, John Foster, 1868–1936.
        Panama, l'oeuvre gigantesque. Adapté de
        l'anglais par Georges Feuilloy. Paris, P. Roger
        [1913]
        251 p.   plates, map.   21 cm.

6782 Frédeux, Pierre, 1897–
        Herman Melville. [Paris] Gallimard [1950]
        283 p.   illus., ports., maps.   21 cm.

6783 Freeport, Andrew, pseud.
        The case of the Hudson's Bay company. In a
        letter to Lord Palmerston... London, Edward
        Stanford, 1857.
        18 p.   21 cm.

6784 Fröbel, Julius, 1805–1893.
        Seven years' travel in Central America, northern
        Mexico, and the far West of the United States. By
        Julius Froebel ... London, R. Bentley, 1859.
        xiv p., 1 l., 587 p. illus., 8 pl. (incl. front.)
        22 cm.

6785 Frost, John, 1800–1859.
        The history of Mexico and its wars. Comprising
        an account of the Aztec empire, the Cortez conquest,
        the Spaniards' rule, the Mexican revolution, the

164

Texan war, the war with the United States, and the
Maximilian invasion. Together with an account of
Mexican commerce, agriculture... and the social
condition of the people. By John Frost... The
revisions and additions up to the present time, by
the publisher. Embellished with 550 engravings,
from designs of W. Groome and other... artists...
New Orleans, La., A. Hawkins, 1886.
xii, 13-706, [8] p. incl. illus., plates,
ports., plans. front., fold. map. 23 1/2 cm.

6786 Froude, James Anthony, 1818-1894.
The English in the West Indies; or, The bow of
Ulysses, by James Anthony Froude; with illustrations
engraved on wood by G. Pearson, after drawings by
the author. New York, C. Scribner's sons, 1888.
x p., 1 l., 373 p. front., plates. 20 1/2 cm.

6787 Frýd, Norbert.
Mexiko je v Americe. [Črty a snímky z cest. 1.
vyd.] Praha, Práce, vydavatelstvo ROH, 1952.
173 p. illus. 20 cm.

6788 Fuente, Beatriz de la.
La escultura de Palenque. Mexico, Imprenta
Universitaria, 1965.
223 p. 22 cm.

6789 Fuentes y Guzmán, Francisco Antonio de, 1643 (ca.)-
1699 or 1700.
... Historia de Guatemala; ó Recordación floreda;
escrita el siglo XVII por el capitán d. Francisco
Antonio de Fuentes y Guzmán... que publica por
primera vez con notas é ilustraciones d. Justo
Zaragoza... Madrid, L. Navarro, 1882-83.
2 v. fold. map. 23 cm.

6790 Fulton, Hugh R
Genealogy of the Fulton family; being descendants
of John Fulton, Nottingham, Pa., with descendants
of Hugh Ramsey of Nottingham, and Joseph Miller of
Lancaster County, Pa. Lancaster, Pa., New Era
printing company, 1900.
238 p. 17 cm.

6791   Furber, George C
       The twelve months volunteer; or, Journal of a
       private, in the Tennessee regiment of cavalry, in
       the campaign, in Mexico, 1846-47; comprising four
       general subjects: I. A soldier's life in camp;
       amusements; duties; hardships; II. A description
       of Texas and Mexico, as seen on the march; III.
       Manners; customs; religious ceremonies of the
       Mexicans; IV. The operations of all the twelve
       months volunteers: including a complete history
       of the war with Mexico ... engravings, from draw-
       ings by the author. By George C. Furber, of Company
       G. Cincinnati, J. A. & U. P. James, 1849.
       xi, [13]-640 p. incl. illus., plates, plans.
       front., plates, fold. map.   24 cm.

6792   The future of the country, by A patriot. [n.p.,
       n.d.]
       28 p.

                              G

6793   Gaceta de Caracas. 1808-1810. Paris, Établissements
       H. Dupuy et c^{ie}, 1939.
       6 v.   22-37 cm.
       Facsimile edition with prefatory note by the
       Comisión editora on p. [7]-[11] of v. 1.

6794   Gaceta del govierno del Perú. Periódico del gobierno de
       Simón Bolívar. Prólogos por Cristóbal L. Mendoza
       [y] Felix Denegri Luna. Explicación preliminar por
       Pedro Grases. Caracas, Fundación Eugenio Mendoza,
       1967.
       3 v. fronts. (port.: v. 1)   32 cm.

6795   Gadow, Hans Friedrich, 1855-
       Through southern Mexico, being an account of the
       travels of a naturalist, by Hans Gadow ... With
       over one hundred and sixty full page and other

illustrations and maps. London, Witherby & co.;
New York, C. Scribner's sons, 1908.
   xvi, 527 p. incl. illus., plates. front., fold.
map.   22 1/2 cm.

6796   Gage, Thomas, 1603?-1656.
        A new survey of the West-Indies. Being a journal
of three thousand and three hundred miles within
the main land of America. By Tho. Gage... Setting
forth his voyage from Spain to S. John de Ulhua:
and thence to Xalapa, Tlaxcalla, the City of Angels,
and Mexico ... Likewise his journey thence through
Guaxaca, Chiapa, Guatemala, Vera Paz, &c. with his
abode XII. years about Guatemala, his wonderful
conversion and calling to his native country: with
his return through Nicaragua and Costa Rica, to
Nicoya, Panama, Porto Bello, Cartagena, and Havana
... With an account of the Spanish navigation
thither; their government, castles, ports, commodi-
ties, religion, priests and friers, Negro's, mulatto's,
mestiso's, Indians; and their feasts and solemnities.
With a grammar, or some few rudiments of the Indian
tongue, called Poconchi or Pocoman. The 4th ed.
enlarg'd by the author, with an accurate map.
London, Printed by B. Motte, for T. Horne, 1711.
   4 p.l., 477, [18] p. front. (fold. map)   18
1/2 cm.

6797   Gage, Thomas, 1603?-1656.
        A new survey of the West India's... 2d ed. ...
London, Printed by E. Cotes, and sold by John
Sweeting, M.DC.LV.
   5 p.l., 220, [1] p. front., maps.   29 cm.

6798   Gage, Thomas, 1603?-1656.
        Nieuwe ende seer naeuwkeurige reyse door de
Spaensche West-Indien van Thomas Gage; met seer
curieuse soo land-kaerten als historische figueren
verciert ende met twee registers voorsien. Overgeset
door H. V. Q. Utrecht, J. Ribbius, 1682.
   6 p.l., 450, [66] p. 8 pl., 3 maps.   20 1/2 cm.

6799   Gage, Thomas, 1603?-1656.
        Nouvelle relation, contenant les voyages de Thomas
Gage dans la Nouvelle Espagne, ses diverses avantures,

& son retour par la province de Nicaragua, jusques
à la Havane. Avec la description de la ville de
Mexique, telle qu'elle étoit autrefois, & comme
elle est à present, ensemble une description exacte
des terres & provinces que possedent les Espagnols
en toute l'Amerique, de la forme de leur gouvernement ecclesiastique & politique, de leur commerce,
de leurs moeurs, & de celles des criolles, des
metifs, des mulatres, des Indiens, & des negres.
4 ed., rev. & cor. Amsterdam, P. Marret, 1720.
   2 v. fold. plates, fold. maps.   17 cm.

6800 Gage, Thomas, 1603?-1656.
      Relation du Mexique, et de la Nouvelle Espagne.
Traduite de l'anglois. (In Thévenot, Melchisédech.
Relations de divers voyages curieux. Novv. éd.
Paris, 1696. 36 cm. v. 2 [no. 15] 40 p.)

6801 Gago de Vadillo, Pedro.
      Luz de la verdadera cirugia... Pamplona, Juan
Micòl, 1692.
      292 p., 4 l.   24 cm.

6802 Galindo y Villa, Jesús.
      Reseña histórico-descriptiva de la ciudad de
México que escribe Jesús Galindo y Villa, regidor
del Ayuntamiento, por encargo del señor presidente
de la misma corporación D. Guillermo de Landa y
Escandón, y expresamente para los delegados á la
Segunda conferencia internacional americana.
México, Impr. de F. Díaz de León, 1901.
      viii, 243 p. illus., plates, ports., fold. map,
plans, facsims.   27 1/2 cm.

6803 Gall, Francis.
      Belice, tierra nuestra. Guatemala, Centro
Editorial "José de Pineda de Ibarra", 1962.
      197 p., facsim., maps.   19 cm.

6804 Gallegos, Estevan José, d. 1787.
      El doctor don Estevan Joseph Gallegos prebendado,
de esta santa Iglesia, uno de los opositores a la
canongia penitenciaria vacante, en conformidad
del auto proveydo por V. S. en que manda, aleguen
los opositores sus meritos, representa lo siguiente.
[Colophon: Con licencia del ordinario. Impresso

en Lima, En la imprenta que esta en la plazuela de
San Christoval. Año de 1751]
[7] p.   20 cm.

6805   Gallinda y Villa, Jesús.
Geografía de la Republica Mexicana ...   México,
Sociedad de edición y librería franco-americana,
1926-1927.
2 v. illus., diags., maps.   22 cm.

6806   Gallo Sopuerta, Francisco.
... Defensa en grado de segunda suplicacion por
d. Diego Martin Gutierrez de la Arena, natural de
la ciudad de Mondoñedo en Galicia, vecino de Cartagena,
con la Archicofradia del Santisimo Sacramento, sita
en la santa Iglesia de México: sobre la succesion
en propiedad del vínculo fundado de parte de sus
bienes por el capitan d. Francisco Fernandez del
Corral, vecino que fué de México. Pretende d. Diego
Martin n. 17. la revocacion de las sentencias de
vista y revista dadas por la Real audiencia de
México á 7 de agosto de 1775, y 13 de enero de
1777, y se le declare successor legítimo en dicho
mayorazgo. Madrid, Por la viuda de don Joaquin
Ibarra, 1796.
1 p.l., 14 numbered. 1.   22 cm.

6807   Gallup map & supply co.
Highway atlas. A map of every state in the
United States, also southern Canada and Mexico
with index to towns showing population. Kansas
City, Mo., Gallup map and supply co., ᶜ1936.
76 (i.e. 80) p. incl. 90 maps. (part col.)
36 cm.

6808   Galvan [Rivera, Mariano]
Kurze statistische notizen über die Vereinigten
Staaten von Mexico. Aus dem mexicanischen handkalender
von Galvan für das jahr 1833 übersetzt von I. F. G.
Schwalbe. Berlin, Lüderitz'sche buch- und kunsthand-
lung (E. H. Schröder) 1833.
29, [1] p.   19 1/2 cm.

6809   Gálvez, Juan de, 1750-1807.
Modos con que podran los christianos desagraviar a

169

Nuestro Señor Jesu-Christo Sacramentado, de los
ultrages que le han hecho los impios convencionistas
franceses, en la presente guerra. Sermon moral, que
la ilustre y venerable Hermandad de la esclavitud del
santisimo sacramento de la Iglesia parroquial del
señor san Pedro, de esta nobilisima ciudad de
Arcos de la Frontera, consagra en honor del dulcisimo
corazon de Jesus, Nuestro Divino Redentor. Dixolo
en dicha parroquia el dia 27 de junio de este
presente año de 1794. el r. p. fr. Juan de Galvez
... Con licencia: Cadiz: Por d. Manuel Ximenez
Carreño, calle Ancha [1794]
80 p.   25 cm.

6810 Gannon, Frederic Augustus, 1881-
A story of the Arbella, of Pioneer Village, and
of Lincoln's address... Salem, Mass., Cassino
press, [1945]
11 p. illus.   20 cm.

6811 Gante, Pablo C   de.
La ruta de occidente; las ciudades de Toluca y
Morelia, por Pablo C. de Gante. México, D. F.,
D.A.P.P., 1939.
95, [1] p. illus. (incl. maps, plan)   21 1/2 cm.

6812 Garber, Mrs. Virginia (Armistead)
The Armistead family, 1633-1910. Richmond,
Va., Whittet & Shepperson, printers, 1910.
319 p.   22 cm.

6813 Garcés, Francisco Tomás Hermenegildo, 1738-1781.
On the trail of a Spanish pioneer; the diary and
itinerary of Francisco Garcés (missionary priest)
in his travels through Sonora, Arizona, and California, 1775-1776; translated from an official
contemporaneous copy of the original Spanish manuscript, and ed. with copious notes, by Elliott
Coues... New York, F. P. Harper, 1900.
2 v. fronts., 8 pl., 2 port., 2 maps, plan, 5
facsims.   23 1/2 cm.

6814 García Camba, Andrés.
Memorias para la historia de las armas españolas
en el Perú. Madrid, Editorial-América [1916]

2 v.   23 cm.

6815   García Cubas, Antonio, 1832-1912.
        Album del Ferrocarril mexicano. Colección de
        vistas pintadas del natural por Casimiro Castro, y
        ejecutadas en cromolitografía por A. Sigogne, C.
        Castro, etc., con una descripción del camino y de
        las regiones que recorre, por Antonio García
        Cubas ... Album of the Mexican railway. A col-
        lection of views taken from nature... Translated
        from the Spanish by George F. Henderson. México,
        V. Debray y cª., 1877.
        1 p.l., 56 p. col. plates, fold. map.   35 x
        49 cm.

6816   García Cubas, Antonio, 1832-1912.
        Atlas metódico para la enseñanza de la geografía de
        la República Mexicana, formado y dedicado á la
        Sociedad mexicana de geografía y estadística por el
        ingeniero Antonio García Cubas... México, Sandoval
        y Vasquez, 1874.
        54 p. front. (port.), maps.   27 cm.

6817   García Cubas, Antonio, 1832-1912.
        Cuadro geográfico, estadístico, descriptivo é
        histórico de los Estados Unidos Mexicanos. Mexico,
        Oficina Tip. de la Secretaría de Fomento, 1884.
        xxxi, 474, iii p. illus., map.   24 cm.

6818   García Cubas, Antonio, 1832-1912.
        Diccionario geográfico, histórico y biográfico
        de los Estados Unidos Mexicanos, por Antonio García
        Cubas... México, Antigua impr. de Murguía, 1888-91.
        5 v. illus.   31 cm.

6819   García Cubas, Antonio, 1832-1912.
        ... El libro de mis recuerdos; narraciones his-
        tóricas, anecdóticas y de costumbres mexicanas
        anteriores al actual estado social, ilustrada con
        más de trescientos fotograbados... Mexico, Impr.
        de A. García Cubas, hermanos sucesores, 1904.
        635 p. illus. (incl. ports., plans, facsim)
        28 1/2 cm.

6820   García de Escañuela, Bartholomé, bp., d. 1684.

Exemplar religioso. Propvesto en la vida, y mverte del reverend^mo padre fray Andres de Gvadalvpe... En vn sermon fvnebre, qve en svs exeqvias dezia fr. Bartholome Garcia de Escañuela ... Dedicado al excelentissimo señor d. Gaspar de Baracamonte y Guzman, conde de Peñaranda... Con licencia. En Madrid, En la Imprenta real, 1668.
6 p.l., 20 numbered l.   21 cm.

6821   García Gravados, Rafael.
Diccionario biográfico de historia antiqua de Mejico.   Mejico, Instituto de Historia, 1952-1953.
3 v.   24 cm.

6822   Gardiner, Abraham Sylvester.
Tom Quick, or, The foundation and the capstone. Pioneer enterprise and national independence... Chicago, Knight & Leonard co., printers, 1889.
75 p.   front. (port.), illus.   19 cm.

6823   Gardner, Frank Augustine, 1861-
Thomas Gardner, planter (Cape Ann, 1623-1626; Salem, 1626-1671) and some of his descendants, giving Essex county Massachusetts, and northern New England lines to the eighth generation and Nantucket lines through the fourth generation. Comp. and arranged by Frank A. Gardner...   Salem, Mass., Essex Institute, 1907.
iv, 343 p.   front. (port.), plates.   23 cm.

6824   Gardner, James Henry.
The lost captain.   [Oklahoma City, 1943]
35 p.   front. (port.), illus.   23 cm.

6825   Garneau, François Xavier, 1809-1866.
Histoire du Canada.   7. éd., rev., annotée et publiée avec introduction et des appendices, par son petit-fils Hector Garneau.   Préface de M. Gabriel Hanotaux.   Paris, F. Alcan, 1920-28.
2 v.   24 cm.

6826   Garnett, James Mercer, 1840-1916.
Biographical sketch of Hon. Charles Fenton Mercer, 1778-1858.   M.C. 1817-1840, of Aldie, Loudoun County,

Virginia, son of Hon. James Mercer, judge of Court
of appeals of Virginia. By James Mercer Garnett,
Richmond, Va., Priv. print. by Whittet & Shepperson,
1911.
95 p. front., pl., ports. 23 cm.

6827 Garrett, R B
An interesting letter about the death of John Wilkes
Booth, written by the Rev. R. B. Garrett to General
A. R. Taylor... Peoria, Ill. [privately printed]
1934.
23 p. illus. facsim. 20 cm.

6828 Garzo, José.
... El arcobispo, dean, y Cabildo de la santa
iglesia de Lima, dizen: que los indios de aquel
arçobispado siguieron pleyto en el consejo con el
dean, y Cabildo, suponiendo en sus pedimientos,
que pagauan dos diezmos... [n.p., 1666?]
3 numb l., [3] p. 21 cm.

6829 Gaspé, Philippe Aubert de.
Mémoires par Philippe A. de Gaspé, auteurs des
"Anciens canadiens". Québec, N. S. Hardy, Libraire-
éditeur, 1885.
563 p. 21 cm.

6830 Gates, Arnold Francis.
Amberglow of Abraham Lincoln and Ann Rutledge, by
Arnold Francis Gates. West Leisenring, Pa., The
Griglak printery [c1939]
2 p.l., 3-15 p., 1 l. illus. (port.) 17 cm.

6831 Gates, Arnold Francis.
Amberglow of Abraham Lincoln and Joshua Speed.
West Leisenring, Pa., Griglak printery [1941]
15 p. 20 cm.

6832 Gaztaneta y de Iturribálzga, Antonio, 1656-1728.
Norte de la navegación... Sevilla, Juan
Francisco de Blas, 1692.
187 l. maps., diags. 25 cm.

6833 Gay, Sydney Howard, 1814-1888.
... James Madison... New York, Houghton, Mifflin

and company, 1884.
vi, 342 p.   18 cm.

6834   Geiger, John Lewis.
A peep at Mexico: narrative of a journey across
the republic from the Pacific to the Gulf in
December 1873 and January 1874. By John Lewis
Geiger... London, Trübner & co., 1874.
xiv, 353 p. front., pl., fold. maps.   22 cm.

6835   Gemelli Careri, Giovanni Francesco, 1615-1725.
Las cosas más considerables, vistas en la Nueva
España, por el doctor don Juan Francisco Gemelli
Carreri. Traducción de José María de Agreda y
Sánchez, revisada por los editores a la vista de la
edición original. Prólogo de Alberto María Carreño.
México, Ediciones Xochitl, 1946.
3 p.l., [9]-204 p., 3 l. illus. (incl. ports., map.
23 x 17 1/2 cm.

6836   Genealogy of the Henry Adams family. Keene, N. H.,
Sentinel printing company, 1894.
9 p.   23 cm.

6837   Gentry, Thomas Benton.
Memoirs of General Richard Gentry, a Missouri
pioneer and soldier... Kansas City, Mo., 1899.
19 p. front. (port.)   26 1/2 cm.

6838   George, Alfred.
... Holidays at home and abroad. By Alfred
George... London, W. J. Johnson, printer, 1877.
xxiii, [1], 199 p.   21 1/2 cm.

6839   George, Marian M   , 1865-
A little journey to Mexico, for intermediate and
upper grades, by Marian M. George. Chicago, A.
Flanagan company [c1901]
123 p. col. front., illus. (incl. port.), map.
19 1/2 cm.

6840   George, Marian M   , 1865-
A little journey to Mexico and Central America,
for home and school, intermediate and upper grades,
by Marian M. George. Chicago, A. Flanagan company,

174

1929.
    x p.l., 3-186 p.   illus.   19 1/2 cm.

6841 George, Paul.
    Das heutige Mexiko und seine kulturfortschritte.
    Von Paul George... Mit 34 tafeln...   Jena, G.
    Fischer, 1906.
        3 p.l., 133, [1]-p. front. (port.), 33 pl.
    33 1/2 cm.

6842 George Washington's physician; their friendship and
    his treatment during the President's last illness.
    [n.p., n.d.]
        cover-title, [14] p.   illus.   15 cm.

6843 Geschichte der englischen kolonien in Nord-Amerika
    von der ersten entdeckung dieser   lander durch
    Sebastian Cabot, bis auf den frieden 1763 ...   Aus
    dem englischen. Leipzig, C. Fritsch, 1775-76.
        2 v. fold. map.   16 1/2 cm.
    Translated by Anton Ernst Klausing.

6844 Gevers Deynoot, William Theodorus.
    Aanteekeningen op eene reis door de Vereenigde
    Staten van Nord Amerika en Canada, in 1859...
    's-Gravenhage, M. Nijhoof, 1860.
        6 p.l., 264 p. col. plates.   24 1/2 cm.

6845 The gibbet of Regina. The truth about Riel. Sir
    John A. Macdonald before public opinion. By one who
    knows. New York, Thompson and Moreau, printers and
    publishers, 1886.
        200 p. illus.   23 cm.

6846 Gibbon, Eduardo A
    Guadalajara (la Florencia mexicana) Vagancias y
    recuerdos. El salto de Juanacatalán y El Mar Chap-
    alico... Guadalajara, Ediciones del Banco Indus-
    trias de Jalisco [1967]
        cover-title, 371 p.   21 1/2 cm.

6847 Giger, Henry Douglas, comp.
    ... The story of the Sangamon County court house
    ... Springfield, Ill., Phillips bros., [1901]
        25 p. illus.   23 cm.

175

6848   Gilbert, C   E
       Two presidents: Abraham Lincoln, Jefferson
Davis; origin, cause and conduct of the War
between the States, the truth of history belongs
to posterity. [Houston? Tex.] 1927.
       82 p.   19 cm.

6849   Gilbert, James Stanley, 1855-1906.
       Panama patchwork: poems by James Stanley Gil-
bert. 6th ed. Cristobal and Colon, Isthmus of
Panama, J. V. Beverhoudt, 1920.
       3 p.l., ix-xxii p., 1 l., 170 p.   19 1/2 cm.

6850   Giles Pretel, Juan de.
       Por la señora d. Ana Francisca Colon de Portugal,
viuda del señor don Diego de Cardenas y Valda, del
consejo de guerra de Su Mag. que tambien lo fue
del de Indias, y capitan general del exercito de
Cantabria. En el pleyto de propiedad, pendiente
en dicho real Consejo de Indias. Sobre. el estado de
duque de Veragua, y de la Vega, marques de Iamaica,
y demas bienes, y rentas, de que fundo vinculo, y
mayorazgo don Christoual Colon, primer descubridor,
y almirante de las Indias. Con don Pedro Colon
de Portugal, que oy possee el dicho estado, que
primero se siguiò con su abuelo don Nuño Colon de
Portugal, y despues con su padre don Aluaro de
Portugal. Y con don Francisco Colon de Cordoua y
Bocanegra, marques de Villamayor. Y con don Diego
Colon de Toledo y Larreatigui, cauallero de la
Orden de Santiago. En vista. Replicase a las
informaciones en derecho, que han dado las otras
partes. [n.p., 17--]
       91 numbered l. [18] p.   24 cm.

6851   Giles Pretel, Juan de.
       Señor. El marques de Mancera, virrey, y capitan
general en los reinos del Peru, y en su nombre, y
con su poder Simõ Aluarez de Prado. Dize, que en
diferentes memoriales, que a dado à V. M. en que ha
respondido, y satisfecho à los capitulos, que dio,
en los suyos don Iuã de Medina Avila... [n.p.,
16--]
       [6] p.   21 cm.

6852   Gillespie, Joseph, 1809-1885.
        Recollections of early Illinois and her noted
        men... Chicago, Fergus prtg. co., 1880.
        50 p. illus. 20 cm.

6853   Gilliam, Albert M   , d. 1859.
        Travels in Mexico, during the years 1843 and
        44; including a description of California, the
        principal cities and mining districts of that
        republic; the Oregon territory, etc. By Albert
        M. Gilliam... A new and complete ed. Aberdeen,
        G. Clark and son; etc., etc. 1847.
        vi, 7-312 p. 19 1/2 cm.

6854   Gilliland, Thaddeus Stephens, 1834-   , ed.
        History of Van Wert County, Ohio. and represen-
        tative citizens; ed. and comp. by Thaddeus S. Gilli-
        land... Chicago Ill., Richmond & Arnold, 1906.
        803 p. incl. illus., plates, ports. port.
        28 x 23 1/2 cm.

6855   Gillpatrick, Owen Wallace.
        The man who likes Mexico; the spirited chronicle
        of adventurous wanderings in Mexican highways and
        byways, by Wallce Gillpatrick; illustrated with
        photographs. New York, The Century co., 1911.
        10 p.l., 3-374 p. incl. plates, port. front.
        21 1/2 cm.

6856   Gillpatrick, Owen Wallace, 1862-
        Wanderings in Mexico; the spirited chronicle of
        adventure in Mexican highways and byways, by Wallace
        Gillpatrick... London, E. Nash, 1912.
        10 p.l., 3-374 p. incl. plates, port. front.
        21 1/2 cm.

6857   [Gilmer, Elizabeth (Meriwether)] 1861-1951.
        Mexico, by Dorothy Dix [pseud.] Gulfport,
        Miss., C. Rand, ᶜ1934.
        [13] p. 21 1/2 cm.

6858   Glazier, Willard, 1841-1905.
        Peculiarities of American cities. By Captain
        Willard Glazier ... Philadelphia, Hubbard brothers,
        1885.

4 p.l., v-xv, 25-558 p.   front. (port.) plates.
19 1/2 cm.

6859   Glover, Livingston Maturin, 1819-1880.
The character of Abraham Lincoln: a discourse
delivered April 23rd, 1865 at... Jacksonville,
Illinois. Jacksonville, Ill., Journal Book & Job
Office, 1865.
21 p.   23 cm.

6860   Godfrey, Edward K
The island of Nantucket, what it was and what it is
being a complete index and guide to this noted
resort... including its history, people, agriculture,
botany, conchology and geology... compiled by
Edward K. Godfrey. Boston, Lee and Shepard; New
York, C. T. Dillingham, 1882.
vi, 365 p. 2 fold. maps (incl. front.)   17 cm.

6861   [Godoy Alcayaga, Lucila] 1889-   , ed.
... Lecturas para mujeres. [Mexico] Secretaría
de educación, 1923.
1 p.l., 7-395, [1] p., 1 l.   illus.   22 cm.

6862   Goldman, Edward Alphonso, 1873-1946.
Biological investigations in Mexico. Washington,
Smithsonian Institution, 1951.
xiii, 476 p. plates, fold. col. map.   24 cm.

6863   Gómara, Francisco López de, 1510-1560?
The conquest of the West India (1578) by Francisco
López de Gómara; with an introduction by Herbert
Ingram Priestly ... New York, N. Y., Scholars'
facsimiles & reprints, 1940.
xxi p., facsim.: 6 p.l., 405, [3] p.   17 1/2 cm.

6864   Gómara, Francisco López de, 1510-1560?
Histoire generalle des Indes Occidentales et
terres neuves. Paris, Chez Michel Sonnus, 1590.
354 p.   25 cm.

6865   [González, José Antonio] comp.
Album de México monumental. [Mexico] "Excelsior"
cía. editorial, s.a. [1926?]
cover-title, 176 p.   illus.   28 1/2 x 36 1/2 cm.

6866   González, Juan Vicente, 1810-1866.
      ... Biografía del general José Félix Ribas, primer
teniente de Bolívar en 1813 y 1814 (época de la guerra
á muerte)   Madrid, Editorial-América [1918?]
302 p.   22 1/2 cm.

6867   González Peña, Carlos, 1885-
      Entre el polvo del camino.   México, Editorial
Stylo [1950]
272 p.   19 cm.

6868   González Suarez, Federico, abp., 1844-1917.
      Historia general de la República del Ecuador
... 2. ed.   Quito, D. Cadena A., 1931.
7 v. and atlas (xiii, 210 p., xliv pl.   incl.
plans)   25 cm.

6869   Goodrich, Frederick Elizur, 1843-1925.
      The life and public services of Grover Cleveland,
with incidents of his boyhood and an account of his
rise to eminence in his profession; also containing
his addresses and official documents as mayor of
the city of Buffalo and governor of the state of
New York...   By Frederick E. Goodrich...   With
an introduction by Hon. Frederick O. Prince...
Portland, Me., H. Hallett & co. [c1884]
     504 p.   incl. plates. 2 port. (incl. front.)
20 cm.

6870   Goodsir, Robert Anstruther.
      An arctic voyage to Baffin's bay and Lancaster
Sound in search of friends with Sir John Franklin
...   London, John van Voorst, 1850.
viii, 152 p.   illus., map.   24 cm.

6871   Gorman, Samuel.
      Abraham Lincoln, late President of the United
States, fallen in the defense of his country:
sermon... delivered April 16, 1865.   New York,
C. A. Alvord, 1865.
22 p.   20 cm.

6872   Gostkowski, [G   baron de]
      De Paris à Mexico par les Etats-Unis...   Paris,
P. V. Stock, 1899.

2 p.l., 432 p.   front., pl. port.

6873   Gourlay, Robert Fleming, 1778-1863.
Statistical account of Upper Canada, compiled
with a view to a grand system of emigration, by
Robt. Gourlay...   London, Simpkin & Marshall, 1822.
2 v.   3 maps (incl. fronts., 1 fold.)   22 cm.

6874   Gouy-d'Arcy, Louis-Henri-Marthe, marquis de, 1753-1794
Précis remis... aux commissaires auxquels l'
Assemblée nationale a renvoyé l'examen de la demande
faite par les représentans de la colonie [de Saint-
Domingue] pour obtenir provisoirement la liberté de
se procurer des farines, dont elle manque absolument
[Versailles, Chez Baudouin] 1789.
12 p.   20 cm.

6875   Graham, Albert Alexander, 1860-
Mexico, with comparisons and conclusions.   By
A. A. Graham...   1st ed.   Topeka, Kan., Crane &
company, 1907.
283 p.   front. (port.)   20 cm.

6876   Graham, Frederic Ulric.
Notes of a sporting expedition to the far west
of Canada, 1847...   Explanatory notes by Jane
Hermione Graham.   London, printed for private
circulation only, 1898.
120 p.   illus., maps.   25 cm.

6877   Grand Army Hall and Memorial Association of Illinois.
Fiftieth annual Lincoln birthday service...
February 12, 1949, Memorial Hall, Chicago, Illinois.
[Chicago, The Association, 1949]
24 p.   illus.   20 cm.

6878   Grand Army of the Republic.
Abraham Lincoln, the saviour of the freedom of
mankind.   Lincoln, Nebraska, G. A. R., 1918.
[3] p.   20 cm.

6879   Grand Army of the Republic.
Pilgrimage of the G. A. R. to the tomb of Lincoln,
September 29, 1887: souvenir from the home of Lin-
coln.   Springfield, Ill., H. W. Bokker, printer, 188

[4] p. illus. 20 cm.

6880 Grandfort, Marie (Fontenay) de.
      The New world: tr. from the French by E. C.
      Wharton. New Orleans, Sherman, Wharton, 1855.
      144 p. 21 cm.

6881 Grant, Andrew.
      History of Brazil, comprising a geographical
      account of that country, together with a narrative
      of the most remarkable events which have occurred
      there since its discovery. London, H. Colburn,
      1809.
      304 p. 21 cm.

6882 Grant, Jeannette A
      Through Evangeline's country, by Jeannette A.
      Grant... Boston, Joseph Knight company, 1894.
      x, 100 p. incl. illus., plates, ports., map.
      col. front. 20 1/2 cm.

6883 Gray, Albert Zabriskie, 1840-1889.
      Mexico as it is: being notes of a recent tour
      in that country; with some practical information
      for travellers in that direction, as also some
      study on the church question, by Albert Zabriskie
      Gray... New York, E. P. Dutton, & co., 1878.
      148 p. incl. front., illus., plates. port.
      18 1/2 cm.

6884 Gray, Hugh.
      Letters from Canada, written during a residence
      there in the years 1806, 1807, and 1808, showing
      the present state of Canada and its productions -
      trade - commercial importance and political relations
      ... London, Printed for Longman, Hurst, Reese,
      and Orme, 1809.
      16, 406 p. front. (fold. map) 23 cm.

6885 Gt. Brit. Parliament.
      Exploration - British North America. Papers
      relative to the exploration by Captain Palliser
      in that portion of British North America which lies
      between the northern branch of the river Saskatchewan
      and the frontier of the United States; and between

the Red River and Rocky Mountains. Presented to
both Houses of Parliament by command of Her Majesty,
June 1859. London, Printed by George William Eyre
and William Spottiswoode for Her Majesty's Sta-
tionery Office, 1859.
   64 p.   map.   24 cm.

6886   Gt. Brit. Parliament.
      Exploration - British North America. Further
papers relative to the exploration by the expedition under Captain Palliser of that portion of
British North America which lies between the
northern branch of the river Saskatchewan and the
frontier of the United States: and between the Red
river and the Rocky mountains, and thence to the
Pacific ocean. Presented to both houses of Parliament by command of Her Majesty, 1860. London,
Printed by George Edward Eyre and William Spottiswoode, 1860.
   75 p.   maps.   23 cm.

6887   Gt. Brit. Parliament.
      Exploration - British North America. The journals
detailed reports, and observations, relative to the
exploration, by Captain Palliser, of that portion
of British North America, which, in latitude, lies
between the British boundary line and the height
of land or watershed of the northern or frozen
ocean respectively, and, in longitude, between
the western shore of Lake Superior and the Pacific
Ocean, during the years 1857, 1858, 1859, and 1860.
Presented to both houses of Parliament by command of
Her Majesty, 19th May 1863. London, Printed by
George Edward Eyre and William Spottiswoode, 1863.
   325 p.   illus., fold. maps.   24 cm.

6888   Greeley, Horace, 1811-1872.
      A political textbook for 1860: comprising a brief
view of presidential nominations and elections including all national platforms ever yet adopted;
also a history of the struggle respecting slavery
... [etc.] comp. by Horace Greeley and John F.
Cleveland. New York, Tribune association, 1860.
   248 p.   23 cm.

6889 Green, Frank William.
Notes on New York, San Francisco, and old
Mexico, by Frank W. Green. Wakefield, Eng., E.
Carr, 1886.
3 p.l., 173 p. 21 1/2 cm.

6890 Green, William Spotswood, 1847-
Among the Selkirk glaciers; being the account
of a rough survey in the Rocky Mountain regions of
British Columbia, by William Spotswood Green...
London and New York, Macmillan and co., 1890.
xv, 1 l., 251 p. incl. front. 8 pl., fold. map.
19 1/2 cm.

6891 Greenhow, Robert, 1800-1854.
The history of Oregon and California, and the
other territories on the north-west coast of North
America; accompanied by a geographical view and map
of those countries, and a number of documents as
proofs and illustrations of the history... Boston,
Charles C. Little and James Brown, 1844.
xviii p., 1 l., 482 p. 22 cm.

6892 Greenough, William Parker, 1830?-1900.
Canadian folk-life and folk-lore, by William
Parker Greenough, "G. de Montauban." With illus-
trations by Walter C. Greenough. New York, G. H.
Richmond, 1897.
xii, 199 p. illus., plates, port. 22 cm.

6893 Gregg, Josiah, 1806-1850?
Karawanenzüge durch die westlichen prairieen und
wanderungen in Nord-Mejico. Nach dem tagebuche des
Amerikaners Josias Gregg, bearb. von M. B. Lindau
... 2. ausg. ... Dresden und Leipzig, Arnold, 1848.
2 v. in 1. fronts., 2 maps (1 fold.) 18 1/2 cm.

6894 Gregg, Josiah, 1806-1850?
Scenes and incidents in the western prairies:
during eight expeditions, and including a residence
of nearly nine years in northern Mexico... By
Josiah Gregg... Philadelphia, J. W. Moore, 1856.
2 v. in 1. illus., 3 pl., map. 19 1/2 cm.

6895 Gregg, Josiah, 1806-1850?

Wanderungen durch die prairien und das nördliche
Mexiko. Von dem Amerikaner Josias Gregg. Aus dem
englischen übertragen von Gottlob Fink... Stuttgart
Franckh, 1847.
2 v. in 1. 15 1/2 x 12 cm.

6896 Grégoire, Henri-Baptiste, constitutional bp. of Blois,
1750-1831.
Lettre aux philanthropes, sur les malheurs, les
droits et les réclamations des gens de couleur de
Saint-Domingue, et des autres îles françoises de
l'Amérique... Paris, Belin [etc.] 1790.
1 p.l., 21 p. 19 1/2 cm.

6897 Grégoire, Henri-Baptiste, constitutional bp. of Blois,
1750-1831.
Mémoire en faveur des gens de couleur ou
sangmêlés de St.-Domingue, & des autres isles
françoises de l'Amérique, adressé à l'Assemblée
nationale. Paris, Chez Belin, 1789.
52 p. 20 cm.

6898 Gregory, Samuel.
Gregory's history of Mexico. A history of Mexico
from the earliest time to the present... geographica
view of the country... state of society... anecdotes
and incidents of Mexican life, etc. By Samuel
Gregory, A. M. Boston, F. Gleason, 1847.
2 p.l., 9-100 p. incl. pl. 27 1/2 cm.

6899 Grenfell, Sir Wilfred Thomason, 1865-1940.
Adrift on an ice-pan... illustrated from photographs by Dr. Grenfell and others. Boston and
New York, Houghton Mifflin company, 1909.
xxv, [1] p., 1 l., 68, [2] p. front. (port.)
7 pl. 19 cm.

6900 Grenfell, Sir Wilfred Thomason, 1865-1940.
Down north on the Labrador... New York, Chicago
[etc.] Fleming H. Revell company [c1911]
229 p. front., 11 pl. 19 1/2 cm.

6901 Grenfell, Sir Wilfred Thomason, 1865-1940.
Labrador, the country and the people, by Wilfred
T. Grenfell... and others. New York, The MacMillan

Co., 1909.
        xii p., 1 l., 497 p.   incl. illus., maps. front.,
plates, map.   20 cm.

6902   Grenier, Edouard, 1819-1901.
        The death of President Lincoln: a poem, by
Edouard Grenier... Tr. by Mrs. C. L. Botta. First
published in Harpers weekly, October 19th, 1867...
New York, C. F. Heartman, 1918.
        2 p.l., [1], 7 p.   23 cm.

6903   Greswell, William Henry Parr, 1848-1923.
        History of the Dominion of Canada, by the Rev.
William Parr Greswell... Under the auspices of
the Royal Colonial Institute. Oxford, Clarendon
press, 1890.
        xxxi, [1], 339 p.   maps (part fold.)   19 1/2 cm.

6904   Grier, Thomas Graham, 1865-
        Letters from Cuba, by a son to his mother.
Chicago, Wagner & Hanson [1906]
        77 p.   illus.   21 cm.

6905   Griffin, Solomon Bulkey, 1852-
        Mexico of today by Solomon Bulkey Griffin. ...
New York, Harper & brothers, 1886.
        4 p.l., 267 p.   incl. illus., plates, port.,
maps. fold. front.   19 1/2 cm.

6906   Grone, Carl von d. 1849.
        Briefe über Nord-Amerika und Mexiko und den
zwischen beiden geführten krieg, von Carl von
Grone... Nach dessen tode herausgegeben und mit
einem vorworte begleitet von A. C. E. von Grone.
Braunschweig, Druck von G. Westermann; New-York, G.
& B. Westermann brothers, 1850.
        viii, p., 1 l., 110 p.   22 1/2 cm.

6907   Grose, Howard Benjamin, 1851-
        Advance in the Antilles; the new era in Cuba and
Porto Rico, by Howard B. Grose ... [New York]
Council of women for home missions, 1910.
        xii, 256 p.   incl. front. (port.), plates, fold.
col. map.   19 1/2 cm.

6908 Guatemala (City) Escuela normal central para varones.
      ... Guatemala, breve panorama de su cultura.
      Guatemala, C. A., Tipografía nacional, 1944.
         212 p.   18 cm.

6909 Guatemala. Dirección General de Caminos.
         Guía kilométrica de la República de Guatemala.
         2. ed., corr. y aumentada. Guatemala, C. A., 1949.
         2 v.   diagrs., maps.   19 cm.

6910 Guerra, Eduardo.
         Historia de la Laguna. Torreón, su origen y sus
         fundadores. [Saltillo, Mex., Impresora de Coahuila]
         1932.
         366 p.   illus.   24 cm.

6911 Guest, Moses.
         Poems on several occasions. To which are annexed,
         Extracts from a journal, kept by the author while
         he followed the sea, and during a journey from New-
         Brunswick, in New-Jersey, to Montreal and Quebec.
         By Moses Guest. Second edition. Cincinnati,
         Looker & Reynolds, printers......1824.
         1 p.l., iv (i.e. vi), [7]-160 p.   17 1/2 cm.

6912 Guide to Havana, Mexico and New York. A descrip-
         tion of the principal cities of the island of
         Cuba and of Mexico ... Also Guía de Nueva York y
         los Estados Unidos... By W. F. Smith & co. New
         York, W. F. Smith & co., 1885.
         1 p.l., 78 p.   23 1/2 cm.

6913 Guillemin-Tarayre, Edmond, 1832-1920.
         Description des anciennes possessions mexicaines
         du nord. [1. livraison. Paris, Impr. Nationale,
         1871]
         216 p.   illus. 11 plates, maps (part fold., part
         col.)   37 cm.

6914 Guillemin-Tarayre, Edmond, 1882-1920.
         Exploration minéralogique des régions mexicaines,
         suivie de notes archéologiques et ethnographiques,
         par m. E. Guillemin-Tarayre... rapport adressé à
         son excellence m. Duruy... Paris, Imprimerie
         impériale, 1869.

ix, [1], 304 p. illus., double col. pl.,
maps (part fold.), plans (part double)
23 1/2 cm.

6915 [Gunby, A   L   ]
... Life and services of David French Boyd...
New Orleans, T. H. Thomason, 1904.
36 p.   23 cm.   (University bulletin, Series
II, June, 1904. No. 2. Louisiana State Uni-
versity, Baton Rouge, La.)

6916 Gunn, Benjamin Jesse, 1865-
Life of Abraham Lincoln in verse... delivered
by the author at Lincoln's tom the thirtieth
anniversary of his death... [Great Bond, Kansas,
Gunn's print shop] c1914.
32 p.   13 cm.

6917 Günther, Erich.
Illustriertes handbuch von Mexico, Mit be-
sonderer berücksichtigung der deutschen in-
teressen, von Erich Günther ... Mexico, E.
Günther [etc., etc.] 1912.
4 p.l., [7]-371 p. illus., fold. map.
23 1/2 cm.

6918 Gurley, Phineas Densmore, 1816-1868.
The voice of the rod; a sermon preached...
June 1, 1865, in the New York Avenue Presbyter-
ian Church, Washington, D. C. Washington, W.
Ballentyne, 1865.
16 p.   22 cm.

6919 Gurney, Joseph John, 1788-1847.
Familiar letters to Henry Clay of Kentucky,
describing a winter in the West Indies. By
Joseph John Gurney ... New-York, Press of M.
Day & co., 1840.
203 p.   23 cm.

6920 Haas, Elise S
    Letters from Mexico [by] Elise S. Haas. San
Francisco, Priv. print., 1937.
    1 p.l., 37, [1] p., 1 l.   24 1/2 cm.

6921 [Hackett, Karleton] ed.
    In memory of Bert Leston Taylor (B.L.T.) Program
and records of a public meeting held in the Black-
stone Theatre, March 27, 1921. Chicago, Walter M.
Hill, 1922.
    43 p.   20 cm.

6922 Hadfield, Joseph, 1759-1851.
    An Englishman in America, 1785, being the diary
of Joseph Hadfield; edited and annotated by
Douglas S. Robertson. Toronto, The Hunter-Rose
co., limited, 1933.
    ix, 232 p. front. (port.)   24 cm.

6923 Hagen, Hermann Bessel, 1889-
    ... Mexico, by Hermann B. Hagen... [Washington?
D. C., n.d.]
    caption-title, 116 numbered l., 1 l.   26 1/2 cm.

6924 Haiti.
    Le moniteur haitien. February, 1845 - November,
1849. Port-au-Prince, 1845-1849.
    1 v.   30 cm.

6925 Hakluyt, Richard, 1552?-1616.
    The voyages of the English nation to America.
Collected by Richard Hakluyt, preacher, and ed. by
Edmund Goldsmid... Edinburg, E. & G. Goldsmid,
1889-90.
    4 v.   23 cm.

6926 Hale, Edward Everett, 1822-1909.
    A family flight through Mexico. By Rev. E. E.
Hale and Miss Susan Hale... Boston, D. Lothrop &
co. [c1886]
    301 p. incl. front., illus., pl., port.   23 cm.

6927 Hale, Susan, 1833-1910.
        Mexico. New York, G. P. Putnam, 1901.
        428 p. illus., ports., fold. map. 20 cm.

6928 Hall, Alfred Bates, 1875-1936.
        Panama and the canal, by Alfred B. Hall ... and
        Clarence L. Chester ... New York, Newson and com-
        pany [c1910]
        ix, 236 p. incl. front., illus. 19 1/2 cm.

6929 Hall, Basil, 1788-1844.
        Extracts from a journal, written on the coasts of
        Chile, Peru, and Mexico, in the years 1820, 1821,
        1822, by Captain Basil Hall... Philadelphia, E.
        Littell, 1824.
        2 v. fold. chart. 19 cm.

6930 Hall, Basil, 1788-1844.
        Voyage au Chili, au Pérou, et au Mexique,
        pendant les années 1820, 1821 et 1822, par le
        capitaine B. Hall ... Paris, A. Bertrand, 1825.
        2 v. fold. chart. 20 1/2 cm.

6931 Hall, Fayette.
        The Copperhead; or, The secret political history
        of our civil war unveiled; showing the falsity of
        New England... how Abraham Lincoln came to be
        president... New Haven, Conn., F. Hall, 1902.
        22 p. illus. 23 cm.

6932 Hall, Francis, d. 1833.
        Travels in Canada, and the United States, in
        1816 and 1817. By Lieut. Francis Hall ... Boston:
        Re-published from the London edition by Wells and
        Lily... 1818.
        332 p. illus. 21 1/2 cm.

6933 Hall, Gordon, 1823-1879.
        President Lincoln's death; its voice to the
        people; A discourse by Gordon Hall... preached
        in the First church, Northampton, April 19, 1865.
        Northampton, Mass., Trumbull & Gere, printers,
        1865.
        16 p. 22 1/2 cm.

6934 Hall, Nathaniel, 1805-1875.
       The proclamation of freedom: A sermon preached
    in Dorchester, January 4, 1803, by Nathaniel Hall
    ... Boston, Crosby and Nichols; E. Clapp, 1863.
       15 p.   23 1/2 cm.

6935 Hall, Newman, 1816-1902.
       A sermon on the assassination of Abraham Lincoln;
    preached at Surrey chapel, London... May 14, 1865.
    Boston, Bartlett & Halliday, 1865.
       16 p.   24 cm.

6936 [Hall, William Henry Bullock] 1837-
       Across Mexico in 1864-5. By W. H. Bullock.
    London and Cambridge, Macmillan and co., 1866.
       vi p., 1 l., 396 p. front. (map), plates,
    port.   19 cm.

6937 Halpin, Will R
       Two men in the West. By Will R. Halpin. [Pitts-
    burgh? Pa., Shaw bros.? 1898]
       108 p. 16 pl.   16 cm.

6938 Halstead, Murat, 1829-1908.
       Caucuses of 1860: a history of the national
    political conventions of the current presidential
    campaign... Columbus, Follett, Foster, & co.,
    1860.
       232 p.   23 cm.

6939 Hamburg-südamerikanische dampfschifffahrtsgesellschaft.
       Compañia Hamburgo-sud americana. "Cap Polonio",
    10 enero, 1928, gran crucero de turismo a las 3
    Américas. Buenos Aires, A. M. Delfino & cía.
    (s.a.) [1927]
       1 p.l., 52 p. illus., map.   30 1/2 cm.

6940 Hamilton, Dorothy.
       Dorothy Hamilton presents Mexico and her people
    through pictures. [Phoenix, Ariz., c1940]
       3 p.l., 20 mounted phot.   29 cm.

6941 Hamilton, James Cleland, 1836-
       The prairie province; sketches of travel from
    Lake Ontario to Lake Winnipeg, and an account of

the geographical position, climate, civil institutions, inhabitants, production and resources of the
Red River Valley... By J. C. Hamilton... Toronto,
Belford Bros., 1876.
vii, 259 (i.e. 255) p. incl. front., illus.,
plates, 2 fold. maps, fold. plan. 18 1/2 cm.

6942 Hamilton, Leonidas Le Cenci.
Border states of Mexico: Sonora, Sinaloa,
Chihuahua and Durango. With a general sketch of
the republic of Mexico; and Lower California,
Coahuila, New Leon, and Tamaulipas. A complete
description of the best regions for the settler,
miner, and advance guard of American civilization
... By Leonidas Hamilton. San Francisco, Bacon
& company, printers, 1881.
2 p.l., 3-162, vii p. 2 fold. maps (incl. front.)
23 cm.

6943 Hamilton, Leonidas Le Cenci.
Border states of Mexico: Sonora, Sinaloa,
Chihuahua and Durango. With a general sketch of
the republic of Mexico, and Lower California,
Coahuila, New Leon and Tamaulipas. A complete
description of the best regions for the settler,
miner and the advance guard of American civilization... By Leonidas Hamilton. 4th ed., rev. and
enl. New York, 1883.
2 p.l., [3]-226, xii p. 4 pl. 22 1/2 cm.

6944 Hamilton, Leonidas Le Cenci.
Hamilton's Mexican handbook; a complete description of the Republic of Mexico, its mineral and
agricultural resources, cities and towns of every
state, factories, trade, imports and exports...
tariff regulations, duties, etc., etc., and a commercial directory of the principal business men...
by Leonidas Le Cenci Hamilton... Boston, D. Lothrop
& co., 1883.
1 p.l., 281, xiii p. plates, ports. 24 cm.

6945 [Hamilton, Thomas] 1789-1842.
Men and manners in America. By the author of
"Cyril Thornton," etc. ... Philadelphia, Carey,
Lea & Blanchard, 1833.

vi, 410 p.   23 cm.

6946   [Hamilton, Thomas] 1789-1842.
        Men and manners in America.   By the author of Cyril
        Thornton, etc. ... 2d American ed.   Philadelphia,
        Carey, Lea & Blanchard, 1833.
            2 v.   19 1/2 cm.

6947   [Hamilton, Thomas] 1789-1842.
        Men and manners in America.   By the author of Cyril
        Thornton, etc. ... 2d ed.   Edinburgh [etc.] W.
        Blockwood [etc.] 1834.
            2 v.   20 cm.

6948   Hamm, Margherita Arlina, 1871-1907.
        Porto Rico and the West Indies.   By Margherita
        Arlina Hamm ...   London, New York, F. T. Neely,
        [1899]
            vi, [9]-230 p.   front., plates, port.   19 1/2 cm.

6949   Hanks, N   C
        Up from the hills.   Chicago, W. B. Conkey
        [c1921]
            32 p.   20 cm.

6950   Hanley, Mrs. May Carr.
        With John Brun in òld Mexico, by Mrs. May Carr
        Hanley.   Mountain View, Calif., Kansas City, Mo.
        [etc.] Pacific press publishing association
        [c1924]
            127 p.   incl. front., illus., map.   20 cm.

6951   Hannay, James, 1842-1910.
        The history of Acadia, from its first discovery
        to its surrender to England by the Treaty of Paris.
        St. John, N. B., Printed by J. & A. McMillen, 1879.
            vii, 440 p.   22 cm.

6952   Hardin County (Ky.) Historical Society.
        Who was who in Hardin county; compiled and pre-
        pared by Hardin county historical society.   Elizabeth
        town, Ky., Priv. print. by the Elizabethtown news
        for Hardin county historical society [1946]
            2 v.   illus. (ports.)   29 x 24 1/2 cm.

6953 Harding, George Canady, 1829-1881.
The miscellaneous writings of George C. Harding.
Indianapolis, Carlon & Hollenbeck, printers, 1882.
2 p.l., 358 p. front. (port.) 20 1/2 cm.

6954 Hardy, Campbell.
Forest life in Acadie. Sketches of sport and
natural history in the lower provinces of the
Canadian Dominion. London, Chapman & Hall, 1869.
viii, 371 p. plates. 23 cm.

6955 Hardy, Robert William Hale, d. 1871.
Travels in the interior of Mexico, in 1825, 1826,
1827, & 1828. By Lieut. R. W. H. Hardy, r.n.
London, H. Còlburn and R. Bentley, 1829.
xiii, [1] 540 p. illus., plates, 2 maps (incl.
fold. front.) 21 1/2 cm.

6956 Haring, Clarence Henry, 1885-
... Los bucaneros de las Indias occidentales en
el siglo XVII. 2. ed., hecha por la Academia
nacional de la historia (Caracas, Venezuela)...
Traducción especial del inglés para el "Boletín
de la Cámara de comercio de Caracas." Paris,
Brajas, Desclée, de Brouwer, 1939.
4 p.l., [11]-274 p., 1 l. fold. map. 20 cm.

6957 Harlan, James, 1820-1899.
The constitution upheld and maintained. Speech
of Hon. James Harlan, of the United States Senate.
[Washington, Union congressional committee, 1864]
7 p. 22 cm.

6958 Harman, S   W
Belle Starr, the female desperado. Houston, Tex.,
Frontier Press of Texas, 1954.
59, [5] p. illus. 21 cm.

6959 Harper, Henry Howard, 1871-
A journey in southeastern Mexico; narrative of
experiences, and observations on agricultural and
industrial conditions... Boston, Priv. printed for
the author by the DeVinne press, N. Y., 1910.
xiii, 100 p. front. 24 1/2 cm.

6960   Harris, George Washington, 1814-1869.
       Sut Lovingood travels with old Abe Lincoln [by]
       George Washington Harris; introduction by Edd
       Winfield Parks.   Chicago, The Black cat press,
       1937.
       2 p.l., 7-44 p., 1 l.

6961   Harris, William Richard, 1847-1923.
       Days and nights in the tropics, by Dean Harris.
       Toronto, Morang & co., limited, 1905.
       xi, 230 p.   front. (port.), plates.   23 1/2 cm.

6962   Hart, Charles Henry, 1847-1918.
       A biographical sketch of His Excellency, Abraham
       Lincoln, late president of the United States; re-
       printed from introd. to Bibliographia Lincolniana.
       Albany, J. Munsell, 1870.
       21 p.   26 cm.

6963   Harte, Bret, 1836-1902.
       The bell-ringer of Angel's, and other stories.
       Boston, Houghton, Mifflin, 1894.
       334 p.   18 cm.

6964   Harte, Bret, 1836-1902.
       Clarence.   Boston, Houghton, Mifflin, 1895.
       2 p.l., 270 p.   18 cm.

6965   Harte, Bret, 1836-1902.
       Colonel Starbottle's client, and some other
       people.   Boston, Houghton, Mifflin, 1892.
       2 p.l., 293 p.   19 cm.

6966   Harte, Bret, 1836-1902.
       Cressy.   Boston, Houghton, Mifflin, 1889.
       2 p.l., 290, 12 p.   19 cm.

6967   Harte, Bret, 1836-1902.
       The crusade of the Excelsior.   Boston, Houghton,
       Mifflin, 1887.
       1 p., 1., iv, 250, 12 p.   front.   18 cm.

6968   Harte, Bret, 1836-1902.
       A first family of Tasajara.   Boston and New
       York, Houghton, Mifflin, 1892.

2 p.l., 301, [14] p.   19 cm.

6969   Harte, Bret, 1836-1902.
        From sand hill to pine. Boston, Houghton,
        Mifflin, 1900.
        3 p.l., 327, [3] p.   18 cm.

6970   Harte, Bret, 1836-1902.
        The heritage of Dedlow Marsh, and other tales.
        Boston, Houghton, Mifflin, 1889.
        259 p.   19 cm.

6971   Harte, Bret, 1836-1902.
        ... In a hollow of the hills, and other tales
        tales, by Bret Harte. Boston and New York, Houghton,
        Mifflin and company [1896]
        3 p.l., 447, [1] p.   19 cm.

6972   Harte, Bret, 1836-1902.
        Mr. Jack Hamlin's mediation, and other stories.
        New York, Metropolitan Magazine co. [1899?]
        289 p.   17 cm.

6973   Harte, Bret, 1836-1902.
        A Sappho of Green Springs, and other stories.
        Boston, Houghton, Mifflin, 1891.
        2 p.l., 294 p.   18 cm.

6974   Harte, Bret, 1836-1902.
        Snow-bound at Eagle's. Boston, Houghton,
        Mifflin, 1886.
        213 p.   16 cm.

6975   Harte, Bret, 1836-1902.
        Stories in light and shadow. Boston, Houghton,
        Mifflin, 1898.
        2 p.l., 304 p., 1 l.   18 cm.

6976   Harte, Bret, 1836-1902.
        Three partners; or, The big strike on Heavy
        Tree Hill.   Boston, Houghton, Mifflin, 1897.
        1 p.l., 342 p.   18 cm.

6977   Harte, Bret, 1836-1902.
        Trent's trust, and other stories.   Boston,

Houghton, Mifflin, 1903.
3 p.l., 264 p.   18 1/2 cm.

6978   Harte, Bret, 1836-1902.
Under the redwoods.   Boston, Houghton, Mifflin,
1901.
2 p.l., 334 p., 1 l.   18 cm.

6979   Harte, Bret, 1836-1902.
A waif of the plains.   Boston, Houghton, Mifflin,
1890.
231 p.   16 cm.

6980   Harte, Bret, 1836-1902.
A ward of the Golden Gate.   Boston, Houghton,
Mifflin, 1890.
1 p.l., 249 p.   18 1/2 cm.

6981   Harthorn, Cyrus M
Harthorn's philosophy.   An appeal to the men of
America, by Cyrus M. Harthorn.   Los Angeles
[Calif.] H. A. Odell [1896]
63 p.   illus.   18 cm.

6982   Hasbrouck, Jacob Louis, 1867-
Lincoln in some of his unheroic hours; paper
... before the Rotary club of Bloomington,
Illinois, February 10, 1938.   Bloomington,
[printed by Daily Pantagraph] 1938.
[16] p.   20 cm.

6983   Haskins, William C   , ed.
Canal Zone pilot, guide to the republic of Panama,
and classified business directory; ed. by William C.
Haskins, pub. by A. Bienkowski ...   Panama, The
Star & herald co., 1908.
1 p.l., iii, iv, 522 p.   front. (port.), illus.
20 1/2 cm.

6984   Hassel, Johann Georg Heinrich, 1770-1829.
Vollständige und neueste erdbeschreibung vom
reiche Mexico, Guatemala und Westindien.   Mit einer
einleitung zur statistik dieser länder.   Bearb. von D
G. Hassel, und J. G. Fr. Cannabich...   Weimar,
Geographisches Institut, 1824.

xiv, 866 p.   22 1/2 cm.

6985   Hasted, Frederick, b. 1793.
          Copy of a letter written from Buffalo... to...
       Abraham Lincoln... [n.p.] 1862.
       [4] p.   20 cm.

6986   Haven, Gilbert, bp., 1821-1880.
          Our next-door neighbor: a winter in Mexico.
       By Gilbert Haven... New York, Harper & brothers,
       1875.
          16 p.l., [17]-467 p. incl. front., illus.,
       plates, map.   22 cm.

6987   Haven, Gilbert, bp., 1821-1880.
          The uniter and liberator of America: a memorial
       discourse on the character and career of Abraham
       Lincoln; delivered in the North Russell Street
       M. E. Church, Boston... April 23, 1865.
          32 p.   23 cm.

6988   Havens, Palmer E   , b. 1818.
          Oration... delivered at Crown Point, July 4,
       1865. Albany, Webb, Parsons & co., 1865.
          36 p.   21 cm.

6989   Hawkins, Sir John, 1532-1595.
          The third troublesome voyage ... to the parts
       of Guinea, and the West Indies, in the yeares
       1567 and 1568 by M. John Hawkins.
          v. 3, 618-623 p.   31 cm.

6990   Hawkins, Sir John, 1532-1595.
          A true declaration of the troublesome voyadge of
       M. John Hawkins to the parties of Guynea and the
       west Indies, in the yeares of our Lord 1567 and
       1568. Imprinted at Londō in Poules Church yarde,
       by Thomas Purfoote for Lucas Harrison, dwelling
       at the signe of the Crane. Anno. 1569 [Mexico,
       D. F., 1926]
          [32] p.   19 cm.

6991   Hawley, Bostwick, 1814-1910.
          Truth and righteousness triumphant; a discourse
       commemorative of the death of President Lincoln;

preached in the Washington Avenue M. E. Church,
April 20, 1865. Albany, N. Y., J. Munsell, 1865.
20 p.   24 cm.

6992 Hawthorne, Julian, 1846-1934.
       Bressant, a novel by Julian Hawthorne. New
York, D. Appleton and co., 1873.
       383 p.   18 1/2 cm.

6993 Hawthorne, Julian, 1846-1934.
       Garth: a novel, by Julian Hawthorne... New
York, D. Appleton and company, 1877.
       291 p.   24 cm.

6994 Hayden, Sidney.
       Washington and his masonic compeers... New York,
Masonic publishing and manufacturing co., 1866.
       407 p.   front., illus. (incl. ports.), fold. facsim
20 cm.

6995 Haydon, Arthur Lincoln, 1872-
       The riders of the plains; adventures and romance
with the North-west mounted police, 1873-1910.
Chicago, A. C. McClurg; London, A. Melrose, 1910.
       xvi, 385, [1] p.   front., illus., plates, ports.,
fold. map, fold. diagr.   24 cm.

6996 Head, Sir Francis Bond, bart., 1793-1875.
       The emigrant. By Sir Francis B. Head, bart.
... 5th ed. London, J. Murray, 1847.
       3 p.l., 441 p.   19 1/2 cm.

6997 Head, Sir Francis Bond, bart., 1793-1875.
       A narrative. By Sir Francis B. Head, bart.
London, J. Murray, 1839.
       viii, 488, 38 p.   22 cm.

6998 Head, Sir George, 1782-1855.
       Forest scenes and incidents, in the wilds of
North America; being a diary of a winter's route
from Halifax to the Canadas, and during four
months' residence in the woods on the borders of
Lakes Huron and Simcoe. 2d. ed. London, J.
Murray, 1838.
       xviii, 363, 56 p.   20 cm.

6999   Heald, Mrs. Jean Sadler.
        Picturesque Panama, the Panama railroad, the
        Panama canal, by Jean Sadler Heald. [Chicago,
        Printed by C. Teich & company, ᶜ1928]
        126 p. incl. front., illus., ports., fold. map.
        23 1/2 cm.

7000   Hearn, Lafcadio, 1850-1904.
        Two years in the French West Indies, by Lafcadio
        Hearn... New York and London, Harper & brothers,
        1890.
        431 p. front., illus., plates.   19 cm.

7001   Heartman, Charles Frederick.
        George D. Smith. G.D.S. 1870-1920. A memorial
        tribute to the greatest bookseller the world has
        ever known. Written by a very small one. Beauvoir
        Community, Miss., Privately printed as a yuletide
        greeting for Charles F. Heartman, 1945.
        31 p. front. (port.), illus.   23 cm.

7002   Heathcote, Charles William, 1882-
        Lincoln in Pennsylvania, by Charles William
        Heathcote... West Chester, Pa. [c1935]
        49 p.   22 cm.

7003   Heitman, Francis Bernard, 1838-1926.
        Historical register of officers of the continental
        army during the War of the Revolution, April, 1775
        to December, 1783. New, rev., and enl. ed.
        Washington, Rare Book Shop Pub. Co., 1914.
        685 p. port.   26 cm.

7004   Heller, Karl Bartholomäus, 1824-1880.
        Reisen in Mexiko in den jahren 1845-1848. Von
        Carl Bartholomaeus Heller. Mit zwei karten, sechs
        holzschnitten und einer lithographie. Leipzig, W.
        Engelmann, 1853.
        xxiv, 432 p. illus., pl., 2 maps (1 fold.)
        23 cm.

7005   Heller, Louie Regina, 1870-   , ed.
        Early American orations, 1760-1824; ed. with an
        introduction and notes by Louie R. Heller ... New
        York, The Macmillan company; London, Macmillan &

co., ltd., 1902.
xvii, 199 p. incl. tab. 14 1/2 cm.

7006 Henderson, John.
The West Indies; painted by A. S. Forrest;
described by John Henderson. London, A. and C.
Black, 1905.
ix, [1], 271, [1] p. 74 col. pl. (incl. front.)
23 cm.

7007 Henderson, John Brooks, 1870-1920.
The cruise of the Tomas Barrera; the narrative
of a scientific expedition to western Cuba and the
Colorados reefs, with observations on the geology,
fauna, and flora of the region, by John B. Henderson
... with 36 illustrations and maps. New York and
London, G. P. Putnam's sons, 1916.
ix, 320 p. front., plates (part col.), ports,
maps. 21 cm.

7008 Hennepin, Louis.
A new discovery of a vast country in America, by
Father Louis Hennepin; reprinted from the second
London issue of 1698, with facsimiles of original
title-pages, maps and illustrations, and the addition of introduction, notes, and index by Reuben
Gold Thwaites... Chicago, A. C. McClurg & co.,
1903.
2 v. fronts., plates, fold. maps. 25 cm.

7009 Henry, Alexander, d. 1814.
New light on the early history of the greater
Northwest. The manuscript journals of Alexander
Henry... and of David Thompson... 1799-1814. Ex-
ploration and adventure among the Indians on the
Red, Saskatchewan, Missouri, and Columbia rivers.
Ed., with copious critical commentary, by Elliott
Coues... New York, F. P. Harper, 1897.
3 v. front. (port.), maps (in pocket) 24 1/2 cm.

7010 Henty, George Alfred, 1832-1902.
Rujub, the juggler. Rahway, N. J., Mershon, 1901.
1 v, 385 p. front. 19 cm.

7011　Henty, George Alfred, 1832-1902.
　　　　The young franc-tireurs and their adventures in
　　　the Franco-Prussian War.　London, Griffith, Farran,
　　　Okeden & Welsh [1882?]
　　　　376 p.　plates.　19 cm.

7012　Hepworth, George Hughes, 1833-1902.
　　　　Starboard and port:　the "Nettie" along shore.
　　　By George H. Hepworth.　New York, Harper & brothers,
　　　1876.
　　　　viii p., 1 l., [11]-237 p.　front. (map) illus.
　　　19 1/2 cm.

7013　Herboso, Pedro.
　　　　Sermon panegyrico, en las fiestas de la publica-
　　　cion del breve, en que la santidad de el sr.
　　　Benedicto XIV. confirmò en patrona principal de
　　　el reyno de la Nueva España, a la milagrosa imagen
　　　de Nuestra Señora de Guadalupe de Mexico.　Dedicalo
　　　en su real, e insigne colegiata, el dia 13. de
　　　diciembre de 1756.　el r. p. fr. Pedro Herboso...
　　　patente el santissimo sacramento, y en presencia
　　　de el excmo. señor vi-rey, Real audiencia, tribunales,
　　　y la sagrada religion de Predicadores. Dalo a luz el
　　　m.r.p. fr. Raymundo de Sequera... quien lo dedica,
　　　a la prodigiosa imagen de Nuestra Señora de la
　　　Piedad, en nombre de su provincia.　Mexico, En
　　　la imprenta de los herederos de doña Maria de
　　　Rivera, en el Empedradillo, 1757.
　　　　17 p.l., 18 p.　incl. diagr.　21 cm.

7014　Heredia y Mieses, José Francisco, 1776-1820.
　　　　... Memorias del regente Heredia (de las reales
　　　audiencias de Caracas y México) divididas en cuatro
　　　épocas:　Monteverde.--Bolívar.--Boves.--Morillo.
　　　Madrid, Editorial-América [1916]
　　　　301 p., 1 l.　22 1/2 cm.

7015　Heres, Tomás de, 1795-1842.
　　　　... Historia de la independencia americana; la eman-
　　　cipación del Perú, según la correspondencia del general
　　　Heres con el Libertador (1821-1830)　Madrid, Edi-
　　　torial-América, 1919.
　　　　495 p.　22 1/2 cm.　(Biblioteca Ayacucho. [XL])

7016 Heriot, George, 1766-1844.
Travels through the Canadas, containing a description of the picturesque scenery on some of the rivers and lakes; with an account of the productions commerce, and inhabitants of those provinces. By George Heriot, esq. ... Philadelphia: Published by M. Carey, no. 122, Market street...1813.
iv, [vii]-xi, [13]-282 p. 19 cm.

7017 Heriot, George, 1766-1844.
... Travels through the Canadas... By George Heriot...
(In Phillips, Sir Richard, pub. A collection of modern... voyages. [1st series] London, 1805-10 22 cm. vol. VII (1808) [no. 3] 232 p. fold. plates)

7018 Hermosa, Jesús.
Compendio elemental de geografía y estadística de la República mejicana, escritos con el título de Manual por Jesus Hermosa. 2. ed. revisada y arreglada á la última división territorial por A. García y Cubas. Paris [etc.] Rosa y Bouret, 1870.
2 p.l., iv, 234 p. 16 cm.

7019 Hernández, Francisco, 1514-1578.
Francisci Hernandi... Opera, cum edita, tum inedita, ad autographi fidem et integritatem expressa... Matriti, ex typographia Ibarrae heredum, 1790.
3 v. 22 cm.

7020 Hernández, Porfirio.
Cumbres y barrancas, viajes a pie y a caballo a través de la República Méxicana. México, 1947.
433 p. illus. 24 cm.

7021 Hernández y Dávalos, Juan E., comp.
... Colección de documentos para la historia de la guerra de independencia de México de 1808 a 1821, coleccionados por J. E. Hernández y Dávalos ... Mexico, J. M. Sandoval, impresor, 1877-1882.
6 v. 22 cm.

7022 Herndon, William Henry, 1818-1891.
Abraham Lincoln, Miss Ann Rutledge, New Salem,

pioneering, and the poem: a lecture delivered in
the old Sangamon county court house, November,
1866, by William H. Herndon. Springfield, Ill.,
1910.
  67 p. front. 29 cm.

7023 Herndon, William Henry, 1818-1891.
      Brief analysis of Lincoln's character: a letter
      to J. E. Remsburg... Sept. 10, 1887. [n.p.] 1917.
      5 p. 20 cm.

7024 Herndon, William Henry, 1818-1891.
      A letter from William H. Herndon to Isaac N.
      Arnold, relating to Abraham Lincoln, his wife, and
      their life in Springfield. [n.p.] 1937.
      [6] p. 20 cm.

7025 Herndon, William Henry, 1818-1891.
      Letter to J. W. Keys, concerning the character of
      Abraham Lincoln. [n.p., 1896]
      [3] p. 20 cm.

7026 Herndon, William Henry, 1818-1891.
      Lincoln and Douglas: the Peoria debates and
      Lincoln's power... Privately printed, 1917.
      1 l. 27 x 41 cm. fold. to 21 cm.

7027 Herndon, William Henry, 1818-1891.
      Lincoln's personal characteristics: a letter
      written Jan. 15, 1874, to an unknown correspondent
      in New York City. Los Angeles, Privately printed
      for H. E. Barker, 1933.
      6 p. 20 cm.

7028 Herndon, William Henry, 1818-1891.
      Lincoln's philosophy of life; a letter written
      to a friend of uncertain identity... Feb. 18, 1886.
      Los Angeles, Privately printed for H. E. Barker,
      1933.
      6 p. 20 cm.

7029 Herndon, William Henry, 1818-1891.
      Lincoln's religion: the text of addresses de-
      livered by William H. Herndon and Rev. James A.
      Reed, and a letter by C. F. B.; edited with an

introductory note, by Douglas C. McMurtrie.
Chicago, The Black cat press, 1936.
    2 p.l., 7-98 p., 1 l.   20 cm.

7030   Herrera y Molina, Alonso de, d. 1644.
    ... Consideraciones de las amenazas del ivizio,
y penas del infierno sobre el ps. 48. Compuesto
por fr. Alonso de Herrera ... Dedicado a la Virgen
Santissima Nru Señora concebida sin macula de peccado
original. Con previlegio real. En Seuilla, Por
Vicent.' Alurez, año de 1618.
    5 p.l., 382 (i.e. 380) numbered l., [31] p.
24 cm.

7031   Herrera y Molina, Alonso de, d. 1644.
    Discvrsos predicables de las excelencias del
nombre de Iesvs, y de los nombres, y atributos de
Christo. Por el padre fray Alonso de Herrera ...
Al ilustrissimo señor don Lonrenço de Grado ...
Con preevilegio real. Impresso en Seuilla; Por
Geronimo de Contreras, a las Siete rebueltas.
Año de 1619.
    4 p.l., 190, 178 numbered l., [40] p.   25 cm.

7032   Herrera y Molina, Alonso de, d. 1644.
    Espeio de la perfeta casada. En qve se contienen
las condiciones que han de tener los buenos casados
para que se con seruen en paz: y como han de criar
sus hijos, y gouernar su familia en amor y temor
de Dios: a cuyo proposito se vá declarando toda
aquella epistola de la sabiduria que canta la
iglesia, y comiença: Mulierem fortem quis inueniet?
Por el padre fray Alonso de Herrera ... A la ilvstre
senora dona Maria Zapata, muger de don Iuan de
Quesada, cauallero de Santiago, hermano del conde
de Garcies. Con licencia. Impresso en Granada, Por
Blas Martinez, mercader, è impressor de libros, año
de 1636.
    6 p.l., 8 numbered l., 9-888, [64] p.   27 cm.

7033   Herrera y Molina, Alonso de, d. 1644.
    Espeio de la perfeta casada. En qve se contienen
las condiciones que han de tener los buenos casados
para que se conseruen en paz, y como han de criar
sus hijos, y gouernar su familia en amor y temor de

Dios: a cuyo proposito se va declarando toda
aquella espistola de la sabiduria que canta la
iglesia, y comiença: Mulierem fortem quis
inueniet? Por el padre fray Alonso de Herrera ...
A la ilvstre senor dona Maria Zapata, muger de
don Iuan de Quesada, cauallero de Santiago, hermano
del conde de Garcies. Con licencia. Impresso en
Granada, Por Andres de Santiago Palomino, impressor
y mercader de libros, Año de 1638.
6 p.l., 8 numbered l., 9-888, [64] p.   28 cm.

7034 Herrera y Tordesillas, Antonio de, 1559-1625.
Descripción de las Indias Occidentales de
Antonio de Herrera, coronista mayor de Su Magd.
de las Indias y Su coronista de Castilla.   Madrid,
Imprenta Real, 1601.
96 p.   25 cm.

7035 Herrera y Tordesillas, Antonio de, 1559-1625.
Historia general de los hechos de los castellanos
en las islas y tierrafirme del mar oceano, escrita
por Antonio de Herrera, coronista mayor de Su Md.
de las Indias y Su coronista de Castilla.   Madrid,
Imprenta real, 1601-1615.
8 v.   25 cm.

7036 Hertz, Emanuel, 1870-
Abraham Lincoln at the climax of the great Lincoln-
Douglas joint debate in Galesburg, Illinois; de-
livered at Galesburg, Illinois, on the 6th day of
October, 1928... [n.p.] 1928.
14 p.   23 cm.

7037 Hertz, Emanuel, 1870-
Abraham Lincoln, what might have been -- let his
contemporaries testify; an address... delivered
before the New York Schoolmasters' Club, February
9, 1929. Printed in the Congressional Record, Fen.
11, 1929... Washington, Government Printing Office,
1929.
12 p.   24 cm.

7038 Hertz, Emanuel, 1870-
How I became a collector of Lincolniana.   New
York, 1926.

7 p.   23 cm.

7039   Hertz, Emanuel, 1870–
       "Pew 89": Lincoln and Beecher.   [n.p., 1929?]
       20 p. illus.   23 cm.

7040   Herzog, K[arl Josef Benjamin]
       Aus Amerika. Reisebrief von C. Herzog... Berlin,
       Puttkammer & Mühlbrecht, 1884.
       2 v.   20 cm.

7041   Hesse-Wartegg, Ernst von, 1854–1918.
       Mexico, land und leute. Reisen auf neuen wegen
       durch das Aztekenland. Von Ernst von Hesse-
       Wartegg. Mit zahlreichen abbildungen und einer
       generalkarte Mexicos. Wien and Olmütz, E. Hölzel,
       1890.
       viii p., 1 l., 463, [1] p. incl. illus., pl.
       fold. map.   24 cm.

7042   Hevia Bolaños, Juan de.
       Laberinto de comercio terrestre y naval...
       Madrid, por Luis Sanchez impressor del rey, 1619.
       664 p.   22 cm.

7043   Hickman, John, 1810–1875.
       ... Political issues and presidential candidates;
       speech... in Concert Hall, Philadelphia, July 24,
       1860.   [Philadelphia? 1860]
       8 p.   22 cm.

7044   Hicks, George, 1835–
       Abraham Lincoln... Kingston, Jamaica, Printed by
       the Educational supply company [1879?]
       21 p.   21 cm.

7045   Hidalgo, Cristobal.
       Guide to Mexico ... San Franciso, The Whitaker &
       Ray co., 1900.
       126 p. illus.   18 cm.

7046   Hill, Alexander Staveley, 1825–1905.
       From home to home: autumn wanderings in the
       Northwest, in the years 1881, 1882, 1883, 1884. By
       Alex. Staveley Hill... Illustrated from sketches

206

by Mrs. Staveley Hill, and photographs by A. S. H.
... New York, O. Judd co., 1885.
   vii, [3], 432 p. front., illus., plates, 2 fold.
maps.   22 1/2 cm.

7047 Hill, Mrs. Emma Shepard.
      Doing Mexico with James, by Emma Shepard Hill.
      Denver, Col., The Bradford-Robinson ptg. co., 1924.
      48 p. front.   19 cm.

7048 Hill, Frederick Trevor, 1866-
      Lincoln's legacy of inspiration, by Frederick
      Trevor Hill... New York, F. A. Stokes company
      [1909]
      6 p.l., 60 p. front.   19 1/2 cm.

7049 Hill, Robert Thomas, 1858-
      Cuba and Porto Rico, with the other islands of
      the West Indies; their topography, climate, flora,
      products, industries, cities, people, political
      conditions, etc., by Robert T. Hill ... New York,
      The Century co., 1898.
      xxviii, 429 p. plates, 2 maps (incl. front.)
      23 1/2 cm.

7050 Hill, S   S
      Travels in Peru and Mexico, by S. S. Hill...
      London, Longman, Green, Longman, and Roberts, 1860.
      2 v.   19 cm.

7051 The historic Lincoln car, located at Columbia
      Heights, Minneapolis. [n.p., n.d.]
      [8] p.

7052 The history of Elgin from 1835 to 1875. Elgin,
      Ill., Published by Lord & Bradford, 1875.
      113 p.   22 cm.

7053 The history of Simon Bolívar, liberator of South
      America. London, Printed by Clayton & co., 1876.
      56 p. incl. front. (port.)   19 cm.

7054 The history of the British dominions in North America:
      from the first discovery of that vast continent by
      Sebastian Cabot in 1497, to its present glorious

establishment as confirmed by the late Treaty of
peace in 1763. In fourteen books. London:
Printed for W. Strahan; and T. Becket and co.,
1773.
2 v. in 1. fronts. (fold. maps)   28 cm.

7055 Hodgenville, Ky. Herald-News.
Lincoln memorial: Hodgenville, Kentucky, "the
birthplace of Lincoln". Hodgenville, Herald-News
[n.d.]
[12] p. illus.

7056 Hoffman, Frederick Ludwig, 1865-
Letters on Mexican trip, by Frederick L. Hoffman,
June-July, 1926. Published in the Boston herald,
July, August, September & October 1926. [Boston,
1926]
1 v.   23 cm.

7057 Hoffmann, Hermann.
Californien, Nevada und Mexiko. Wanderungen eines
polytechnikers, von Hermann Hoffmann. Basel,
Schweighäuser, 1871.
iv, 426, [2] p.   21 1/2 cm.

7058 [Holden, Oliver] 1765-1894.
Sacred dirges, Hymns and anthems, commemorative
of the death of General George Washington, the
guardian of his country, and the friend of man. An
original composition. By a citizen of Massachusetts
Printed at Boston, by J. Thomas and E. T. Andrews,
no. 45, Newberry-Street. [Pref. 1800]
cover-title, score (24 p.)   20 x 23 cm.

7059 Holland, Josiah Gilbert, 1819-1881.
Eulogy on Abraham Lincoln... pronounced at the
City hall, Springfield, Mass., April 19, 1865.
By J. G. Holland. Springfield, L. J. Powers, 1865.
18 p.   23 cm.

7060 Holmes, Mrs. Charlotte (Steevens)
A genealogy of the lineal descendants of John
Steevens, who settled in Guilford, Conn., in 1645,
by Charlotte Steevens Holmes, ed. by Clay W. Holmes.
Elmira, Advertiser press, 1906.

162 p.   22 cm.

7061   Hooper, Samuel, 1808-1875.
A defense of the merchants of Boston against aspersions of the Hon. John Z. Goodrich, ex-collector of customs. By Samuel Hooper. Boston, Little, Brown, and company, 1866.
59 p.   21 1/2 cm.

7062   Hopkins, John Castell, 1864-1923.
Canada; the story of the dominion; a history of Canada from its early discovery and settlement to the present time, by J. Castell Hopkins. New York and London, Cooperative publication society [c1901]
510 p.   front., maps.   20 1/2 cm.

7063   Hornaday, William Temple, 1854-1937.
Camp-fires in the Canadian Rockies, by William T. Hornaday... illustrations by John M. Phillips ... New York, C. Scribner's sons, 1906.
xvii p., 1 l., 353 p.   front., illus., 53 pl., 2 maps.   23 1/2 cm.

7064   Hortop, Job, fl. 1591.
The rare travailes of Job Hortop; being a facsimile reprint of the first edition with an introductory note by G. R. G. Conway. Mexico, 1928.
xi p., facsim: [23] p., 1 l.   facsim.   20 cm.

7065   Hortop, Job, fl. 1591.
The trauailes of Job Hortop ... set on land within the bay of Mexico ... 1568.
(In Hakluyt, Richard. Collection of voyages. London, 1809-12.   31 cm.   v. 3 (1810) p. 578-587)

7066   Houser, Martin Luther, 1871-1951.
Abraham Lincoln, student: his books, by M. L. Houser. [Peoria, Ill.] Priv. print. [Printed by E. J. Jacob, 1932]
47 p.   incl. front., ports., facsims.   25 cm.

7067   Houser, Martin Luther, 1871-1951.
Lincoln and McClellan, by M. L. Houser, prepared for the Lincoln group of Chicago. East Peoria,

Ill., Courier printing company, 1946.
28 p. illus. (maps) 22 cm.

7068 Houser, Martin Luther, 1871-1951.
Lincoln's early political education, by M. L.
Houser. Peoria, Ill., L. O. Schriver, 1944.
2 p.l., 9-35 p., 1 l. illus (incl. facsims.)
port. 24 cm.

7069 Houser, Martin Luther, 1871-1951.
Some religious influences which surrounded
Lincoln. Peoria, Ill., Lester O. Schriver, 1941.
36 p. illus. 24 cm.

7070 Houser, Martin Luther, 1871-1951.
Young Abraham Lincoln and Log College, by M. L.
Houser. Peoria, Ill., L. O. Schriver, 1942.
2 p.l., 9-50 p. illus. (facsims.) 24 cm.

7071 Houser, Martin Luther, 1871-1951.
Young Abraham Lincoln, mathematician, by M. L.
Houser. Peoria, Ill., L. O. Schriver, 1943.
1 p.l., [7]-24 p., 2 l. front. (group port.)
illus. (facsims.) 24 cm.

7072 Howay, Frederic W
... The early history of the Fraser river mines
... Victoria, B. C., Printed by Charles F. Banfield, 1926.
[xviii], 126 p. illus. 24 1/2 cm.

7073 Howe, Beverly Winslow, 1885-
Abraham Lincoln in Great Britain, by Beverly W.
Howe... Chicago, Winslow publishing company, 1940.
51 p. 2 port. (incl. front.) 19 cm.

7074 Howe, Beverly Winslow, 1885-
Two hours and two minutes; or, Lincoln and Everett
at Gettysburg [address delivered before the Lincoln
group of Chicago, Nov. 18, 1937] [n.p., 1937]
23 p. 20 cm.

7075 Howe, Edgar Watson, 1854-
The trip to the West Indies, by E. W. Howe.
Topeka, Crane & company, 1910.

349 p.   illus. (map), plates.   22 cm.

7076   Howe, Elias, 1819-1867.
Before the Hon. Philip F. Thomas, commissioner of
patents. In the matter of application Elias Howe,
jr., for an extension of his sewing machine patent,
dated September 10th, 1846... New York, W. C.
Bryand & co., printers 1860.
cover-title, 97, 9 p.   23 1/2 cm.

7077   Howe, Henry.
Captain Nathan Hale, the hero-martyr of the
American Revolution... New Haven, Conn., Henry
Howe, 1881.
21 p.   illus.   14 cm.

7078   The Hudson's Bay company. What is it? ... London,
A. H. Baily & co., 1864.
81 p.   22 cm.

7079   Hughes, Charles Evans, 1862-1948.
An address by Honorable Charles Evans Hughes,
secretary of state of the United States at the
official memorial exercises in honor of the late
Warren G. Harding held in the hall of the House
of Representatives, Wednesday, February 27, 1924,
at noon. Washington, Government printing office,
1924.
18 p.   25 cm.

7080   Hulbert, Archer Butler, 1873-   , ed.
... Southwest on the turquoise trail; the first
diaries on the road to Santa Fe, edited, with
bibliographical resumé, 1810-1825, by Archer Butler
Hulbert; with maps and illustrations. [Colorado
Springs] The Stewart commission of Colorado college;
[Denver] The Denver public library [1933]
xiv p., 1 l., 301 p.   front., plates, map.
24 1/2 cm.

7081   Hulot, Étienne Gabriel Joseph, baron, 1857-1918.
De l'Atlantique au Pacifique à travers le Canada
et le nord des États-Unis; par le baron Étienne
Hulot ... Paris, E. Plon, Nourrit & c^ie, 1888.
3 p.l., 339 p.   2 fold. maps.   18 1/2 cm.

7082   Humboldt, Alexander, freiherr von, 1769-1859.
        Ensayo politico sobre el reino de la Nueva-
        España. Traducido al español por Vicente Gonzalez
        Arnao. Paris, Rosa, 1822.
        4 v. 2 fold. maps, tables. 20 cm.

7083   Humboldt, Alexander, freiherr von, 1769-1859.
        Ensayo político sobre la isla de Cuba. Nota
        preliminar por Jorge Quintana Rodríguez. Intro-
        ducción por Fernando Ortiz. La Habana, 1960.
        435 p. port. 24 cm.

7084   Humboldt, Alexander, freiherr von, 1769-1859.
        Essai politique sur le royaume de la Nouvelle-
        Espagne; par Alexandre de Humboldt. Avec un atlas
        physique et géographique, fondé sur des observations
        astronomiques, des mesures trigonométriques et des
        nivellemens barométriques ... Paris, F. Schoell,
        1811-12.
        2 v. 34 cm. and atlas of 20 pl. (incl. maps,
        diagrs.) 58 1/2 cm.

7085   Humboldt, Alexander, freiherr von, 1769-1859.
        Essai politique sur le royaume de la Nouvelle-
        Espagne. Par Al. de Humboldt ... Paris, F. Schoell,
        1811.
        5 v. fold. pl., fold. map, tables. 20 cm.

7086   Humboldt, Alexander, freiherr von, 1769-1859.
        The island of Cuba, by Alexander Humboldt.
        Translated from the Spanish, with notes and a pre-
        liminary essay. By J. S. Thrasher. New York,
        Derby & Jackson, Cincinnati, H. W. Derby, 1856.
        xii, [13], 397 p. front. (fold. map) 19 cm.

7087   Humboldt, Alexander, freiherr von, 1769-1859.
        Minerva. Ensayo político sobre el reyno de Nueva
        España, sacado del que publicó en francés Alexandro
        de Humboldt. Por d. P. M. de O. Madrid, Impr. de
        Nuñez [etc.] 1818.
        2 v. 19 1/2 cm.

7088   Humboldt, Alexander, freiherr von, 1769-1859.
        Political essay on the kingdom of New Spain.
        With physical sections and maps founded on astronomi

observations and trigonometrical and barometrical measurements. Translated from the original French by John Black. London, Printed for Longman, Hurst, Rees, Orme, and Brown, 1811.
4 v. fold. maps, diagrs. and portfolio (9 plates; incl. maps, profiles) 24 cm.

7089 Humboldt, Alexander, freiherr von, 1769-1859.
Political essay on the kingdom of New Spain. Book 1 translated and annotated by Hensley C. Woodbridge. Lexington, University of Kentucky Library, 1957.
72 p. 28 cm. (Scripta humanistica Kentuckiensis, 1)

7090 Humboldt, Alexander, freiherr von, 1769-1859.
Selections from the works of the Baron de Humboldt, relating to the climate, inhabitants, productions, and mines of Mexico. With notes by John Taylor ... London, Longman, Hurst, Rees, Orme, Brown, and Green, 1824.
2 p.l., xxxiii p., 1 l., [4], 310 p. front., fold. map. 22 1/2 cm.

7091 Humboldt, Alexander, freiherr von, 1769-1859.
The travels and researches of Alexander von Humboldt; being a condensed narrative of his journeys in the equinoctial regions of America, and in Asiatic Russia:--together with analyses of his more important investigations. By W. Macgillivray... With a map of the Orinoco, and engravings. New-York, Harper & brothers, 1838.
367 p. incl. illus., 2 pl., map. 15 1/2 cm.

7092 Humboldt, Alexander, freiherr von, 1769-1859.
Voyage de Humboldt et Bonpland... Paris, F. Schoell [etc.] 1805-34.
23 v. col. plates, maps, charts. 34 1/2- 58 1/2 cm.

7093 Huntington, Elisha.
An address on the life, character and writings of Elisha Bartlett... Lowell, Mass., S. J. Varney, 1856.
27 p. 23 cm.

7094   Hurd, Duane Hamilton, ed.
         History of Cheshire and Sullivan counties, New
       Hampshire. Ed. by D. Hamilton Hurd. Philadelphia,
       J. W. Lewis & co., 1886.
         ix, 585 p, 410 p. plates, ports., map.   28 1/2 c

7095   Hutchinson, William Francis, 1868-1893.
         Under the Southern Cross; a guide to the sanitariu
       and other charming places in the West Indies and
       Spanish Main. Providence, Ryder & Dearth Co., 1891.
         231 p. illus.   19 cm.

                                  I

7096   Ibáñez, Diego, Franciscan.
         Pvntos primeros [-segvndos] sobre el pleyto qve
       tratan los padres descalços de la prouicia [:]
       de San Diego desta Nueva España, en raçon de
       eximirse de la obediëca de nuestro muy r.p.f.
       Alonso de Montemayor de la Orden de s. Francisco
       ... Son hechos por sv. secretario. el p. fray Diego
       Ybañes ... [Mexico, 1625]
         50 numb. l., 1 l.   24 cm.

7097   Iglehart, Fanny (Chambers) Gooch, 1851-
         Face to face with the Mexicans: the domestic
       life, educational, social, and business ways,
       statesmanship and literature, legendary and general
       history of the Mexican people, as seen and studied
       by an American woman during seven years of inter-
       course with them. By Fanny Chambers Gooch... New
       York, Fords, Howard, & Hulbert [c1887]
         548 p. incl. front., illus., plates (part col.),
       port., facsim.   25 cm.

7098   Illinois. Western Illinois University, Macomb.
         M-4: a travel study tour through Mexico [in
       July and August, 1954. Macomb] 1955.
         95 p. illus., ports., map.   28 cm.

7099   Indiana. Lincoln highway commission.
          Report of the Lincoln ;highway commission to
        Governor Samuel M. Ralston, December 15, 1916;
        commission appointed to determine the route travelled
        through Indiana by Abraham Lincoln and his father's
        family when they removed to Illinois in 1830...
        [Indianapolis] Pub. by the Commission, 1916.
          18 p.   20 cm.

7100   Informe en derecho por la defensa de los procedimientos
        de la Real audiencia de la ciudad de Santiago de
        Chille, en no aver continuado el auxilio, que empezò
        à dàr para la execucion de ciertas patentes,
        dirigidas à los religiosos franciscos de aquella
        provincia, por su comissario general de Indias, y
        en aver estrañado a quatro de dichos religiosos.
        [n.p., 1708?]
          caption-title, 20 p.   23 cm.

7101   Innes et al. vs. Roane et al.
          [Revolutionary officers' pensions. Richmond, Va.?
        1799?]
          20 p.   21 cm.

7102   International American conference. 2d, Mexico, 1901-
        02.
          ... Crónica social 1901. Mexico [F. Laso y comp.,
        impresores, 1902?]
          379 p. illus., plates, photos.   33 cm.

7103   International Bureau of the American republics, Wash-
        ington, D. C.
          ... Mexico. Geographical sketch, natural re-
        sources, laws, economic conditions, actual develop-
        ment, prospects of future growth. Ed. and comp. by
        the International bureau of the American republics.
        1904. Washington, Govt. print. off., 1904.
          454 p. plates.   23 1/2 cm.

7104   International telephone and telegraph corporation.
          Mexico; introduction to Mexico, Mexico in the
        past, leading cities of Mexico, excursions, everyday
        life in Mexico, industry in Mexico, the Mexican
        telephone and telegraph company. New York, Bureau
        of information pro-Iberoamérica of the International

215

telephone and telegraph corporation [c1930]
36 p. illus. 23 cm.

7105 Irigoyen, Ulises.
... Caminos. México, Imprenta mundial, 1934.
283 p., 1 l. incl. illus., port. 21 cm.

7106 Irisarri, Antonio José de, 1786-1868.
... Historia crítica del asesinato cometido en la
persona del gran mariscal de Ayacucho. Madrid,
Editorial-América [1917?]
382 p. 22 1/2 cm.

7107 Irish, Edwin Marshall, 1848-
Abraham Lincoln; Wendell Phillips; addresses.
[n.p.] Printed for private circulation only
[1910]
77 p. 20 cm.

7108 Isequilla Palacio, Juan de la.
Por don Jvan de Hano, vezino de la ciudad de
Mexico, y residente en esta corte. Con don Antonio
de Villa y Hano, vezino, y residente en la misma
ciudad de Mexico, assentista de la real fabrica de
la polvora de ella, y su partido. Sobre que se
declare por nula la determinacion (que con nombre de
sentencia de revista) se pronunciò por el virrey de
la Nueva-España en 30 de março de 704 y que se confirmen las dadas por el dicho virrey, y su auditor
general de la guerra como la dada por este, y el
licenciado d. Ioseph Vribe Castejon, su acompañado,
en revista, en quanto declararon averse contrahido
dicho compañia entre los susodichos, desde el dia
17. de octubre de 701. en que de disolvio de que
dicho don Antonio Villa avia celebrado con d.
Domingo de la Peña con participacion de las perdidas,
ò ganancias que huviesse en dicho assiento; y que
se revoquen estas en lo respectivo à averse considera
por disuelta la compañia desde el dia en que se supone
aver empezado à cobrar esta parte los suplementos, y
capital que tenia puestos en ella, declarandos existi
y permanecer dicha compañia, durante el tiempo porque
se otorgò el referido assiento. [n.p., 170-?]
47 numb. 1. 24 cm.

7109   L'Isle, Joseph Nicolas de, 1688-1788.
        Explication de la carte des nouvelles découvertes
        au nord de la mer du sud... Paris, Chez Desaint
        et Saillant, MDCCLII.
        18 p. fold. map.   20 cm.

7110   Isthmian tourists' guide and business directory a
        directory of the officials of the republic of Panama
        and the cities of Panama and Colon ... business
        directory of the cities of Panama and Colon and
        of the Canal Zone towns; historical and descriptive
        sketches of the Isthmus of Panama; the republic of
        Panama ... a directory of the officials of the
        Isthmian canal commission; the organization of the
        canal force; and the scope of operations of each
        department and division. Historical sketch of the
        Panama canal from its inception until its acquistion
        by the United States; a summary of the operations
        by the Americans to date; and notes of interest to
        tourists of points along the line of the canal.
        Ancon, Canal Zone, Isthmian guide and directory
        company.
        v. illus.   24 cm.

7111   Ixtlilxochitl, Fernando de Alva, ca. 1568-1648.
        Horribles crueldades de los conquistadores de
        México, y de los Indios que los auxiliaron para
        subyugarlo à la corona de Castilla. Ó sea Memoria,
        escrita por D. Fernando de Alva Ixtlilxochitl.
        Publicada por suplemento à la Historia del Padre
        Sahagún, Carlos Maria Bustamente... México, A.
        Valdés, 1829.
        1 p.l., xii, 118 p.   21 1/2 cm.

                              J

7112   Jackson, Julia Newell.
        A winter holiday in summer lands. By Julia
        Newell Jackson. Chicago, A. C. McClurg and company,

1890.
   1 p.l., 221 p. plates. 18 1/2 cm.

7113 Jackson, Samuel Trevena, 1869-
    Lincoln's use of the Bible, by S. Trevena Jackson.
New York. Cincinnati, The Abingdon Press [1914]
    35 p. front. (port.) 17 1/2 cm.

7114 Jamaica. Commissioner at the World's Columbian ex-
    position, Chicago, 1893.
    World's fair. Jamaica at Chicago. An account de-
scriptive of the colony of Jamaica, with historical
and other appendices. Comp. under the direction of
Lt. Col. the Hon. C. J. Ward, C.M.G., honorary
comissioner for Jamaica. New York, W. J. Pell,
printer, 1893.
    95 p. illus., fold. map. 25 1/2 cm.

7115 James, Henry, 1843-1916.
    The ambassadors; a novel. New York and London,
Harper & Brothers, 1903.
    2 p.l., 3-431, [1] p. 21 1/2 cm.

7116 James, Henry, 1843-1916.
    The American. By Henry James, jr. Boston,
Houghton, Mifflin and company, 1877.
    1 p.l., [5]-473 [1] p. 18 1/2 cm.

7117 James, Henry, 1843-1916.
    The Aspern papers, Louisa Pallant, The modern
warning, by Henry James. London and New York,
Macmillan and co., 1890.
    4 p.l., 200 p. 19 1/2 cm.

7118 James, Henry, 1843-1916.
    Embarrassments. The figure in the carpet.
Glasses. The next time. The way it came. By
Henry James. London, W. Heinemann, 1897.
    5 p.l., [3]-263 p. 20 cm.

7119 James, Henry, 1843-1916.
    Essays in London and elsewhere, by Henry James.
New York, Harper & brothers, 1893.
    3 p.l., 305 p. 19 1/2 cm.

7120 James, Henry, 1843-1916.
   The Europeans, A sketch. By Henry James, jr.,
  Boston, and New York, Houghton, Mifflin and company,
  1878.
   1 p.l., 281, [1] p. 19 1/2 cm.

7121 James, Henry, 1843-1916.
   The golden bowl, by Henry James... New York, C.
  Scribner's sons, 1905.
   2 v. 19 1/2 cm.

7122 James, Henry, 1843-1916.
   The lesson of the master, The marriages, The
  pupil, Brooksmith, The solution, Sir Edmund Orme,
  by Henry James. London and New York, Macmillan and
  co., 1892.
   v, 302 p. 19 1/2 cm.

7123 James, Henry, 1843-1916.
   A London life, The Patagonia, The liar, Mrs.
  Temperly. London and New York, Macmillan and Co.,
  1889.
   4 p.l., 366, [2] p. 19 cm.

7124 James, Henry, 1843-1916.
   The portrait of a lady, by Henry James. Boston,
  Houghton Mifflin and co., 1909.
   2 v. front. (port.) 20 cm.

7125 James, Henry, 1843-1916.
   The Princess Casamassima; a novel. London and
  New York, Macmillan and Co., 1886.
   3 v. 19 1/2 cm.

7126 James, Henry, 1843-1916.
   The real thing, and other tales, by Henry James.
  New York and London, Macmillan and co., 1898.
   vii, p., 1 l., 275 p. 19 1/2 cm.

7127 James, Henry, 1843-1916.
   The reverberator [a novel] London and New York,
  Macmillan and Co., 1888.
   2 p.l., 229, [1] p. 18 cm.

7128 James, Henry, 1843-1916.

The sense of the past. New York, Charles
Scribner's sons, 1917.
4 p.l., 358 p.   19 1/2 cm.

7129   James, Henry, 1843-1916.
Tales of three cities. Boston, James R. Osgood,
and company, 1884.
2 p.l., [3]-359 p.   19 cm.

7130   James, Henry, 1843-1916.
The tragic muse. London and New York, Macmillan
and co., 1891.
2 p.l., 488 p.   19 cm.

7131   James, Henry, 1843-1916.
The two magics: The turn of the screw, Covering
end. New York, Macmillan company, London: Macmillan
& co., ltd., 1898.
3 p.l., 3-393, [3] p.   20 cm.

7132   James, Henry, 1843-1916.
Washington Square [a novel] New York, Harper,
1881.
266 p. 7 plates.   18 cm.

7133   James, Henry, 1843-1916.
What Maisie knew, by Henry James. Chicago & New
York, H. S. Stone & co., 1898.
2 p.l., 470 p., 1 l.   19 1/2 cm.

7134   [James, Thomas Horton]
Rambles in the United States and Canada during
the year 1845, with a short account of Oregon by
Rubio [pseud.] 2d. ed. London, J. Ollivier, 1847.
viii, 259 p.   21 cm.

7135   Jameson, Mrs. Anna Brownel (Murphy), 1794-1860.
Winter studies and summer rambles in Canada.
By Mrs. Jameson... London, Saunders and Otley,
1838.
3 v.   19 1/2 cm.

7136   Jameson, Mrs. Anna Brownell (Murphy) 1794-1860.
Winter studies and summer rambles in Canada.
By Mrs. Jameson... New York, Wiley and Putnam

[1839?]
2 v. in 1.   19 1/2 cm.

7137 [Jameson, Robert Francis]
Letters from the Havana, during the year 1820;
containing an account of the present state of the
island of Cuba, and observations on the slave
trade. London, Printed for J. Miller, 1821.
viii p., 1 l., 135 p. map.   20 cm.

7138 Janvier, Francis De Haes, 1817-1885.
The sleeping sentinel. Philadelphia, T. B.
Peterson, 1863.
19 p.   19 cm.

7139 Janvier, Thomas A[llibone]
The Mexican guide by Thomas A. Janvier... 5th ed.
New York, C. Scribner's sons, 1890.
xvi, 531 p. fold. maps.   16 cm.

7140 Jaques, Mary J
Texan ranch life; with three months through
Mexico in a "Prairie schooner." By Mary J. Jaques.
London, H. Cox, 1894.
lx p., 1 l., 363 p. front., illus., plates.
24 cm.

7141 Jay, John, 1745-1829.
The correspondence and public papers of John Jay
... ed. by Henry P. Johnston... New York, London
G. P. Putnam's sons [1890-93]
4 v.   23 1/2 cm.

7142 Jayne, William, 1826-1916.
Abraham Lincoln, personal reminiscences of the
martyred President, by his neighbor and intimate
friend Dr. William Jayne; an address delivered by
Dr. Jayne to the Grand Army Hall and Memorial
Association, February 12, 1900. [Chicago?] Grand
Army Hall and Memorial Association [c1908]
58 p., 1 l. incl. 2 port.   18 cm.

7143 Jean-Louis, Dulciné.
Haïti; choses de la campagne; excursions de Port-
au-Prince à Jacmel... Port-au-Prince, Impr. du

Bulletin officiel de l'agriculture, 1901-06.
2 pt. in 1 v. 20 cm.

7144 [Jebb, Mrs. John Beveridge Gladwyn]
A strange career: life and adventure of John
Gladwyn Jebb, by his widow; with an introduction by
H. Rider Haggard... Edinburgh and London, W.
Blackwood and sons, 1894.
xxv, 335, [1] p. front. (port.), illus. (facsim.)
21 cm.

7145 [Jefferson, Thomas] pres. U. S., 1743-1826.
An act for establishing religious freedom, passed
in the Assembly of Virginia, in the beginning of the
year 1786. [Williamsburg? 1786?]
4 p. 20 cm.

7146 Jefferson, Thomas, pres. U. S., 1743-1826.
Two letters from Thomas Jefferson to his relatives
the Turpins who settled in the Little Miami Valley
in 1797. From the manuscript collection of Robert
Worth Turpin. Edited by Marie Dickore. Oxford,
Ohio, The Oxford Press, 1941.
16 p. facsims. 23 cm.

7147 Jeffery, R
The mission of Abraham Lincoln; a sermon preached
before the Fourth Baptist church, Philadelphia...
June 1st, 1865. Philadelphia, Bryson & son, 1865.
28 p. 20 cm.

7148 Jenkins, Samuel B
The descendants of John Jenkins... [Yarmouthport,
Mass., C. W. Swift] 1929.
59 p. 24 cm.

7149 The Jesuit relations and allied documents: travels
and explorations of the Jesuit missionaries in New
France, 1610-1791; the original French, Latin, and
Italian texts, with English translations and notes;
illustrated by portraits, maps, and facsimiles; ed.
by Reuben Gold Thwaites... Cleveland, The Burrows
brothers company, 1896-1901.
73 v. fronts., illus., pl., port., maps (part
fold.) plans, facsim. (part fold.) 23 cm.

7150   Jesuits.
Por las provincias de la Compáñía de de Iesus de
las Indias occidentales, Nueua-España, prouincias de
Mexico, y en especial de la Puebla de las Angeles.
Con el obispo, dean, y Cabildo de la santa iglesia
de la Puebla de Los Angeles, y arçobispado   de
Mexico. Sobre que se dè sobrecarta de la executoria
que han obtenido estas prouincias la cedula del
año de setenta y seis. [n.p., 16--]
19 numb. l.   23 cm.

7151   Jesuits. Provincia de Mexico.
Catalogus provinciae mexicanae Societatis Jesu,
in quo singulorum nomen, cognomen, patria, actas,
atque ingressus in eamdem continetur. [Colophon:
Mexici: ex regalis, & antiquioris divi Ildefonsi
collegij typis, anno Domini 1758]
caption-title, [25] p.   21 cm.

7152   Jillson, Willard Rouse, 1890-
A chronology of John Magill, Kentucky pioneer
and historian, 1759-1842... Louisville, Ky.,
Standard printing co., 1938.
22 p. front.   22 1/2 cm.

7153   Jillson, Willard Rouse, 1890-
Governor Simeon S. Willis, a biographical sketch
with bibliography... Louisville, Ky., C. T.
Dearing Printing co., 1944.
8 p. front. (port.), illus.   25 cm.

7154   Jillson, Willard Rouse, 1890-
In memory of Stephen Collins Foster, 1826-1864.
Frankfort, Ky., The State Journal Co., 1940.
19 p. front. (port.), illus., facsim., music.
25 1/2 cm.

7155   Jillson, Willard Rouse, 1890-
Irvin S. Cobb at Frankfort, Kentucky...   Carrollton,
Ky., The News-Democrat press, 1944.
8 p.   20 cm.

7156   Johnson, Alexander Bryan, 1786-1867.
The approaching presidential election. Respect-
fully inscribed to the Chicago convention. Utica,

August 18, 1864. [Utica? 1864?]
9 p. 22 cm.

7157 Johnson, Reverdy, 1796-1876.
A reply to the Review of Judge Advocate General
Holt, of the proceedings... of the general court
martial... of Major General Fitz-John Porter...
Baltimore, J. Murphy & co., 1863.
88 p. 23 cm.

7158 Johnson, Stanley Currie, 1878-
A history of emigration from the United Kingdom
to North America, 1763-1912, by Stanley C. Johnson
... New York, E. P. Dutton and co.; London, G.
Routledge & sons, ltd., 1913.
xvi, 387 p. incl. talbes. 22 cm.

7159 Jonckheere, Karel, 1906-
De zevende haven. Oude God, Boekengilde "Die
Poorte" [1942]
270 p. illus. 20 cm.

7160 Jones, Edgar DeWitt, 1876-
Abraham Lincoln still lives; a talk... over the
network of the Columbia Broadcasting Company, on
February 12, 1949. New York, Burton Bigelow, 1949.
[6] p. folder. 24 cm.

7161 Jones, Edgar DeWitt, 1876-
The greatening of Abraham Lincoln; by Edgar
DeWitt Jones. Prize-winning sermon in the Lincoln
sermon contest in memory of the late Rev. John D.
Long, D. D., and based on his book, The life story
of Abraham Lincoln. St. Louis, Mo., The Bethany
press [1946]
3 p.l., 9-38 p., 1 l. incl. 8 port. on 1 l.
26 1/2 cm.

7162 Jones, Lewis Hampton.
Major Thomas ap Thomas Jones of Bathurst,
Virginia. [Louisville, Ky.? 1922?]
12 p. illus., facsim. 25 1/2 cm.

7163 Jones, Thomas A
J. Wilkes Booth: an account of his sojourn in

southern Maryland after the assassination of Abraham
Lincoln, his passage across the Potomac, and his
death in Virginia. Chicago, Laird & Lee, 1893.
126 p. illus. 19 cm.

7164 Jordan, Ebenezer Stevens, 1819-1890.
Death of Abraham Lincoln: a discourse delivered
... June 1, 1865, at the Congregational church,
Cumberland Centre, Me. Portland, Me., printed by
D. Tucker, 1865.
18 p. 24 cm.

7165 Joseph Seaman Cotter, black poet of Kentucky. Lexington, Ky., Erasmus Press, 1973.
[3] p. 22 cm.

7166 Juan de Sante María, brother, d. 1622.
Chronica de la provincia de San Joseph de los
descalços. Parte primera-segunda. Madrid, En la
Imprenta real, 1615-1618.
2 pts. 22 cm.

7167 Juan y Santacilia, Jorge, 1713-1773.
... Noticias secretas de América (siglo XVIII) ...
Madrid, Editorial-América, 1918.
2 v. 21 1/2 cm.

7168 Juana Inés de la Cruz, sor, 1615-1695.
Obras. Barcelona, Joseph Llopis, 1693.
467 p., 3 l. 25 cm.

K

7169 Kaehlig, Theodor.
... Wanderungen in Mexico. Schilderung von land
und volk ... Von Theodor Kaehlig ... Würzburg, L.
Woerl [1880]
2 v. in 1. 15 cm.

7170   Kalm, Pehr, 1716-1779.
En resa til Norra America, på Kongl. swenska weten-
skaps academiens befallning, och publici kostnad,
förrättad of Pehr Kalm ... Stockholm, Tryckt på
L. Salvii kostnad, 1753-61.
3 v. illus., fold. pl. 18 cm.

7171   Kalm, Pehr, 1716-1779.
Travels into North America; containing its natural
history, and a circumstantial account of its plan-
tations and agriculture in general, with the civil,
ecclesiastical and commercial state of the country,
the manners of the inhabitants, and several curious
and important remarks on various subjects. By
Peter Kalm ... Translated into English by John
Reinhold Forster ... London, The editor, 1770-71.
3 v. pl., fold. map. 21 cm.

7172   Kalm, Pehr, 1716-1779.
Travels into North America; containing its natural
history, and a circumstantial account of its planta-
tions and agriculture in general, with the civil,
ecclesiastical and commercial state of the country,
the manners of the inhabitants, and several curious
and important remarks on various subjects. By
Peter Kalm ... Translated into English by John
Reinhold Forster, F. A. S. Enriched with a map,
several cuts for the illustration of natural history,
and some additional notes. The second edition. In
two volumes ... London, Printed for T. Lowndes,
1772.
2 v. plates, fold. map. (v. 2) 21 1/2 cm.

7173   Kane, John Francis, 1881-   , ed.
Picturesque America, its parks and playgrounds,
an illustrated volume with special articles contributed for park and playground sections and numerous
selections from the works of well known authors ex-
pressing the varied appeal of outdoors in America,
edited by John Francis Kane. New York, Resorts and
playgrounds of America, 1925.
521 p., 1 l. col. front., illus., plates (part
col.), maps (part double) 27 cm.

7174   Kate, Herman Frederick Carel ten, 1858-

226

Reizen en onderzoekingen in Noord-Amerika, van
Dr. H. F. C. ten Kate, jr. ... Leiden, E. J.
Brill, 1885.
 5 p.l., 464, [1] p. 2 fold. pl., fold. map.
23 1/2 cm.

7175 Kay, Charles Y
 Lincoln and the debate with Douglas in '58;
written for the Alliance Circle by Chas. Y. Kay;
read at the residence of the secretary, John E.
Morris, Esq., Cleveland, Ohio, September 17, 1915.
[n.p., 1915?]
 34 p. 20 cm.

7176 Kazakova, Liſa Samuilovna.
 От Пиренейских гор до Карибского моря. Рига,
"Лиесма," 1968.
 296 p. with illus. 17 cm.

7177 [Keckley, Betsey] pseud.
 Behind the seams; by a nigger woman who took in
work from Mrs. Lincoln and Mrs. Davis... New York,
National news co., 1868. [Facsimile reprint, 1945,
with prefatory note by A. Lincoln Fann]
 24 p. 23 cm.

7178 Keeling, Robert James, 1828-1909.
 The death of Moses: a sermon preached in
Trinity (P.E.) church, on Sunday evening, April
23, 1865, by Rev. R. J. Keeling, rector, as a tribute
of respect to the memory of Abraham Lincoln...
Washington, D. D. [!] W. H. & O. H. Morrison, 1865.
 16 p. 22 1/2 cm.

7179 The Keim and allied families in America and Europe;
or monthly serial of history, biography, genealogy,
and folklore, ed. by DeB. Randolph Keim. Vols.
1-2, nos. 1-23. Harrisburg, Pa., 1899-1900.
 2 v. 22 cm.

7180 Keith, Elbridge Gerry, 1840-1905.
 A paper on the National republican convention of
1860, read by Hon. Elbridge G. Keith... at the
University of Illinois, June 19, 1904. [Urbana,
Ill., The University, 1904]

19 p.   22 1/2 cm.

7181 Keller, Helen Adams, 1880-1968.
       ... The story of Helen Keller. Told by herself.
       Boston, Perry Mason & Company, 1895.
       15 p. illus.   20 cm.

7182 [Kelley, Mrs. Maria Louisa (Hamilton)] 1860-
       Hamilton family of Charles county, Maryland.
       [Houston, Tex., Standard printing co., 1930]
       3 p.l., 9-75, [1] p.   24 cm.

7183 Kendall, John Jennings.
       Mexico under Maximilian. By J. J. Kendall.
       ... London, T. C. Newby, 1871.
       3 p.l., 354 p. front. (port.), facsim.   20 1/2 cm.

7184 Kendall, John Smith, 1874-
       Seven Mexican cities. By John S. Kendall.   New
       Orleans, La., Picayune job print, 1906.
       63 p. illus.   23 1/2 cm.

7185 Kennedy, John Pendleton, 1795-1870.
       Occasional addresses; and the Letters of Mr.
       Ambrose on the rebellion. By John P. Kennedy.
       New York, G. P. Putnam & sons, 1872.
       2 p.l., [7]-472 p.   19 1/2 cm.

7186 Kennedy, John Pendleton, 1795-1870.
       Political and official papers. By John P.
       Kennedy. New York, G. P. Putnam & sons, 1872.
       614 p.   19 1/2 cm.

7187 Kentucky (Confederate state) Constitution.
       Declaration of independence and constitution of
       the provisional government of the state of Kentucky;
       together with the message of the governor. Bowling
       Green, Ky., U. N. Haldeman, state printer, 1861.
       1 l., [5]-16 p.   22 cm.

7188 Kératry, Émile, comte de, 1832-1904.
       L'élévation et la chute de l'empereur Maximilien:
       intervention français au Mexique, 1861-1867.
       Précédée d'une préface de Prévost-Paradol. Paris,
       Revue Contemporaine, Librairie Internationale, 1867.

[v]-xx, 372 p.   23 cm.

7189   Kerimov, A
       На меридиане дружбы. Декада АзССР на Кубе.
       Баку, Азернешр, 1968.
       138 p., 4 l. of illus.   17 cm.

7190   Kessler, Harry Klémens Ulrich, graf von, 1868-
          Notizen über Mexico, von Harry graf Kessler.
       Berlin, F. Fontane & c⁰, 1898.
          5 p.l., 195, [1] p.   3 pl. (incl. front.)   23 cm.

7191   Key, Helmer, 1864-
          Kaffee, zucker und bananen; eine reise nach Cuba
       und Guatemala, von Helmer Key.   München, Drei
       masken verlag a.-g. [ᶜ1929]
          x, [2], 360 p.   incl. front. (port.), illus.
       2 maps (1 fold.)   23 1/2 cm.

7192   Kingsborough, Edward King, viscount, 1795-1837.
          Antiquities of Mexico...   London, Robert Havell
       and Conaghi, son, and co., etc., etc., 1831-1848.
          9 v.   illus., facsims.   54 cm.

7193   Kingsford, William, 1819-1898.
          The history of Canada.   By William Kingsford.
       Toronto, Roswell & Hutchison; London, Trübner &
       co., 1887-98.
          10 v.   maps (part fold.) tab.   23 1/2 cm.

7194   Kingsley, Charles, 1819-1875.
          At last: a Christmas in the West Indies.   By
       Charles Kingsley... New ed.   London, Macmillan and
       co., 1873.
          xii, 401, [1] p.   incl. front., illus. plates.
       19 1/2 cm.

7195   Kingsley, Charles, 1819-1875.
          At last: a Christmas in the West Indies, by
       Charles Kingsley...   London, Macmillan and co., 1885.
          5 p.l., [ix]-xii, 401, [1] p.   front., illus.,
       plates.   19 cm.

7196   [Kingsley, Rose Georgina]
          South by west; or Winter in the Rocky mountains

and spring in Mexico. Edited with a preface, by the Rev. Charles Kinglsey... London, W. Isbister & co., 1874.
xvii p., 1 l., 411 p. incl. front., illus., fold. map. 22 cm.

7197 Kirke, Henry, 1842-1925.
The first English conquest of Canada; with some account of the earliest settlements in Nova Scotia and Newfoundland. By Henry Kirke, M. A., B. C. L. ... London, Bemrose & sons, 1871.
xi, 227 p. front. (fold. map) 22 cm.

7198 Kirkham, Stanton Davis, 1868-
Mexican trails; a record of travel in Mexico, 1904-07 and a glimpse at the life of the Mexican Indian, by Stanton Davis Kirkham ... illustrated from original photographs by the author. New York and London, G. P. Putnam's sons, 1909.
xvii, 293 p. front., 23 pl. 21 cm.

7199 Kirkwood, John.
An autumn holiday in the United States and Canada.. Edinburgh, A. Elliot, 1887.
272 p. 19 cm.

7200 Kisch, Egon Erwin, 1885-1948.
Objevy v Mexiku. [1. vyd.] Praha, Svoboda, 1947.
228 p. 22 cm.

7201 Knott, James Proctor, 1830-1911.
Andrew Jackson, an address delivered before the Andrew Jackson League at Chicago, Illinois, January 8th, 1890... Louisville, Ky., John P. Morton & company, 1890.
16 p. 23 cm.

7202 Knox, Thomas Wallace, 1835-1896.
The boy travellers in Mexico; adventures of two youths in a journey to northern and central Mexico, Campeachey, and Yucatan, with a description of the republics of Central America, and of the Nicaragua canal; by Thomas W. Knox. New York, Harper & brothers, 1890.
xx, 552 p. incl. col. front., illus., port.,

maps.   23 cm.

7203 Kohl, Johann Georg, 1808-1878.
        Travels in Canada, and through the states of New
      York and Pennsylvania. By J. G. Kohl ... Tr. by
      Mrs. Percy Sinnett. Rev. by the author... London,
      G. Mainwaring, 1861.
        2 v.   19 cm.

7204 Kol, Henri Hubert van, 1852-1925.
        Naar de Antillen en Venezuela, door H. van Kol
      ... Leiden, A. W. Sijthoff, 1904.
        2 p.l., 552, [2] p. illus., 3 pl., 3 fold.
      maps.   26 cm.

7205 Kollonitz, Paula, gräfin, b. 1830.
        The court of Mexico. By the Countess Paula
      Kollonitz... Tr. by J. E. Ollivant... 3d ed.   Lon-
      don, Saunders, Otley & co., 1868.
        xix, 303 [1] p.   22 cm.

7206 Kollonitz, Paula, gräfin, b. 1830.
        Eine reise nach Mexico im jahre 1864... 2. rev.
      aufl. Wien, C. Gerold's sohn, 1867.
        6 p.l., 247 p.   20 cm.

7207 [Koppe, Carl Wilhelm]
        Briefe in die heimath, geschrieben zwischen
      october 1829 und mai 1830, während einer reise
      über Frankreich, England, und die Vereinigten
      Staaten von Nordamerica nach Mexico ... Stuttgart
      und Tübingen, J. G. Cotta, 1835.
        x, 201, [1] p.   22 cm.

7208 [Koppe, Carl Wilhelm]
        Mexicanische zustände aus den jahren 1830 bis
      1832. Vom verfasser der "Briefe in die heimath,
      geschrieben zwischen october 1829 und marz 1830,
      während einer reise über Frankreich, England und
      die Vereinigten Staaten von Nord-amerika nach
      Mexico..." Stuttgart und Augsburg, Cotta, 1837.
        2 v.   22 1/2 cm.

7209 Kotzebue, Otto von.
        A voyage of discovery, into the South sea and

Bering's strait... 1815-1818... London, Longman,
Hurst, Rees, Orme, and Brown, 1821.
  3 v. illus., maps. 25 cm.

7210 Kowalski, Henri, 1841-
  A travers l'Amérique; impressions d'un musicien.
Paris, E. Lachaud, 1872.
  xi (i.e. ix), 260 p. 23 cm.

7211 Krebs, Ernst Hugo.
  A sermon in memory of Abraham Lincoln...
assassinated... April 14, 1865 A. D. ... Delivered
April 19, 1865... in the Church of the Holy Ghost
in St. Louis, Mo., from the German... tr. by a lady
hearer. [St. Louis, 1865]
  8 p. 20 cm.

7212 Krishna Iyer, V   R   , 1915-
  കൃബ; യാത്രാവിവരണം. ഗ്രന്ഥകാരാ വി. ആർ, കൃഷ്
ണയ്യർ. കോട്ടയം, സാഹിത്യപ്രവചന സഹകരണസ
ഘം; Sales Dept. നാഷനൽ ബുക്ക്സ്റ്റാൾ ,1967,
  191 p. 18 cm.

7213 Krzywicka-Adamowicz, Helena.
  Meksyk: orzeł, wąż i opuncja. [Wyd. 1. Warszawa
Wiedza Powszechna, 1963.
  277, [3] p. illus., maps (2 fold.) 18 cm.

                          L

7214 Laboulaye, Edouard René Lefebvre de, 1811-1883.
    Professor Laboulaye, the great friend of America,
  on the presidential election [translation] of a
  paper received at the Department of State from the
  American consul at Paris. The election of the
  President of the United States. Washington, Printed
  for the Union Congressional Committee, 1864.
    14 p. 24 cm.

7215 La Brosse, Jean Baptiste de, 1724-1782.
Nehiro-iriniui aiamihe massinahigan, shatshegutsh,
mitinekapitsh, iskuamiskutsh, netshekatsh, misht',
assinitsh, shekutimitsh, ekuanatsh, ashuabmushuanitsh,
piakuagamitsh... Uabistiguiatsh, Massinahitsetuau,
Broun gaie Girmor, 1767.
96 p. 4to.

7216 La Brosse, Jean Baptiste de, 1724-1782.
[Primer in Montagnais dialect] Uabistiguiatsch,
Massinahitsetuau, Broun gaie Girmor, 1767.
8 p. 4to.

7217 Lacarrière, Marguerite.
J'ai redécouvert l'Amérique; ou, 18.000 kms en
six semaines. [Paris] Editions de la Plume d'Or
[1955?]
143 p. 19 cm.

7218 La Condamine, Charles Marie de, 1701-1774.
A succinct abridgment of a voyage made within the
inland parts of South-America. To which is annexed,
a map of the Maranon, or river of Amazons, drawn
by the same. London, E. Withers [etc.] 1747.
xii, 108 p. front. (fold. map) 21 1/2 cm.

7219 Ladrón de Guevara, Antonio.
Noticias de los poblados de que se componen
el Nuevo Reino de León, provincia de Coahuila,
Nueva-Extramadura, y de Texas. Monterrey, México,
Instituto Tecnológico y de Estudios Superiores de
Monterrey, 1969.
xxiv, 134 p. fold. table., fold. map. 25 cm.

7220 Ladrón de Guevara, Baltazar, d. 1804.
Manifiesto, que el real Convento de religiosas
de Jesus Maria de Mexico, de el real patronato,
sujeto a el Orden de la purissima e immaculada
concepcion, hace a el sagrado Concilio provincial,
de las razones que le assisten, para que se digne
de declarar ser la que siguen vida comun, y conforme
á su regla, y que no se debe hacer alguna novedad en
el méthodo, que les prescribió el illmo. y exemó.
sr. d. frai Payo Enriquez de Rivera: cuya resolucion
pretenden que à mayor abundamiente se apruebe, y

el que han observado en los demás puntos que se
expressen. Lo dictò el lic. d. Bálthazar Ladron de
Cuevara... [Mexico] Impr. de d. Felipe de Zúñiga
y Ontiveros, 1771.
1 p.l., 217 p.   29 cm.

7221   Laet, Joannis de, 1593-1649.
Novvs orbis, seu descriptionis Indiae occidentalis
libri xviii... Lugdunum Batavorum, apud Elzevirios,
1633.
[40], 690, [19] p.   maps.   25 cm.

7222   Lahontan, Louis Armand de Lon d'Arce, baron de,
1666-1715?
... Dialogues curieux entre l'auteur et un sauvage
de bon sens qui a voyagé, et Mémoires de l'Amérique
septentrionale, publiés par Gilbert Chinard.   Avec
7 reproductions des gravures originales.   Baltimore,
Maryland, The Johns Hopkins press; Paris, A.
Margraff [etc., etc.] 1931.
2 p.l., 268 p., 3 l.   front., plates.   25 1/2 cm.

7223   Lahontan, Louis Armand de Lom d'Arce, baron de,
1666-1715?
New voyages to North-America... which is added,
a dictionary of the Algonkine language, which is
generally spoke in North-America.   Illustrated with
twenty-three maps and cuts.   Written in French by
the Baron Lahontan... Done into English.   The 2d
ed. ... A great part of which never printed in
the original ...   London, Printed for J. Osborn,
1735.
2 v.   fronts., plates (part fold.), maps (part
fold.)   20 cm.

7224   Lahontan, Louis Armand de Lom d'Arce, baron de,
1666-1715?
New voyages to North-America, by the Baron de
Lahontan; reprinted from the English edition of
1703, with facsimiles of original title-pages,
maps, and illustrations, and the addition of introduction, notes, and index, by Reuben Gold Thwaites
...   Chicago, A. C. McClurg & co., 1905.
2 v.   fronts., plates (1 fold.), maps (part fold.)
22 cm.

7225 Lahontan, Louis Armand de Lom d'Arce, baron de, 1666-1715?
Voyages du baron de Lahontan dans l'Amerique Septentrionale, qui contiennent une rélation des différens peuples qui y habitent ... l'avantage que l'Angleterre peut retirer de ce païs, étant en guerre avec la France ... 2, éd., revuë, corrigée, & augmentée. Amsterdam, Chez François l'Honoré, 1728.
3 v. front., plates (part fold.) fold. maps.
16 1/2 x 9 1/2 cm.

7226 Lalcaca
The assassination of Abraham Lincoln: speech of Mr. Lalcaca, a Parsee gentleman of India, at St. George's Hall, Liverpool, England, Thursday, April 27, 1865... [Portland, Me.] Privately printed [Southworth Press] 1925.
[3] p. 31 cm.

7227 Lamb's biographical dictionary of the United States; ed. by John Howard Brown... Boston, Mass., James H. Lamb company, 1900-1903.
7v fronts., illus., ports. 27 1/2 cm.

7228 Lambert de Sainte-Croix, Alexandre, 1854-
Onze mois au Mexique et au Centre-Amérique par Lambert de Sainte-Croix... Paris, E. Plon, Nourrit & cie., 1897.
viii, 202 p. fold. map. 18 cm.

7229 Lambert, John, fl. 1811.
Travels through Canada, and the United States of North America, in the years 1806, 1807, & 1808. To which are added, biographical notices and anecdotes of some of the leading characters in the United States. By John Lambert... With a map and numerous engravings ... 2d ed., cor. and improved. London, Printed for C. Cradock and W. Joy; Edinburgh, Doig and Stirling; and M. Keene, Dublin, 1813.
2 v. col. fronts, plates (part col.), maps (1 fold.) 21 cm.

7230 Lamberton, James McCormick, 1856-1915.
Washington as a freemason... Philadelphia, Printed

by J. B. Lippincott company, 1902.
61 p.   25 cm.

7231   Landa, Diego de, 1524-1579.
Relation des choses de Yucatan de Diego de
Landa; texte espagnol et traduction française en
regard, comprenant les signes du calendrier et
de l'alphabet hiéroglyphique de la langue maya,
accompagné de documents divers historiques et
chronoliques, avec une grammaire et un vocabulaire
abrégés français-maya; précédés d'un essai sur les
sources de l'histoire primitive du Mexique et de
l'Amérique Centrale, etc., d'apres les monuments
égyptiens, et de l'histoire primitive de l'Egypte
d'après les monuments, américains, par l'abbé
Brasseur de Bourbourg... Paris, A. Durand, 1864.
2 p.l., xcii, 516 p.   illus.   26 cm.

7232   Landenberger, Emil.
... Wanderjahre in Mexiko; mit 86 abbildungen und
einer karte. Leipzig, F. A. Brockhaus, 1925.
304 p., 1 l.   front., plates, port., map.
19 cm.

7233   Landívar, Rafael, 1731-1793.
Georgicas mexicanas; versión métrica del poema
latino del padre Rafael Landívar, s.j., Rusticatio
mexicana. Por el presbítero Federico Escobedo ...
México, Depto. editorial de la Sria. de educación,
1924 [i.e. 1925]
xxix, 423 p.   20 1/2 cm.

7234   Landívar, Rafael, 1731-1793.
Geórgicas mexicanas; traducción en verso castellano
del poema latino del R. P. Rafael Landívar, Rusticati
mexicana, por Federico Escobedo. 2. ed., corr. y
aumentada. Puebla, Editorial J. M. Cajica, Jr.
[1969]
614 p.   22 cm.

7235   Landívar, Rafael, 1731-1793.
... Por los campos de México. Prólogo, versión y
notas de Octaviano Valdés. México, Ediciones de
la Universidad nacional autónoma, 1942.
xxv, [1], 217, [1] p., 1 l.   illus.   20 cm.

7236   Landívar, Rafael, 1731-1793.
         Por los campos de México.   Introducción, versión
       y notas de Octaviano Valdés.   Selección de Alberto
       Delgado Pastor.   México, Secretaría de Educación
       Pública [1950]
         112 p.   18 cm.

7237   Landívar, Rafael, 1731-1793.
         Raphaelis Landivar Rusticatio mexicana.   Editio
       altera auctior, et emendatior ...   Bononiae, ex
       typographia S. Thomas Aquinatis, 1782.
         xxviii, 209, [1] p.   3 pl.   20 cm.

7238   Landívar, Rafael, 1731-1793.
         Rusticación mejicana, de Rafael Landívar;
       traducción literal y directa de la segunda edición
       de Bolonia, 1782, por Ignacio Loureda ...   México,
       Sociedad de edición y librería franco americana,
       s.a., 1924.
         vii, 311 p.   24 1/2 cm.

7239   Lange, Max, 1832-1899.
         Abraham Lincoln, der Wiederhersteller der
       nordamerikanischen Union...   Leipzig, O. Spamer,
       1866.
         260 p.   illus.   21 cm.

7240   Lanman, Charles, 1819-1895.
         Adventures in the wilds of the United States
       and British American provinces.   By Charles Lanman
       ...   Illustrated by the author and Oscar Bessau
       ... with an appendix by Lieut. Campbell Hardy ...
       Philadelphia, J W. Moore, 1856.
         2 v.   front., plates.   23 cm.

7241   Lardizábal y Uribe, Miguel de, 1744-1820.
         Apologia por los agótes de Navarra, y los chuetas
       de Mallorca, con una breve digresion á los vaqueros de
       Asturias.   Escrita por d. Miguel de Lardizabal y
       Uribe ...   Madrid, Por la viuda de Ibarra, hijos y
       compañia, 1786.
         1 p.l., 139 p.   24 cm.

7242   Lardizábal y Uribe, Manuel de, 1744-1820.
         Discurso sobre las penas, contrahido á las leyes

criminales de España, para facilitar su reforma.
Por don Manuel de Lardizabal y Uribe... Madrid,
J. Ibarra, 1782.
1 p.l., xiv, 293 p. 17 cm.

7243 La Rochefoucauld Liancourt, François Alexandre
Frédéric, duc de, 1747-1827.
La Rochefoucauld-Liancourt's travels in Canada,
1795; with annotations and strictures by Sir David
William Smith ... Ed. with notes by William Renwick
Riddell ... [Toronto, A. T. Wilgress, 1917]
viii, 196 p. front., pl., ports. 24 1/2 cm.

7244 La Rochefoucauld Liancourt, [François Alexandre
Frédéric] duc de, 1747-1827.
Travels through the United States of North
America, the country of the Iroquois, and Upper
Canada, in the years 1795, 1796, and 1797; with an
authentic account of Lower Canada. By the Duke
de La Rochefoucault Liancourt... London, R.
Phillips, 1799.
2 v. 3 fold. maps (incl. fronts.) vi fold. tab.
21 cm.

7245 Larrazábal, Felipe, 1816-1873.
... Vida del libertador Simón Bolívar. Nueva
edición modernizada, con prólogo y notas de R.
Blanco-Fombona. Madrid, Editorial-América [1918]
2 v. fronts. (port.), fold. maps, fold. geneal.
tab. 23 cm.

7246 Lasaga, Juan Lucas De, y Otro.
Señor, Los Vasallos de V. M. dueños de minas en
el Reino de la. Nueva España, y empleados en este
importante egercicio, ván a exponer á la Piedad de
V. M. ... sus justos reclamos, ... [Mexico, 1774]
12 p. 22 cm.

7247 Latham, Allen.
A roll of the officers in the Virginia line of the
Revolutionary army who have received land bounty in
the states of Ohio and Kentucky: to which is added,
a list of non-commissioned officers and privates
whose claims, if not assigned, are well worthy of
attention. By Latham and Leonard. Chillicothe,

Ohio, February 16, 1822.
20 p.   18 cm.

7248   Latorre, Germán.
... Relaciones geográficas de Indias (contenidas
en el Archivo general de Indias de Sevilla).   La
Hispano-América del siglo XVI: Virreinato de Nueva
España. (Mexico.--Censos de población).   Colección
y publicación hecha por Germán Latorre...   Sevilla,
Tip. Zarzuela, 1920.
119 p., 1 l.   7 mounted maps.   24 cm.

7249   Latrobe, Charles Joseph, 1801-1875.
The rambler in Mexico.   MDCCCXXXIV.   By Charles
Latrobe...   New York, Harper & bros., 1836.
vi, [7]-228 p.   19 cm.

7250   Laurens, Henry, 1724-1792.
Correspondence of Henry Laurens, of South
Carolina.   New York, Printed for the Zenger club,
1861.
240 p.   22 cm.

7251   Leach, Josiah Granville, 1842-1922.
Memoranda relating to the ancestry and family
of Hon. Levi Parsons Morton, vice-president of the
United States (1889-1893).   By Josiah Granville
Leach...   Cambridge, Printed at the Riverside press,
1894.
4 p.l., 191 p.   front., plates, fold. geneal. tab.
24 1/2 cm.

7252   LeBeau, C   , avocat.
Aventures du S^r. C. LeBeau... ou, Voyage
curieux et nouveau, parmi les sauvages de l'Amerique
Septentrionale.   Dans le quel on trouvera une
description du Canada, avec une relation tres
particuliere des anciennes coutumes, moeurs &
façons de vivre des barbares qui l'habitent & de
la maniere dont ils se comportent aujourd'hui...
Amsterdam, H. Uytwerf, 1738.
2 v.   6 fold. pl., fold. map.   15 1/2 cm.

7253   LeClercq, Chretien, fl. 1641-1695.
New relation of Gaspesia, with the customs and

religion of the Gaspesian Indians, by Father
Chrestien LeClercq, tr. and ed., with a reprint of
the original, by William F. Ganong... Toronto,
The Champlain society, 1910.
xv, 452 p. illus., plates (part fold.), maps
(part fold.), facsims. 24 cm.

7254 Leclerq, Jules Joseph, 1848-1928.
Un été en Amérique, de l'Atlantique aux montagnes
Rocheuses, par Jules Leclerq. 2 ed. Paris, E.
Plon et cie, 1866.
2 p., l., 414 p., 1 l. front., plates. 18 1/2
cm.

7255 Leclercq, Jules Joseph, 1848-1928.
Voyage au Mexique, de New York à Vera-Cruz, en
suivant les routes de terres; par Jules Leclercq
... Ouvrage contenant 36 gravures et 1 carte.
Paris, Hachette et cie., 1885.
3 p.l., 446 p., 1 l. incl. illus., plates. fold.
map. 19 cm.

7256 Lee, Mrs. S   M
Glimpses of Mexico and California, by S. M. Lee.
Boston, G. H. Ellis, printer, 1887.
3 p.l., 9-124 p. 18 cm.

7257 Leech, Robert.
The Jones family in Ireland, a chapter of hitherto
unwritten genealogical history. Yonkers, N. Y.,
M. H. Clark, printer, 1886.
81 p. 16 cm.

7258 Leeds, Samuel Penniman, 1824-1910.
Remarks made by the pastor in "The Congregational
church at Dartmouth College" on the Sunday (March
9, 1862) after the President's Emancipation message.
[n.p.] 1862.
[2] p.

7259 Lees, James Arthur.
B. C., 1887. A ramble in British Columbia, by
J. A. Lees and W. J. Clutterbuck... with map and 75
illustrations from sketches and photographs by the
authors. London and New York, Longmans, Green, and

co., 1888.
viii, 387 p. front., illus., 15 pl., fold. map.
19 cm.

7260 Leffingwell, Samuel L   comp.
Sketch of the life and labors of Thomas D. Jones,
sculptor... Columbus, O., Columbus Prtg. co., 1871.
44 p.   19 cm.

7261 Léger, Jacques Nicolas, 1859-
Haïti, son histoire et ses détracteurs... New
York and Washington, The Neale publishing company,
1907.
411 p. front., 14 pl.   22 1/2 cm.

7262 Lejeune, Louis.
Terres mexicaines. México, M. Guillot, 1912.
404 p.   19 cm.

7263 Lemmon, George T
Lincoln in the light of his age: a centenary
memorial... with special contributions by William
Jennings Bryan, John Sharp Williams [and others]
[New York, Cochrane pub. co., 1909]
15 p.   23 cm.

7264 Le Moyne, Auguste, b. 1800.
Viajes y estancias en América del Sur; La Nueva
Granada, Santiago de Cuba, Jamaica y el Istmo de
Panamá. Bogotá [Ministerio de Educación de
Colombia, 1945]
432 p.   20 cm.

7265 Lempriere, Charles, 1818-1901.
Notes in Mexico, in 1861 and 1862; politically
and socially considered. By Charles Lempriere...
London, Longman, Green, Longman, Roberts, & Green,
1862.
4 p.l., 480 p. front., illus., 6 pl., fold. map,
facsim. 19 cm.

7266 Lenglet du Fresnoy, Nicolas, 1674-1755.
A geography of children: or, A short and easy
method of teaching or learning geography... London,
Printed for Edward Littleton and John Hawkins, 1737.

129 p.   16 cm.

7267   Lerner, Ira T
         See exotic Mexico, the key to Latin America.
         Cover   by J. Horna.   Mexico [1956]
         192 p.   illus.   24 cm.

7268   Lescarbot, Marc.
         Histoire de la Nouvelle-France, par Marc Lescarbot,
         suivie des Muses de la Nouvelle-France.   Nouv. ed.,
         pub. par Edwin Tross, avec quatre cartes geographi-
         ques...   Paris, Librarie Tross, 1866.
         3 v.   4 fold. maps.   20 cm.

7269   Lettre des colons résidens à St.-Domingue, au roi
         [le 31 mai 1788] [n.p., 1788]
         15 p.   20 cm.

7270   Lettres au docteur Priestley, en Amérique... tr. de
         l'anglais...   Londres, 1798.
         v, [7]-20 p.   21 1/2 cm.

7271   Levanto, Leonardo, fl. 1741-1776.
         Crisis americana, sobre el canonicato regular de
         s^{to} Domingo de Guzman, en la santa iglesia cathedral
         de Osma.   Asserto historical apologetico, dividido
         en trece dissertaciones, y respuestas à quarenta
         dudas.   Contra el doctor Arguleta, y maestro Noriega,
         Su autor el m.r.p. maestro fray Leonardo Levanto
         ...   Madrid, Por Gabriel Ramirez, plazuela de la
         Aduana, 1741.
         14 p.l., 484 p.   coat of arms.   22 cm.

7272   Levinge, Sir Richard George Augustus, 7th bart., 1811-
         1884.
         Echo's aus den Urwäldern; oder, Skizzen trans-
         atlantischen Lebens.   Nach englischen Quellen bearb.
         von Fr. Gerstäcker.   Leipzig, W. Gerhard, 1847.
         viii, 263 p.   15 cm.

7273   Leyva, Antonio de.
         Señor El Capitan D. Antonio de Leyva, puesto à
         los Reales pies de V. M. dize: Que aviendose
         visto vn Memorial... etc. [n.p., ca. 1690]
         4 p.   21 cm.

7274 L'Honoré Naber, Samuel Pierre, 1865-   , ed.
... Piet Heyn en de zilvervloot, bescheiden uit
Nederlandsche en spaansche archieven bijeenverzameld
en uitg. door S. P. L'Honoré Naber en Irene A.
Wright. Utrecht, Kemink & zoon, 1928.
2 v. in 1.   port., fold. map, fold. tab., diagr.
22 1/2 cm.

7275 El Liberal.   Redactor de las sesiones del Soberano
Congreso.   Redactor extraordinario del Soberano
Congreso.   Notas sobre las operaciones del Congreso
de Chile.   Contestaciones.   1823-1824.   Santiago,
Biblioteca Nacional, 1965.
522 p.   28 cm.
A reissue of four periodicals published in
Santiago.   The first, El Liberal, an irregular
weekly, is in 48 numbers and 2 supplements
issued July 28, 1823-Feb. 4, 1825 (except Jan.
23-Aug. 10, 1824)   Included in the vol. are five.
"Contestaciones al 'Liberal'".   The second periodical,
Redactor de las sesiones del Soberano Congreso, is in
18 numbers covering the ordinary and extraordinary
sessions, Aug. 13-Dec. 1, of the Congress of 1823.
The third, Redactor extraordinario del Soberano
Congreso, in its single number, covers later,
Dec. 29-31, sessions of the Congress of 1823.
The fourth, Notas sobre las operaciones del Congreso
de Chile, is in five numbers issued Sept. 11-Nov.
12, 1823.

7276 Liberty Hall, Inc., Louisville, Ky.
Liberty Hall, Frankfort, Kentucky, built in
1796 by Hon. John Brown, son of Rev. John Brown and
Margaret Preston Brown.   [Louisville, Ky., 1947?]
16 p.   illus.   19 1/2 cm.

7277 Life of Cornelius Heeney, 1754-1848.   [Brooklyn,
N. Y.]   Brooklyn Benevolent Society, 1948.
[14] p.   17 cm.

7278 Lighthall, William Douw, 1857-
Montreal after 250 years, by W. D. Lighthall,
M. A. Montreal, F. E. Grafton & sons, 1892.
7 p.l., 149 p., 1 l.   front. (port.), illus.,
plates, plans.   19 1/2 cm.

7279   Lincoln, Abraham, pres. U. S., 1809-1865.
        Abraham Lincoln and Mary Owen: three letters,
Lincoln to Mrs. O. H. Browning, I. N. Arnold to
O. H. Browning, O. H. Browning to I. N. Arnold
... Springfield, Ill., Privately printed, Barker's
art store, 1922.
        [12] p.   21 cm.

7280   Lincoln, Abraham, pres. U. S., 1809-1865.
        Abraham Lincoln: his autobiographical writings
now brought together for the first time and pre-
faced with an introductory comment, by Paul M. Angle
Kingsport, Tenn., Priv. print. at Kingsport Press
[c1947]
        63 p.   col. port., facsim.   26 cm.

7281   Lincoln, Abraham, pres. U. S., 1809-1865.
        Abraham Lincoln on prohibition... New York,
Prohibition Educational League of New York county
[n.d.]
        4 p.   20 cm.

7282   Lincoln, Abraham, pres. U. S., 1809-1865.
        Abraham Lincoln's letter to Major General Joseph
Hooker, dated January 26, 1863.   [Chicago, The
Caxton Club, 1942]
        [7] p., facsim, [4] p.   27 cm.

7283   Lincoln, Abraham, pres. U. S., 1809-1865.
        The address of the Hon. Abraham Lincoln, in
vindication of the policy of the framers of the
Constitution and the principles of the Republican
party, delivered at Cooper institute, February 27th,
1860, issued by the Young men's Republican union
... with notes by Charles C. Nott & Cephas Brainerd
... New York, G. F. Nesbitt & co., printers, 1860.
        32 p.   23 cm.

7284   Lincoln, Abraham, pres. U. S., 1809-1865.
        ... The campaign in Illinois: last joint debate;
Doublas and Lincoln at Alton, Illinois. Washington,
printed by L. Towers, 1858.
        32 p.   22 1/2 cm.

7285   Lincoln, Abraham, pres. U. S., 1809-1865.

A letter from President Lincoln to General Joseph
Hooker, January 26, 1863. Philadelphia, 1879.
31. 21 cm.

7286 Lincoln, Abraham, pres. U. S., 1809-1865.
... The letters of President Lincoln on questions
of national policy... New York, H. H. Lloyd & co.,
1863.
22 p. 19 cm.

7287 Lincoln, Abraham, pres. U. S., 1809-1865.
Lincoln the poet: poems by Abraham Lincoln,
compiled by the poet Hunter [pseud.] Chicago, Ill.,
P. H. Dodge [c1940]
[46] p. illus. (ports.) 21 1/2 cm.

7288 Lincoln, Abraham, pres. U. S., 1809-1865.
Lincoln's account of the Hampton Roads conference,
with facsimiles from the original documents in the
collection of Judd Stewart. [n.p.] 1910.
18 p. 20 cm.

7289 Lincoln, Abraham, pres. U. S., 1809-1865.
Lincoln's autobiography... [n.p., Northwestern
National Life Insurance co.,]
[4] p. folder facsimile, port. (Northwestern
national life insurance co., Historical series, no.
31)

7290 Lincoln, Abraham, pres. U. S., 1809-1865.
Opinions on 'slavery' and 'reconstruction of the
union' as expressed by President Lincoln; with brief
notes by Hon. William Whiting. [New York] Printed
for the Union Congressional committee by J. A. Gray
and Green [1864]
16 p. 23 cm.

7291 Lincoln, Abraham, pres. U. S., 1809-1865.
A strange affair [by] Abraham Lincoln... ed. by
Roger W. Barrett. [Peoria, Ill., printed by E. J.
Jacob, c1933]
17 p. illus. 23 cm.

7292 Lincoln campaign songster, for the use of clubs;
containing all of the new popular songs. Phil-

adelphia, Mason & co., 1864.
16 p.   20 cm.

7293   The Lincoln catechism, wherein the eccentricities
and beauties of despotism are fully set forth: a
guide to the presidential election of 1864.   New
York, J. F. Feeks [c1864]
46 p.   20 cm.

7294   ... Lincoln, 1864--McKinley, 1900.   The Democratic
party's parallel--Imperialism and "militarism", then
and now--"Consent of the governed" applied to the
seceded states--"The war a failure"--The same
charge of surrendering to Plutocracy--Expansion
south of Mason and Dixon's line denounced.   [n.p.]
1900.
[8] p.   20 cm.

7295   Lincoln Fellowship, Hamilton, Ontario.
The hallowed trail, by Kenneth C. Cameron [etc.]
being the substance of addresses delivered before
the Lincoln Fellowship of Hamilton, Ontario...
February 13, 1956.   [Hamilton, Ontario? 1956?]
16 p.   port.   20 cm.

7296   Lincoln Fellowship of Wisconsin.
The Lincoln statue at the University of Wisconsin,
erected 1909:   addresses at ceremonies of acceptance and of dedication of the only replica of
statue by Adolph A. Weinman at Hodgenville, Kentucky.   Madison, 1950.
17 p.   illus., ports.   26 cm.

7297   Lincoln Fellowship of Wisconsin.
Lincoln visits Beloit and Janesville, Wisconsin:
contemporary accounts of anti-slavery speeches of
October 1, 1859.   Madison, 1949.
20 p.   illus., port.   27 cm.

7298   Lincoln Guard of Honor.
Organization and objects of the London guard of
Honor, and first memorial service, held on the
fifteenth anniversary of the death of Abraham
Lincoln, Springfield, Illinois, April 15th, 1880.
[Springfield, State journal printers, 1880]

14 p.   illus.   23 cm.

7299   The Lincoln Memorial, Washington, D. C.
       Alexandria, Va., Action Publication, c1950.
       30 p.   illus., ports.   23 cm.

7300   Lincoln, Mrs. Mary (Todd) 1818-1882.
       Mary Lincoln, a letter to her cousin, Elizabeth
       Todd Grimsley, Sept. 29, 1861. [n.p.] Privately
       printed, 1917.
       [7] p.   20 cm.

7301   The Lincoln monument in memory of Scottish-American
       soldiers; unveiled in Edinburgh, August 21, 1893.
       Edinburgh & London, William Blackwood & Sons, 1893.
       98 p.   illus.   20 cm.

7302   Lincoln, Solomon, 1804-1881.
       Notes on the Lincoln families of Massachusetts;
       with some account of the family of Abraham Lincoln,
       late president of the United States. By Solomon
       Lincoln... Boston, D. Clapp & son, printers, 1865.
       10 p.   24 1/2 cm.

7303   Linton, J   F
       Some unrecorded history of the Army of the
       Patomac [!] [n.p., n.d.]
       8 p.   22 cm.

7304   Lippé, Joseph Alfred, 1865-
       Le tour de Mexique; mon journal de voyage, par
       l'abbé J.-A. Lippé... Montréal, Arbour & Dunpont,
       1907.
       271 p.   front., plates.   19 cm.

7305   Lloréns Torres, Luís.
       América (estudios históricos y filológicos) ...
       Colección de artículos escritos y ordenados por d.
       Luís Lloréns Torres, con una carta-prólogo de d.
       Antonio Cortón. Madrid, V. Suárez; [etc., etc.,
       1898]
       204 p.   21 cm.

7306   Llorente Vázquez, Manuel.
       Cuadros americanos: Venezuela, Brasil, California,

Guatemala, Montevideo y Ecuador, por Manuel Llorente
Vázquez ... con un prólogo de Luis Vidart. Madrid,
F. Fe, 1891.
2 p.l., [vii]-xxiii, 432 p. 18 1/2 cm.

7307 Lloyd George, David, 1863-1945.
Abraham Lincoln: an address before the Midday
luncheon club... Springfield, Ill., Thursday,
October 18, 1923. Cleveland, printed for S. W.
Tener, April, 1924.
13 p. 24 cm.

7308 Loaisaga, Manuel De.
Historia de la milagrosissima imagen de nuestra
Señora de Occotlan... Puebla, Viuda Miguel de
Ortega Bonilla, 1745.
182 p. 25 cm.

7309 [Lobato, José G   ]
Consideraciones generales sobre la geografía,
meteorología y climatología de la zona intertropical
de la República Mexicana con relación á la
aclimatación del hombre. Mexico, Impr. de J. M. A.
Ortiz, 1874.
57 p. 22 1/2 cm.

7310 Lochon, Henri.
En 2 [i.e. deux] CV chez les primitifs, Indiens
Tarahumaras de la Sierra mexicaine. Photos
[par] Eric de Waubert de Genlis. Lyon, E. Vinay
[1956]
223 p. illus. 21 cm.

7311 Lodge, Henry Cabot, 1850-1924.
... Alexander Hamilton... Boston, New York,
Houghton, Mifflin and company, 1883.
vi, 306 p. 18 cm.

7312 Logan, John Alexander, 1826-1886.
Fitz-John Porter: speech in the Senate of the
United States... March 13, 1884. [Washington,
Govt. Prtg. Office] 1884.
112 p. 23 cm.

7313 Logan, Walter Seth, 1847-1906.

The siege of Cuautla, the Bunker Hill of Mexico
... New York, The Knickerbocker press, 1893.
27 p.   21 cm.

7314   Løkken, Thomas Olesen, 1877-
Danmark i Amerika.   Omslagstegning of Einar Gross.
København, Uhlmanske forlag, 1950.
296 p.   fold. map.   23 cm.

7315   Lombardo Toledano, Humberto.
Construyendo México, 1910-1946.   México, 1946.
cover-title, 1 v. (unpaged)   illus., ports.   30 cm.

7316   Long, Orie William.
Thomas Jefferson and George Ticknor, a chapter
in American scholarship.   Williamstown, Mass.,
The McClelland Press, 1933.
39 p.   24 cm.

7317   Longfellow, Samuel, 1819-1892, ed.
Life of Henry Wadsworth Longfellow, with
extracts from his journals and correspondence; ed.
by Samuel Longfellow...   Boston and New York,
Houghton, Mifflin and company, 1891.
3 v.   fronts., illus., plates, ports., facsims,
19 1/2 cm.

7318   López Cordero, Fr. Antonio, 1678 or 9-1730.
Vida de la esclarecida Virgen Dulcissima Esposa
de N. Señor Jesu Christo.   Santa Ines de Monte-
policiano...   Puebla, Viuda Miguel de Ortega
Bonilla, 1744.
314 p.   26 cm.

7319   Lopez de Avilés, José.
Debido recverdo de agradecimiento leal a los
beneficios hechos en Mexico por sv dignissimo, y
amadissimo prelado: el ill.mo r.mo y ex.mo
senor maestro d. fr. Payo Enriqvez, Afan de Ribera
... Dedicado al ex.mo s.or d.   Thomas, Antonio,
Lorenço, Manuel de la Cerda, Manrique de Lara,
Enriquez, Afan de Ribera, Portocarrero, y Cardenas:
conde de Paredes, marqués de la Laguna... Escribialo
el b.r Ioseph Lopez de Aviles... Año de 1682...
Con licencia de los supiriores [!], impresso < à

costa de los affectos de su señoria illustrissma >
en Mexico, año de 1684. En la imprenta de la viuda
de Francisco. Rodriguez Luperçio; en cuya tienda
se hallara, junto a la puente de Palacio.
   2 p.l., 120 p.   27 cm.

7320 López, Elpidio.
   ... Geografía de México, para uso de las escuelas
primarias, por los profesores Elpidio López y Jorge
Casahonda; redactada bajo la supervisión de la
Comisión editora popular de la S. E. P. 2. ed.,
corr. México, D. F., Ediciones encuadernables El
Nacional, 1940.
   109, [3] p. incl. illus., maps.   20 x 29 cm.

7321 López, Herrero, Juan Antonio.
   ... Por el curador ad litem de d.ª Maria Josepha
Alfonso Pimentel, Tellez Giron Enriquez de
Cabrera, condesa-duguesa de Benavente, y Gandía,
num. 164. con D.ª Gertrudiz Gallo Villavicencio, num.
145, vecina de la ciudad de México, viuda de D.
Juan Parada Fonseca Enriquez, como madre, tutora, y
curadora de la persona, y bienes de D. Juan Maria
Gomez de Parada Fonseca Enriquez, su hijo, num. 153.
D. Pedro de Alcantara Fernandez de Hijar, Porto-
carrero y Sylva, duque de Hijar, num. 150. D.
Bernardino Fernandez de Velasco Pimentel Vigil de
Quiñones, duque de Frias num. 161. D. Joaquin de
Toledo y Rivera Quiñones Enriquez y Pimentél,
marqués de Mancera, num. 163. D. Fabricio Mathias
Piñateli de Aragon Cortes Pimentél Quiñones, duque
de Terra-Nova, num. 165. D. Hermenegildo Manuel
Hurtado de Mendoza Enriquez de Guzmán, marqués de
Gelo, y Villamayna, num. 146, y el curado ad litem
de d. Joseph Ramon Enriquez de Guzman, menor, num.
133. Sobre la tenuta, y possession del mayorazgo
de Alva de Aliste, fundado por D., Enrique Enriquez,
n. 3. primer conde de este titulo, en su testamento
de 24. de julio de 1480. Con ius unidos, y
agregados, vacante, por muerte de D. Francisco
Alphonso Pimentél, conde de Benavente, n. 159.
[Madrid? 1770]
   1 p.l., 19 numb: l.   21 cm.

7322 López, Manuel Antonio, b. 1803.

... Recuerdos históricos de la guerra de la independencia. Colombia y el Perú (1819-1826) Madrid, Editorial-América, 1919.
328 p. plans. 22 cm.

7323 López Velarde, Ramón, 1888-1921.
... La suave patria. Comentario final de Francisco Monterde, grabados en madera de Julio Prieto.
México, Imprenta universitaria, 1944.
19, [1] p., 1 l. illus. 32 1/2 cm.

7324 Lord, John Keast, 1818-1872.
The naturalist in Vancouver Island and British Columbia... London, R. Bentley, 1866.
2 v. fronts., plates. 21 cm.

7325 Lord, Theodore A
A summary of the case of General Fitz-John Porter. 2d ed. San Francisco, 1883.
84 p. 2 maps. 23 cm.

7326 Lorenzana y Butrón, Francisco Antonio, cardinal, 1722-1804.
Cartas, edictos, y otros obras sueltas del excelentisimo señor don Francisco Antonio Lorenzana, arzobispo de Toledo, primado de las Españas. Toledo, Por Nicolás de Almanzáno, impresor de la real Universidad, 1786.
[254] p. 27 cm.

7327 Lorenzana y Butrón, Francisco Antonio, cardinal, 1722-1804.
Coleccion de las pastorales y cartas del excelentisimo señor don Francisco Antonio Lorenzana, arzobispo de Toledo, primado de las Españas.
Madrid, Por d. Joachin Ibarra, 1779.
[303] p. 27 cm.

7328 Lotz, James Robert, comp.
Yukon bibliography. Preliminary ed. Ottawa, Northern Co-ordination and Research Centre, Dept. of Northern Affairs and National Resources, 1964.
vii, 155 p.

7329 Louisville, Ky. Congregation Adath Israel.

Lincoln centenary services, 1909: Temple Adath
Israel, Louisville, Ky. [Louisville, Courier-
Journal, 1909]
38 p. front. 22 cm.

7330 Louisville, Ky. University. J. B. Speed memorial
museum.
Catalogue of Lincoln: books, pamphlets, magazines.
Louisville, J. B. Speed Memorial museum, [1942]
19 p. 20 cm.

7331 Lovell's gazetteer of British North America: containing the latest and most authentic descriptions
of over six thousand cities, towns and villages...
and general information... as to the names... &c.,
of over fifteen hundred lakes and rivers, with a
table of routes... Ed. by P. A. Crossby. Montreal,
J. Lovell; Rouse's Point, J. Lovell & sons, 1873.
2 v. in 1. 19 cm.

7332 Low, Seth, 1850-1916.
Speech of Hon. Seth Low, at Lincoln dinner, in
Brooklyn, February 13, 1888... New York, Henry
Bessey, 1888.
14 p. 20 cm.

7333 Lowe, Charles, 1828-1874.
Death of President Lincoln: a sermon delivered
in the Unitarian Church in... Charleston, S. C.
... April 26, 1865. Boston, American Unitarian
Association, 1865.
24 p. 20 cm.

7334 Löwenstern, Isidor, 1810-1858.
Le Mexique; souvenirs d'un voyageur, par Isidore
Löwenstern ... Paris, A. Bertrand; [etc., etc.]
1843.
viii, 466 p., 1 l. 22 cm.

7335 Lowrey, Grosvenor Porter.
The commander-in-chief: a defense upon legal
grounds of the proclamation of emancipation; and an
answer to ex-Judge Curtis' pamphlet, entitled
"Executive power". New York, G. P. Putnam, 1862.
31 p. 19 cm.

7336   Lowry, Thomas, 1843-1909.
       Personal reminiscences of Abraham Lincoln.
       London, Privately printed... 1910 [Minneapolis,
       1929]
          32 p.   22 cm.

7337   Lozada, Jesús Rodolfo, 1892-
       ... Información turística sobre México.   México,
       D. F., D.A.P.P., 1939.
          3 p.l., 9-175 p.   fold. maps.   23 1/2 cm.

7338   Lucas, Daniel Bedinger, 1836-1909.
       Nicaragua: war of the filibusters, by Judge
       Daniel B. Lucas... with introductory chapter by
       Hon. Lewis Baker... The Nicaraguan canal, by Hon.
       W. A. MacCorkle... The Monroe doctrine, by J.
       Fairfax McLaughlin, LL.D. Richmond, Va., B. F.
       Johnson publishing company, 1896.
          216 p.   front. (port.), pl., map.   19 1/2 cm.

7339   Luccock, John.
       Notes on Rio de Janeiro, and the southern parts
       of Brazil; taken during a residence of ten years
       in that country, from 1808 to 1818. London, S.
       Leigh, 1820.
          viii, 639, [1] p.   3 maps.

7340   Lumholtz, Karl [Sofus] 1851-
       El México desconocido; cinco años de exploración
       entre las tribus de la Sierra Madre occidental; en
       la tierra caliente de Tepic y Jalisco, y entre los
       Tarascos de Michoacán; obra escrita en inglés por
       Carl Lumholtz ... y traducida al castellano por
       Balbino Dávalos ... Ed. ilustrada. Nueva York,
       C. Scribner's sons, 1904.
          2 v.   fronts. (ports.), illus., plates (partly
       col.), fold. maps.   25 cm.

7341   Lumholtz, Karl Sofus, 1851-
       Unknown Mexico; a record of five years' exploration
       among the tribes of the western Sierra Madre; in the
       tierra caliente of Tepic and Jalisco; and among the
       Tarascos of Michoacan, by Carl Lumholtz ...   New
       York, C. Scribner's sons, 1902.
          2 v.   fronts. (v. 2: double facsim.), illus. (incl.

music), plates (part col.), ports., fold. maps.
25 cm.

7342 Lummis, Charles Fletcher, 1859-
The awakening of a nation; Mexico of to-day; by
Charles F. Lummis ... New York and London, Harper
& brothers, 1898.
xi p., 1 l., 179 p. front., plates, ports., fold.
map. 21 cm.

7343 Luzac, S
... Manchitas de color centroamericanas. Santiago
de Chile, 1946.
85 p., 1 l. col. plates. 21 cm.

7344 Lyell, Sir Charles, 1797-1875.
Charles Lyell's Reisen in Nordamerika, mit beobach-
tungen über die geognostischen verhältnisse der
Vereingten Staaten, von Canada und Neu-Schottland
Deutsch von dr. Emil Th. Wolff ... Halle, C.
Graeger 1846.
xii, 395, [1] p. front. (fold. map) plates
(partly fold.) 21 cm.

7345 Lyell, Sir Charles, 1797-1875.
... Lyell's travels in North America in the years
1841-2; abridged and ed. by John P. Cushing ... New
York, C. E. Merrill co. [c1909]
172 p. 17 cm.

7346 Lyell, Sir Charles, 1797-1875.
Travels in North America; with geological
observations on the United States, Canada, and Nova
Scotia. By Charles Lyell ... London, J. Murray,
1845.
2 v. col. fronts., illus., plates (part fold.)
maps (part fold.) facsims. 19 1/2 cm.

7347 Lyell, Sir Charles, 1797-1875.
Travels in North America, in the years 1841-2;
with geological observations on the United States,
Canada, and Nova Scotia. By Charles Lyell ... New
York, Wiley and Putnam, 1845.
2 v. in 1. 5 pl. (part fold., incl. col. front.,
v. 1) 2 maps (incl. front., v. 2) 19 1/2 cm.

7348   Lyon, George Francis, 1795-1832.
        Journal of a residence and tour in the republic of
        Mexico in the year 1826. With some account of the
        mines of that country. By Capt. G. F. Lyon ...
        London, J. Murray, 1828.
        2 v. illus. 19 1/2 cm.

7349   Lyon, G[eorge] F[rancis]
        The sketch-book of Captain G. F. Lyon, R.N., during
        eight months residence in Mexico. No. 1 [and 2]
        [London] J. Dickinson, 1827.
        cover-title, 1 p.l., 5 pl., 1 l., 5 pl.   37 cm.

                                    M

7350   [McAdam, J   T   ]
        Canada; the country, its people, religions,
        politics, rulers, and its apparent future, being a
        compendium of travel from the Atlantic to the
        Pacific, the Great Lakes, Manitoba, the Northwest,
        and British Columbia... by Captain "Mac" [pseud.]
        Enl. ed., Montreal, 1882.
        353 p. illus.   23 cm.

7351   McCallen, Robert Seth.
        Strangled liberty; or, Rome and ruin; a bombshell
        to the McKinley administration, a revelation to the
        Protestant world. St. Louis, Columbia Book Concern,
        1900.
        256 p. illus.   20 cm.

7352   McCamant, Wallace, 1867-
        Lincoln in the winter of '60-'61: an address
        ... to the joint session of the twenty-ninth
        legislature of Oregon, on February twelfth, nine-
        teen hundred seventeen. [n.p., 1917]
        7 p.   23 cm.

7353   McCamant, Wallace, 1867-

                                  255

Thaddeus Stevens: an address delivered... before
the Pennsylvania club of Portland, Oregon, on April
4th, 1916... [n.p.] 1916.
32 p. 20 cm.

7354 McCarty, Joseph Hendrickson, 1830-1897.
Two thousand miles through the heart of Mexico.
By Rev. J. Hendrickson McCarty ... New York,
Phillips & Hunt; Cincinnati, Cranston & Stowe, 1886.
288 p. front., pl. 19 cm.

7355 McClellan, George Brinton, 1826-1885.
... The Democratic platform: General McClellan's
letter of acceptance. New York, [Democratic Party
Headquarters] 1864.
8 p. 20 cm.

7356 McClure, Alexander Kelly, 1828-1909.
... Col. McClure tells of Lincoln's journey:
veteran relates true story of famous midnight trip
taken by President from Harrisburg to Washington.
Reprinted from Philadelphia press, Jan. 19, 1908.
[n.p., 1908?]
[4] p. folder. 20 cm.

7357 McClure, Alexander Kelly, 1828-1909.
Lincoln as a politician. Putnam, Conn.,
Privately printed for G. A. Tracy, 1916.
21 p. 23 cm.

7358 McClure, Alexander Kelly, 1828-1909.
To the Pacific and Mexico, by A. K. McClure...
Philadelphia & London, J. B. Lippincott company,
1901.
162 p. front., (port.), 5 pl., map. 20 cm.

7359 McConnell, H   H
Five years a cavalryman; or Sketches of regular
army on the Texas frontier, twenty odd years ago.
By H. H. McConnell... Jacksboro, Tex., I. N.
Rogers & co., printers, 1889.
viii p., 1 l., [11]-319 p. 20 cm.

7360 Macdonald, Duncan George Forbes, 1823?-1884.
British Columbia and Vancouver's Island, com-

prising a description of these dependencies, their physical character, climate, capabilities, population, trade, natural history, geology, ethnology, gold-fields, and future prospects: also an account of the manners and customs of the native Indians. 2d. ed. London, Longman, Green, Longman, Roberts & Green, 1862.
   xiii, 524 p. fold. map. 22 cm.

7361 McDougall, William.
   Red River insurrection. Hon. Wm. McDougall's conduct reviewed. Montreal, Printed by John Lovell, 1870.
   69 p. 22 cm.

7362 McElroy, Clarence L   , 1903-
   Seventeen days in the Mexican jungle, by Clarence L. McElroy ... Greenfield, Ind., The Mitchell company, 1933.
   172 p. plates, ports., map. 19 cm.

7363 Macfie, Matthew.
   Vancouver Island and British Columbia, their history, resources, and prospects. London, Longman, Green, Longman, Roberts & Green, 1865.
   574 p. illus., fold. maps. 22 cm.

7364 McGary, Elizabeth Visére.
   An American girl in Mexico, by Elizabeth Visére McGary... New York, Dodd, Mead & company, 1904.
   3 p.l., 159 p. front., 14 pl., facsim. 19 1/2 cm.

7365 MacGowan, Robert.
   The significance of Stephen Collins Foster. Indianapolis, Privately printed, 1932.
   25 p. 20 cm.

7366 McGowen, M
   [Letter to Thomas Robertson, Esq.] [n.p.] 1864.
   [4] p. 23 cm.

7367 M'Gregor, John, 1797-1857.
   British America. By John M'Gregor, esq. ...
   Edinburgh, William Blackwood; and London, T. Cadell,

1832.
2 v. maps (part fold., incl. fronts.) 23 cm.

7368 MacGregor, John, 1797-1857.
The progress of America, from the discovery by
Columbus to the year 1846... London, Whittaker and
co., 1847.
2 v. 24 1/2 cm.

7369 McGuire, J   A
In the Alaska-Yukon game-lands, by J. A. McGuire;
introduction by William T. Hornaday (photographs by
the author) Cincinnati, S. Kidd company [1921]
215 p. plates, ports., map. 21 cm.

7370 McHatton-Ripley, Elizabeth.
From flag to flag. A woman's adventures and
experiences in the South during the war in Mexico,
and in Cuba. New York, D. Appleton and company,
1889.
296 p. 12 cm.

7371 M'Ilvaine, William, jr.
Sketches of scenery and notes of personal adventure
in California and Mexico. Containing sixteen
lithographic plates. By William M'Ilvaine, jr.
Philadelphia [Smith & Peters, printers] 1850.
44 p. 16 pl. (incl. front.) 25 1/2 cm.

7372 Mackay, Charles, 1814-1889.
Life and liberty in America: or, Sketches of a
tour in the United States and Canada in 1857-8.
By Charles Mackay... with ten illustrations. New-
York, Harper & brothers, 1859.
1 p.l., [v]-viii, [9]-413 p. incl. plates. front.
20 cm.

7373 Mackay, Charles, 1814-1889.
Life and liberty in America; or, Sketches of a
tour in the United States and Canada, in 1857-8.
By Charles Mackay ... 2d ed. London, Smith, Elder
and co. [1859]
2 v. in 1. front., pl. 20 cm.

7374   Mackenzie, George Norbury, 1851-1919, ed.
        Colonial families of the United States of America,
     in which is given the history, genealogy and
     armorial bearings of colonial families who settled
     in the American colonies from the time of the
     settlement of Jamestown, 13th May, 1607, to the
     battle of Lexington, 19th April, 1775; edited by
     George Norbury Mackenzie ... New York, Boston,
     The Grafton press, 1907-
               v. illus. (coat of arms)   25 1/2 cm.
        Vols. II-VII have imprint: Baltimore, Md.,
     The Seaforth press.
        "List of 'The Ark' and 'The Dove' passengers":
     v.5, p. 593-606.
        "List of 'Mayflower' passengers," and "Compact
     signed in the cabin of the 'Mayflower'": v.5,
     p. 607-614.
        Vols. VII-   edited by Nelson Osgood Rhoades.

7375   McKinley, William, pres. U. S., 1843-1901.
        Abraham Lincoln: an address... before the
     Marquette club, Chicago, February 12, 1896...
     [Chicago? 1896]
        27 p.   20 cm.

7376   Mackoy, Harry Brent.
        Simon Kenton as soldier, scout, and citizen...
     An address delivered Wednesday, August 19, 1936,
     at the Blue Licks Battlefield State Park, Robertson
     County, Kentucky, on the occasion of the 154th anni-
     versary of the Battle of the Blue Licks and commemora-
     tion of the centenary of the death of General Simon
     Kenton. Lexington, Ky., 1930.
        30 p.   22 1/2 cm.

7377   McLaughlin, Joseph R
        The jury trial of 1900 in the court of public
     opinion; Bryan vs. McKinley, Judge Samuel Levelhead,
     on the bench. The people's cause presented in crisp,
     sparkling argument by the leading men of the day.
     Chicago, Laird & Lee [1900]
        294 p.   illus.   19 cm.

7378   McLean, Archibald.
        Alexander Campbell as a preacher... New York

[etc.] Fleming H. Revell Company [c 1908]
46 p. front. (port.) 18 cm.

7379 McLeod, Robert Randall.
Markland or Nova Scotia; its history, natural
resources and native beauties, by Robert R.
McLeod. [Berwick, N. S.] Markland publishing
company, 1903.
603 p. incl. map, diagrs. front., plates, ports.
25 1/2 cm.

7380 McMurtrie, Douglas Crawford, 1888-1944.
The early career of Joseph Charless, the first
printer in Missouri. Colombia, Mo., Privately
printed, 1932.
14 p. 23 cm.

7381 McMurtry, Robert Gerald, 1906-
Confederate General Ben Hardin Helm, Kentucky
brother-in-law of Abraham Lincoln; a condensation
of the original study; address at annual meeting,
Lincoln Fellowship of Wisconsin, Madison, Feb. 12,
1958. [Madison, 1959]
18 p. ports.

7382 [McMurtry, Robert Gerald] 1906-
Let's talk of Lincoln, of his life, of his
career, of his deeds, of his immortality. Harrogate, Tenn., Department of Lincolniana, Lincoln
memorial university, 1939.
2 p.l., 41 p. illus. 19 cm.

7383 McMurtry, Robert Gerald, 1906-
Lincoln's friend, Douglas: a Lincoln day address.
[St. Louis, Principia Corporation, c1946]
19 p. 20 cm.

7384 Macoun, John, 1831-1920.
Manitoba and the great North-west; the field
for investment; the home of the emigrant, being
a full and complete history of the country... by
John Macoun... to which has been added the educational & religious history of Manitoba & the
North-west, by George M. Grant... also Montana
and the Bow River district compared for grazing

purposes, by Alexander Begg... also sketch of the
rise and progress of Winnipeg, by J. C. McLagan...
to which has been added an appendix of statistics
of the Dominion of Canada... Guelph, Ont., The
World publishing company, 1882.
   3 p.l., [v]-xxii, [17]-687 p.   front., illus.,
plates, fold. maps, fold. plan, col. diagr.
24 1/2 cm.

7385   McReady, John Dudley.
      The collected works of James Lane Allen.   [New
York, 1922]
      49 p., [1] l.   28 cm.

7386   McSherry, Richard, 1817-1885.
      El puchero; or, A mixed dish from Mexico, em-
bracing General Scott's campaign, with sketches of
military life, in field and camp, of the character
of the country, manners and ways of the people,
etc. By Richard M'Sherry... Philadelphia, Lippincott, Grambo & co., 1850.
      2 p.l., xi, [13]-247 p.   front., plates, fold.
plan.   19 1/2 cm.

7387   Madariaga, Salvador de, 1886-
      ... Hernan Cortés.   Buenos Aires, Editorial
sudamericana [1943]
      3 p.l., [9]-739 p., 1 l. port., 2 maps (1 fold)
22 cm.

7388   Madeleine, pseud.
      Tage in Mexico.   [Berlin] 1925.
      80 p. illus.   20 cm.

7389   Madison, Dorothy (Payne) Todd, 1768-1849.
      Memoirs and letters of Dolly Madison, wife of
James Madison... ed. by her grand-niece [Lucia B.
Cutts] Boston and New York, Houghton, Mifflin and
company, 1886.
      1 p.l., 210 p.   18 cm.

7390   Magie, James K   , b. 1827.
      ... Historical, political and educational lecture
on Lincoln before he was president, by Major James
K. Magie... [Washington, 1892]

[4] p.   illus. (ports.)   28 cm.

7391   Magruder, Henry R
         Sketches of the last year of the Mexican empire,
       by Henry R. Magruder...   Illustrated with ten
       woodcuts by the author. 1st ed. [Wiesbaden,
       Printed by C. Ritter, 1868?]
         viii, 135 p. incl. illus., plates.   21 cm.

7392   Mair, Charles, 1838-
         Through the Mackenzie Basin; a narrative of the
       Athabasca and Peace River Treaty Expedition of 1899.
       With a map of the country ceded and numerous photo-
       graphs of native life and scenery.   Toronto, W.
       Briggs, 1908.
         149 p. illus.   25 cm.

7393   Majó Framis, Ricardo.
         Vidas de los navegantes, conquistadores y
       colonizadores españoles de los siglos XVI, XVII y
       XVIII.   Madrid, Aguilar, 1962.
         2 v. illus.   19 cm.

7394   Malespine, A
         Les États-Unis en 1865; d'après les documents
       officiels communiqués au Congrès, par A. Malespine.
       Paris, E. Dentu, 1865.
         48 p.   24 cm.

7395   Malouet, Pierre-Victor, baron, 1740-1814.
         Examen de cette question: Quel sera pour les
       colonies de l'Amérique le résultat de la révolution
       françoise, de la guerre qui en est la suite, & de
       la paix qui doit la terminer?...   [Londres] Imp.
       de Baylis, 1797.
         29 p.   21 cm.

7396   Malte-Brun, Conrad, originally Malthe Conrad Bruun,
       1775-1826.
         Les États-Unis et le Mexique; histoire et géographie
       par Malte-Brun; illustrations de Gustave Doré; cinq
       cartes géographiques coloriées, dressées par A.-H.
       Dufour...   Paris, G. Barba [1862]
         cover-title, 72 p. illus., 5 maps.   29 1/2 cm.

7397 Malvar y Pintos, Sebastián.
El juez de ciencia, de conciencia, y de
desinteres. Oracion funebre en las exequias, que
la grande Universidad de Salamanca celebró en su
real capilla de San Geronymo el 16, de junio de
1770. honrando la piadosa memoria de su ilustre
hijo el señor d. Martin Davila... Dixola el illmo.
y rmo. sr. d. fr. Sebastian Malvar, y Pintos...
Reimpresa a expensas del sr. d. Joaquin Norberto
Davila y Cotes, marques de Zafra, hijo primogenito
de dicho señor. Valladolid, En la oficina de la
viuda de d. Tomas de Santandér, 1784.
55 p. 22 cm.

7398 Mamamtavrishvili, D   G
В гостях у мексиканских хирургов. Тбилиси, Сабчота
Сакартвело, 1960.
82 p. illus. 21 cm.

7399 Mañas, Uldarica.
... Tres conferencias, leídas en el Lyceum, la
Habana ... [Habana, Imp. El Siglo xx, A. Muñiz y
hno., 1936]
3 p.l., 5-37 p. 24 cm.

7400 Mancisidor, José, 1894-   , ed.
Angulos de México, selección, prólogo y notas de
José Mancisidor. México, Secretaría de Educación
Pública, 1946.
93 p. 20 cm.

7401 Mangino, Fernando Joseph, d. 1806.
Proyecto para el establecimiento en Mexico de
una Academia de las tres nobles artes. [n.p.,
1781]
[12] p. 19 cm.

7402 Marble, Manton, 1834-1917.
Letter to Abraham Lincoln. By Manton Marble,
editor of "The World"... New York, Priv. print.,
1867
25 p. 25 cm.

7403 Margati, José, 1841-1887.
A trip to the city of Mexico. By José Margati

...   Boston, Putnam, Messervy & co., 1885.
88 p.   fold. map.   18 cm.

7404   Margry, Pierre, 1818-1894, ed.
Découvertes et établissements des français dans
l'ouest et dans le sud de l'Amérique Septentrionale
(1614-1754) Mémoires et documents originaux
recueillis et pub. par P. Margry... [Paris, Impr.
D. Jouaust, 1876-86]
6 v.   fronts. (v. 1, 4, 5: ports.)   25 1/2 cm.

7405   Marín de Alfocea, Juan.
Alegacion de los protectores y administradores
de los bienes, acciones y derechos, de las pias
memorias que fundó el arcediano de México don
Joseph de Torres, como fideicomisario de don Juan
Caballero, para el pleyto que se sigue en el
consejo con el marques de Rivascacho, y el bachiller
don Manuel de Flores, sobre cumplimiento de la
executoria librada á consequencia de lo determinado
por el consejo declarando haber habido lugar al
recurso de injusticia notoria que se introduxo
por el administrador de la obra pia, mandándole
adjudicar á ésta 45 sitios para ganados con el
servicio de 6 ₣ 500 pesos. Pretende la obra pia
que se desprecien los recursos, y se castiguen los
artificios con que dicho Flores ha entorpecido
el cumplimiento des despacho executorio del consejo,
y que se le mande devolver para que lo tenga en
todas sus partes con la posesion de los sitios,
y el entero en caxas que se decretó con arreglo á
la ordenanza: con imposicion de las costas causadas
desde la oposicion de Flores y devolucion de la
cantidad depositada. Madrid, En la oficina de
don Benito Cano, Año de MDCCXCVII.
1 p.l., 25 numb. l.   27 cm.

7406   Marín de Alfocea, Juan.
Memorial ajustado hecho con citacion de las
partes en virtud de decreto del consejo de 25 de
agosto de 1792, del recurso de injusticia notoria
introducido por don Joseph Sanchez Espinosa, administrador de la Pia memoria que fundó el arcediano
de la catedral de México don Joseph de Torres y
Vergara, fideicomisario de don Juan Caballero, de

sentencias de vista y revista de la Real audiencia
de Guadalaxara, en autos seguidos con el marques
de Rivascacho: sobre la adjudicacion en virtud de
denuncias de 45 sitios de tierras realengas, y
de la nueva instancia que á conseqüencia de la
declaracion hecha por el consejo en el citado recurso
y despacho librado en su virtud, ha introducido d.
Joseph Manuel de Flores, presbitero, del obispado de
Guadalaxara, poseedor de los expresados sitios, en
virtud de compra hecha al marques antes de intro-
ducirse en el consejo el recurso de injusticia
notoria, sobre que se le ha mandado oir. Madrid,
Por la viuda de don Joaquin Ibarra, 1795.
1 p.l., 75 numb. l. 27 cm.

7407 Mariscal, Ignacio, 1829-1910.
Bravo en 1812; artículo escrito para el album
conmemorativo de Don Nicolás Bravo; con algunos
otros conceptos sobre el asunto leidos en la
Academia Mexicana correspondiente con la Española.
México, Oficina Tip. de la Secretaría de Fomento,
1886.
25 p. 24 cm.

7408 Markens, Edward Wasgate.
Lincoln and his relations to doctors. Reprint
from the Journal of the Medical society of New
Jersey, 1922. [n.p., 1922?]
11 p. 20 cm.

7409 Markens, Isaac.
Abraham Lincoln and the Jews. New York, Printed
for the author, c1909.
60 p. 22 cm.

7410 Markens, Isaac.
President Lincoln and the case of John Y. Beall.
New York, Printed for the author, 1911.
11 p. port. 25 cm.

7411 Markham, Sir Clements Robert, 1830-1916.
Zwei reisen in Peru. Von Clements R. Markham.
Leipzig, G. Senf, 1865.
viii, [9]-316 p. 19 1/2 cm.

7412   Markham, Edwin, 1852-
       Edwin Markham's The man with the hoe; (D'r mon
mit d'r hock); Lincoln, the man of the people
(D'r Lincoln, de leit era mon) and other poems,
translated into the Pennsylvania-German dialect
by A. Monroe Aurand, jr. Harrisburg, Pa., Priv.
print., the Aurand press, 1934.
       25, [1] p., 1 l. incl. front. (2 port.)   23 cm.

7413   Marmier, Xavier, 1809-1892.
       Les États-Unis et le Canada. Tours, A. Mame,
1877.
       238 p. plates.   26 cm.

7414   Marquez, Pedro [José] 1741-1820.
       Due antichi monumenti di architettura messicana,
illustrati da D. Pietro Marquez ... Roma, Presso
il Salomoni, 1804.
       1 p.l., iv, 47 p. iv fold. pl.   22 1/2 cm.

7415   Marraro, Howard Rosario, 1897-
       Lincoln's Italian volunteers from New York.
Reprinted from New York history, January, 1943.
[n.p., 1943]
       30 p. illus.   20 cm.

7416   Marsh, Edward Sprague, 1857-
       Stephen A. Douglas: a memorial; a description of
the dedication of the monument erected to his memory
at Brandon, Vermont... Brandon, Vt., Privately
printed, 1914.
       121 p. illus.   25 cm.

7417   Marshall, Logan.
       The story of the Panama Canal; the wonderful
account of the gigantic undertaking commenced by the
French, and brought to triumphant completion by the
United States; with a history of Panama from the
days of Balboa to the present time. [n.p., 1913]
       286 p. illus. (part col.), maps.   23 cm.
       Chapters 1-8 and the greater portion of Appendices
taken from "Panama, the isthmus and the canal, by
Forbes Lindsay", pub. in 1912.

7418   Martín, Enrico, d. 1632.

Reportorio de los tiempos, y historia natvral
desta Nveva España. Compuesto por Henrico Martinez
... [tomo 1.] En México, En la emprenta del mismo
autor, 1606.
12 p.l., 277 (i.e. 371), [1] p. illus.
19 1/2 cm.

7419 Martín, Enrico, d. 1632.
Repertorio de los tiempos e historia natural de
Nueva España. Introd. de Francisco de la Maza.
Apéndice bibliográfico de Francisco González de
Cossío. México, Secretaría de Educación Pública,
1948.
xlvii, 317 p. facsims. 24 cm.

7420 Martin, Franklin.
Major General William Crawford Gorgas, N. C.,
U.S.A. ... Chicago, Gorgas Memorial Institute
[n.d.]
76 p. front. (port.) 19 cm.

7421 Martin, Percy Falcke, 1861-
Mexico of the twentieth century, by Percy F.
Martin ... London, E. Arnold, 1907.
2 v. fronts., plates, ports., 2 fold. maps.
22 cm.

7422 Martin, Percy Falcke, 1861-
Mexico's treasure-house (Guanajuato) an illustrated
and descriptive account of the mines and their
operations in 1906, by Percy F. Martin ... 44
pages illustrations, 6 panoramic views, 2 maps and
diagrams. New York, The Cheltenham press, 1906.
4 p.l., 7-259, ix p. fold. front., plates (part
fold.), ports., fold. maps. diagrs. 25 1/2 cm.

7423 Martin, Robert Montgomery.
The Hudson's Bay territories and Vancouver's
island, with an exposition of the chartered rights,
conduct and policy... London, T. & W. Boone, 1849.
175 p. fold. map. 20 cm.

7424 Martineau, Harriet, 1802-1876.
Retrospect of western travel. By Harriet Martineau
... London, Saunders and Otley; New York, Sold by

Harper & brothers, 1838.
2 v.   21 cm.

7425   Martineau, Harriet, 1802-1876.
Society in America. By Harriet Martineau...
2d. ed. London, Saunders and Otley, 1837.
3 v.   19 1/2 cm.

7426   Martínez de Diego, Cayetano.
Formulario instructivo para que los administradores generales del real estanco ordenen, y metodizen
los libros en que deben llevar la cuenta de la
entrada, y salida de las especies de sus consumos,
y caudales; como la que han de seguir, y ajustar
á los particulares de su comprehension, y las
tercenas, y estanquillos de las ciudades. Que
dá don Cayetano Martinez de Diego, contador general
de la intervencion, y administracion de la real
renta del tabaco de estos reynos del Perú, y
Chile, y secretario de la real junta por S. M.
en virtud de la ordenanza 15. de su título.
Lima En la oficina que está en la Casa de los
niños huerfanos, 1770.
[33] p.   22 cm.

7427   Martínez de la Parra, Juan, 1655-1701.
Luz de verdades católicas, y explicacion de la
doctrina christiana, que siguiendo la costumbre
de la casa professa de la Compañia de Jesus de
Mexico, todos los jueves del año ha explicado en
su iglesia el p. Juan Martinez de la Parra...
Contiene tres tratados... Dedicada al glorioso
apostol de las Indias San Francisco Xavier en esta
vltima impression corregida, y emmendada; y con
coordinación de los tres indices de los tratados
a un indice general, que hasta ahora no havia
salido... Sevilla, En la imprenta castellana, y
latina de la viuda de Francisco Lorenzo de Hermosilla
en calle de Vizcainos, 1729.
5 p.l., 450 p.   30 cm.

7428   Marvin, Donald Mitchell, 1893-
Canada and the twentieth century, by Donald M.
Marvin... and J. Edwin van Buskirk... Montreal
[Mercury press limited] 1926.

143, [1] p.   incl. front., illus., tables.
28 cm.

7429   Mason, Augustus, Lynch.
Joseph Brant and the Mohawks... [Fort Wayne,
Ind., Public Library of Fort Wayne and Allen
County, n.d.]
63 p.   illus., map.   21 cm.

7430   Mason, R   H
Pictures of life in Mexico.   By R. H. Mason.
With etchings by the author...   London, Smith,
Elder and co., 1852.
2 v.   fronts., plates.   19 cm.

7431   Mason, Robert C
George Mason of Virginia, citizen, statesman,
philosopher... An address commemorative of the
launching of the S. S. "Gunston Hall" at Alexandria
Virginia, January, 1917.   New York, Oscar Aurelius
Morgner, 1919.
56 p.   front. (port.), illus. facsim.   20 1/2 cm.

7432   Masseras, E
L'exemple de l'Amérique: Washington et son
oeuvre... Paris, E. Plon, Nourrit et c^{ie}, 1889.
xii, 302 p., 1 l.   18 1/2 cm.

7433   Massey, George Valentine, 1903–
Boyce and allied families, compiled for Willard
David Boyce.   Dover, Del., 1945.
v.   plates, ports., coat of arms, facsims.
28 cm.

7434   Massey, George Valentine, 1903–
Excerpts from the de Rapelje, Remsen (van der
Beeck) Swain, Clark, Clayton, Morgan, Boyce, Naudain,
Steel and Stockton genealogies. [n.p.] 1948.
77 l.   plates, ports., facsim.   29 cm.

7435   Massey, George Valentine, 1903–
James Cannon of Nanticoke and descendants, including the allied families of Cordry, Adams, Hooper,
Obier and Ward.   Compiled for Arthur R. Cannon.
[n.p.] 1948.

217 l. plates, facsims. 28 cm.

7436 Masústegui, Pedro.
Arte de construccion: por el m.r^{do}. p.mro.
fray Pedro Masustegui... Con licencia, Sevilla,
En la imprenta de Manuel Nicolás Vazquez, y
compañia, en calle Genova, 1777.
124 p. 23 cm.

7437 Matthews, John, of London, ed.
... Matthews' American armoury and blue book.
Ed. and pub. by John Matthews... London, J.
Matthews [1901]
vii, [1], 416, xvi p. illus. 25 1/2 cm.

7438 [Maude, John]
Visit to the falls of Niagara in 1800. London,
Longman, Rees, Orme, Brown & Green, 1826.
viii p., 1 l., v, 313, xxvi p. plates. 24 cm.

7439 Maudslay, Anne Cary (Morris)
A glimpse at Guatemala, and some notes on the
ancient monuments of Central America, by Anne
Cary Maudslay and Alfred Percival Maudslay. London, J. Murray, 1899.
xvii, 289 p., illus., fold. maps

7440 Maya, Augustin.
México moderno. Fotografías de: Augustin Maya,
Rodrigo Moya y Ursula Bernath. Mexico, Editorial
Grijalbo, 1967.
1 v. (unpaged) 18 cm.

7441 Maya, Augustin.
México prehispánico y colonial. Fotografías
de: Augustin Maya, Rodrigo Moya y Ursula Bernath.
Mexico, Editorial Grijalbo, 1967.
1 v. (unpaged) 18 cm.

7442 Maya, Augustin.
Puebla. Fotografías de: Agustin Maya, Rodrigo
Moya y Ursula Bernath. Mexico, Editorial Grijalbo,
1967.
1 v. (unpaged) 18 cm.

7443 Mayer, Brantz, 1809-1879.
Mexico as it was and as it is: by Brantz Mayer
... With numerous illustrations on wood, engraved
by Butler from drawings by the author... New-York,
J. Winchester; [etc., etc.] 1844.
3 p.l., [v]-xii, 390 p. front., illus., plates,
plan, facsim. 23 1/2 cm.

7444 Mayer, Brantz, 1809-1879.
Mexico, Aztec, Spanish and republican: a historical, geographical, political, statistical and
social account of that country from the period of
the invasion by the Spaniards to the present time;
with a view of the ancient Aztec empire and civilization; a historical sketch of the late war; and
notices of New Mexico and California, by Brantz
Mayer... Hartford, S. Drake and company, 1852.
2 v. front. (port.), illus., pl., map, facism.
24 cm.

7445 Maynard, Mrs. Henrietta Sturdevant (Colburn) 1841-
1892.
Reminiscences of the war of the rebellion. Did
Abraham Lincoln receive aid from the spirit world?
Some extracts from "Was Abraham Lincoln a spiritualist?" [Relay, Md., W. H. Plummer, c1912]
4 p. 23 cm.

7446 Maynard, Mrs. Henrietta Sturdevant (Colburn) 1841-
1892.
Was Abraham Lincoln a spiritualist? or, Curious
revelations from the life of a trance medium, by
Mrs. Nettie Colburn Maynard... Philadelphia, R.
C. Hartranft, 1891.
xxiv, 255 p. illus. 19 cm.

7447 Maynard, Horace, 1814-1882.
How, by whom, and for what was the war begun?
Speech of Hon. Horace Maynard, of Tennessee, in
the city of Nashville, March 20, 1862. [n.p.]
1862.
24 p. 20 cm.

7448 Mayo, Amory Dwight, 1823-1907.
The nation's sacrifice. Abraham Lincoln. Two

discourses, delivered... April 16, and April 19, 1865, in the Church of the Redeemer, Cincinnati, Ohio... Cincinnati, R. Clarke & co., 1865.
    28 p.   22 cm.

7449   Medrano, Pedro de, 1649-1725.
    Gazophylacium divinae dilectionis. Petra pretiosior coeli, soli, et sali. Scilicet, sanctus Petrus princeps apostolorum apposite, ac dilucide elucidatus, ad eximium exemplum boni pastoris Christi domini... ex Sacra Scriptura, concilijs sacris, & sanctis patribus: vbi plura ad conciones conspicua continentur. Cum indice tripartito. Authore r.p. Petro de Medrano... [Matriti?] Ex typographia Francisci del Hierro, 1720.
    16 p.l., 328 p., 16 l.   24 cm.

7450   Meese, William Augustus, 1856.
    Abraham Lincoln: incidents in his life relating to waterways. [Moline, Ill., Desaulniers & co., 1908]
    53 p. illus.   23 cm.

7451   [Mejía Deras, Ismael]
    Policarpo Bonilla; algunos apuntes biográficas, por Aro Sanso [pseud.] Un estudio del dr. Ricardo D. Alduvín y esquema para una biografía, por Rafael Heliodoro Valle. México, Imprenta mundial, 1936.
    xlv, 558 p., 1 l. ports.   23 1/2 cm.

7452   Mejia, José Victor.
    Geografía de la República de Guatemala. 2. ed. Guatemala, Centro-America [Tipografía nacional] 1927.
    399, iv p.

7453   Meléndez, Juan.
    Señor. El maestro fray Ivan Melendez, del Orden de predicadores, difinidor, y procurador general en ambas curias de su prouincia de s. Iuan Baptista del Perù, de la misma orden, y especialmente diputad para las causas de beatificacion, y canonizacion del venerable siervo de Dios maestro fray Vicente Vernedo, religioso de dicha su religion, dize ...

[n.p., 1680?]
[4] p.   21 cm.

7454 Melish, John, 1771-1822.
A description of the British possessions in North
America, and of the most important places along the
lines in the United States: intended as an ac-
companiment to Melish's Map of the seat of war in
North America. 3. ed. enl. & improved; and illustrated by a map of the country between Lakes Erie
and Ontario. Philadelphia, Printed by T. and G.
Palmer, 1813.
26 p.   col. fold. map.   23 1/2 cm.

7455 Memoirs of Allegheny county, Pennsylvania; personal
and genealogical... Madison, Wis., Northwestern
historical association, 1904.
2 v.   illus. (ports.)   26 1/2 cm.

7456 ... Memorial ajustado, hecho de orden del real, y
supremo Consejo de Indias, con citacion, y
asistencia de las partes: en el pleyto seguido
en él por d. Geronymo Maria de Motezuma Oca,
Nieto de Silva, Sarmiento, y Zuñiga, conde de
Motezuma, de Tultengo, vizconde de Ilucan, señor de
Tula, num.26. Con don Ventura Osorio de Moscosoo
Sarmiento de Valladares, marqués de Astorga, conde
de Altamira, y Santa Marta, duque, y señor de
Artrisco, num. 25. Sobre la pertenencia en pro-
priedad de una merced de 4℣ pesos de renta
annual perpetua, concedida por real decreto de 31.
de enero del año pasado de 1699. y asismismo de
otras anteriores encomiendas vitalicias, que
componen, la cantidad de 8℣ 250. ducados de plata,
perpetuadas, por real resolucion de S.M. de 25. de
agosto de 1705. [Madrid? 1770]
181 p.   fold. geneal. tab.   27 cm.

7457 Memorial of the people of Red River to the British
and Canadian governments, with remarks on the
colonization of Central British North America, and
the establishment of a great territorial road
from Canada to British Columbia. Submitted to the
Canadian government, by Sandford Fleming. Printed
by order of the Legislative assembly. Quebec,

273

Printed for the contractors by Hujter, Rose & co.,
1868.
57 p.   22 cm.

7458   Memorials of the life and character of Stephen
T. Logan... Springfield, Ill., H. W. Rokker, 1882.
87 p. front.   21 cm.

7459   Mendoza, Juan de, fl. 1656-1686.
Relacion de el santvario de Texaxique, en que
está colacada la milagrosa imagen de Nuestra
señora de los Angeles. Noticia de los milagros
qve el Señor ha obrado en gloria de esta santa
imagen. Devocion grande con que se frequenta esta
santuario. Qve por mandado de n.r^{mo}.p.f. Juan de
Luzuriaga... Escrive el p.fr. Iuan de Mendoza...
y qve dedica at b.^{r}d. Antonio de Samano y Ledezma
... con licencia en Mexico, Por Juan de Ribera
impressor, y mercader de libros, 1684.
8 p.l., 18 numb. l.   21 cm.

7460   Menzies, Archibald, 1754-1842.
... Menzies' journal of Vancouver's voyage,
April to October, 1792. Edited, with botanical
and ethnological notes, by C. F. Newcombe, M.D.,
and a biographical note by J. Forsyth... Victoria,
B.C., Printed by William H. Cullin, 1923.
xx, 171 p. illus., facsims.   23 cm.

7461   Mera, Francisco de.
Por el Colegio real de San Fernando, qve en la
civdad de Quito del reyno del Perù fundò la religion
de predicadores. En el pleyto qve en el Consejo
real de las Indias sigue con el Colegio seminario
de San Luis, de la misma ciudad, cuya administracion
està à cargo de los padres de la Compañia de Jesus.
Sobre la preferencia en todas las concurrencias
publicas, y actos literarios. [n.p., 1709?]
10 numb. l.   20 cm.

7462   Mercier, Honoré.
Discours prononcé... à l'Assemblée legislative de
Québec le 7 mai 1886 sur la question Riel. Québec,
Imprimerie de l'Electeur, 1886.
58 p.   20 cm.

7463   Mercurio peruano [de historia, literatura, y
        noticias públicas] Lima, 1791-95.
        12 v. illus. 21 cm.

7464   Mercurio peruano; revista mensual de ciencias
        sociales y letras... Lima, Sanmartí y cia.,
        impresores, 1918-1931.
        20 v. illus. plates (part col.) ports., maps,
        facsims. 24 cm.

7465   Mérida, Mexico.
        Periódico constitucional del gobierno de Mérida.
        Mérida, 1821.
        1 v. 25 cm.

7466   Merrick, Richard Thomas, 1826-1885.
        The Emancipation proclamation: state rights
        national convention: speech of Richard T. Merrick,
        before the Young men's Democratic Invincible Club,
        Chicago, Dec. 11, 1862. [n.p.] 1862.
        16 p. 20 cm.

7467   Merwin, Samuel, 1874-1936.
        The road to Frontenac, by Samuel Merwin. New
        York, Doubleday, Page & co., 1901.
        vi p., 1 1., 404 p. front., 3 pl. 20 1/2 cm.

7468   Mesas Redondas sobre Problemas de las Zonas Aridas
        de México, Mexico, 1955.
        Mesas Redondas sobre Problemas de las Zonas
        Aridas de México, Biblioteca Central de la Ciudad
        Universitaria, 24 a 28 de enero de 1955. México,
        Ediciones del Instituto Mexicano de Recursos
        Naturales Renovables, 1955.
        vi, 262 p. 2 fold. col. maps, col. diagr.
        23 cm.

7469   Mesas Redondas sobre Problemas del Trópico Mexicano,
        Mexico, 1955.
        Mesas Redondas sobre Problemas del Trópico
        Mexicano, Anfiteatro "Bolívar" de la Escuela
        Nacional Preparatoria, 10 al 14 de octubre de 1955.
        México, Ediciones del Instituto Mexicano de Re-
        cursos Naturales Renovables, 1955.
        vi, 322 p. fold. map, tables. 23 cm.

7470   Meserve, Frederick Hill, 1865-   , comp.
        Lincolniana and historical photographs. New
        York, Privately printed, 1917.
        28 p.   20 cm.

7471   Meserve, Frederick Hill, 1865-
        This is Abraham Lincoln; with an introd. by
        Carl Sandburg. Harrogate, Tenn., Lincoln Memorial
        university, 1941.
        19 p.   20 cm.

7472   Mexican Isthmus Land Co., Inc., Kansas City, Mo.
        A picture journey through tropical Mexico.
        Kansas City, Mo. [1912]
        unpaged.   20 cm.

7473   Mexican journeys (firm, travel agency, Austin, Tex.)
        Mexican Journeys. [Austin, Tex., Mexican Journeys
        c1940]
        cover-title, 28 p.   illus.   26 1/2 cm.

7474   Mexican National Railroad.
        Tropical tours to Toltec towns in Mexico ...
        [New York] Mexican National Railroad, 1893.
        60, [3] p.   incl. front., illus. (part col.)
        17 cm.

7475   Mexican National Railroad.
        Tropical tours to Toltec towns in Mexico; pre-
        sented with compliments of the Mexican National R.R.
        (Laredo route) ...   [Chicago, Rogers & Smith co.,
        c1898]
        78 p., 1 l.   incl. front., illus., map.   17 cm.

7476   Mexican Revolution Party.
        ... The second six year plan 1941-1946. Text
        approved in the National assembly held in the city
        of Mexico on the 1st., 2nd. and 3rd. days of No-
        vember 1939 and several documental speeches, de-
        livered by General Manuel Avila Camacho ...   [n.p.,
        n.d.]
        144 p.   19 cm.

7477   Mexican typical view album. New York, The Albertype
        co., c1889.

1 p.l., 12 pl.   13 x 19 cm.

7478   Mexico (City)
Celebra la muy noble, y leal ciudad de Mexico,
con magestuoso aparato, singular regocijo, y pompa
festiva juramento de defender la immaculada concepcion de la Virgen Maria Nuestra Señora, el
tercero dia del novenario que se celebrò en el
Convento de el seraphico padre san Francisco,
el dia siete de octubre de 1653.   Con assistencia
del excmo. sr. d. Francisco Fernandez de la Cueva,
duque de Alburquerque...   Mexico, Por la viuda
de Bernardo Calderon, en la calle de San Augustin,
1733.
[4] p.   19 cm.

7479   Mexico (City)
Triumphal pompa, y festivo aparato en que bajo
la idea del dios Apolo, se sombrearon las heroycas
empressas de el exc^{mo}. señor d. Juan Francisco de
Guemes, y Horcasitas... virrey, governador, y capitan
general de esta Nueva-España... en el sumptuoso
arco, que para su publico ingresso erigio el
afectuoso esmero de la nobilissima, e imperial
corte mexicana.   Mexico, En la imprenta real del
superior govierno, y del nuevo rezado de doña Maria
de Rivera, en el Empedradillo, 1746.
24 p.   21 cm.

7480   Mexico.   Comisión de limites.
Diario de viage de la Comision de limites que
puso el gobierno de la Republica, bajo la direccion
del exmo.sr.general de division d. Manuel de
Mier y Teran.   Lo escribieron por su órden los
individuos de la misma Comision d. Luis Berlandier
y d. Rafael Chovel.   México, Tip. de J. R. Navarro,
1850.
298 p., 1 l.   port.   23 1/2 cm.

7481   Mexico.   Comisión nacional de caminos.
... Los caminos de México.   The roads of Mexico.
[Mexico] 1931.
140 p.   incl. front., illus. (incl. maps) ports.,
tables.   16 1/2 x 23 1/2 cm.

7482   Mexico. Congreso. Cámara de Diputados.
       ... Un continente, un pueblo, un hombre.
       Mexico, D.F., 1941.
         4 p.l., 13-146 p. illus. (incl. ports.)
       23 1/2 cm.

7483   Mexico. Departamento de Antropología.
         Introduction, synthesis and conclusions of the
       work The population of the Valley of Teotihuacan,
       by Manuel Gamio, director of anthropology. México,
       Tall. Gráf. de la Nación, 1929.
         xcviii p. illus., maps (part fold.), diagrs.
       29 cm.

7484   Mexico. Departamento de Antropología.
         Traduction of the introduction, synthesis and
       conclusions of the work The population of the Valley
       of Teotihuacán, by Manuel Gamio, director of anthro-
       pology. México, Tall. Gráf. de la Nación, 1922.
         [3], xcviii p. illus., maps (part fold.), diagrs.
       30 cm.

7485   Mexico. Departamento de Turismo.
         Así es México. Departamento de Turismo de la
       Secretaría de Gobernación [y] Asociación Mexicana
       de Turismo. [Texto de Eduardo de Ontañón] [Mexico,
       194]
         36 p. illus.   22 cm.

7486   Mexico. Dirección de antropología.
         ... La población del valle de Teotihuacán; re-
       presentativa de las que habitan las regiones rurales
       del distrito federal y de los estados de Hidalgo,
       Puebla, Mexico y Tlaxcala. [Mexico, Dirección de
       talleres gráficos, 1922]
         2 v. in 3. illus., plates (part col.), ports.,
       fold. maps, plans (part fold.), facsims., fold.
       tables, diagrs. (part fold.)   29 cm.

7487   Mexico. Dirección general de correos.
         Coleccion de itinerarios y leguarios formada
       por la Seccion de estadistica militar, que se
       manda imprimir de orden del supremo gobierno, para
       que rectificada por las autoridades y personas a
       quienes corresponde, pueda servir a los usos de la

Administracion general de correos de la republica.
Mexico, Impr. de Y. Cumplido, 1850.
2 p.l., 204 p.   22 1/2 cm.

7488   Mexico. Dirección General de Geografía y Meteorología.
Bibliografía geográfica de México. Recopilación
y ordenamiento de Angel Bassols Batalla, geógrafo.
México [1955]
652 p.   21 cm.

7489   Mexico. Estado mayor del ejército.
Colección de itinerarios para diferentes puntos
de la Republica Mexicana, formados por la Sección
de geográfia y estadística de la Plana mayor del
ejército, mandada imprimir por orden del supremo
gobierno de 14 de marzo de 1844. México, Impr. de J.
M. Lara, 1844.
28, 9 p.   31 cm.

7490   Mexico. Inspección y conservación de monumentos
arqueológicos de la República Mexicana.
Archaeological explorations in Escalerillas
street, city of Mexico, by Leopoldo Batres, general
inspector of archaeological monuments, year 1900.
Mexico, J. Aguilar Vera & co., printers, 1902.
cover-title, 58 p., 1 l.   illus., 2 col. pl.,
3 port., 2 fold. plans.   32 cm.

7491   Mexico. Inspección y conservación de monumentos
arqueológicos de la República Mexicana.
... Exploración arqueológica del oriente del
Valle de México, por Leopoldo Batres. Tlaloc?
Año de 1903. [México, Imprenta Gante, 1903]
19 p. illus., viii (i.e. 9) pl.   28 1/2 cm.

7492   México moderno. Revista mensual de letras y arte.
Mexico, 1920-23.
3 v.   24 cm.

7493   México; síntesis geográfica y económica. México,
1955.
106 p.   44 illus., ports.   21 cm.

7494   Le Mexique, au début du xxe siècle, par mm. le prince
Roland Bonaparte, Léon Bourgeois, Jules Claretie,

d'Estournelles de Constant, A. de Foville, Hippolyte
Gomot, O. Gréard, Albin Haller, Camille Krantz,
Michel Lagrave, Louis de Launay, Paul Leroy-
Beaulieu, E. Levasseur, le général Niox, Alfred
Picard, Élisée Reclus ...   Paris, C. Delagrave
[1904]
    2 v.   illus., plates, maps (part fold.)   30
1/2 cm.

7495 Mier, Gregorio.
    Por parte de d. Pedro de Villar y Zuviaur, del
Orden de Santiago, albasea tenedor de bienes, y
heredero de doña Juana Villaverde, su muger, quien
lo fuè de don Simon Ruydiaz, del mismo orden, se
ponen en consideracion de V.S. los fundamentos de
derecho, que hacen à su favor, para que se sirva
de concurrir con su dictamen, à que se confirme el
auto definitivo, prounciado por esta Real audiencia
en la causa que sigue Petronila Ruydiaz, hija
natural de don Simon, sobre la sexta parte, en que la
instituyò por heredera; por el que se declarò no have
lugar el mandamiento de mission en possession,
pedido por dicha hija natural. Y manda se lleven
los autos al contador entrepartes [!] para que
arreglado al computo de gananciales, que reza el
instrumento otorgado por d. Pedro à favor de doña
Juana en el pueblo de Late en 3. de mayo del año
de 755. proceda à formar la hijuela de division, y
particion, sacando las mandas, y legados, con preferencia à la sexta parte, en que es instituida la
hija natural, y que del resto que quedasse, le
deduzga la sexta parte. [Lima, 1758]
    [62] p.   24 cm.

7496 Mier Noriega y Guerra, José Servando Teresa de,
      1765-1827.
    ... Memorias de fray Servando Teresa de Mier, del
Convento de Santo Domingo, de México ... ... Prólogo
de don Alfonso Reyes. Madrid, Editorial-América
[1917?]
    xxii p., 1 l., 430 p.   23 cm.

7497 Miles, Thomas Jefferson.
    "To all whom it may concern"; the conspiracy of
leading men of the Republican party to destroy the

American union proved by their words and acts antecedent and subsequent to the rebellion. New York, J. Walter & co., 1864.
35 p.   22 cm.

7498   Military Order of the Loyal Legion of the United States.   Iowa Commandery.
... Songs compiled for use of the Commandery, State of Iowa. Des Moines, P. C. Kenyon, 1887.
127 p.   20 cm.

7499   Military Order of the Loyal Legion of the United States.   Massachusetts Commandery.
The invitation as issued for April 15th, 1927: You are invited to be present with ladies of your family at the installation of the Saint Gaudens bronze statue of Abraham Lincoln at the head-quarters of the Massachusetts Commandery, Cadet Armory Boston, at 3 o'clock on the afternoon of Friday, April 15, 1927. [Boston? 1927]
15 p.   20 cm.

7500   Military Order of the Loyal Legion of the United States.   Massachusetts Commandery.
... Register of the Commandery of the state of Massachusetts, November 1, 1912. Cambridge [Mass.] The University press, 1912.
xxxvi, 522 p.   26 cm.

7501   Military Order of the Loyal Legion of the United States.   Minnesota Commandery.
... Songs compiled for use of Minnesota Commandery. St. Paul, Pioneer press co., 1886.
74 p.   20 cm.

7502   Military Order of the Loyal Legion of the United States.   Missouri Commandery.
Songs compiled for use of Missouri Commandery. St. Louis, Woodward & Tiernan, 1887.
129 p.   20 cm.

7503   Military Order of the Loyal Legion of the United States.   New York Commandery.
Addresses delivered before the Commandery of the state of New York... February 3, 1909... in ob-

281

servance of... President Abraham Lincoln. [New York, 1909]
    31 p.   24 cm.

7504 Military Order of the Loyal Legion of the United States. Ohio Commandery.
    The commemoration of the Lincoln centenary by the Ohio Commandery of the Military Order of the Loyal Legion of the United States, at their headquarters February 12, 1909. Douglas A. Brown, official reporter. [Cincinnati, 1909]
    31 p.   22 1/2 cm.

7505 Military Order of the Loyal Legion of the United States. Pennsylvania Commandery.
    Ceremonies at the twenty-fifth anniversary. American Academy of Music, Philadelphia, April 15, 1890. Philadelphia, Privately printed, 1890.
    78 p.   20 cm.

7506 Miller, John, biographer.
    ... Memorias del general Miller, al servicio de la República del Perú. Escritas en inglés por Mr. John Miller, y tr. al castellano por el general Torrijos ... Madrid, Editorial-América [1918?]
    2 v.   22 1/2 cm.

7507 Millet, Thomas.
    Nouvel examen du rapport de M. Barnave sur l'affaire de Saint-Domingue, d'après celui qu'il a fait imprimer (project de constitution pour la partie française de Saint-Domingue [14 juin 1791]) Paris, De l'impr. de la rue d'Argenteuil [1799]
    109 p.   20 cm.

7508 [Milliken, James]
    A voyager's letters from Mexico. 1876. Printed for private circulation. Philadelphia, Press of J. B. Lippincott & co., 1876.
    36 p.   17 cm.

7509 Miner, James.
    Abraham Lincoln: personal reminiscences of the martyr-emancipator, as he appeared in the memorable campaign of 1854, and in his subsequent career...

read at the Lincoln Day celebration in the Winchester (Illinois) high school... February 12, 1912. [Winchester, Ill.? 1912?]
8 p.   20 cm.

7510   Minnesota. Legislature.
Northwest British America and its relations to the State of Minnesota, by James W. Taylor, St. Paul, Newson, Moore, Foster & company, Printers, 1860.
42 p.   23 cm.

7511   Mirabeau, Honoré-Gabriel de Riqueti, comte de, 1749-1791.
Discours... dans la séance de ce matin 11 juin [1790] sur la mort de Benjamin Franklin. [n.p., 1790]
3 p.   20 cm.

7512   Miranda Fonseca, Mariano.
Monografía de la República mexicana, por el profr. Mariano Miranda Fonseca. Texto oficial para uso de los alumnos de las escuelas de 2a. enseñanza. 2. ed. México, D. F. [Porrua hnos. y cía., 1943]
233, [2] p. illus., maps (1 fold.)   20 cm.

7513   [Mitchell, James]
Letter on the relation of the white and African races in the United States, showing the necessity of the colonization of the latter; addressed to the President of the U. S. Washington, Govt. prtg. off., 1862.
28 p.   20 cm.

7514   Moler, Arthur Bass, 1866-
Mexico; the diary of a trip taken by A. B. Moler and wife, February 1912; illustrations courtesy National railways of Mexico. [Chicago, Printed by Legal news co.] c1912.
[16] p. illus.   27 1/2 cm.

7515   Molina Enriquez, Andrés.
... Esbozo de la historia de los primeros diez años de la revolución agraria de Mexico (de 1910 a 1920) hecho a grandes rasgos, por el lic. Andrés

Molina Enriquez... Mexico, Talleres gráficos del
Museo nacional de arqueología, historia y etnografía,
1937.
5 v. in 1. illus., plates (part col.), ports.,
maps, facisms. 19 1/2 cm.

7516 [Molina y Saldívar, Gaspar de, marqués de Ureña]
1741-1806.
El imperio del piojo recuperado. Por don
Severino Amaro [pseud.] Con licencia. En
Sevilla, En la imprenta de Vázquez, Hidalgo, y
compañia. Año de 1784.
31 p. 22 cm.

7517 Monge Alfaro, Carlos.
... Geografía social y humana de Costa Rica. 2.
ed. De acuerdo con el programa vigente de segunda
enseñanza. San José de C. R., A. C., Imprenta y
librería universal, 1943.
129 p., 3 l. 25 1/2 cm.

7518 Monroy Padilla, Salvador.
Prontuario geográfico de la República Mexicana,
para el 4.e año de instrucción primaria. [México,
19]
48 p. illus., maps. 19 x 29 cm.

7519 [Monsalve, Miguel de]
Señor. El marques de Leganès, puesto a los
reales pies de V. M. dize: que siruio al rey
nuestro señor, padre de V. M. de gloriosa memoria,
que està en el cielo, mas de veinte años... [n.p.,
1650?]
22 numbered l. 23 cm.

7520 Monte Carmelo, Fr. Juan del.
Señor, I. Fray Juan del Montecarmelo, como
Procurador General de la Provincia de Carmelitas
Descalzos de Nueva-España, ... hace presente à
los Reales Pies de V. Mag. ... [n.p., 18 th century]
3 p. 20 cm.

7521 Montgomery, George Washington, 1804-1841.
Narrative of a journey to Guatemala, in Central
America, in 1838, by G. W. Montgomery. New York,

Wiley & Putnam, 1839.
vii, [9]-195 p.   22 cm.

7522   Montgomery, Sir James.
Substance of the speech of Sir James Montgomery,
bart., in the House of commons, 24th of June 1819,
on bringing forward his motion relative to the
petition of Mr. John Pritchard, of the Red River
settlement. London, Printed by J. Brettell, 1819.
53 p.   20 cm.

7523   [Monti, Luigi] 1830-1914.
Adventures of a consul abroad. By Samuel Sample-
ton [pseud.]... Boston, Lee and Shepard; New
York, C. T. Dillinghan, 1878.
270 p.   18 cm.

7524   Montoto de Sedas, Santiago, 1890-   , ed.
Colección de documentos inéditos para la historia
de Ibero-América... Madrid, Editorial Ibero-
Africano-Americana [1927]
427 p., 1 1. facsims.   25 cm.

7525   Montpetit, Édouard, 1881-
... Les survivances françaises au Canada.
Conférences faites a l'École libre des sciences
politiques les 13 et 20 juin 1913, précédées des
discours prononcés par m. Étienne Lamy ... et m.
Louis Madelin. Paris, Typographie Plon-Nourrit
et cie, 1914.
2 p.l., 91 p.   19 cm.

7526   Montreal Herald.
This was Montreal in 1814, 1815, 1816, and 1817;
life in Canada's metropolis as called verbatim
from the editorial, news, and advertising columns
of the Montreal herald, a four-page weekly newspaper published nearly 150 years ago. Compiled by
Lawrence M. Wilson, [1st ed. Montreal] [Priv.
print. for Château de Ramezay, 1960]
205 p. illus., ports., map (on lining paper),
fold. facsim (in pocket)   24 cm.

7527   Moodie, Susannah (Strickland) 1803-1885.
Roughing it in the bush; or, Life in Canada. By

Susannah Moodie...　New York, De Witt & Davenport
[1852]
　　2 v. in 1.　19 cm.

7528　Moodie, Susannah (Strickland), 1803-1885.
　　Roughing it in the bush; or, Forest life in
Canada.　Illus. in colour by R. A. Stewart.
Toronto, Bell & Cockburn, 1913.
　　568 p.　illus. (part col.)　22 cm.

7529　Moore, H　　　　Judge.
　　Scott's campaign in Mexico; from the rendezvous
on the island of Lobos to the taking of the city,
including an account of the siege of Puebla, with
sketches of the country, and manners and customs of
the inhabitants.　By H. Judge Moore, of the Palmetto
regiment.　Charleston, J. B. Nixon, 1849.
　　xii, 234 p.　19 1/2 cm.

7530　Moore, Joseph Hampton, 1864-
　　With Speaker Cannon through the tropics; a
descriptive story of a voyage to the West Indies,
Venezuela and Panama; containing views of the
speaker upon our colonial possessions, the Panama
canal and other great governmental problems; an
illustrated history and guide book for statesmen,
travelers and students, with conclusions by the
author.　By J. Hampton Moore...　Philadelphia, The
Book print, 1907.
　　xi, [1], 410 p.　incl. front. (port.), illus.,
plates.　20 1/2 cm.

7531　[Morales, Juan Bautista] 1788-1856.
　　El Gallo Pitagórico.　[Colleción de artículos
crítico-políticos y de costumbres]　[Mexico]　Impr.
lithog. de Cumplico, 1845.
　　280 [1] p.　front. (port.), illus.　20 cm.

7532　Morales, Vicente.
　　El Señor Root　en Mexico; crónica de la visita
hecha en octubre de 1907 al pueblo y al gobierno
de la República Mexicana, por Su Excelencia el
Honorable Señor Elihu Root, secretario de estado
del gobierno de los Estados Unidos de América.　La
escriben:　Vicente Morales y Manuel Caballero, por

acuerdo de la Comisión organizadora de festejos
en honor del Sr. Root. Mexico, Impr. de "Arte y
letras," 1908.
    314, [1] p. incl. illus., ports.   26 1/2 x 19 cm.

7533   Morand, Paul, 1888-
       ... Hiver caraïbe, documentaire. Paris, E.
       Flammarion [ᶜ1929]
       259 p., 1 l.   19 cm.

7534   Morelet, Arthur, 1809-
       Travels in Central America, including accounts
       of some regions unexplored since the conquest; from
       the French of the Chevalier Arthur Morelet, by Mrs.
       M. F. Squier. Introduction and notes by E. Geo.
       Squier. New York, Leypoldt, Holt & Williams, 1871.
       xvii, [19]-430 p. incl. front., illus., plates.
       plates, map.   20 cm.

7535   Morelìa, Mexico. Ordinances, etc.
       Ordenanza, que para el establecimiento de alcaldes
       de barrio en esta ciudad de Valladolid de Michoacán,
       ha extendido su corregido intendente en virtud de
       superiores órdenes del exmo señor virrey. México,
       Por don Mariano Joseph de Zúñiga y Ontiveros, calle
       del Espíritu santo, 1796.
       1 p.l., 8, [7] p. fold. map.   20 cm.

7536   Morfi, Juan Agustín, d. 1783.
       Viaje de indios y diario del Nvevo México,
       por el rev. fray Jvan Agvstín de Morfi; con vna
       introducción biobibliográfica y acotaciones por
       Vito Alessio Robles. 2. ed., con adiciones, de la
       impresa por la sociedad "Bibliófilos mexicanos".
       México, Antigua libería Robredo de J. Porrúa e hijos,
       1935.
       caption title, 3 p.l., [9]-306 p., 1 l. front.,
       plates (1 fold.), maps (1 fold.), fold. plans.
       24 cm.

7537   Morgan, Matthew Somerville, 1839-1890.
       The American war: cartoons by Matt Morgan and
       other English artists; with illustrative notes.
       London, Chatto & Windus, 1874.
       unpaged.   25 cm.

7538   Morgan, William Ferdinand, 1817-1888.
        Joy darkened: sermon preached in St. Thomas
        church, New York... April 16, 1865, by the rector.
        New York, Baker & Godwin, 1865.
        47 p.   20 cm.

7539   Morice, Adrian Gabriel, 1859-1938.
        The history of the northern interior of British
        Columbia (formerly New Caledonia) 1660-1880.
        London, J. Lane, The Bodley Head, 1906.
        368 p.   illus., map (fold.)   24 cm.

7540   Morrill, Gulian Lansing, 1857-
        The devil in Mexico, by G. L. Morrill ("Golightly"
        ... Lowell L. Morrill, photographer. [Minneapolis,
        c1917]
        5 p.l., 346 p. front. (port.) plates.   20 cm.

7541   Morrill, Gulian Lansing, 1857-
        Rotten republics; a tropical tramp in Central
        America, by G. L. Morrill ("Golightly") ... Photos
        and illustrations by Lowell L. Morrill. Chicago,
        M. A. Donohue & co. [c1916]
        5 p.l., 302 p. front. (port.), plates.   20 cm.

7542   Morris, Alexander.
        The Hudson's Bay and Pacific territories. A
        lecture... Montreal, John Lovell, printer and pub-
        lisher, 1859.
        57 p.   22 cm.

7543   Morris, [Ida Dorman] "Mrs. J. E. Morris."
        A tour in Mexico, by Mrs. James Edwin Morris;
        illustrated from photographs taken en route by James
        Edwin Morris. New York, London [etc.] The Abbey
        press [1902]
        1 p.l., 322 p. front., pl.   20 cm.

7544   Mortier, Michel.
        Biographical notice of Madame Adelina Patti...
        [New York, Steinway & sons, 1881?]
        14 p. front. (port.)   22 cm.

7545   El Mosaico. Bogotá, 1858-1865.
        4 v.   24 cm.

7546   Motezuma, Diego Luis de, 1619-1699.
        Corona mexicana; 6 Historias de los nueves
        Motezumas, por el P. Diego Luis de Motezuma...
        Edición y prólogo por Lucas de Torre...   Madrid,
        Biblioteca Hispania, 1914.
        viii, 505, [6] p.   23 cm.

7547   Moxon, Joseph.
        A brief discourse of a passage by the North-
        Pole to Japan, China, &c. Pleaded by three ex-
        periments: and answers to all objections that can
        be urged against a passage that way... With a
        map of all discovered lands nearest to the Pole
        ... London, Printed for Joseph Moxon, 1674.
        6 p. map.   22 cm.

7548   Mühlenpfordt, Eduard.
        Versuch einer getreuen schilderung der republik
        Mejico, bezonders in beziehung auf geographie,
        ethnographie und statistik... Hannover, C. F.
        Kius, 1844.
        2 v.   21 cm.

7549   Müller, J[ohann] W[ilhelm] von, 1824-1866.
        Reisen in den Vereinigten Staaten, Canada und
        Mexico, von baron J. W. von Müller ... Leipzig,
        F. A. Brockhaus, 1864-65.
        3 v. fronts. (v. 1-2), illus., plates, maps,
        diagr.   23 cm.

7550   Mulvaney, Charles Pelham.
        The history of the North-west rebellion of 1865,
        comprising a full and impartial account of the
        origin and progress of the war... including a
        history of the Indian tribes of North western
        Canada... Toronto, Published by J. R. Hovey &
        co., 1885.
        viii, [17]-424 p. illus., map.   20 cm.

7551   Muñoz, Joaquín.
        Guatemala, ancient and modern, by Joaquin Muñoz and
        Anna Bell Ward. New York, The Pyramid press [1940]
        5 p.l., xv-xviii, 19-318 p. front. (port.)
        illus.   23 1/2 cm.

7552 Muñoz, Joaquin.
Guatemala, from where the rainbow takes its
colors; ancient, historical, colorful, picturesque,
modern. [3d ed. Guatemala City] Printed by Tip.
Nacional de Guatemala [1952]
328 p. illus., port., fold. maps. 23 cm.

7553 The murder of Abraham Lincoln planned and executed
by Jesuit priests. Indianapolis, Ironclad age,
1893.
11 p. 18 cm.

7554 [Murillo, Gerardo] 1884-
... El paisaje (un ensayo) México, 1933.
1 p.l., 24 p., 1 l. incl. 5 col. mounted pl.
32 pl. 25 x 30 1/2 cm.

7555 Murillo, Gerardo, 1884-
Valles y montañas de México, 80 dibujos del
doctor Atl [pseud.] Obras de 1904 a 1948.
Exposición del Museo Nacional de Artes Plásticas,
marzo-abril 1948. México [Departamento de Artes
Plásticas, Instituto Nacional de Bellas Artes, 1948]
16 p. illus., port. 29 cm.

7556 Murray, David Christie, 1847-
The Cockney Columbus; by David Christie Murray.
London, Downey & co., 1898.
xiv, 202 p. 19 1/2 cm.

7557 Murray, Henry Anthony, 1810-1865.
Lands of the slave and the free: or, Cuba, the
United States, and Canada. By the Hon. Henry A.
Murray ... London, J. W. Parker and son, 1855.
2 v. plates, maps (1 fold.) 19 1/2 cm.

7558 Murray, Henry Anthony, 1810-1865.
Lands of the slave and the free: or, Cuba, the
United States, and Canada. By Captain the Hon.
Henry A. Murray, R.N. London, New York, G. Routledge & co., 1857.
xxiii, 480 p. front., plates, maps (1 fold.)
19 1/2 cm.

7559 Murray, Samuel, 1865-

From clime to clime; why and how I journeyed
21,630 miles, by Samuel Murray. New York, C. P.
Young co., printers [1905]
   141, [1] p.   map.   17 1/2 cm.

7560   Mutis, José Alestino, 1732-1808.
   Instruccion forma la por un facultativo existente
por muchos años en el Perú, relativa de las
especies y virtudes de la quina... Cadiz, Por Don
Manuel Ximenez Carreño, 1792.
   19 p.   20 cm.

7561   Myers, Leonard, 1827-1905.
   Abraham Lincoln: a memorial address delivered
... June 15th, 1865, before the Union League of the
thirteenth ward. Philadelphia, King & Baird, 1865.
   15 p.   23 cm.

                              N

7562   Nadal, Bernard Harrison, 1812-1870.
   National reconstruction: a discourse delivered
at Wesley chapel, Washington, D. C., on the 1st day
of June, 1865. By the pastor, B. H. Nadal, D.D.
Washington, D. C., W. H. Moore, printer, 1865.
   15 p.   21 1/2 cm.

7563   Nason, Elias, 1811-1887.
   Eulogy on Abraham Lincoln... delivered before
the New England Historic-Genealogical Society, Boston,
May 3, 1865. Boston, W. V. Spencer, 1865.
   28 p.   24 cm.

7564   National Lincoln monument association.
   National Lincoln monument association, incor-
porated by act of Congress, March 30th, 1867.
Washington, Printed at the Great republic office,
1867.
   12 p.   18 cm.

7565   National Union Association of Ohio.
   ... Dayton speech of Hon. John Brough. President

Lincoln's response relative to the arrest of
Vallandingham. Cincinnati, Moore, Wilstach,
Keys & co., 1863.
  31 p.   23 cm.

7566 National Union Convention. Baltimore, June 7-8, 1864.
    Presidential election, 1864: proceedings of the
National Union Convention, held in Baltimore, Md.,
June 7th and 8th, 1864, reported by D. F. Murphy.
New York, Baker & Godwin, 1864.
  94 p.   20 cm.

7567 Navarrete, Martín Fernández de, 1765-1844.
    Colección de los viages y descubrimientos que
hicieron por mar los españoles desde fines del
siglo xv, con varios documentos inéditos concerniente
á la historia de la marina castellana y de los
establecimientos españoles en Indias, coórdinada é
ilustrada por don Martin Fernandez de Navarrete ...
Madrid, Imprenta real, 1825-37.
  5 v. port., fold. maps. 22 cm.

7568 Navarro y Rodrigo, Carlos, 1833-1903.
    ... Vida de Agustin de Iturbide. Memorias de
Agustin de Iturbide. Madrid, Editorial-América,
1919.
  362 p.   23 cm.

7569 Nebel, Carl.
    Viaje pintoresco y arqueolojico sobre la parte
mas interesante de la Republica Mejicana, en los
años transcurridos desde 1829 hasta 1834, por el
arquitecto Don Carlos Nebel. 50 laminas litografiadas con su texto explicativo. Paris y
Mejico [Impr. de P. Renouard] 1839.
  [60] p. 49 col. pl., plan. 56 cm.

7570 Nebel, Carl.
    Voyage pittoresque et archéologique dans la partie
la plus intéressante du Mexique, par C. Nebel...
50 planches lithographiées avec texte explicatif.
Paris, M. Moench [etc.] 1836.
  [82] p., 1 l. 49 pl. (part col.), plan. 55
1/2 cm.

7571   Nelson, Henry Addison, 1820-1906.
          The divinely prepared ruler, and The fit end
       of treason, two discourses delivered at the First
       Presbyterian church, Springfield, Illinois...
       May 7, 1865.   Springfield, Baker & Phillips, 1865.
          39 p.   22 cm.

7572   Nelson, Robert, missionary in China.
          Reminiscences of the Right Rev. William Meade,
       D.D., bishop of the Prot. Epis. Church in Virginia,
       from August 19th 1829, to March 14th 1862...
       Shanghai, "Ching-Foong" general printing office,
       1873.
          60 p.   front. (port.)   17 1/2 cm.

7573   Nelson, Wilbur.
          Obadiah Holmes, ancestor and prototype of
       Abraham Lincoln.   [n.p., 1932]
          20 p.   illus.   20 cm.

7574   New Jersey. Legislature.
          Celebration of the bi-centennial anniversary of
       the New Jersey Legislature, 1683-1883.   Trenton,
       N. J., Naar, Day, & Naar, 1883.
          55 p.   23 cm.

7575   A new route from Europe to the interior of North
       America with a description of Hudson's Bay and
       Straits.   Issued by Nelson valley railway and
       transportation company, Montreal.   Montreal,
       Printed by John Lovell & son, 1881.
          19 p.   fold map.   22 cm.

7576   The new west. Extending from the Great lakes across
       plain and mountain to the golden shores of the
       Pacific...   Winnipeg, Manitoba, Canadian historical
       publishing co., 1888.
          205 p.   map, illus.   22 cm.

7577   New York (City)
          Addresses of the city of New York to George
       Washington, with his replies.   New York, 1867.
          viii, 14 p.   front. (port.), fold. facsim.   26 cm.

7578   New York (State) University. Division of visual

instruction.
... Slides and photographs: Mexico. [Albany,
N. Y., 1916]
caption title, 16 p.   23 cm.

7579   Newcombe, C   F
... The first circumnavigation of Vancouver
Island...   Victoria, B.C., Printed by William H.
Cullin, 1914.
69 p.   maps (part fold.)   24 1/2 cm.

7580   Newman, Francis William, 1805-1897.
The good cause of President Lincoln.   [London]
Emancipation society [1863]
24 p.   17 cm.

7581   Newman, John B
Texas and Mexico in 1846; comprising the history
of both countries, with an account of the soil,
climate and productions of each...   New York, J. K.
Wellman, 1846.
32 p.   fold. map.   20 cm.

7582   Niccolls, Samuel Jack, 1838-
In memoriam: a discourse on the assassination
of Abraham Lincoln...   St. Louis, April 23rd, 1865.
St. Louis, S. Spencer, 1865.
16 p.   22 cm.

7583   Nicholas, Francis Child, 1862-
... Around the Caribbean and across Panama;
illustrated with maps and half-tones from rare
photographs.   Boston & New York, H. M. Caldwell
company [c1903]
7 p.l., 373 p.   front., 35 pl., 4 maps.   21 cm.

7584   Nichols, James Thomas, 1865-
The new South and old Mexico, by James T.
Nichols ... with a chapter on Mexico--country of
contrasts, by John F. Case ...   Des Moines, Ia.,
Nichols book and travel co. [c1927]
128 p.   pl.   20 cm.

7585   Niles, Henry Edward, 1823-1900.
Address... on the occasion of President Lincoln's

funeral obsequies in York, Pa.   York, H. Young
[1865]
   8 p.   22 cm.

7586   Ninety years ago, June 16, 1858, the Illinois Republican state convention met in Springfield,
   Illinois; Photographic reproduction of the original
   copy of the proceedings as published a few days
   after the convention... [n.p.] 1948.
   19 p.   illus. facsim.   20 cm.

7587   Noble, Mason, 1809-1881.
   Sermon delivered in the United States Naval
   Academy, on the day of the funeral of the late
   President, Abraham Lincoln...   Newport, G. T.
   Hammond, 1865.
   16 p.   22 cm.

7588   Noriega, Eduardo.
   Geografía de la República Mexicana, por Eduardo
   Noriega ...   México, La V^{da} de C. Bouret, 1898.
   543 p.   illus. (incl. ports., maps)   18 cm.

7589   Norman, Benjamin Moore, 1809-1860.
   Rambles by land and water, or Notes of travel in
   Cuba and Mexico; including a canoe voyage up the
   river Panuco, and researches among the ruins of
   Tamaulipas... By B. M. Norman ...   New York, Paine
   & Burgess; New Orleans, B. M. Norman, 1845.
   xvii p., 1 l., [21]-216 p.   illus., plates.   19 cm.

7590   Norman, Benjamin Moore, 1809-1860.
   Rambles in Yucatan; or Notes of travel through
   the peninsula, including a visit to the remarkable
   ruins of Chi-Chen, Kabha, Zayi, and Uxmal...
   Fourth ed. New York, J. & H. G. Langley, 1844.
   304 p.   front., illus., plates, map, plans.
   23 cm.

7591   The North Georgia gazette and winter chronicle.
   London, John Murray, 1821.
   133 p.   illus.   24 cm.

7592   Northend, William Dummer, 1823-1902.
   Speeches and essays upon political subjects,

from 1860 to 1869. By William D. Northend.
Salem, H. P. Ives, 1869.
viii, [9]-268 p. 21 1/2 cm.

7593 Northwest Company of Canada, defendant.
Report of proceedings connected with the disputes
of the Earl of Selkirk and the Northwest Company
at the assizes held at York in Upper Canada,
October 1818. From minutes taken in court.
Montreal, Printed by James Lane and Nahum Mower,
1819.
218, xlviii p. 22 cm.

7594 Norton, Anthony Banning.
The great revolution of 1840. Reminiscences of the
log cabin and hard cider campaign, by A. B. Norton
... Mount Vernon, O., and Dallas, Tex., A. B.
Norton & co., 1888.
376 p. incl. front. 19 cm.

7595 Notes and sketches collected from a voyage in the
North-west by a Sister of Charity of Montreal.
Montreal, P. Callahan, book and job printer, 1875.
23 p. 20 cm.

7596 Noticias sobre que deben infomar los subdelegados
de jurisdicciones donde haya reales de minas.
[n.p., 1791?]
caption title, [3] p. 18 cm.

7597 Notman (William) & son.
48 specially selected views of the Canadian
Rockies. Montreal, Valentine & Sons [1907]
plates. 24 x 29 cm.

7598 Nouvelles de Saint-Domingue, du 9 au 14 mars 1790.
[n.p., 1790]
8 p.

7599 Nova Scotia. Commissioner of public records.
Selections from the public documents of the
province of Nova Scotia. Pub. under a resolution
of the House of assembly passed March 15, 1865. Ed.
by Thomas B. Akins, D. C. L., commissioner of
public records. The translations from the French

by Benj. Curren, D. C. L. Halifax, N. S., C.
Annand, 1869.
   1 p.l., ii, 755 p. fold. pl., 2 fold. facism.
22 cm.

7600   Nova Scotia. Executive Council.
        [Resolutions of the governor in council re-
specting the calling of an assembly in that province... Halifax? John Bushell? 1757?]
        Broadside. 2 cols.   18 x 14 inches.

7601   Nova Scotia. Governor, 1752-1756 (Hopson)
        Proclamation for the forming of a militia.   By
His Excellency Peregrine Thomas Hopson, Esq.
captain-general and governor in chief, in... Nova
Scotia, ... Halifax, Printed by J. Bushell,
Printer to the government, 1753.
        Broadside, 37 lines.   34 1/2 x 23 cm.

7602   Nova Scotia. Governor, 1756-1761 (Lawrence)
        By Charles Lawrence, Esq; a proclamation given
in the Council chamber at Halifax, this fourteenth
day of November 1758... Halifax, John Bushell,
1758.
        Broadside.   34 x 18 cm.

7603   Nova Scotia. Governor, 1756-1761 (Lawrence)
        By His Excellency Charles Lawrence, Esq.,
captain-general·and governor in chief in... Nova
Scotia... a proclamation. Given... at Halifax,
this twelfth day of October, 1758... Halifax, J.
Bushell, Printer to the government, 1758.
        Broadside, 37 lines.   36.8 x 18.4 cm.

7604   Nova Scotia historical society, Halifax, N.S.
        Collections. Halifax, Morning Herald office
[etc.] 1879-1914.
        18 v. in 15. maps., tables.   21 cm.

7605   Nova Scotia. House of assembly.
        Journal and votes of the House of assembly for
the province of Nova-Scotia. Halifax, Robert
Fletcher, 1767.
        4 p.   24 cm.

7606   Nova Scotia. House of assembly.
       Journal and votes of the House of assembly for
the province of Nova-Scotia... Halifax, Robert
Fletcher, 1767.
       52 p.   30 cm.

7607   Nova Scotia. Laws, statutes, etc.
       The perpetual acts of the general assemblies of
His Majesty's province of Nova-Scotia... Halifax,
Robert Fletcher, 1767.
       206 p.   30 cm.

7608   Nova Scotia. Laws, statutes, etc.
       The temporary acts of the general assemblies of
His Majesty's province of Nova-Scotia... Halifax,
Robert Fletcher, 1767.
       65 p.   30 cm.

7609   Novo, Salvador, 1904-
       Este y otros viajes. México, Editorial Stylo
[1951]
       188 p.   19 cm.

7610   Noyes, Theodore Williams, 1858-
       War of the metals. Washingtoniana. Mexico,
Hawaii and Japan. By Theodore W. Noyes... Washington, D. C., T. W. Cadick, printer, 1899.
       3 p.l., 3-151 p.   23 cm.

7611   Nuncibay Carrillo, Francisco.
       Defensa en derecho que a su favor haze el doc. d.
Francisco Nuncivay Carrillo, abogado de esta Real
audiencia. En la causa executiua, que sigue d.
Antonio Sancho Davila Bermudes, posseedor de las
haziendas nombradas Santa Cruz de Carabamba, y
San Juan de Julcan Citas en la provincia de
Guamachuco. Para que se rescinda el arrendamiento,
que de ellas le otorgò, por la lession enorme, y
enormissima, que contubo, y que reducido à justicia,
declarado el justo precio à que deviò correr, sele
[:] condene à la restitucion de el excesso per-
cebido. Declarando por nullo el embargo actuado
en vienes de el expressado d.d. Francisco. Con
licencia del superior govierno. En Lima, En la
plazuela de San Christobal, 1759.

[157] p.   15 cm.

7612   Núñez Rochet, Daniel.
       CL [i.e. Centésimo-quincuagésimo] aniversario
       de la independencia de México. [Homenaje del
       pueblo de los Estados Unidos de América al pueblo
       de México, en el CL aniversario de su independencia
       nacional, 1810-1960. México, 1960]
       cover-title, [48] p. 22 plates.   31 cm.

7613   Nursey, Walter R   , 1847-1927.
       The story of Isaac Brock, hero, defender and
       saviour of upper Canada, 1812, by Walter R.
       Nursey... Toronto, W. Briggs, Chicago, A. C.
       McClurg & co., 1909.
       ix, 11-181 p. col. front., plates (part col.),
       ports., plan.   20 cm.

                              O

7614   Oakleaf, Joseph Benjamin, 1858-
       Lincoln as a criminal lawyer [an address... at
       the banquet of Illinois State's Attorney's Association
       ... December 7, 1912... [Chicago] Augustana, Illi-
       nois, Augustana book concern, 1923.
       15 p. port.   20 cm.

7615   Oakleaf, Joseph Benjamin, 1858-
       National Union convention of 1864 and why Lincoln
       was not nominated by acclamation.   Moline, Ill.,
       Carlson prtg. co., 1924.
       11 p.   19 x 16 cm.

7616   Ober, Frederick Albion, 1849-1913.
       A guide to the West Indies and Bermudas, by
       Frederick A. Ober ... with maps and many illustra-
       tions. New York, Dodd, Mead & company, 1908.
       ix, 525 p. front., plates, fold. maps.   17 cm.

7617   Ober, Frederick Albion, 1849-1913.
       A guide to the West Indies, Bermuda and Panama.
       By Frederick A. Ober ... New York, Dodd, Mead &

company, 1913.
ix, 533 p. front., plates, fold. maps. 17 cm.

7618 Ober, Frederick Albion, 1849-1913.
Our West Indian neighbors; the islands of the
Caribbean Sea, "America's Mediterranean": their
picturesque features, fascinating history, and
attractions for the traveler, nature-lover, settler
and pleasure-seeker; by Frederick A. Ober ... New
York, J. Pott & company, 1904.
5 p.l., 433 p. front., 53 pl., fold. map.
20 1/2 cm.

7619 Ober, Frederick Albion, 1849-1913.
Travels in Mexico and life among the Mexicans.
By Frederick A. Ober ... Boston, Estes & Lauriat,
1884.
xxii, [23]-672 p. incl. front., illus., pl.,
maps. 23 1/2 cm.

7620 Obregón Lizano, Miguel, 1861-1935.
... Geografía general de Costa Rica, por M.
Obregón L. ... San José, Imp. Lines, A. Reyes,
1932-
v. Illus., fold. plates, maps (part fold.)
23 1/2 cm.

7621 Obsequies of Abraham Lincoln in Union square, New
York, April 25, 1865. Printed for the Citizens'
committee, by D. Van Nostrand, 1865.
32 p. 20 cm.

7622 Observations d'un habitant des colonies, sur le
mémoire en faveur des gens de couleur... par M.
Grégoire [le 16 décembre 1789] [n.p., 1789]
68 p. 20 cm.

7623 The Observer. Belice, British Honduras, 21 February
1885 - 13 February 1886.
Unique file of scattered numbers in British
Museum.

7624 Och, Joseph, 1725?-1773.
[P. Joseph Och's... Nachrichten von Seinen
reisen nach dem spanischen Amerika...] (In Murr,

Christoph G. von, ed. Nachrichten von verschiedenen ländern des spanischen Amerika. Halle, 1809-[1811] 21 1/2 cm. 1 th., p. 1-292.

7625 O'Connor, Francisco Burdett, 1791-1871.
... Independencia americana. Recuerdos de Francisco Burdett O'Connor, coronel del ejército, libertador de Colombia y general de división de los del Perú y Bolivia. Los publica su nieto F. [i.e. T.] O'Connor d'Arlach. Madrid, Sociedad española de librería [1915?]
2 p.l., [7]-416 p., 1 l. 23 cm.

7626 Oda, que para dar principio a un nuevo certámen de amor compuso una colegiala del real Colegio de niñas de san Ignacio de Loyola de esta ciudad de Mexico, y la ofrece en nombre del mismo colegio a los amables reyes Carlos quarto y Luisa de Borbon ... México, Por don Felipe de Zuñiga y Ontiveros, 1791.
[20] p. 19 cm.
"Oda dirigida al exmô. señor conde de Revilla Gigedo": p. [11- 12]

7627 Odell, Ruth.
Helen Hunt Jackson ("H.H.") Abstract of a dissertation presented to the Graduate College in partial fulfillment of the requirements for the degree of doctor of philosophy. Department of English, June 1937. [Lincoln] Published by the University of Nebraska, 1942.
9 p. 23 cm.

7628 Ogden, John Cosens, 1751-1800.
A tour through Upper and Lower Canada. By John C. Ogden ... Containing, a view of the present state of religion, learning, commerce, agriculture, colonization, customs and manners, among the English, French, and Indian settlements. 2d ed. Wilmington, Printed by Bonsal and Niles, for the author, 1800.
117 p. 17 cm.

7629 Ogilby, John, 1600-1676.
America; being the latest, and most accurate description of the New world; containing the

original of the inhabitants, and the remarkable
voyages thither, the conquest of the vast empires
of Mexico and Peru and other large provinces in
those parts. Also their cities, fortresses, towns,
temples, mountains and rivers; their habits, customs,
manners and religions; their plants, beasts, birds,
and serpents. With an appendix containing, besides
several other considerable additions, a brief survey
of what hath been discover'd of the unknown south-
land and the Arctick region. Collected from most
authentick authors, augmented with later observations, and adorn'd with maps and sculptures. London,
Printed by the author, 1671.
674 p., illus., 32 pl. (part fold.) 6 port.,
19 maps (part fold.)   43 cm.

7630 Ogilvie, William, 1846-1912.
Early days of the Yukon & the story of its gold
finds by William Ogilvie... Ottawa, Thorburn &
Abbott, 1913.
xii, 306 p. front., plates, ports.   19 cm.

7631 O'Higgins, Bernardo, supreme director of Chile, 1778-
1842.
... Epistolario de d. Bernardo O'Higgins, capitán
general y director supremo de Chile, gran mariscal
del Perú, y brigadier de las Provincias unidas del
Río de la Plata ... Anotado por Ernesto de la
Cruz ... Madrid, Editorial-América, 1920.
2 v.   22 cm.

7632 Old Abe's jokes, fresh from Abraham's bosom, containing all iss [!] issues, excepting the "green-
backs", to call in some of which, this work is
issued. New York, T. R. Dawley [1864]
135 p. front.   20 cm.

7633 Oldroyd, Osborn Hamiline, 1842-1930.
The centenary of Abraham Lincoln's birth. [n.p.,
n.d.]
[4] p.

7634 Oldroyd, Osborn Hamiline, 1842-1930.
The mystic number seven in the life of Abraham
Lincoln... Washington, D. C., 1930.

12 p.   18 cm.

7635 O'Leary, Daniel Florencio, 1800-1854.
      Bolívar y la emancipación de Sur-América;
      memorias del general O'Leary, tr. del inglés por
      su hijo Simón B. O'Leary... Madrid, Sociedad
      española de librería [pref. 1915]
      2 v.   23 cm.

7636 O'Leary, Daniel Florencio, 1800-1854, comp.
      ... Correspondencia de extranjeros notables con
      el Libertador ... Madrid, Editorial-América, 1920.
      2 v.   23 cm.

7637 O'Leary, Daniel Florencio, 1800-1854.
      ... Últimos años de la vida pública de Bolívar;
      memorias del general O'Leary. Tomo apendice (1826-
      1829) Prologo de R. Blanco-Fombona. Madrid, Edi-
      torial-América [1916]
      580 p., 1 l.   23 cm.

7638 Oliphant, Laurence, 1829-1888.
      Minnesota and the far West. Edinburgh, W.
      Blackwood, 1885.
      xiii, 306 p. illus.   21 cm.

7639 Olivares, José de.
      Our islands and their people as seen with camera
      and pencil; introduced by Major-General Joseph
      Wheeler ... with special descriptive matter and
      narratives by José de Olivares ... Edited and
      arranged by William S. Bryan ... photographs by
      Walter B. Townsend ... St. Louis, New York [etc.]
      N. D. Thompson publishing co. [1899-1900]
      2 p.l., [3]-776 p. col. front., illus., col.
      plates, port., maps.   41 x 29 1/2 cm.

7640 Oliveira Lima, Manuel de, 1865-1928.
      ... Formación histórica de la nacionalidad
      brasileña; traducción y prólogo de Carlos Pereyra.
      Madrid, Editorial-América, 1918.
      278 p.   22 1/2 cm.

7641 Oliver, Edmund Henry, 1882-1935, ed.
      The Canadian North-west, its early development

and legislative records; minutes of the councils
of the Red river colony and the Northern department
of Rupert's land... Ed. by Prof. E. H. Oliver
... Pub. by authority of the secretary of State
under the direction of the archivist. Ottawa,
Government printing bureau, 1914-15.
2 v. 6 fold. maps. 25 cm.

7642 Onstott, R   J
New Salem, the home of Abraham Lincoln, 1831-
1837: its history complete... Mason City, Ill.,
The author [1927]
4 p. 20 cm.

7643 Ontañón, Eduardo de, 1904-
... Manual de México. México, Ediciones Xochitl
[1946]
2 p.l., 3-201, [1] p., 1 l. plates. 23 1/2 cm.

7644 Oquino, Juan.
Defenza al cargo qve resvlto en la residenica, que
de orden de S. Mag. tomó el señor doctor don
Alvaro Bernardo de Quiros, oydor de la Real
audiencia de Lima al señor yntendente. d. Juan
Oquino. Licencia del superior govierno. [Lima]
En la imprenta de Ignacio de Luna [1724]
[34] p. 24 cm.

7645 Order of United American Mechanics. State Council of
Pennsylvania.
... In memoriam: Abraham Lincoln, President of
the United States. Philadelphia, G. Hawkes, 1865.
88 p. front. 15 cm.

7646 Ordoñez de Ceballos, Pedro, b. 1550?
Historia y viage del mundo. Madrid, J. Garcia
Infanzon, a costa de F. Sayeclon, 1691.
6 p.l., 432, [7] p. 21 1/2 cm.

7647 Orendian, Leopoldo I
Cosas de viejos papeles. Guadalajara, Jal.,
1968.
103 p. 23 1/2 cm.

7648 Oria y Senties, Enrique de.

... Tierra de promisión: Brazil--Argentina--
Paraguay--Uruguay--Chile--Bolivia--Perú--Colombia
--México--Guatemala. Madrid, Impr. de. J. Pueyo,
1931.
297 p., 1 l.   19 cm.

7649   Orozco y Berra, Manuel, 1816-1881.
Apuntes para la historia de la geografía en
México, por Manuel Orozco y Berra. México,
Impr. de F. Diaz de Leon, 1881.
503 p.   24 cm.

7650   Orrego Luco, Augusto, 1848?-
... La cuestión del Pacífico: Tacna y Arica
... Santiago de Chile, Soc. Impr.-lit. Barcelona,
1919.
49 p.   17 1/2 cm.

7651   Orrego Luco, Luís, 1866-
Chile contemporáneo... Santiago de Chile, Impr.
Cervantes, 1904.
232 p.   23 cm.

7652   Osborn, Sherard.
Stray leaves from an Arctic journal; or, Eighteen
months in the polar regions, in search of Sir John
Franklin's expedition, in the years 1850-51. By
Lieut. Sherard Osborn, commanding H.M.S. vessel
"Pioneer"... London, Longman, Brown, Green and
Longmans, 1852.
vii p., 1 l., 329 p. col. front., illus., col.
plates, fold. map.   19 1/2 cm.

7653   Osborne, John, of the Royal mail steam packet co.
Guide to the West Indies, Madeira, Mexico,
northern South America, &c., &c., compiled from
documents specially furnished by the agents of
the Royal mail steam packet company, the Board of
trade, and other authentic sources ... By John
Osborne ... 3d ed., containing the company's latest
regulations essential to passengers and merchants.
London [Royal mail steam packet co.] 1845.
xliv, 310 p. illus., maps, tab.   18 cm.

7654   Österreichischer touristen-klub, Vienna. Sektion für naturkunde.

Festschrift anlässlich des fünfundzwanzigjährigen bestandes der Sektion für naturkunde des Österreichischen touristen-klubs, im auftrage des ausschusses hrsg. von E. Kittl. Wien, Verlag der Sektion für naturkunde des Österreichischen touristen-klubs, 1906.

2 p.l., 3-40 p. illus. (incl. ports.) 28 1/2 cm.

7655 Oswald, Felix Leopold, 1845-1906.

Summerland sketches, or Rambles in the backwoods of Mexico and Central America... By Felix L. Oswald. With numerous illustrations by H. F. Farny and Hermann Faber. Philadelphia, J. B. Lippincott & co., 1880.

425 p. incl. front., illus. 21 1/2 cm.

7656 Outram, Sir James, 1869-1925.

In the heart of the Canadian rockies, by James Outram... New York, The Macmillan company; London, Macmillan & co., ltd., 1906.

xii p., 1 l., 466 p. incl. front., illus., plates. 3 maps (1 fold.) 23 cm.

7657 Oviedo y Valdés, Gonzalo Fernández de, 1478-1557.

Historia general y natural de las Indias, islas y tierrafirme del mar océano... Publicada la Real academia de la historia, cotejada con el códice original, enriquecida con las enmiendas y adiciones del autor, é ilustrada con la vida y el juicio de las obras del mismo por d. José Amador de los Rios ... Madrid, Impr. de la Real academia de la historia 1851-55.

3 pt. in 4 v. 29 cm.

7658 Owen, Robert, 1771-1858.

Robert Owen's opening speech, and his reply to the Rev. Alex. Campbell, in the recent public discussion in Cincinnati, to prove that the principles of all religions are erroneous, and that their practice is injurious to the human race. Also, Mr. Owen's Memorial to the republic of Mexico, and a narrative of the proceedings thereon ... for the purpose of establishing a new political and moral system of government, founded on the laws of nature,

as explained in the above debate with Mr. Campbell.
Cincinnati, Pub. for R. Owen, 1829.
    6 p.l., [v]-xiii, [15]-226 p., 1 l.   21 1/2 cm.

P

7659 Pacheco, José Ramón.
        Lettres sur le Mexique. Par J. R. Pacheco ...
      Lettre première. Bordeaux, C. Lawalle neveu, 1833.
        50 p.   22 cm.
        No more published?

7660 Packard, Roy Dwight, 1889-
        The love affairs of Abraham Lincoln, by R. D.
      Packard... Cleveland, O., Carpenter printing co.
      [1947]
        1 p.l., 14 p.   23 cm.

7661 Packard, Roy Dwight, 1889-
        The riddle of Lincoln's religion, by R. D.
      Packard... Cleveland, O., Printed by E. O. Hodge
      co. [1946]
        1 p.l., 12 p.   front.   23 cm.

7662 Paddock, Wilbur Fisk, 1831-1903.
        A great man fallen! A discourse on the death of
      Abraham Lincoln, delivered in St. Andrew's Church,
      Philadelphia... April 23, 1865. Philadelphia,
      Sherman & co., 1865.
        24 p.   23 cm.

7663 Páez Brotchie, Luis, 1893-
        Guadalajara de Indias, y otras monografías
      históricas regionales. Guadalajara, Ediciones
      del Banco Industrial de Jalisco, 1957.
        xiii, 233 p.   maps, coats of arms, facsims.
      23 cm.

7664 Páez, José Antonio, pres. Venezuela, 1790-1873.
        ... Memorias del general José Antonio Páez,
      autobiografía; apreciación de Páez, por José Martí.
      Madrid, Editorial-América [1916?]

307

481 p., 1 1.   23 cm.

7665   Páez, Pedro, 1564-1622.
Copia de vna carta del padre Pedro Paez de la
Compañía de Iesus, escrita en Etiopia a seys de
iulio de.1618, para vn padre de la prouincia de
Toledo de la misma Compañia de Iesvs. Da cuenta com
en aquella tierra se hã reduzido a la fè el emperado
y otros muchos principes, y las guerras que han
tenido vnos con otros por esta causa; y como los-
dichos [¡] han ya fundad [sic] alli seminarios.
Lima, Por Francisco Lasso, 1619.
[4] p.   21 cm.

7666   Palafox y Mendoza, Juan de, bp., 1600-1659.
Año espiritual, dividido en meses, y semanas, que
comprehende en el invierno el temor de las postrim-
erias. En la primavera la hermosura de las virtudes
En el estio el fervor de los afectos. En el otoño
la madurez de los frutos. Parte primera. Offrecela
al mayor aprovechamiento espiritual de los fieles,
el ilustrissimo y reverendissimo señor don Juan de
Palafox y Mendoza... Brusselas, Por Francisco
Foppens, impressor, y mercader de libros, 1662.
61 p.l., 151 p.   24 cm.

7667   Palafox y Mendoza, Juan de, bp., 1600-1659.
Carta que el illmo exmo, y ve. sr. d. Juan de
Palafox y Mendoza... escribiò al p. Horazio
Carochi, preposito de la casa professa de la
Compañia de Jesus. Sacada de su original, que se
halla en el noviciado de carmelitas descalzos de la
Puebla de los Angeles de la Nueba España. En
Lovaina, Por Egidio Daníque, 1723 [i.e. 176-?]
183 p.   25 cm.

7668   Palafox y Mendoza, Juan de, bp., 1600-1659.
Gemidos del corazon, tiernos afectos, amorosos
suspiros, y vivos sentimientos de una alma contrita,
y arrepentida de sus pecados. Sacados de la Vida
interior del ilustrisimo, excelentisimo, y venerable
señor don Juan de Palafox y Mendoza, obispo de Osma.
Dedicado a la excelentisima señora duquesa de
Medina-Coeli. En Madrid, Por Joseph Doblado, 1778.
4 p.l., 150 p. 1 1.   24 cm.

7669 [Palafox y Mendoza, Juan de, bp.] 1600-1659.
Memorial al rei nvestro señor. Sobre la execvcion
del breve de la santidad de Inocencio x. en la dif-
erencia ivrisdicional, i sacramental. Entre los
religiosos de la Compañia de Iesvs de la Nveva-
España, i la ivrisdicion eclesiastica del obispado
de la Pvebla de los Angeles. [n.p., 1650?]
5 p.l., 127 p.   25 cm.

7670 Palafox y Mendoza, Juan de, bp. 1600-1659.
El pastor de noche buena. Practica breve de las
virtudes. Conocimiento facil de los vicios.
Corregido, añadido, y emmendado por su autor el
ilvstr. y reverend, señor don Jvan de Palafox, y
Mendoza, obispo de Osma, del consejo de Su Magestad.
Con licencia. Barcelona, Por Pablo Campins, 1721.
16 p.l., 257, 7 p.   25 cm.

7671 Palafox y Mendoza, Juan de, bp., 1600-1659.
El pastor de noche buena. Practica breve de las
virtudes. Conocimiento facil de los vicios.
Corregido, añadido, y enmendado por su autor el
ilustrmo. y revermo. señor don Juan de Palafox y
Mendoza... Barcelona, Por Juan Piferrer, 1730.
16 p.l., 266 [6] p.   26 cm.

7672 Palafox y Mendoza, Juan de, bp., 1600-1659.
Peregrinacion de Philotea al santo templo, y
monte de la Crvz. Del ilvstrissimo, y reverendissimo
señor don Ivan de Palafox y Mendoza... A los principes de la iglesia san Pedro, y san Pablo. Con
licencia; En Zaragoça, Diego Dormer, 1661.
20 p.l., 219, [1] p.   25 cm.

7673 Palafox y Mendoza, Juan de, bp. 1600-1659.
Varon de deseos, en que se declaran las tres
vias de la vida espiritual purgativa, iluminativa y
unitiva. Ofrecido al aprovechamiento espiritual
de las almas devotas. Por el ilustrisimo y reveren-
dísimo don Juan de Palafox y Mendoza, obispo de la
Puebla de los Angeles. Con las licencias necesarias.
Madrid, En la imprenta de Benito Cano, 1786.
6 p.l., 408 p.   28 cm.

7674 Palma y Freites, Luis de la.

Por las religiones de santo Domingo, san Francisco
y san Agustin de la provincias de la Nueva-España.
En defensa de las doctrinas, de que fueron remouidos
de hecho sus religiosos doctrineros: por el illus-
trissimo señor don Iuan de Palafox y Mendoza, obispo
de Tlaxcala, del consejo de Su Magestad en el real y
supremo de las Indias. [Colophon: En Madrid, En la
Imprenta real. 1664]
34 numb. l. 25 cm.

7675 Palmer, Frederick, 1873–
Central America and its problems; an account of
a journey from the Rio Grande to Panama, with introductory chapters on Mexico and her relations to
her neighbors, by Frederick Palmer, F.R.G.S. New
York, Moffat, Yard & company, 1910.
xiv, 347 p. front., plates, fold. map. 22 cm.

7676 Palmer, Robert M , 1820-1862.
Washington and the union: oration delivered...
at the reception of President Lincoln at Harrisburg
... on the 22d day of February, 1861. [Harrisburg,
1861]
17 p. 23 cm.

7677 Pan American tourist bureau, Laredo, Texas.
Power's guide to Mexico for the motorist, published
by the Pan American tourist bureau, Laredo, Texas.
11th ed. Laredo, Texas, 1936.
3-66 p. incl. illus., maps. 26 cm.

7678 Pan American union.
Mexico; a general sketch, comp. by the Pan
American union, John Barrett, director general,
Francisco J. Yánes, assistant director. Washington, D. C. [Press of B. S. Adams] 1911.
389, xvii p. front. (port.), illus., 2 pl., 4
fold. maps. 23 1/2 cm.

7679 [Pan American union. Travel division]
... Mexico. [Washington, 1943]
11, [1] p. illus. (incl. maps) 23 x 10 1/2 cm.

7680 Pan American Union. Travel Division.
Visit Honduras. [Rev. ed.] Washington [1958]

22 p.   illus.   23 cm.

7681   Pan American Union.   Travel Division.
Visit Panama.   [Rev. ed.]   Washington [1958]
cover-title, 32 p.   illus., fold. map.   23 cm.

7682   Pani, Alberto J   , 1878-
En camino hacia la democracia, por Alberto J.
Pani ...   México, Depto. de aprovisionamientos
generales, Dirección de talleres gráficos, 1918.
4 p.l., 11-156 (i.e. 163), [1] p., 3 1.   24
1/2 cm.

7683   Papel periódico ilustrado.   Bogotá, Imprenta de
Silvestre y compañia [etc. 1881-88]
5 v.   illus. (incl. ports., facsims.), fold.
plates.   32 1/2 cm.

7684   Papeles de Nueva España, publicados de orden y con
fondos del gobierno mexicano por Francisco del Paso y
Troncoso...   Segunda serie: Geografía y estadística
...   Madrid, Establecimiento tip.   "Sucesores de
Rivadeneyra,"   1905-
v.   illus., plates (part fold.)   24 cm.
Contents.--I. Suma de visitas de pueblos por orden
alfabético; manuscrito 2,800 de la Biblioteca nacional
de Madrid, anónimo de la mitad del siglo xvi.--

7685   Paraíba.   Conselho estadual de cultura.
Paraíba cultural.   [João Pessoa?]   Govérno do
estado, Secretaria da educação e cultura [n.d.]
3 v.   22 cm.

7686   Pardo, J   Joaquin.
Guía de antigua Guatemala [por] J. Joaquín Pardo,
Pedro Zamora Castellanos, [y] Luis Lujan Muñoz.
Liminar: Francis Gall.   2. ed. [Guatemala City]
Editorial "José de Pineda Ibarra," 1968.
281 p.   illus., facsims., maps.   17 cm.

7687   Parker, Sir Gilbert, 1862-1932.
Old Quebec, the fortress of New France, by
Gilbert Parker and Claude Glennon Bryan...   New
York, London, The Macmillan company, 1904.
xxiv p. 1 1., 486 p.   incl. illus., plates,

311

ports., plan. 25 port. (incl. front.), 4 maps.
23 cm.

7688   Parker, Sir Gilbert, 1862-1932.
  The seats of the mighty; being the memoirs of
Captain Robert Moray, sometime an officer in the
Virginia regiment, and afterwards of Amherst's
regiment, by Gilbert Parker... New York, D. Appleton and company, 1896.
  x p., 1 l., 376 p. front., plates, ports, map.
19 cm.

7689   Parker, Sir Gilbert, 1862-1932.
  The United States and this war: a word in
season: speech delivered... to the Pilgrim's
Society... London, on the 15th April, 1915, on
the... 50th anniversary of the death of Abraham
Lincoln. London, Darling & son, 1915.
  10 p.   21 cm.

7690   Parker, Henry Elijah, 1821-1896.
  Discourse the day after the reception of the
tidings of the assassination of President Lincoln,
preached in the South Congregational church, Concord, N. H., April 16, 1865. By the pastor, Rev.
Henry E. Parker. Concord, Printed by McFarland &
Jenks, 1865.
  15 p.   23 cm.

7691   Parker, Joel, 1816-1888.
  The war powers of Congress, and of the president:
an address delivered before the National club of
Salem, March 13, 1863. Cambridge, H. O. Houghton,
1863.
  60 p.   20 cm.

7692   Parkman, Francis, 1823-1893.
  ... France and England in North America... by
Francis Parkman. Boston, Little, Brown, and company, 1910.
  7 v. in 9. fronts. (incl. 3 ports.) maps (part
double), plans.   21 1/2 cm.
  Contents.--pt. 1. Pioneers of France in the New
World. - pt. 2. The Jesuits in North America in
the seventeenth century. - pt. 3. La Salle and the

discovery of the Great West. - pt. 4. The old regime
in Canada. - pt. 5. Count Frontenac and New France
under Louis XIV. - pt. 6. A half-century of con-
flict. 2 v. - pt. 7. Montcalm and Wolfe. 2 v.

7693   Parra, Antonio.
Discurso sobre los medios de connaturalizar y
propagar en España los cedros de la Havana, y
otros arboles, asi de construccion, como de
maderas curiosas y frutales.   Por don Antonio
Parra...   Madrid, viuda de Ibarra, 1799.
1 p.l., 36 p.   24 cm.

7694   Parra, Jacinto de.
La Bienaventurada Rosa Pervana de S. María, de
la Tercera Orden de Santo Domingo Sv admirable
vida, y preciosa mverte...   Madrid, Melchor
Sanchez, 1668.
28 p.l., 471 p.   26 cm.

7695   Parry, William Edward.
Journal of a second voyage for the discovery of
a north-west passage from the Atlantic to the Pacific;
performed in the years 1819-20, in Her Majesty's
ships Hecla and Griper...   London, John Murray, 1821.
310, cccixp., 7 pl.   illus., maps.

7696   Parry, William Edward.
Journal of a second voyage for the discovery of
a north-west passage from the Atlantic to the
Pacific; performed in the years 1821-22-23, in His
Majesty's ships Fury and Hecla.   London, John
Murray, 1824.
xxx p., 1 l. 592 p.   fold. maps, plates.   25 cm.

7697   Parry, William Edward.
Journal of a third voyage for the discovery of a
north-west passage from the Atlantic to the Pacific;
performed in the years 1824-25, in His Majesty's
ships Hecla and Fury...   London, John Murray, 1826.
186, 151 p.   illus., maps.   24 cm.

7698   Pastor, M   H
... Impresiones y recuerdos de mis viajes á
México. San Sebastián [Spain] La Voz de Guipúzcoa,

1900.
2 p.l., [9]-225, [3] p.   19 cm.

7699   Patterson, Adoniram Judson, 1827-1909.
Eulogy on Abraham Lincoln, delivered in Portsmouth,
N. H., April 19, 1865. Portsmouth, C. W. Brewster
& son, 1865.
30 p.   22 cm.

7700   Patterson, James Willis, 1823-1893.
Memorial address on the life and character of
Abraham Lincoln, delivered at Concord, N. H., June
1, 1865... Concord, Cogswell & Sturtevant, 1865.
24 p.   23 cm.

7701   Patterson, Richard S
Henry C. J. Heusken, interpreter to the first
American consular and diplomatic posts in Japan
... Washington, 1948.
19 p.   20 cm.

7702   Patterson, Robert Mayne, 1832-1911.
The character of Abraham Lincoln. By Robert
M. Patterson, pastor of the Great Valley Presbyterian
church. Philadelphia, J. S. Claxton, 1865.
44 p.   22 1/2 cm.

7703   Paul, Almarin B
A letter from Gold Hill, Nevada, April 23, 1865:
presented to F. Ray Risdon by Glen Dawson, February
12, 1950. [n.p.] Privately printed, 1950.
6 p.   20 cm.

7704   Paxton, W   M
The Paxtons: their origin in Scotland, and their
migrations through England and Ireland to the colony
of Pennsylvania. Platte City, Mo., Landmark print.,
1903.
420, 65 p.   22 cm.

7705   Payno, Manuel.
Compendio de geografía de Mexico, precedido de
breves nociones de astronomía y cosmografía, escrito
por Manuel Payno para el uso de los establecimientos
de educación primaria. México, F. Díaz de León y

314

S. White, 1872.
128 p.   fold. map.   14 1/2 cm.

7706   Payno y Flores, Manuel, 1810-1894.
Tardes nubladas; colección de novelas, por Manuel
Payno.   México, Impr. de F. Díaz de León y S. White,
1871.
478, [2] p.   19 1/2 cm.

7707   Paz, Ireneo, 1836-1924.
Nueva guía de Mexico, en inglés, francés y
castellano, con instrucciones y noticias para
viageros y hombres de negocios, por Ireneo Paz y
Manuel Tornel.   Año de 1882.   México, Impr. de I.
Paz [1882?]
912 p.   front. (fold. plan), fold. tab.   16 cm.

7708   Paz, José María, 1791-1854.
... Memorias póstumas del general José María
Paz.   Madrid, Editorial-América [1917]
491 p.   23 cm.

7709   Paz Soldán, Mariano Felipe, 1821-1886.
... Historia del Perú independiente (1822-1827)
...   Madrid, Editorial-América, 1919.
2 v.   23 cm.

7710   Peabody, Henry Greenwood.
In the footsteps of Cortes, an illustrated lecture
by Henry G. Peabody.   [Pasadena, Cal., H. G. Peabody,
c1918]
1 p.l., 21 p.   23 cm.

7711   Peabody, Henry Greenwood, 1855-
Mexican scenery and architecture, an illustrated
lecture by Henry G. Peabody.   [Pasadena, Calif.,
H. G. Peabody, c1932]
23 p.   23 cm.

7712   Peacock, Thomas Brower.
... Buffalo Bill.   Thrilling adventures of Col.
W. F. Cody...   Denver, Col. [n.d.]
28 p.   illus.   19 cm.

7713   Peck, George Record, 1843-1923.

Abraham Lincoln: an address at Janesville, Wisconsin, at the celebration of the Centennial anniversary of Abraham Lincoln's birth, February 12, 1909. [n.p., 1909?]
15 p. 20 cm.

7714 Peck, George Record, 1843-1923.
Abraham Lincoln: a response at the annual banquet of the Marquette club, of Chicago, on the birthday of Abraham Lincoln. February 12th, 1895, by George R. Peck. Chicago, 1895.
12 p. 23 cm.

7715 [Peel, Bruce Braden]
The Saskatoon story 1882-1952. Dedicated to Saskatoon's pioneers by M. A. East. Saskatoon, Printed by General printing and bookbinding limited, 1952.
86 p. illus. 32 cm.

7716 Pellowe, William Charles Smithson, 1890-
The royal road to Mexico; a travel log--an interpretation--a plea for friendship, by William C. S. Pellowe. Detroit, Mich., The Watergate publishing company, 1937.
168 p., 1 l. illus. 18 1/2 cm.

7717 Pemex travel club, Mexico.
Mexico's western highways, including the cities of Toluca, Morelia, Pátzcuaro, Uruapán, Guadalajara. Presented by Pemex travel club (division of Petróleos mexicanos) Mexico city [Talleres gráficos de la nación, 1940?]
112 p. incl. illus., 37 maps, plans. 21 cm.

7718 Peña Montenegro, Alonso de la, bp. d. 1688.
Itinerario para parochos de indios, en que se tratan las materias mas particulares, tocantes à ellos, para su buena administracion... Amberes, Juan Bautista Verdussen, 1726.
784 p. 28 cm.

7719 Peñalosa y Zúñiga, Clemente.
El honor militar, causas de su origen, progresos y decadencia; ó, Correspondencia de dos hermanos

desde el exercito de Navarra de S.M:C., por Don
Clemente Peñalosa y Zúñiga... [t.1] [Madrid] B.
Cano, 1795.
5 p.l., 207 p.   20 cm.

7720 Pendleton, George Hunt, 1825-1889.
Hear Hon. George H. Pendleton. [Richmond, 1864?]
8 p.   23 cm.

7721 Pennell, Orrin Henry.
Religious views of Abraham Lincoln.   Alliance,
Ohio, R. M. Scranton prtg. co. [1899]
52 p. front.   22 cm.

7722 Pennington, Edgar Legare.
George White, teacher, historian, priest.
Hartford, Conn., Church missions publishing company, 1943.
23 p.   22 1/2 cm.

7723 Pennsylvania. General assembly. House of representatives.
Addresses on the consideration of resolutions
relative to the death of Abraham Lincoln, president
of the United States, delivered in the House of
representatives of Pennsylvania, January 23, 1866;
together with the last inaugural address of President
Lincoln. Harrisburg, Singerly & Myers, state printers, 1866.
24 p.   24 cm.

7724 [Pennsylvania railroad company]
Pennsylvania tour to Mexico, affording four weeks
in the land of the Aztecs... [Philadelphia, Allen,
Lane & Scott, c1891]
58 p. front., illus., fold. map.   20 x 15 1/2 cm.

7725 Percival, Olive.
Mexico City; an idler's note-book, by Olive Percival. Chicago, H. S. Stone and company, 1901.
5 p.l., 208 p. front., plates.   17 1/2 cm.

7726 Percy, Algernon Heber.
Journal of two excursions in the British North
West territory of North America by Algernon Heber

Percy and Mrs. Heber Percy, 1877 & 1878. Market
Drayton, Shropshire, Printed for private circulation
by Bennion & Horne [1879?]
33 p. illus., fold. map. 22 cm.

7727 Pereda y Victoria, Victorino.
Explicacion breve de oraciones, con el conocimiento
de tiempos, recogida de varios authores, por d.
Victorino Pereda, y Victoria, preceptor en un tiempo
de latinidad en México, y despues cathedratico de
élla en el real ilustre Colegio de s. Francisco de
Sales, de la villa de S. Miguel el Grande. A cuyas
expensas sale â luz nuevamente, para el uso de sus
grammaticos alumnos. Reimpressa en Mexico: En la
imprenta del lic d. Joseph Jauregui. Ano de 1777.
[36] p. 23 cm.

7728 Pereda y Victoria, Victorino.
Explicacion de generos, y preteritos, segun el
arte, y clasicos authores. Por d. Victorino Pereda,
y Victoria, preceptor en un tiempo de latinidad en
México, y despues cathedratico de élla en el real
ilustre Colegio de s. Francisco de Sales, de la villa
de S. Miguel el Grande. A cuyas expensas sale â
luz nuevamente, para el uso de sus grammaticos
alumnos. Reimpressa en Mexico: En la imprenta del
lic. d. Joseph Jauregui. Año de 1777.
[48] p. 27 cm.

7729 Pérez de Amézaga, Juan.
Relacion de las novedads qve Iuan Perez de
Ameçaga, agente de negocios del real Consejo de
las Indias, ha sacado para sus amigos de su diario,
sucedidas desde 14. de julio de 1678. que salieron a
navegar galeones para Tierrafirme, y flota para
Nueva-España. [Lima, 1680?]
4 numb. l. 21 cm.

7730 Perez de Arteaga, Diego.
Relación de Misantle, por Diego Perez de Arteaga,
1579. (Notas de David Ramírez Lavoignet) [Xalapa,
Universidad Veracruzana, 1962]
193 p. fold. pl. 18 cm.

7731. Pérez de Lara, Alfonso, fl. 1608-1629.

Compendio de las tres gracias de la santa cruzada,
subsidio, y escusado, que su santidad concede a la
sacra catolica real magestad del rey don Felipe
III. nuestro señor, para gastos de la guerra contra
infieles, y la pratica dellas, assi en el consejo,
como en los iuzgados de los subdelegados. Re-
copilado de mandado del señor don Martin de Cordoua
... Por el licenciado Alonso Perez de Lara ...
Madrid, En la Imprenta real, MDCX.
    10 p.l., 333 (i.e. 332), 146, [19] p.   25 cm.
    Erros in pagination: no. 53-58 (2d group) omitted;
several pages misnumbered; one blank leaf inserted
after p. 146.

7732 Pérez de Lara, Alfonso, fl. 1608-1629.
    De anniversariis, et capellaniis, libri dvo.
Qvibus vltra generalem anniuersariorum & capellaniarum
materiam, specialiter disputatur de annuo relicto:
pro virginibus maritādis: pro infantibus expositis
nutriendis: pro redimendis captiuis: pro relaxādis
carceratis: pro mōte pietatis: pro celebrādo festo
Corporis Christi, cum praecedentijs processionis: de
trāsferēdis cadaueribus, absquè tributo. De quarta
funerali: de probatione generis & qualitatis sanguinis
ad capellaniam requisitae, et ad alia statuta. Opvs
qvidem, vt pivm et practicabile, ita & vtile vtroque
foro versantibus, iudicibus, aduocatis, clerisis, &
monachis, & quibuscunque alijs piorum executorib
Avthore licenciato Illephonso Perez de Lara...
Matriti, ex typographia Illephonsi Martini, anno
M.DCVIII.
    10 p.l., 478 (i.e. 474) p., 1 l.   27 1/2 cm.

7733 Pérez de Lara, Alfonso, fl. 1608-1629.
    ... Opera omnia in tres tomos distributa.
[Lugduni, sumptibus Rochi Deville, & L. Chalmette.
MDCCXXXIII]
    v. 1, 9 p.l., 151, [9] p.; v. 2, 4 p.l., 221
(i.e. 219), [46] p.; v. 3, 1 p.l., 158, [35] p.
26 cm.
    Errors in pagination: v. 2, no. 184 and 218
omitted.

7734 Pérez de Lazcano, Diego.
    Proposicion, y manifiesto, qve el contador Diego

319

Perez de Lazcano, que lo es de las cuentas finales, y visita de la reales caxas de la villa imperial de Potosi, haze al rey nvestro señor: explicando el medio de introducir el aumento del valor de la plata, conforme à la real pragmatica de 14. de octubre del ano de 1686. à la plata en pasta, y barras de todas leyes, para que su real hazienda perciba los aumentos quantiosos, y evidentes, que se siguen de concederse a las Indias el aumento del valor de la plata, y labor, y vso de la moneda nueva, conforme a dicha pragmatica. En que comprueba, que solo en el reyno del Perù tendrà Su Magestad (que Dios guarde) de aumento al año 400ᵾ 973 ps. 7 rs. de a ocho de la nueva moneda, y que utilizaràn sus vassallos, vn millon quatrocientos y cincuenta y quatro mil y ciento y ochenta y dos pesos de a ocho, segun el estado presente; y que concedido dicho aumento, y moneda nueva, seràn mayores estos aumentos, y vtilidades. [Lima, 1691]
5, [3] p., 32 numb. 1.   23 cm.

7735   Perez y Hernandez, José María, ed.
Diccionario geográfico estadístico, histórico, biográfico de industria y comercio de la República mexicana... Mexico, 1874-75.
4 v.   30 cm.

7736   Périgny, Maurice, comte de. 1877-
... Les Etats-Unis du Mexique; préface de M. Marcel Dubois... Paris, E. Guilmoto [1912]
3 p.l., [ix]-xi, 310 p.   fold. map.   23 cm.

7737   Peter, Robert, 1805-1894.
Obituary sketch of Ethelbert Dudley, M.D. ... Delivered at the request of physicians of Lexington, Kentucky. [Lexington, 1862?]
[8] 1.   25 cm.

7738   Pétition nouvelle des citoyens de couleur des îles françoises, à l'Assemblée nationale, précédées d'un avertissement sur les manoeuvres employées pour faire échouer cette pétition, et suivie des pièces justificatives... Paris, Desenne [etc.] 1791.
xii, 19 p.   19 1/2 cm.

7739 Petrarca, Francesco, 1304-1374.
      Los sonetos y canciones del poeta Francisco
      Petrarcha, que traduzia Henrique Garces de lengua
      thoscana en eastellana. Dirigido a Philippo
      Segundo deste nombre, manarcha [sic] primero de
      las Españas, è Indias Oriental, y Occidental. En
      Madrid, Impresso en casa de Guillermo Droy impres-
      sor de libros, ano 1591.
      14 p.l., 178 numbered l.   26 cm.

7740 [Pferdekamp, Wilhelm] 1901-
      Auf schiffen, schienen, pneus ... eine reise,
      von Arnold Nolden [pseud.]... Berlin, Volksverband
      der bücherfreunde, Wegweiser-verlag g.m.b.h.
      [c1930]
      383, [1] p. incl. map.   18 1/2 cm.

7741 [Pferdekamp, Wilhelm] 1901-
      ... Auf schiffen schienen pneus... roman einer
      abenteuerlichen reise. Hamburg, Der neue sieben
      stäbe verlag [c1935]
      287, [1] p.   19 1/2 cm.
      Author's pseud., Arnold Nolden, at head of title.

7742 [Philadelphia. Union League]
      ... Abraham Lincoln. [Philadelphia, Crissey &
      Markley, 1864]
      12 p.   23 cm.

7743 Philadelphia. Union League.
      The will of the people. [n.p.] 1864.
      8 p.   20 cm.

7744 Phillips, Wendell, 1811-1884.
      An address, delivered in Tremont temple,
      Boston, April 19th, 1865. Worcester, C. Hamilton
      [1865]
      8 p.   22 cm.

7745 The picket line and campfire stories: a collection
      of war anecdotes, both grave and gay, illustrative
      of the trials and triumphs of soldier life, with
      ... humorous stories, told of and by Abraham Lin-
      coln, together with a full collection of Northern
      and Southern war songs, by a member of G. A. R.

New York, Hurst [n.d.]
various pagings.   20 cm.

7746   Pickett, LaSalle Corbell, "Mrs. G. E. Pickett,"
1848-1931.
An historic letter by LaSalle Corbell Pickett
about Abraham Lincoln: facsimile of original
letter laid in.   [Chicago, National Republican
club, 1947]
[4] p.   folder.   20 cm.

7747   Picó, Rafael.
Nueva geografía de Puerto Rico: física,
económica, y social, por Rafael Picó.   Con la
colaboración de Zayda Buitrago de Santiago y
Héctor H. Berrios.   [San Juan]   Editorial Universitaria, Universidad de Puerto Rico, 1969.
xviii, 400 p.   illus. (part col.), maps.   24 cm.

7748   The picturesque tourist: being a guide through the
state of New York and Upper and Lower Canada, including a Hudson river guide; giving an accurate
description of cities and villages, celebrated
places of resort, etc. ...   New York, J. Disturnell,
1858.
1 p.l., ix, [10]-298 p.   front., illus., plates,
3 maps (1 fold.)   16 cm.

7749   Pierrepont, Edwards, 1817-1892.
Argument... to the jury, on the trial of John H.
Surratt for the murder of President Lincoln.
Washington, Govt. printing office, 1867.
122 p.   22 cm.

7750   Pim, Bedford Clapperton Trevelyan, 1826-1886.
Dottings on the roadside, in Panama, Nicaragua,
and Mosquito.   By Bedford Pim ... and Berthold
Seemann ...   London, Chapman and Hall, 1869.
xvi, 468 p.   col. front., illus., 5 col. pl.,
2 maps.   23 cm.

7751   Pim, Bedford Clapperton Trevelyan, 1826-1886.
The gate of the Pacific.   By Commander Bedford
Pim   ...   London, L. Reeve & co., 1863.
xiii, [1], 432 p.   incl. col. front. plates (part

322

col.) maps.   22 1/2 cm.

7752   Pinilla, Sabino, 1851-1909.
       ... La creación de Bolivia; prólogo y notas de
       Alcides Arguedas.   Madrid, Editorial-América [1917]
       371 p.   23 cm.

7753   Pittman, Hannah (Daviess) 1840-   , ed.
       Americans of gentle birth and their ancestors;
       a genealogical encyclopedia ... embracing many
       authenticated lineages and biographical sketches
       of the founders of the colonies and their descen-
       dants found in all parts of the United States.
       Mrs. H. D. Pittman, editor ...   Saint Louis, Mo.,
       Buxton & Skinner, 1903-07.
       2 v.   fronts., plates (part col.), ports., col.
       coats of arms.   26 1/2-30 cm.

7754   Plummer, Mary Wright, 1856-
       Roy and Ray in Mexico, by Mary Wright Plummer
       ...   New York, H. Holt and company, 1907.
       ix, 403 p.   front. (port.), 15 pl., map.   21 cm.

7755   Poe, John William, 1850-1923.
       The true story of the killing of "Billy the Kid"
       (notorious New Mexico outlaw) as detailed by John
       W. Poe, a member of Sheriff Pat Garrett's posse,
       to E. A. Brininstool, in 1919.   Los Angeles, Cal.,
       Priv. print. by E. A. Brininstool [1923?]
       15 p.   incl. port., illus.   22 1/2 cm.

7756   Poinsett, Joel Roberts, 1779-1851.
       Notes on Mexico, made in the autumn of 1822.
       Accompanied by an historical sketch of the revolu-
       tion, and translations of official reports on the
       present state of that country.   By J. R. Poinsett,
       esq. ...   London, J. Miller, 1825.
       viii, 298 p., 1 l., 138 p.   front. (fold. map)
       22 1/2 cm.

7757   Polk, J   M   , 1838-
       The North and South American review, by J. M.
       Polk...   Austin, Tex., Press of Von Boeckmann-
       Jones co., printers, 1912.
       61 p.   incl. front. (port.), illus.   22 1/2 cm.

323

"A genealogical tree of the Polk family,"
folded chart 43 1/2 x 56 1/2 cm, inserted at end.

7758 Pollard, Hugh Bertie Campbell, 1888-
A busy time in Mexico; an unconventional record
of Mexican incident, by Hugh B. C. Pollard. New
York, Duffield and company, 1913.
vii, 243 p. front., plates, port. 23 cm.

7759 [Poole, Mrs. Annie Sampson]
Mexicans at home in the interior. By a resident.
London, Chapman & Hall, 1884.
viii, 183, [1] p. front. (port.) 19 1/2 cm.

7760 Portrait and biographical album of Henry county,
Iowa, containing full page portraits and biographical
sketches of prominent and representative citizens
of the county, together with portraits and biogra-
phies of all the governors of Iowa, and the presidents of the United States. Chicago, Acme publishing
company, 1888.
4 p.l., [17]-694 p. incl. plates (part double)
ports. 28 cm.

7761 Posada Gutiérrez, Joaquín, 1797?-1881.
... Memorias histórico-políticas. Últimos días
de la gran Colombia y del Libertador ... Madrid,
Editorial-América, 1920-21.
3 v. 22 cm.

7762 Posadas, Gervasio Antonio de, 1757-1832.
... Memorias de Gervasio Antonio Posadas,
director supremo de las provincias del Rio de la
Plata en 1814. Memorias de un abanderado (Nueva
Granada: 1810-1819) por José María Espinosa.
Madrid, Editorial-América, 1920.
400 p. 22 cm.

7763 Posselt, Louis.
Louis Posselt's kreuz- und querzüge durch Mexiko
und die Vereinigten Staaten von Nord-Amerika.
Nach tagebuchaufzeichnungen bearbeitet von F.
Maurer. Heidelberg, C. Winter, 1882.
ix, 253 p. 20 1/2 cm.

7764   Pote, William, 1718-1755.
        The journal of Captain William Pote, jr., during
        his captivity in the French and Indian war from May,
        1745, to August, 1747. New York, Published by Dodd,
        Mead, & co., MDCCCXCVI.
        xxxvii p., 1 l., 223 p. front., pl., ports.,
        maps, facsim. and atlas.   23 1/2 cm.

7765   Potter, William James, 1830-1893.
        The national tragedy: four sermons delivered
        before the First Congregational society, New
        Bedford, on the life and death of Abraham Lincoln.
        New Bedford, Mass., A. Taber & brother, 1865.
        67 p.   22 cm.

7766   Pouchot, Pierre, 1712-1767.
        Mémoires sur la dernière guerre de l'Amérique
        Septentrionale, entre la France et l'Angleterre.
        Suivis d'observations, dont plusieurs sont rela-
        tives au théatre actuel de la guerre, & de nouveaux
        détails sur les moeurs & les usages des sauvages,
        avec des cartes topographiques. Yverdon, 1781.
        3 v. fold. map, 2 fold. plans.   16 cm.

7767   Poussin, Guillaume Tell, 1794-1876.
        The United States; its power and progress.
        By Guillaume Tell Poussin... 1st American, from
        the 3d Paris ed. Tr. from the French, by Edmund
        L. DuBarry... Philadelphia, Lippincott, Grambo
        & co., 1851.
        xxiv, [33]-488 p.   22 1/2 cm.

7768   Pozo y Honesto, José del.
        Demonstracion legal en defensa de d. Joseph del
        Pozo y Honesto, tesorero, y oficial real de la
        real hazienda de la ciudad, è isla de S. Juan de
        Puerto Rico, en Indias, representando el derecho
        del patrimonio real, y en defensa de los cargos que
        se le han fulminado. Y por don Francisco de
        Allendez y Melendez, d. Pedro Montañès y Lugo, don
        Juan Antonio Bruno y Guerrero; y los demàs, que
        fueron capitulares en los años de setecientos diez
        y nueve, y setecientos y veinte. Y por el sargento
        mayor reformado d. Bartholome Alonso Montero, los
        capitanes don Juan Baptista Butron y Muxica, don

Laurdano [!] de Arroyo, y el capitan Andrès Antonio
Gonçalez; y por los demàs militares y vezinos de
dicha ciudad, que consultaron en los expressados
años de setecientos y diez y nueve, y setecientos
y veinte. Con el señor fiscal del svpremo Consejo
de Indias, y con el capitan Migvel Enriqvez, vezino
de dicha ciudad, contador don Antonio Paris Negro,
y otros. Sobre que se confirme la sentencia de
vista, dada por los señores de sala de justicia
de dicho real, y supremo Consejo de Indias, en
la causa, que à instancia del dicho don Joseph del
Pozo, y demàs que se suponen delatores, pende en
dicho supremo Consejo en grado de suplicacion,
aumentandose las penas, y multas en ella contenidas
à lo que el arbitrio del consejo fuere servido,
mandando se le resarzan à d. Joseph del Pozo todos
los daños, interesses, perjuizios, y menoscabos, que
por esta razon se le han seguido, y à los demàs, que
se suponen delatores. [Madrid?] 1723.
61 numb. l.   23 cm.

7769   Prantl, Adolfo.
... La ciudad de México novísima guía universal
de la capital de la República Mexicana; directorio
clasificado de vecinos, y prontuario de la organiza-
cion y funciones del gobierno federal y oficinas
de su dependencia. Obra ilustrada con fotograbados
de Ulderigo Tabarracci ... y acompañada de un plano
topográfico de la ciudad. México, J. Buxó y
compañía, 1901.
4 p.l., [xi]-xxiv p., 1 l., 1005, [2] p. plates,
ports., fold. map, plan, tables (part fold.)
20 x 15 1/2 cm.

7770   Prat de Saba, Onogre, 1733?-1810.
Vicennalia sacra peruviana; sive, De viris
peruvianis religione illustribus hisce viginti
annis gloriosa morte functis. Ab Onuphrio Prat
de Saba sac. hispano. Ferrariae, ex typografia
Francisci Pomatelli, 1788.
xvi, 200 p.   20 cm.

7771   [Pratt, Harry Edward] 1901-
Lincoln's Springfield: a guide book & brief
history... [Springfield, Ill., The Abraham Lincoln

association, 1938]
cover-title, [28] p. illus. 16 cm.

7772 Prentis, Noble Lovely, 1839-1900.
South-western letters. By Noble L. Prentis.
Topeka, Kan., Kansas publishing house, 1882.
133 p., 1 l. 20 1/2 cm.

7773 Presbrey, O   F
Abraham Lincoln, the patriot and Christian.
Saratoga Springs, N. Y., The author [1900]
8 p. 20 cm.

7774 Prescott, William Hickling, 1796-1859.
History of the conquest of Mexico, by William H.
Prescott ... Ed. by John Foster Kirk ... Philadelphia, J. B. Lippincott company [1902]
3 v. fronts., plates, maps. 19 1/2 cm.

7775 Prescott, William Hickling, 1796-1859.
Mexico and the life of the conqueror Fernando
Cortes... New York, Peter Fenelon Collier, 1898.
2 v. illus. 21 cm.

7776 Preston, William Thomas Rochester, 1851-
The life and times of Lord Strathcona, by W. T.
R. Preston... London, E. Nash, 1914.
ix, [2], 13-324 p. front. (port.) 23 cm.

7777 Price, Sir Rose Lambart, bart., 1837-1899.
The two Americas; an account of sport and travel.
With notes on men and manners in North and South
America. By Major Sir Rose Lambart Price, bart.
... Philadelphia, J. B. Lippincott & co., 1877.
viii, 368 p. front., plates. 21 1/2 cm.

7778 Price, Thomas W
Brief notes taken on a trip to the city of Mexico
in 1878, by Thomas W. Price ... [n.p., 1878?]
iv p., 1 l., [7]-103 p. 19 1/2 cm.

7779 Prida y Arteaga, Francisco de la, 1850-
... Le Mexique, tel qu'il est aujourd'hui; ouvrage
orné de quatre portraits par Aristle Boulineau et
d'une carte gravée par Ehrard. Paris, A. Savine,

327

1891.
3 p.l., xv, 376 p. incl. 3 port. front., fold.
map. 23 cm.

7780 Pritchard, John.
Narratives of John Pritchard, Pierre Chrysologue
Pambrun and Frederick Damien Heurter, respecting
the aggressions of the North-West Company, against
the Earl of Selkirk's settlements upon Red river.
London, John Murray, 1819.
91 p. 22 cm.

7781 Proclamation of emancipation: presented to the subscribers to the Proclamation of emancipation.
Lithographed by Rosenthal, and published by L.
Franklin Smith. Philadelphia, Pa., 1863.
15 p. 20 cm.

7782 Proctor, Addison Gilbert, 1838-
Lincoln and the convention of 1860... [Chicago
Historical Society, 1918]
29 p. front. 23 cm.

7783 Providence. City Council.
Proceedings of the City council of Providence on
the death of Abraham Lincoln, with the oration
delivered... June 1, 1865, by William Binney, esq.
Providence, Knowles, Anthony & co., 1865.
56 p. 26 cm.

7784 Prowse, Daniel Woodley.
A history of Newfoundland from the English,
colonial, and foreign records, by D. W. Prowse...
with a prefatory note by Edmund Gosse... London
and New York, Macmillan and co., 1895.
xxiii, 742 p. illus., plates, ports., plans,
maps (part fold.) 25 1/2 cm.

7785 Prud'homme, Louis Arthur.
Notes historiques sur la vie de P. E. de Radisson.
[Ottawa?] Imprimerie de l'agriculture [1892?]
62 p. 22 cm.

7786 Pullen-Burry, Bessie, 1858-
Jamaica as it is, 1903; by B. Pullen-Burry...

London, T. F. Unwin, 1903.
xiv p., 1 l., 240 p. incl. front., facsim.
7 pl., map. 19 1/2 cm.

7787 Putnam, George, 1807-1878.
... An address delivered before the city government, and citizens of Roxbury, on occasion of the
death of Abraham Lincoln... April 19, 1865. Roxbury, L. B. & O. E. Weston, printers, 1865.
14 p. 23 cm.

7788 Putnam, George Haven, 1844-1930.
Abraham Lincoln, the great captain; personal
reminiscences by a veteran of the Civil War, a
lecture delivered at Oxford, May 7, 1928. Oxford,
Clarendon press, 1928.
32 p. 20 cm.

Q

7789 Osuna, Joaquin. (Misfiling; should follow 7654)
El iris celeste de las catolicas Españas, la
aparicion, y patrocinio de N.S. de Guadalupe, en
las Indias occidentales. [n.p.] 1745.
22 p.l., 31 p. illus. (coat of arms) 22 cm.

7790 Que ceux qui ont une âme lisent ceci [à Saint-Domingue,
ce 20 février 1789] Au Cap, Isle Saint-Domingue,
1789.
12 p. 20 cm.

7791 Quebec, Province. Laws, statutes, etc.
Ordinances, made for the province of Quebec...
Quebec, Imprimées par Brown & Gilmore, 1767.
81 p. 30 cm.

7792 Quesada, Vicente Gregorio, 1830-1913.
... Recuerdos de mi vida diplomática, misión en
México (1891) ... Buenos Aires, J. Menéndez, 1904.
164 p. 26 cm.

7793 La question Riel. [n.p., 1886?]

329

67 p.   20 cm.

7794   Quevedo y Zubieta, Salvador, 1859-
... México.   Recuerdos de un emigrado, con prólogo
de Don Emilio Castelar.   Madrid, Est. tip. de los
Sucesores de Rivadeneyra, 1883.
xxiv, 397, [2] p.   19 cm.

7795   Quijano Quesada, Alberto.
... Costa Rica ayer y hoy, 1800-1939.   San José,
Costa Rica, Editorial Borrasé hermanos, 1939.
771, [1] p.   illus. (incl. ports.)   26 1/2 cm.

7796   Quill Lake, Sask.   School.
... Quill Lake history.   A tribute to the community
and its builders.   Regina, Sask., Public press, ltd.
[1955?]
47 p.   28 1/2 cm.
At head of title: 1905-1955.   Saskatchewan golden
jubilee.

7797   Quincy, Edmund, 1808-1877.
Life of Josiah Quincy of Massachusetts.   By his
son Edmund Quincy.   Boston, Ticknor and Fields,
1867.
xii, 560 p.   2 port. (incl. front.)   21 cm.

R

7798   Rabe, Johann E
Eine erholungsfahrt nach Texas und Mexico.   Tage-
buchblätter von Joh. E. Rabe.   Mit initialen von
A. T. Bargum.   Hamburg und Leipzig, L. Voss, 1893.
2 p.l., 284 p.   23 1/2 cm.

7799   Radisson, Peter Esprit, 1656-1685 (?)
Voyages of Peter Esprit Radisson, being an account
of his travels and experiences among the North
American Indians, from 1652 to 1684.   Transcribed
from original manuscripts in the Bodleian Library
and the British Museum.   With historical illustrations and an introduction, by Gideon D. Scull...

[n.p., 1885]
385 p.   22 cm.

7800   Raleigh, Walter, 1552?-1612.
The discoverie of the large, rich, and bevvtifvl
empyre of Gviana, with a relation of the great and
golden citie of Manoa (which the Spanish call El
Dorado) and of the prouinces of Emeria, Arromaia,
Amapaia, and other countries, with their riuers,
adioyning... London, Robert Robinson, 1596.
[16], 112 p.   22 1/2 cm.

7801   [Ramírez de Aguilar, Fernando] 1887-
... Estampas de México. México, 1930.
4 p.l., xi, 320 p.   23 1/2 cm.

7802   Ramírez, José Fernando, 1804-1871, ed.
Extracto de las relaciones de los viajeros y
misioneros, que han explorado el territorio
situado al norte de México del 26⁰ al 29⁰; ó,
Noticias del suelo, clima, producciones, costumbres,
ritos, creencias, lenguas, de las tribus indígenas
que lo ocupan y de las ruinas y rastros de sus
antiguos pobladores, q'se encuentran diseminados
en aquellos desiertos. Sacadas de la colección de
mss. del Archivo General. México, 1847. México,
Vargas Rea, 1949.
96 p.   illus.   20 cm.

7803   Ramsing, H   U
The family of Alexander Hamilton's mother. Translated by S. Vahl from Historisk Tidsskrift (Copenhagen)
1939. [n.p.] 1951.
54, 9 p.   28 cm.

7804   Randolph, Innis.
O I'm a good old rebel. [n.p., n.d.]
4 p.   illus., music.   16 cm.

7805   Rankin, Jeremiah Eames, 1828-1904.
Moses and Joshua: a discourse on the death of
Abraham Lincoln, preached in the Winthrop church,
Charlestown, Wednesday noon, April 19, 1865. Boston,
Dakin and Metcalf [1865]
16 p.   23 cm.

7806 Raster, Hermann, 1827-1891.
      Reisebriefe von Hermann Raster. Mit einer
      biographie und einem bildniss des verfassers.
      Berlin, Buchdr. Gutenberg (F. Zillessen) 1891.
      318 p. front. (port.)   19 1/2 cm.

7807 Ratzel, Friedrich, 1844-1904.
      Aus Mexico. Reiseskizzen aus den jahren, 1874
      und 1875. Von dr. Friedrich Ratzel ... Mit einer
      karte in farbendruck. Breslau, J. U. Kern (M.
      Müller) 1878.
      xiii, 426 p. fold. map.   23 cm.

7808 Rawlings, Thomas.
      The confederation of the British North American
      provinces; their history and future prospects; in-
      cluding also British Columbia and Hudson's Bay
      territory; with a map, and suggestions in reference
      to the true and only practicable route from the
      Atlantic to the Pacific ocean... London, Sampson
      Low, son, and Marston, 1865.
      244 p. illus., fold. map.   22 cm.

7809 Rawlings, Thomas.
      What shall we do with the Hudson's Bay territory?
      Colonize the "fertile belt," which contain forty
      millions of acres... London, A. H. Baily & co.,
      1866.
      83 p.   22 cm.

7810 Raymond, Samuel.
      Genealogies of the Raymond families of New England,
      1630-1 to 1886, with a historical sketch of some of
      the Raymonds of early times, their origin, etc.
      New York, Press of J. J. Little & co., 1886.
      299 p.   22 cm.

7811 Rea, Alonso de la.
      Cronica de la orden N. Serafico P.S. Franscisco,
      provincia de San Pedro y San Pablo de Mechoacan
      en la Nueva España. Compuesta por el P. lector
      de teologia Fr. Alonso de la Rea de la misma pro-
      vincia... Dedicada á N.P. Fr. Cristóbal Vaz, ministro
      provincial de ella. Año de 1639. Con privilegio.
      En México por la viuda de Bernardo Calderon. Año de

1643. Ed. de la "Voz de México." Mexico, Impr. de
J.R. Barbedillo y c.ª, 1882.
   xv, 488 p.   19 1/2 cm.

7812 Reasons to show that there is a great probability of a
   navigable passage to the western American ocean
   through Hudson's streights, and Chesterfield inlet
   ... London, Printed for J. Robinson, 1749.
      23 p.   22 cm.

7813 Reavis, Logan Uriah, 1831-1889.
      The life and public services of Richard Yates,
   the war governor of Illinois: a lecture delivered
   in the hall of the House of representatives,
   Springfield, Illinois, Tuesday evening, March 1st,
   1881. By Hon. L. U. Reavis... St. Louis, J. H.
   Chambers & co., 1881.
      3 p.l., 37 p. front. (port.)   23 1/2 cm.

7814 Rebullosa, Jaime.
      Descripcion de todas las provincias, reynos, y
   estados, y ciudades principales del mundo...
   Gerona, Jaime Bro, 1748.
      456 p.   20 cm.

7815 Réclamations pour les colonies des Antilles, adressées
   au roi et à la nation... [Paris, 1789]
      42 p.   21 cm.

7816 Reed, H   B
      The back-bone of Illinois in front and rear, from
   1861 to 1865, and Memorial Hall, Springfield,
   Illinois. Springfield, Illinois, H. W. Rokker,
   1886.
      51 p.   20 cm.

7817 Reed, Seth, 1823-
      A discourse delivered on the occasion of the
   funeral obsequies of President Lincoln, April 19,
   1865... Boston, G. C. Rand & Avery, 1865.
      24 p.   24 cm.

7818 Reed, William Bradford, 1806-1876.
      Speech... on the presidential question, delivered
   before the National Democratic association, Phil-

adelphia, September 4, 1860. [Philadelphia, 1860]
   20 p.   23 cm.

7819 Rees, Thomas, 1850-1933.
      Spain's lost jewels: Cuba and Mexico, by Thomas
      Rees ...   Springfield, Ill., Illinois state register
      [c1906]
         3 p.l., 13-398 p. front. (ports.), plates.
      20 1/2 cm.

7820 Reese, Mary E
      Genealogy of the Reese family in Wales and
      America. Richmond, Va., Whittet & Shepperson, 1903.
         322 p.   18 cm.

7821 Reiche, Karl Friedrich, 1860-
      Kreuz und quer durch Mexiko; aus dem wanderbuch
      eines deutschen gelehrten, von prof. dr. Karl
      Reiche. Leipzig, Deutsche buchwerkstätten g.m.b.h.,
      1930.
         128 p. front., plates.   25 cm.

7822 Reid, R   L
      ... The assay office and the proposed mint at
      New Westminster. A chapter in the history of the
      Fraser River mines... Victoria, B.C., Printed by
      Charles F. Banfield, 1926.
         101 p. illus. (part fold.)   24 1/2 cm.

7823 Reider, J   H
      A digest of tropical Mexico. This volume will
      be a helpful guide to all who seek a better knowledge
      of our little sister republic, Mexico. By Dr. J.
      H. Reider ... Los Angeles, Grafton publishing cor-
      poration, 1913.
         xv, [17]-196 p. incl. front. plates, port., fold.
      map.   17 1/2 cm.

7824 Rejano, Juan, 1903-
      ... La esfinge mestiza, crónica menor de México.
      Portada e ilustraciones de Miguel Prieto ...
      [México, Editorial Leyenda, s.a., 1945]
         3 p.l., 9-292 p., 3 l. illus.   24 cm.

7825 Relaçam verdadeira dos trabalhos q̄ ho gouernador dō
     Fernādo de souto e certos fidalgos portugueses
     passarom no descobrimēto da Frolida. Evora, Andree
     de Burgos, 1557.
          unpaged. 23 cm.

7826 Relacion sucinta en que se explica sencillamente el
     nuevo descubrimiento de sacar el aceyte del
     cacahuete ó manî de América, y de lo demas, que se
     sabe en el dia de este fruto. [Valencia, 1798.
     Colophon: Por Josef Estévan, impresor del ilmo.
     señor arzobispo]
          16 p. 22 cm.

7827 Relacion verdadera de todos los sucessos y encuentros
     que ha tenido la real armada de la flota, en la
     carrera de las Indias, con los olandeses, desde
     catorze de enero, hasta tres de março de mil y
     seiscientos y quarenta y vno. viniendo por gen-
     erales don Geronimo de Sandoual, y don Iuan de Vega
     Baçan. Con licencia. Madrid, Por Iuan Sanchez,
     1641.
          [4] p. 21 cm.

7828 Relation du séjour de M. de Blanchelande, lieutenant
     pour le roi au gouvernement général de Saint-
     Domingue, au Port-au-Prince, par un créole. Port-
     au-Prince, Impr. nat., F. Chaidron & compagnie,
     1792.
          21 p. 1 p.l. 17 1/2 cm.

7829 Religious Tract Society, London.
          Abraham Lincoln. London, Religious Tract Society
     [n.d.]
          32 p. 21 cm.

7830 Reminiscences of a bungle. By one of the bunglers.
     Toronto, Grip printing & publishing co., 1887.
          66 p. 23 cm.

7831 Reminiscences of the Red River rebellion of 1869.
     [n.p., n.d.]
          45 p. 20 cm.

7832 Remsburg, John Eleazer, 1848-

The fathers of our republic: Paine, Jefferson,
Washington, Franklin. A lecture delivered before
the tenth annual congress of the American secular
union, in Chickering Hall, New York, November 13,
1886... Boston, J. P. Mendum, 1887.
vi, [7]-45 p. 18 cm.

7833 El Renacimiento; periódico literario. México,
Impr. de F. Díaz de León y Santiago White, 1869.
2 v. 24 cm.

7834 El Renacimiento; periódico literario. 2. época.
México, Impr. de F. Díaz de León sucesores, 1894.
3 p.l., 403, [1] p. plates, ports., music.
30 1/2 cm.

7835 Repertorio americana; semanario de cultura hispánica.
San José, Costa Rica, C. A., J. García Monge,
1920-1934.
29 v. illus. (incl. ports.) 29 1/2 x 34 cm.
Semimonthly, Sept. 1919-May 1, 1921; 3 no. a
month, May 10-Aug. 1921; weekly, Sept. 1921-

7836 El Repertorio pintoresco, miscelánea instructiva y
amena, consagrada á la religion, la filosofía, la
industria y las bellas letras. Mérida de Yucatán,
1863.
586, vii p.

7837 La República Mexicana. Estados del Norte: Sonora--
Chihuahua--Coahuila. Nuevo Leon--Tamaulipas.
Paris, Mexico, Vda. de C. Bouret, 1910.
5 v. in 1. illus. (incl. tables), 5 col. maps.
32 x 25 1/2 cm.

7838 Republican Convention, Richmond, Va., 18 March 1839.
Proceedings of the Republican Convention.
Monday, March 18, 1839. [Richmond, Va.? 1839?]
24 p. 21 cm.

7839 Republican Party. Illinois. Convention, 1858.
Proceedings of the Republican state convention,
held at Springfield, Illinois, June 16, 1858.
Springfield, Bailhache & Baker, [1858]
12 p. 27 cm.

7840   Republican Party. National Convention, 2d, Chicago,
        1860.
        ... Proceedings of the National Republican
        Convention, held at Chicago, May 16th, 17th and
        18th, 1860... Chicago, Press & Tribune office, 1860.
        44 p.   21 cm.

7841   Réveillaud, Eugène, 1851-
        Histoire du Canada et des Canadiens français de
        la découverte jusqu'à nos jours, par Eug.
        Réveillaud. Paris, Grassart [1884]
        4 p.l., 551 p. fold. map.   23 cm.

7842   Revere, Joseph Warren, 1812-1880.
        Keel and saddle: a retrospect of forty years
        of military and naval service. By Joseph W. Revere.
        Boston, J. R. Osgood and company, 1872.
        xiii, 360 p.   19 1/2 cm.

7843   Reverente satisfaccion, que a su Reverendissimo
        Padre Maestro General dà en nombre de su Provincia
        de Mexico de Religiosos Augustinos Calzados, el
        Padre Procurador General de ella. [n.p., ca. 1753]
        57 p.   24 cm.

7844   Revista azul; el domingo de "El Partido liberal".
        Mexico, Tipografía de "El Partido Liberal," 1895-
        1896.
        5 v. ports.   32 1/2 cm.

7845   Revista cubana, periódico mensual de ciencias,
        filosofía, literatura y bellas artes. Havana,
        Soler, Álvarez y comp., 1885-1895.
        21 v. pl., ports.   26 1/2 cm.

7846   Revista de bibliografía chilena y extranjera.
        Santiago de Chile, 1913-1918.
        6 v.   23 cm.

7847   Revista de Bogotá. Literatura, ciéncias, filosofía,
        historia, viajes, teatro, memorias, etc. Bogotá,
        1871-1872.
        1 v.   24 cm.

7848   Revista de Chile. Santiago, Imprenta Gutenberg,

1881.
2 v.   25 cm.

7849   Revista de Cuba; periódico mensual de ciencias,
derecho, literatura y bellas artes ... Director:
Dr. José Antonio Cortina. Havana, Est. tip. de
Soler, Alvarez y comp. [etc] 1877-84.
16 v.   25 cm.

7850   Revista de La Habana. Havana, Impr. del Tiempo,
1853-57.
9 v.   illus., pl., port.   23-31 cm.

7851   Revista de Santiago. Santiago de Chile, 1855.
1 v.   23 cm.

7852   Revista de Santiago. Santiago de Chile, 1872-1873.
3 v.   23 cm.

7853   Revista del Rio de la Plata; periódico mensual de
historia y literatura de América. Publicado por
Andrés Lamas. Vicente Fidel Lopez y Juan María
Gutierrez. Buenos Aires, Mayo, 1871-[77]
13 v.   21 cm.

7854   Revista moderna. Arte y ciencia. Mexico, 1898-
1903.
6 v.   23 cm.

7855   Revista moderna. Mexico, 1903-1911.
15 v.   23 cm.

7856   Revista nueva; ciencias, literatura y artes.
Panamá, 1916-1919.
6 v.   23 cm.

7857   Revista peruana, fundada por Mariano Felipe Paz
Soldán. Carlos Paz Soldán, editor. Lima, M.
Fernandez, 1879-1880.
5 v. pl.   26 1/2 cm.

7858   Reybaud, Louis.
Marines et voyages... Paris, Michel Lévy frères,
1854.
400 p.   19 cm.

7859 Reyes, Rafael, pres. Colombia, 1851-1931.
    Misión diplomática y militar, 1903-04. Bogotá,
Imprenta nacional [1904]
    77 p.   24 cm.

7860 Reyna, Francisco de, d. 1708.
    Señor. El maestro fray Francisco de Reyna, de
la Orden de predicadores, procurador general de su
provincia de San Hipolito martyr, valle de Oaxaca,
ocurre à V. Mag. con el motivo de los procedimientos,
inquietudes, y discordias que fomentò el reverendo
obispo don fray Angel de Maldonado, con siniestros
informes à V. Mag. y al virrey por despojar à la
provincia, de las doctrinas que tiene a su cargo...
[n.p., 1708?]
    6 numb. l.   20 cm.

7861 Reynolds, Lewis Gardner.
    A wonderful hour with Abraham Lincoln. [n.p.]
1929.
    [4] p.   illus.   22 cm.

7862 Rhys, Horton.
    A theatrical trip for a wager! through Canada and
the United States. By Captain Horton Rhys ("Morton
Price") ... London, Pub. for the author by C.
Dudley, 1861.
    3 p.l., [3]-140 p.   3 col. pl.   22 cm.

7863 Ribas, Manual José de la.
    Grammatical construcción de los hymnos eclesiasticos
... Madrid, Andrés Ramirez, 1776.
    1 p.l., 244 p., 4 l.   21 cm.

7864 Rice, John H
    Mexico: our neighbor, by John H. Rice.   New
York, J. W. Lovell co. [c1888]
    124 p.   front., port.   19 cm.

7865 Richard, Edouard, 1844-1904.
    ... Acadia; missing links of a lost chapter in
American History, by an Acadian... New York, Home
book company; Montreal, J. Lovell & son, 1895.
    2 v.   fronts. (v.1, port.; v.2, map)   23 1/2 cm.

7866   Richards, Augustus Long.
        Steuben the pionner. An address given before the
        Steuben Old Home Day Association, August 24, 1835
        ... [Steuben, N. Y.?] Steuben Old Home Day
        Association, 1936.
        32 p. front. (port.), illus., map. 23 cm.

7867   Richardson, Albert Deane, 1833-1869.
        Garnered sheaves from the writings of Albert
        Deane Richardson collected and arranged by his wife
        [Mrs. Abby (Sage) Richardson: to which is added a
        biographical sketch of the author... pub. by
        subscription only. Hartford, Conn., Columbian book
        co.; Toledo, O., W. E. Bliss: [etc., etc.], 1871.
        4 p.l., [17], 430 p. front. (port.), illus.,
        plates. 22 1/2 cm.

7868   Rickard, Thomas Arthur, 1864-
        Journeys of observation, by T. A. Rickard ...
        San Francisco, Dewey publishing company, 1907.
        xvi, 255, vii, 130 p. front., illus., plates,
        maps. 24 1/2 cm.

7869   Riedel, Emil.
        Practical guide of the city and valley of Mexico.
        With excursions to Toluca, Tula, Pachuca, Puebla,
        Cuernavaca, etc., and two maps by Emil Riedel ...
        City of Mexico, I. Epstein, 1892.
        2 p.l., iv, 427 p. 2 fold. maps. 14 cm.

7870   Riker, Carroll L
        On to Washington; the National party and its
        platform. By Carroll L. Riker ... Chicago, Ill.,
        National political review association [C1894]
        191 p. incl. port. 19 1/2 cm.

7871   Ripley, Edward H
        The capture and occupation of Richmond, April
        3d, 1865. New York, Putnam, 1907.
        31 p. illus. 22 cm.

7872   Riva Palacio, Mariano, 1803-1880.
        Memorandum sobre el proceso del archiduque
        Fernando Maximiliano de Austria, por los CC.
        Mariano Riva Palacio y Lic. Rafael Martinez de la

Torre. Mexico, Impr. de F. Díaz de León y S.
White, 1867.
92, 49 p. front. (port.) 23 cm.

7873 Riva Palacio, Vicente, 1832-1896, ed.
México a través de los siglos. Historia general
y completa del desenvolvimiento social, político,
religioso, militar, artístico, científico y
literario de México desde la antigüedad más remota
hasta la época actual... pub. bajo la dirección
del general D. Vicente Riva Palacio... Barcelona,
Espasa y compañia 1888-89.
5 v. illus., plates (partly col.) maps, facsims.
35 cm.

7874 River Plate Publishing Company.
Guide to México, illus. for the tourist and bus-
inessman. Autorizada por la Secretaría de Gober-
nación. Raul Sapia M., editor. 2d ed. Mexico, New
York, 1942.
xvi, 178 p. illus. (part col.), ports., maps
(part fold.) 21 cm.

7875 Rivera, Luis Manuel del.
México en 1842. Madrid, Imprenta y fundición
de D. Eusebio Aguado, 1844.
321 p. 22 cm.

7876 Rivera y Sanromán, Agustín, 1824-1916.
Los hijos de Jalisco: o sea, Catálogo de los
catedráticos de filosofía en el Seminario conciliar
de Guadalajara desde 1791 hasta 1867, con expresión
del año en que cada catedrático acabo de enseñar
filosofía, i de los discípulos notables que tuvo.
Escrito por Agustín Rivera. 2. ed. Guadalajara,
Escuela de artes i oficios, taller de tipografía
dirigido por J. Gómez Ugarte, 1897.
133 p. 23 1/2 cm.

7877 Rivera y Sanromán, Agustín, 1824-1916.
Principios críticos sobre el virreinato de la
Nueva España i sobre la revolución de independencia
... San Juan de los Lagos, Jal., Tipografía de José
Martín Hermosillo, etc., 1884-1888.
3 v. 22 cm.

341

7878 Rivera y Villalón, Pedro de, fl. 1740.
... Diario y derrotero de lo caminado, visto y
observado en la visita que hizo a los presidios
de la Nueva España Septentrional el brigadier
Pedro de Rivera. Con una introd. y notas por Vito
Alessio Robles. México, Taller Autográfico, 1946.
244 p. fold. maps. 25 cm.

7879 Rivero, Nicolás, 1849-
... Recuerdos de Méjico, 1910. Habana, Impr. de
Rambla y Bouza, 1911.
xi, 159 p. plates. 23 1/2 cm.

7880 Roberts, Bernie K
Richardville, chief of the Miamis [Fort Wayne,
Ind., Public Library of Fort Wayne and Allen County,
1956?]
11 p. illus. 21 cm.

7881 Roberts, Sir Charles George Douglas, 1860-1943.
A sister to Evangeline; being the story of Yvonne
de Lamourie, and how she went into exile with the
villagers of Grand Pré. Boston, Lamson, Wolffe,
1898.
viii, 289 p. map. 20 cm.

7882 Roberts, Edwards.
With the invader: glimpses of the Southwest.
By Edwards Roberts. San Francisco, S. Carson &
co., 1885.
3 p.l., [5]-156 p. front., illus. 17 1/2 cm.

7883 Roberts, Orlando W
Narratives of voyages and excursions on the east
coast and in the interior of Central America;
describing a journey up the river San Juan, and
passage across the lake of Nicaragua to the city of
Leon: pointing out the advantages of a direct
commercial intercourse with the natives. By Orlando
W. Roberts ... With notes and observations by Edward
Irving. Edinburgh, Printed for Constable & co.;
[etc., etc.] 1827.
xxiii, [25]-302 p. front. (fold. map) 15 cm.

7884 Robinson, Charles Seymour, 1829-1899.

The martyred president: a sermon preached in
the First Presbyterian church, Brooklyn, N. Y.
... April 16th, 1865. New York, J. F. Trow, 1865.
31 p. 23 cm.

7885 Robinson, Elrie.
James M. Bradford, pioneer printer... St.
Francisville, La., St. Francisville Democrat,
1938.
54 p. 23 cm.

7886 Robinson, Henry M
The great fur land; or Sketches of life in the
Hudson's bay territory, by H. M. Robinson, with
numerous illustrations from designs by Charles
Gasche. New York, G. P. Putnam's sons, 1879.
x p., 1 l., 348 p. illus. 20 cm.

7887 Robinson, John Hovey, 1825–
... Nick Whiffles, the trapper guide. A tale of
the Northwest. By Dr. J. H. Robinson, New York,
G. W. Carleton & co. [etc.] 1877.
412 p. 18 1/2 cm.

7888 Robinson, Luther Emerson, 1867–
Ephraim Elmer Ellsworth, first martyr of the Civil
war. [Springfield, Ill., 1923]
24 p. 22 cm.

7889 Robinson, Stuart, 1814-1881.
Rev. Stuart Robinson to President Lincoln.
[n.p.] 1865.
8 p. 20 cm.

7890 Robinson, Thomas Hastings, 1828-1906.
The unveiling of divine justice in the great
rebellion: a sermon... June 1, 1865. [n.p., 1865?]
35 p. 22 cm.

7891 Robles, Antonio de, 1645?-17--.
Diario de sucesos notables (1665-1703) Edición y
prólogo de Antonio Castro Leal. Mexico, Editorial
Porrua, 1946.
3 v. 19 cm.

7892   Rockwell, John Arnold, 1803-1861.
        Reasons against sustaining the Republican party,
        in two letters... published in the Norwich Courier
        on the 20th and 31st of July, 1860, and the answer
        of the editor of the Courier. Norwich, Conn.,
        Courier, 1860.
        16 p.   22 cm.

7893   Rodríguez Cerna, José.
        Tierra de sol y de montaña, por José Rodríguez
        Cerna. 2. ed., corr., con un juicio de Cansinos
        Assens. Guatemala, C. A., 1945.
        271 p., 1 l.   20 1/2 cm.

7894   Rodriguez de Leon Pinelo, Antonio, d. 1660.
        Discorso sobre la importancia, forma, y disposicion
        de la Recopilacion de leyes de las Indias Occiden-
        tales... [n.p., ca. 1623]
        57 p.   24 cm.

7895   Rodríguez de Rivas y Velasco, Diego, bp., d. 1771.
        Carta pastoral, que il ill.^{mo} señor doctor d.
        Diego Rodriguez Rivas, obispo de la ciudad de
        Guadalajara, en el Nuevo Reyno de Galicia, escribió
        a su clero secular, y regular, encargandole el
        cumplimiento de su obligacion en la enseñanza de
        la doctrina de Christo en el pulpito, y los con-
        fesionarios, y el exercico de la caridad con los
        pobres, y personas miserables. Madrid, Por Joachin
        Ibarra, 1768.
        71 p.   22 cm.

7896   Rodríguez de San Miguel, Juan.
        La República Mexicana en 1846, ó sea Directorio
        general de los superiores poderes, y de las principal
        autoridades, corporaciones y oficinas de la nación
        ... México, Imprenta de J. M. Lara, 1845.
        198, 125, 146, 192 p.   20 cm.

7897   Rodríguez Villa, Antonio, 1843-1912.
        ... El teniente general don Pablo Morillo primer
        conde de Cartagena, marqués de la Puerta (1778-
        1837) ... Madrid, Editoria-América, 1920.
        2 v.   22 cm.

7898   Rodway, James.
    The West Indies and the Spanish Main, by James
Rodway. London, T. F. Unwin, 1896.
    1 p.l., vii-xxiv, 371, [1] p. front., illus.,
fold. map. 20 cm.

7899   Rogers, John Davenport, 1857-1914.
    ... Canada--pt. III, geographical, by J. D.
Rogers... Oxford, Clarendon press, 1911.
    v, [2], 302 p. incl. maps. 19 cm.

7900   Rogers, Joseph Morgan, 1861-
    The true Henry Clay... Philadelphia and London,
J. B. Lippincott company, 1904.
    3 p.l., 11-388 p. front., plates, ports., facsims.
20 1/2 cm.

7901   Rogers, Thomas L
    Mexico? Si, Señor. By Thos. L. Rogers...
Boston [Collins press] 1893.
    1 p.l., 294 p. illus., plates, 3 maps (1 double)
20 1/2 cm.

7902   Rojas, Isidro.
    Progreso de la geografía en México en el primer
siglo de su independencia. Estudio presentado en
nombre de la Sociedad Mexicana de Geografía y
Estadística. México, Tip. de la Viuda de F. Díaz
de León, Sucs., 1911.
    50 p. 23 cm.

7903   Romero de Terreros y Vinent, Manuel, marqués de
San Francisco, 1880-
    El barón Gros y sus vistas de México. México,
Impr. Universitaria, 1953.
    16 p. plates. 23 cm.

7904   Romero, Matías, 1837-1898.
    Geographical and statistical notes on Mexico by
Matias Romero. New York and London, G. P. Putnam's
sons, 1898.
    xiv p., 1 l., 286 p. pl., map. 25 1/2 cm.

7905   Romero, Matias, 183701898.
    Mexico and the United States; a study of subjects

affecting their political, commercial, and social
relations, made with a view to their promotion.
v. 1. New York & London, G. P. Putnam's sons, 1898.
xxxv p., 1 l., 759 p. 2 pl., map., facsim.
25 1/2 cm.

7906 Romig, Mrs. Edna (Davis) 1889-
Lincoln remembers. Philadelphia, Dorrance,
[c1930]
76 p. 20 cm.

7907 Romo de Vivar y Torres, Joaquín, 1841-1899.
Guadalajara. Apuntes históricos, biográficos,
estadísticos y descriptivos de la capital del estado
de Jalisco, según obra publicada por su autor en
1888. Guadalajara, Jal., Ediciones del Banco Industrial de Jalisco [1964]
172 p. port. 23 cm.

7908 Rosa, Luis de la, d. 1856.
Impresiones de un viage de México á Washington
en octubre y noviembre de 1848. Por d. Luis de la
Rosa. Nueva-York, Impr. de W. G. Stewart [1849]
1 p.l., iv, [7]-54 p. 21 1/2 cm.

7909 Rosillo de Lara, Juan.
Por don Antonio de Villa y Hano, assentista
general de la polvora de la ciudad de Mexico. Con
don Juan Antonio de Hano, vezino de dicha ciudad.
Sobre que se mande dar despacho, para que se exe-
cute la sentencia de revista, pronunciada por el
duque de Alburquerque, virrey, y capitan general
del reyno de Mexico, con acuerdo, y pareceres de
los licenciados don Miguel Calderon de la Barca,
don Joseph de Luna, y don Balthasar de Tobar, oydores
de la Real audiencia de la dicha cuidad, por la qual
revocò la de vista, que avia dado. con acuerdo de
don Francisco de Valençuela y Venegas su auditor de
guerra, y que se desestime la nulidad, ò revocacion,
que en contrario se pretende de la dicha sentencia
de revista. [n.p., 1708?]
28 numb. l. 22 cm.

7910 Rosillo de Lara, Juan.
Por d. Diego Manuel de Olavarria, juez, oficial

real del Tribunal de las reales caxas de Mexico,
vezino de dicha ciudad, como heredero de doña Ynès
de Belarde y Neyra, su muger. Con doña Rosa
Fernandez de Saravia, como madre, tutora, y curadora
de d. Manuel Cayetano de Elizaga su hijo, y de
Domingo de Elizaga su marido, vezinos de dicha
ciudad. Sobre qve en el grado de segunda suplicacion, que interpuso d. Diego, en tiempo, y en forma
de vna executoria, pronunciada por la Real audiencia
de dicha ciudad, se declare, que contuvo injusticia
dicha executoria, y sentencia de revista, y que se
debe mandar executar la de vista, que en dicho
pleyto se avia pronunciado à su favor. [n.p., 1709?]
    11 numb. l.   21 cm.

7911 Ross, Sir John, 1777-1856.
      Narrative of a second voyage in search of a north-
west passage, and of a residence in the Arctic
regions during the years 1829, 1830, 1831, 1832,
1833. By Sir John Ross... Including the reports of
... James Clark Ross... and the discovery of the
northern magnetic pole. London, A. W. Webster, 1835.
      2 v. front. (port., v. 2), plates, (part col.),
maps (part fold.), col. plan.   31 cm.

7912 Ross, Sir John, 1777-1856.
      A voyage of discovery, made under the orders of
the Admiralty, in His Majesty's ships Isabella and
Alexander, for the purpose of exploring Baffin's
Bay, and inquiring into the probability of a north-
west passage. By John Ross... London, J. Murray,
1819.
      2 p.l., xxxix. [1], 252 p., 1 l., cxliv. p.
front., plates (part col., part fold.), fold. maps,
tables.   28 cm.

7913 Rouhaud, Hippolyte.
      Les régions nouvelles; histoire du commerce et de
la civilisation au nord de l'océan Pacifique, par
Hippolyte Rouhaud ... Paris, E. Dentu, 1868.
      2 p.l., vi, 404 p.   23 cm.

7914 Routier, Gaston, 1868-
      ... Le Mexique; limites géographiques.--Orographie.
--Hydrographie.--L'agriculture, la flore, la faune et

les mines. L'industrie et le commerce. Avec une
préface de Ignacio Altamirano ... et une carte du
Mexique dressée par les soins de la Société de
géographie de Lille, d'après les derniers documents
officiels. Paris, H. Le Soudier, 1891.
    2 p.l., [3]-110 p. fold. map. 25 cm.

7915 [Roy, Just Jean Étienne] 1794-1870.
    Excursion d'un touriste au Mexique pendant
l'année 1854. Publiée par Just Girard [pseud.]
Tours, A. Mame et c^{ie}, 1859.
    2 p.l., 188 p. front. 21 1/2 cm.

7916 Roy, Pierre Georges.
    Les noms géographiques de la province de Québec,
par Pierre-Georges Roy. Lévis [Impr. par "La Cie
de publication le Soleil"] 1906.
    514 p., 1 l. 22 1/2 cm.

7917 [Royal geographical society, London]
    [Papers read before the Royal geographical
society. Central America. London, J. Murray, 1841]
    [76]-107 p. fold. map. 23 cm.
    Papers iii-vi, detached from the Journal of the
Royal geographical society, v. 11.

7918 Rúa, Hernando de la.
    Manifestacion breve, radical, y fvndamental de la
persecucion que ha padecido, y padece la religion
serafica en las provincias de Nueva-España. Noticia,
y razon de los litigios que se han motiuado por la
dignidad episcopal, y defendido por permission, ò
influxo de fray Hernando de la Rua, comissario general, que haze à nuestro reuerendissimo padre general
de toda la orden, sucessor de nuestro serafico padre
s. Francisco. Dado a la estampa por el padre predicador fray Francisco de Ayeta, hijo de la Prouincia
de el santo euangelio de Mexico. [n.p., 1671?]
    34 numb. l. 23 cm.

7919 Rudeen, E   F
    Lincoln a Christian, though not a "Campbellite"
... [n.p., 1923?]
    [4] p. 21 cm.

7920   Ruiz de la Peñuela, Francisco.
       Por don Garcia Sarmiento de Mendoça, conde de
Salvatierra, marques de Sobroso, gentil-hombre de la
camara de Su Magestad virrey, y capitan general que
fue del Pirù, y comendador de la encomienda de los
santos de la Orden de Santiago. Con don Manvel de
los Cobos y Luna, marques de Camarasa, don Baltasar,
y don Alvaro Sarmiento sus hijos; y con el señor don
Diego Sarmiento de Mendoça, hermano del dicho conde,
del consejo de guerra de'Su Mágestad, y commissario
general de la infanteria de España. Sobre la
tenvta, y possession del mayorazgo, estado, y condado de Ribadavia, que fundaron don Iuan Hurtado
de Mendoca, y doña Maria Sarmiento su muger, el año
de 1530. [n.p., 16--]
       38 numb. 1.   23 cm.

7921   Ruiz de Montoya, Antonio, 1585-1652.
       Lexicon hispano-guaranicum. "Vocabulario de la
lengua guarani," inscriptum a reverendo patre
jesuita Paulo Restivo secundum Vocabularium Antonii
Ruiz de Montoya anno MDCCXXII in civitate S.
Mariae Majoris denuo editum et adauctum, sub
auspiciis augustissimi domini Petri Secundi Brasiliae
imperatoris posthac curantibus illustrissimis ejusdem
haeredibus ex unico qui noscitur imperatoris
beatissimi exemplari redimpressum necnon praefatione
notisque instructum opera et studiis Christiani
Frederici Seybold... Stuttgardiae, in aedibus
Guilielmi Kohlhammer, 1893.
       x p., 1 1., 545 p.   20 1/2 cm.

7922   Russell, Alex J
       The Red River country, Hudson's Bay & north -
west territories, considered in relation to Canada.
With the last report of S. J. Dawson, Esquire, C. E.,
on the line of route between Lake Superior and the
Red River settlement... Ottawa, Published by G. E.
Desbarats, 1869.
       201 p.   map.   23 cm.

7923   Russell, Sir William Howard, 1820-1907.
       Canada: its defences, condition and resources.
Being a second and concluding volume of "My diary,
North and South." Boston, T. O. H. P. Burnham, 1865.

xii, 311 p.   20 cm.

7924   Rutherford, Mildred Lewis, 1852-1928.
         Address... Wrongs of history righted. Savannah,
         Georgia... Nov. 13, 1914. [Athens, Ga., McGregor
         co., 1914]
         34 p.   23 cm.

7925   Rutherford, Mildred Lewis, 1852-1928.
         Jefferson Davis, the president of the Confederate
         States, and Abraham Lincoln, the president of the
         United States, 1861-1865. [Richmond, Va., Virginia
         stationery co., 1916]
         48 p.   23 cm.

7926   Rutherford, Mildred Lewis, 1852-1928, ed.
         Miss Rutherford's historical notes (formerly
         Scrap book): Contrasted lives of Jefferson
         Davis and Abraham Lincoln. v. 1-6; Jan.-June 1927.
         Athens, Ga., Mildred L. Rutherford, 1927.
         cover-title: 40, 20, 23, 32, 20, 20 p.   24 cm.

7927   Rutherford, Mildred Lewis, 1852-1928.
         The South must have her rightful place in his-
         tory... Athens, Georgia, 1923.
         50 p.   230 cm.

7928   Rutherford, Mildred Lewis, 1852-1938, comp.
         Truths of history, presented by Mildred Lewis
         Rutherford... a fair, unbiased, impartial, unprejudic
         and conscientious study of history. Object: to
         secure a peaceful settlement of the many perplexing
         questions now causing contention between the North
         and the South. [Athens? Ga., 1920?]
         cover-title, 13, xi, 114 p.   23 cm.

7929   Rvbi (Ship)
         Navio nombrado el Rvbi capitana. Sv cventa. De
         los gastos pagados por la recavdacion de la plata,
         frutos, y mas efectos, que se sacaron de dicho navio
         capitana de la flota, del cargo del señor gefe de
         esquadra don Rodrigo de Torres, que varo en los
         cayos de Boca de Canal de Bahama, en 15.de julio de
         1733. Havana, años de 1733. y 1734. Contadvria del
         comercio de España. A cargo don Joseph Diaz de

350

Gvytian. [n.p., 1734]
29 p.   21 cm.

7930 Sabin, Edward.
Remarks on the account of the late voyage of
discovery to Baffin's Bay, published by Captain J.
Ross, R. N. ... London, Printed by Richard and
Arthur Taylor for John Book, 1810.
40 p.   38 cm.

7931 Sahagun, Bernardino de, c. 1499-1590.
Histoire générale des choses de la Nouvelle-
Espagne... Traduite et annotée par D. Jourdanet
et Remi Siméon. Paris, G. Masson, 1880.
lxxix, 898 p.   27 cm.

7932 Sahagún, Bernardino de, c.1499-1590.
Historia general de las cosas de Nueva España, por
el m.r.p. fr. Bernardino de Sahagún, de la Orden de
los frayles menores de la observancia... Mexico,
D. F., P. Robredo, 1938.
5 v. front. (port.), illus. (facsims.), plates
(part col.), tables (part fold.)   24 cm.

7933 Saint-Domingue. Assemblée Provinciale du Sud.
Extrait des registres des délibérations... et de
sa séance du 16 mai 1790, imprimé par ordre de
l'Assemblée nationale. [Paris, Chez Baudouin, 1790]
8 p.   20 cm.

7934 Saint-Domingue (colony) Chambre d'agriculture du Cap.
Lettre bien importante... adressée aux membres
du Comité Colonial, séant a Paris [10 décembre 1788]
[n.p., 1789]
16 p.   20 cm.

7935 Saint-Domingue. Comité colonial à Paris.
Extrait du registre des délibérations... du 27
janvier 1789 (extrait des registres de la Chambre
d'agriculture du Cap, Séance du 7 novembre 1788)

n.p., 1789]
7 p.   20 cm.

7936   Saint-Domingue. Commissaires.
Lettre des commissaires de la colonie de Saint-
Domingue, au roi [el août 1788] [Paris, Chez Clousie?
1788]
8 p.   20 cm.

7937   Saint-Domingue. Commissaires.
Premier recueil de pièces intéressantes, remises
par les commissaires de la colonie de Saint-
Domingue, à MM. les notables, le 6 novembre 1788.
[n.p., 1788]
7, 8, 6, 6, 47 p.   20 cm.

7938   Saint-Domingue. Conseil supérieur.
Réclamation de M. l'intendant de Saint-Domingue
[Barbé-Marbois] enregistrée au conseil supérieur de
cette colonie. [n.p., 1789]
14 p.   20 cm.

7939   Saint-Domingue. Conseil supérieur.
Remontrances de monsieur de [Barbé] Marbois,
intendant de Saint-Domingue, contre l'arrêt d'en
registrement de l'acte intitulé: Ordonnance de M.
le gouverneur-général, concernant la liberté du
commerce pour la partie du sud de Saint-Domingue.
[Paris, se trouve chez M. Louis, 1789]
11 p.   20 cm.

7940   Saint-Domingue. Députés à l'Assemblée nationale.
Précis remis... aux six commissaires du Comité
d'agriculture et de commerce, chargés de rendre
compte à l'Assemblée nationale de l'affaire relative
à l'approvisionnement de cette isle. [Versailles,
chez Baudouin, 1789]
4 p.   20 cm.

7941   Saint-Domingue. Gouverneur-général.
Correspondance de M. le marquis [Marie-Charles]
du Chilleau ... avec M. le comte de La Luzerne,
ministre de marine, & M. de Marbois, intendant...
relativement à l'introduction des farines étrangeres
dans cette colonie. [n.p., 1789]

37 p.   chart.   20 cm.

7942 St. John's River society.
Whereas it has been thought expedient, for the
information of the proprietors of sundry tracts of
land, situate [:] in the province of Nova-Scotia,
or Acadia, to make known the tenor of the several
grants under which the said lands are held, there-
fore the following extracts are printed... Quebec,
Brown and Gilmore [1766?]
2 l.   79 lines (recto of l. 1)   32 1/2 x 21
1/2 cm.

7943 Saldías, Adolfo, 1850-1914.
... La evolución republicana durante la revolución
argentina. Madrid, Editorial-América, 1919.
400 p.   23 1/2 cm.

7944 Salm-Salm, Felix Constantin Alexander Johann Nepomuk,
prinz zu, 1828-1870.
My diary in Mexico in 1867, including the last
days of the Emperor Maximilian; with leaves from
the diary of the Princess Salm-Salm, etc. By Felix
Salm-Salm... London, R. Bentley, 1868.
2 v.   front., pl., port., map, facsim.   20 1/2 cm.

7945 Salter, William, 1821-1910.
The life of James W. Grimes, governor of Iowa,
1854-1858; a senator of the United States, 1859-
1869. By William Salter. New York, D. Appleton
and company, 1876.
xii, 398 p.   front. (port.), illus., pl.   22
1/2 cm.

7946 Salvaalegre, Juan Pio de Montúfar y Frasco, marqués de.
Razon que sobre el estado y gubernacion politica
y militar de las provincias, ciudades, villas y
lugares que contiene la jurisdiccion de la Real
audiencia de Quito, da al excelentisimo señor don
Josef de Solis Folch de Cardona ... virrey,
gobernador y capitan general del Nuevo Reyno de
Granada, don Juan Pio de Montufar y Frasco...
marques de Salvaalegre... gobernador y capitan
general de las provincias de Quito. [Madrid, 1790]
52 p.   22 cm.

7947   Sampson, Flem D
Abraham Lincoln - the Kentuckian: delivered
before the National Republican club of New York
City, February 12, 1929.   [n.p.] 1929.
18 p.   20 cm.

7948   San Alberto, José Antonio de, abp., 1727-1804.
Carta pastoral que el ilustrisimo y reverendisimo
señor d. fr. Joseph Antonio de S. Alberto, obispo
del Tucumán, dirige a sus diocesanos con ocasión
de publicar una instruccion para los seminarios de
niños y niñas, donde por lecciones, preguntas y
respuestas se enseñan las obligaciones que un
vasallo debe á su rey y señor. Con licencia. En
Madrid en la Imprenta real. Año de M.DCC.LXXXVI.
210 p., 3 1.   25 cm.

7949   San Martin, José de, 1778-1850.
... San Martín, su correspondencia (1823-1850)
Madrid, Editorial-América, 1919.
368 p.   23 cm.

7950   San Martin Súarez, José de.
Tablas modernas, de la situacion que tienen,
en latitud, y longitud todas las costas de Tierra
Firme, è islas de Barlovento, con sus adyacentes.
Sondas, viriles baxos, arrecifes, canales, puertos,
ensenadas, y lo mas notable del seno mexicano.
Recopiladas en este puerto de la Havana. Por don
Josef de San Martin Suarez, teniente de navio de la
real armada, ayudante, y piloto mayor de derrotas.
Con junta de primeros, y segundos pilotos de esta
esquadra. Celebrada, por disposicion, de el exmo.
s^r. d. Josef Solano y Bote... Año de 1781. Con
licencia. Barcelona, En la imprenta de Bernardo
Pla impresor, en la calle de los Algodoneros [1784]
3 p.l., 80, 31, [1] p.   22 cm.

7951   San Salvador. Museo Nacional "David J. Guzman."
Anales. San Salvador, El Salvador, Imprenta
Nacional, 1903-1911.
5 v.   23 cm.

7952   Sanborn, Helen Josephine, 1857-1917.
A winter in Central America and Mexico, by Helen

J. Sanborn. Boston, Lee and Shepard; New York,
C. T. Dillingham, 1886.
iv, 321 p. 18 cm.

7953 Sánchez Sorondo, Matías Guillermo, 1880-
... La cuestión de límites con Bolivia; discurso
pronunciado en el Senado de la nación el 6 de
septiembre de 1938. Buenos Aires [1938]
15 p. fold. map. 28 1/2 cm.

7954 Sánchez Valverde, Antonio, d. 1790.
El predicador. Tratado dividido en tres partes,
al qual preceden unas reflexiones sobre los abusos
del púlpito y medios de su reforma: por don
Antonio Sanchez Valverde... Madrid MDCCLXXXII.
Por don Joachin Ibarra, impresor de camara de
S.M. Con las licencias necesarias.
4 p.l., 1 v, 152 p. 26 cm.

7955 Sandiel y Palacios, Mariano Buenaventura.
Çlarissimo viro augustinensis familiae alumno...
r^{mo}. p. m^{tro}. fr. Lucae Centeno, Grato, & obsequenti:
animo theoreticae medicinae theses D.O.C. pro ad
implenda constit. CXLIX. D. Marianus Bonaventura
Sandiel, et Palacius... Defendentur in reg. ac.
pontif. Mexico academia... sub praesidio d.d.d.
Josephi Maximiliani Rosales a Velasco... Mexici, ex
typographia Bibliotec. Mexic. lic. d. Joseph. â
Jauregui, in via Sancti Bernardi [1771?]
broadside. illus. 30 x 25 cm.

7956 Santa Fé y Bogotá. Bogotá, 1923-1930.
13 v. 22 cm.

7957 Santa María, José de.
... Trivnfo del agva bendita: a el ill.^{mo} i r.^{mo}
don Iuan de Palafox i Mendoça... el m.r.p.d. Ioseph
de Santa Maria... Con privilegio. Sevilla, Simon
Fajardo, 1642.
23 p.l., 243 numbered l. [32] p. 27 cm.

7958 Santibáñez, Enrique, 1869-
Geografía nacional de México, escrita por Enrique
Santibañez ... Mexico, Compañía nacional editora
"Aguilas", s.a. [1923?]

295 p.   incl. illus., ports., maps, col. diagr.
23 cm.

7959   Sanz de Monroy, Miguel Elias.
Memorial ajustado hecho con citacion, y asistencia
de los procuradores de las partes. En el pleito
que en la Real chancilleria de Valladolid se sigue
entre don Antonio Enriquez de Guzman, vecino de la
ciudad de Salamanca, num. 153. Doña Gertrudis Gallo
Villavicencio, vecina de la ciudad de Megico,
viuda de don Juan Gomez de Parada, Fonseca y
Enriquez... don Pedro Alcantara Tellez y Giron,
marques de Peñafiel ... y don Diego Fernandez de
Velasco, Enriquez de Guzman, Lopez, Pacheco, Giron,
Gomez de Sandobal, y Roxas, duque de Frias, conde
de Alba de Liste, año 1786. Sobre la subcesion en
propiedad del estado, y mayorazgo de Alba de Liste
... [Valladolid? 1789]
1 p.l., 177 numb. l.   25 cm.

7960   Sapia Martino, Raúl.
Guatemala: Mayaland of eternal spring. 3. ed.
ilustrada castellano-inglés. 3d illustrated edition,
Spanish-English. Ciudad de Guatemala [1963]
unpaged. illus. (part col.), maps.   24 cm.

7961   Sapper, Carl.
Das nördliche Mittelamerika nebst einem Ausflug
nach dem Hochland von Anahuac. Reisen und Studien
aus den Jahren 1888-1895... Braunschweig, Verlag
von Friedrich Vieweg und Sohn, 1897.
xii, 429, [8] p. front. (port.), map.   22 cm.

7962   Saravia, Manuel de.
Alegación en derecho por la Archiofradia
sacramental, sita en la santa Iglesia catedral de
México, como patrona del Colegio de colegialas huér-
fanas titulado de Nuestra Señora de la Caridad de la
misma ciudad en el pleyto, que en grado de segunda
suplicación pende en el Supremo consejo de las
Indias, con d. Diego Martin Gutierrez de la Arena,
natural de la ciudad de Mondoñedo, y vecina de
Cartagena: sobre pertenencia en propiedad del
mayorazgo fundado en virtud de real facultad por
el capitan d. Francisco Fernandez de Corral, vecino

que fué de la misma ciudad de México. Pretende
la archicofradía que se confirmen las dos sentencias
de vista y revista dadas á su favor por la Real
audiencia de México en 7 de agosto de 1775, y 13
de enero de 1777, con las condenaciones que son
consiguientes à la calidad de la instancia.
Madrid, Por la viuda de don Joaquin Ibarra, 1796.
1 p.l., 19 numb. l.   20 cm.

7963 Saravia, Manuel de.
... Memorial ajustado, hecho con citacion y
asistencia de las partes, de mandato de los señores
del real y supremo Consejo de las Indias, del
pleyto que sigue en grado de segunda suplicacion
d. Diego Martin Gutierrez de la Arena, natural
de la ciudad de Mondoñedo en Galicia, y vecino de
Cartagena, con la Archiofradía del santísimo
sacramento, sita en la santa Iglesia catedrál de
México, sobre la pertenencia y succesion de cierto
vínculo ó mayorazgo fundado por el capitan don
Francisco Fernandez del Corral, vecino que fue de
dicha ciudad de Mexico. [Madrid, 1794]
1 p.l., 32 numbered l. fold. geneal tab.   23 cm.

7964 Sarmiento de Gamboa, Pedro.
History of the Incas, by Pedro Sarmiento de
Gamboa, and the execution of the Inca Tupac Amaru,
by Captain Baltasar de Ocampo. Translated and
edited with notes and an introduction by Sir
Clements Markham. Cambridge, Printed for the
Hakluyt Society, 1907.
xxii, 395 p. fold. maps, facsims.   22 cm.

7965 Sartorius, C[hristian] i.e. Carl Christian Wilhelm,
1796-1872.
Mexico. Landscapes and popular sketches by C.
Sartorius. Ed. by Dr. Gaspey. With 18 steel
engravings by distinguished artists, from original
sketches by Moritz Rugendas. Darmstadt, G. G.
Lange; New-York, Lange & Kronfeld [etc., etc.]
1858.
4 p.l., [v]-vi, 202 p. front., plates.   28 1/2
x 22 1/2 cm.

7966 Sartorius, Christian, i.e. Carl Christian Wilhelm,

357

1796-1872.
   Mexiko. Landschaftsbilder und skizzen aus dem
volksleben, von C. Sartorius. Mit stahlstichen
vorzüglicher meister nach original-aufnahmen von
Moritz Rugendas. Darmstadt, G. G. Lange; New-
York, Lange & Kronfeld [etc., etc.] 1855.
   4 p.l., [v]-viii, 364 p. front., plates.   23
1/2 cm.

7967 Satin, Mark Ivor, 1946-
   Manual for draft-age immigrants to Canada.
Edited by Mark Satin, 4th rev. ed. [Toronto]
Toronto Anti-draft Programme [cover 1970, c1968]
   vi, 98 p.   21 cm.

7968 Saunders, Rolfe S
   An oration on the death of Abraham Lincoln, late
president of the United States: By Rolfe S.
Saunders, delivered on Island 40, April 25, 1865.
Memphis, W. A. Whitmore, printer, 1865.
   16 p.   23 cm.

7969 Saussure, Henri Louis Frédéric de, 1829-1905.
   Coup d'eil sur l'hydrologie du Mexique, principale-
ment de la partie orientale; accompagné de
quelques observations sur la nature physique de ce
pays. Par Henri de Saussure ... Genève, Impr.
de J.-G. Fick, 1862.
   196 p.   2 fold. maps.   24 1/2 cm.

7970 Sauvalle, Paul Mare, 1857-
   ... Louisiane--Mexique--Canada. Aventures cos-
mopolites. Montréal, Desaulniers et Leblanc, impr.,
1891.
   3 p.l., 308 p., 1 l.   18 1/2 cm.

7971 Savage, James, 1784-1873.
   A genealogical dictionary of the first settlers
of New England, showing three generations of those
who came before May, 1692, on the basis of Farmer's
Register... By James Savage... Boston, Little,
Brown and company, 1860-62.
   4 v.   24 1/2 cm.
   A genealogical cross index of the four volumes
of the Genealogical dictionary of James Savage.

By O. P. Dexter... New York, O. P. Dexter, 1884.
38 p. 24 cm.

7972 Scadding, Henry, 1813-1901.
Toronto of old: collections of the early settlement and social life of the capital of Ontario...
Toronto, Adam, Stevenson & co., 1873.
xii, 594 p. 2 port. (incl. front.) 23 cm.

7973 Scarritt, Winthrop Eugene, 1857-
Mexico and her opportunities, by Winthrop E.
Scarritt... [New York? 1906]
cover-title, 16 p. illus. 25 1/2 cm.

7974 Scherger, Carl.
Wanderungen durch die mittel-amerikanischen
Freistaaten Nicaragua, Honduras und San Salvador
... Braunschweig, Druck und Verlag von Georg
Westermann, 1857.
516 p. 22 cm.

7975 Schiess, Wilhelm.
Quer durch Mexiko vom Atlantischen zum Stillen
ocean, von dr. Wilhelm Schiess. Mit 55 illustrationen
und 16 lichtdrucktafeln. Berlin, D. Reimer (E.
Vohsen) 1902.
xii, [1], 233, [1] p. front., illus., pl.,
fold. map. 25 1/2 cm.

7976 Schlözer, Kurd von, 1822-1894.
Mexikanische briefe, von Kurd von Schlözer,
1869-1871; hrsg. von Karl von Schlözer. Stuttgart
und Berlin, Deutsche verlags-anstalt, 1913.
xviii, 97, [1] p. 22 cm.

7977 Schmidel, Ulrich.
Vierte Schiffart. Warhafftige Historien einer
wunderbaren Schiffart. Editio Secvnda. Noribergae,
Impensis Levini Hulsij, 1602.
103 p. illus., fold. map. 20 1/2 cm.

7978 Schoolings, Sir William, 1860-
The Governor and company of adventurers of
England trading into Hudson's bay during two hun-
dred and fifty years, 1670-1920... London, The

Hudson's bay company, 1920.
xvi, 129 1 p. incl. col. front., illus. plates
(part col.), ports. (part col.), maps (part fold.),
facsim. 28 x 23 cm.

7979 Schott, Carl.
... Landnahme und kolonisation in Canada am
beispiel Südontarios... Kiel, 1936.
xv, 330 p. illus., maps, tables, diagrs.
24 cm.

7980 Schriver, Lester Osborne, 1891-
Lincoln and Vandalia, by Lester O. Schriver and
Joseph C. Burtschi. Peoria, Ill., 1946.
36 p. mounted illus. (incl. port., facsim.)
24 cm.

7981 Schroeder, Osw
... Republic of Mexico, by Osw. Schroeder ...
Denver, New York, Press Buedingen art pub. co.,
1902.
1 p.l., 56 p. illus. 33 1/2 cm.

7982 Schwatka, Frederick, 1849-1892.
Along Alaska's great river. A popular account
of the travels of the Alaska exploring expedition of
1883, along the great Yukon river, from its source
to its mouth, in the British Northwest territory,
and in the territory of Alaska. By Frederick
Schwatka... New York, Cassell & company, limited
[ᶜ1885]
360 p. incl. illus., plates, map. front., 2
fold. maps. 23 1/2 cm.

7983 Scobel, A[lbert] 1851-
Die geographischen und kultur-verhältnisse
Mexico's. Von A. Scobel ... Leipzig, Druck von
O. Mutze, 1883.
cover-title, 20 p. incl. tab. fold. map.
22 cm.

7984 Scoresby, William, 1789-1857.
The Franklin expedition: or, Considerations on
measures for the discovery and relief of our absent
adventurers in the Arctic regions ... With maps.

By the Rev. W. Scoresby ... London, Longman,
Brown, Green, and Longmans, 1850.
  99 p. 2 fold. maps. 21 1/2 cm.

7985 Scott, R   E
    Speech of R. E. Scott of Fauquier, in reply to
  Messrs. Holladay and Boyly, on the subject of the
  reception of the proceeds of the public lands,
  delivered in the House of Delegates of Virginia,
  March 7, 1842. Richmond, Printed by Shepherd and
  Colin, 1842.
    16 p.   21 cm.

7986 Scott, Winfield, 1786-1866.
    Lieut. Gen. Winfield Scott, U.S.A., after hearing
  several addresses made by Mr. Merwin... [n.p.]
  1918.
    [4] p. illus.   21 cm.

7987 Scripps, John Locke, 1818-1866.
    ... 1860 campaign life of Abraham Lincoln:
  annotated. The only biography of himself that
  Abraham Lincoln ever authorized, revised, and
  endorsed. Foreword and notes by M. L. Houser,
  [Peoria, Ill., Edward J. Jacob, 1931]
    74 p. facsim.   25 cm.

7988 [Scudder, Samuel Hubbard] 1837-1911.
    The Winnipeg country; or, Roughing it with an
  eclipse party, by a Rochester fellow [pseud.]
  With thirty-two illustrations and a map. New
  York, N. D. C. Hodges, 1890.
    144 p. illus., plates, fold. map.   18 1/2 cm.

7989 Scully, Everett Graham.
    The story of Robert E. Lee. Portland, Me., L. H.
  Nelson Company, 1905.
    32 p. front. (port.), illus.   25 cm.

7990 Scully, Michael.
    Official motorists' guide to Mexico (Pan-American
  highway) [by] Michael and Virginia Scully. Rev.
  ed., 1937. Dallas, Tex., Turner company [c1937]
    ix, 238, [6] p. front., illus., plates, maps
  (1 fold.), fold. plan.   20 cm.

7991   Sears, Hiram.
        The people's keepsake; or, Funeral address on
        the death of Abraham Lincoln... with the principal
        incidents of his life; delivered... Mount Carmel,
        Illinois... April 23, 1865. Cincinnati, Poe &
        Hitchcock, 1865.
        18 p.   25 cm.

7992   Seaver, Jesse Montgomery, 1890-
        Crawford genealogical data, and suggestions for
        a complete Crawford genealogy, a permanent world
        Crawford association and a national Crawford re-
        union, by J. Montgomery Seaver.   Philadelphia, Pa.
        [1927]
        caption title, [20] p. coat of arms.   32 1/2 cm.

7993   Sebastián de la Parra, Juan, 1546-1622.
        De el bien excellencias y obligaciones de el
        estado clerical y sacerdotal por el r.p.   Ioan
        Sebastian...   Sevilla, Por Matias Clavijo, 1615-
        1620.
        2 v.   23 cm.

7994   Segura, P. Nicolas De.
        Defensa canonica por las Provincias de la
        compañia de Jesus, de la Nueva España, y Philipinas,
        sobre las censuras impuestas, y reagravadas a sus
        religiosas...   [n.p., ca. 1738]
        48 p.   23 cm.

7995   Seixas y Lovera, Francisco De.
        Theatro naval hydrographico ...   Madrid,
        Antonio de Zafra, 1688.
        238 p.   26 cm.

7996   Seler, Frau Caecilie (Sachs) 1855-
        ... Auf alten wegen in Mexiko und Guatemala.
        2. neuberarb. aufl. mit 174 abbildungen auf tafeln
        und im text und 14 plänen und karten. Stuttgart,
        Strecker und Schröder, 1925.
        xvi, 286 p.   front., illus., 107 pl. on 31 l.,
        fold. map.   24 1/2 cm.

7997   Seler, Frau Caecilie (Sachs) 1855-
        Auf forschungsreisen in Mexiko von Cäcilie

362

Seler-Sachs.   Berlin, Ullstein [^{c}1925]
        136, [1] p., 1 l.   incl. maps.   17 1/2 cm.

7998   Seler, Eduard, 1849-1922.
        Ein Wintersemester in Mexico und Yucatan.
      Berlin, Gesellschaft für Erdkunde, 1902.
        477-502 p.   illus.   25 cm.

7999   Selkirk, Thomas Douglas, 5th earl of, 1771-1820.
        A letter to the earl of Liverpool from the earl
      of Selkirk, accompanied by a correspondence with
      the Colonial department (in the years 1817, 1818
      and 1819) on the subject of the Red river settlement
      in North America.   [London] 1819.
        224 p.   23 cm.

8000   Selkirk, Thomas Douglas, 5th earl of, 1771-1820.
        A sketch of the British fur trade in North
      America: with observations relative to the North-
      West company of Montreal. By the Earl of Selkirk.
      London, Printed for J. Ridgway, 1816.
        3 p.l., 130 p.   22 cm.

8001   Semmes, Raphael, 1809-1877.
        The campaign of General Scott, in the valley of
      Mexico: by Lieut. Raphael Semmes... Cincinnati,
      Moore & Anderson, 1852.
        367 p.   front. (plan)   18 1/2 cm.

8002   Semmes, Raphael, 1809-1877.
        Service afloat and ashore during the Mexican
      war: by Lieut: Raphael Semmes... Cincinnati,
      W. H. Moore & co., 1851.
        xii, [7]-480 p.   front. (plan), 6 pl.   21 cm.

8003   Semple, Ellen Churchill, 1863-1932.
        American history and its geographic conditions,
      by Ellen Churchill Semple ... Boston and New York,
      Houghton, Mifflin and company, 1903.
        5 p.l., 466 p., 1 l.   illus., maps (part fold.)
      22 1/2 cm.

8004   Sepulveda, Juan Gines de, 1490-1573.
        Democrates segundo, o, De las justas causas de la
      guerra contra los indios. Edición crítica bilingüe,

traducción castellana, introducción, notas e indices
por Angel Losada. Madrid, Consejo Superior de
Investigaciones Científicas, Instituto Francisco
de Vitoria, 1951.
xlvii, 161 p. port., facsims. 24 1/2 cm.

8005 Sermon de honras funerales, que celebraron a la
memoria del exc.mo senor don Matias de Galvez, en
la iglesia del Convento de Santo Domingo de la
imperial ciudad de Covan (provincia de Verapaz) a
expensas de d. Francisco Xavier de Aguirre, alcalde
mayor de dicha provincia, et trece de diciembre de
mil setecientos ochenta y quatro, predicado por el
prior de el mismo convento. Con licencia. Sevilla,
En la oficina de d. Josef de S. Roman y Codina,
calle de las armas, 1785.
1 p.l., 35 p. 21 cm.

8006 Sesto, Julio.
... El México de Porfirio Díaz (hombres y cosas)
Estudios sobre el desenvolvimiento general de la
República Mexicana después de diez años de permanencia
en ella. Observaciones hechas en el terreno oficial
y en el particular ... Valencia, F. Sempere y
compañía [1909]
xi, [13]-261 p., 1 1. 19 cm.

8007 Seton, Ernest Thompson, 1860-1946.
The Arctic prairies; a canoe-journey of 2,000
miles in search of the caribou; being the account
of a voyage to the region north of Aylmer lake,
by Ernest Thompson Seton... New York, C. Scribner's
sons, 1911.
xvi, 415 p. front., illus., plates. 22 1/2 cm.

8008 Sevilla, Pedro José de.
Gritos del capvchino enfermo a todos los predicadores del orbe, favorezcan al mundo, que perece
miserable, precipitado de su malicia, ò ciego
con su ignorancia. Carta manvscrita al exc.mo.
señor d. Jvan Camargo... por cuyas manos, y poderoso
patrocinio, desea se dilate à todos los ilmos. y
rmos. arzobispos, obispos, y prelados del continente
de nuestro catolico reyno. Escribiola el r.p.f.
Pedro Joseph de Sevilla... Hizola dar a la estampa,

en obsequio à dicho excmo. señor, y para bien de
las almas, juntamente con la carte final (que
otra vez imprimiò) del v.p.fr. Feliciano de
Sevilla, d. Lvcas Brvno de Haro y Vargas... Diego
Lopez de Haro, 1724.
4 p.l., 92 p. 18 cm.

8009 Sevilla, Rafael, d. 1856.
Memorias de un oficial del Ejército español;
campañas contra Bolívar y los separatistas de
América. Apreciación de la obra. por R. Blanco-
Fombona. Madrid, Editorial-América [1916]
309 p. 23 cm.

8010 [Shackleford, John, Jr.]
Brief memoirs of John Shackleford, M.D. [Louis-
ville, Ky., 1885]
22 p. 20 cm.

8011 Shcherbakov, Dmitrii Ivanovich.
Поездка в Мексику; путевые впечатления. Москва,
Гос. изд-во геогр. лит-ры, 1957.
92 p. illus., maps. 20 cm.

8012 Sheldon, Charles, 1867-1928.
The wilderness of the upper Yukon; a hunter's
explorations for wild sheep in sub-arctic mountains,
by Charles Sheldon... New York, C. Scribner's sons,
1911.
xxi, 354 p. col. front., plates (part col.),
maps (1 fold.) 23 1/2 cm.

8013 Sheldon, Lionel Allen, 1831-
Letters of Governor Sheldon written [Nov. 10-28,
1884] to the Santa Fe New Mexican review while on
a visit to the city of Mexico. [n.p., 1885?]
cover-title, 31 p. 25 cm.

8014 Shelvocke, George, fl. 1690-1728.
A voyage round the world, by the way of the great
South Sea: performed in a private expedition during
the war, which broke out with Spain, in the year
1718. By Capt. George Shelvocke. The 2d ed., rev.
and republished by George Shelvocke, esq. London,
Printed for W. Innys and J. Richardson, M. & T.

Longman, 1757.
   3 p.l., iii, [3], 476 p. front. (fold. map),
4 pl. (2 fold.)   21 cm.

8015 Shepard, Ashbel K
   The land of the Aztecs; or, Two years in Mexico.
By A. K. Shepard. Albany, Weed, Parsons & company,
1859.
   209 p.   19 1/2 cm.

8016 Shepherd, William Robert, 1871-
   Papers bearing on James Wilkinson's relations
with Spain, 1788-1789. By William R. Shepherd.
[New York, 1904]
   cover-title, p. [748]-766.   27 cm.

8017 Sheppard, John H
   Reminiscences of the Vaughan family, and more
particularly of Benjamin Vaughan, LL.D. Read
before the New England Historic-Genealogical Society
1865. Boston, D. Clapp & son, printers, 1865.
   40 p.   22 cm.

8018 Sherratt, Harriott Wight.
   Mexican vistas seen from highways and by-ways of
travel, by Harriott Wight Sherratt. Chicago and
New York, Rand, McNally & co., 1899.
   285 p. front., illus., pl., port.   19 1/2 cm.

8019 Shewmake, Oscar Lane.
   The honorable George Wythe. Teacher, lawyer,
jurist, statesman. An address... delivered before
the Wythe Law Club of the College of William and
Mary in Williamsburg, Virginia, on the evening of
December 18, 1921... Second printing, 1954. [William
burg? 1954]
   48 p. front. (port.), illus.   25 cm.

8020 Shoemaker, Michael Myers, 1853-
   The kingdom of the "White woman"; a sketch [by]
M. M. Shoemaker. Cincinnati, R. Clarke & co.,
1894.
   207 p. front., pl.   20 cm.

8021 A short narrative and justification of the proceedings

of the committee appointed by the Adventurers, to
prosecute the discovery of the passage to the
western ocean of America ...   London, J. Robinson,
1749.
    30 p.   20 cm.

8022 A short state of the countries and trade of North
America claimed by the Hudson's Bay company...
London, Printed for J. Robinson, 1749.
    44 p.   23 cm.

8023 Shortt, Adam, 1859-1931, ed.
    Canada and its provinces; a history of the
Canadian people and their institutions, by one
hundred associates. Adam Shortt, Arthur G.
Doughty, general editors... [Archives ed.]
Toronto, Glasgow, Brook and company [etc., etc.]
1914-17.
    23 v. fronts., plates, ports. (part col.) fold.
maps, facsims., tables. f old diagrs. 25 1/2 cm.

8024 Sidney, Henry.
    The travels and extraordinary adventures of Henry
Sidney, in Brazil, and the interior regions of
South America, in the years 1809, 1810, 1811, and
1812. London, Sold by J. Ferguson, 1815.
    iv, 159 p.   18 cm.

8025 Sierra, Justo, 1848-1912, ed.
    Mexico, its social evolution; synthesis of the
political history, administration, military organi-
sation and economical state of the Mexican confederation, its advancements in the intellectual sphere,
its territorial structure, growth of its population,
means of communication both national and international,
its achievements in the fields of industry, agriculture, mining, commerce, etc., etc. Monumental in-
ventory summing up in masterly expositions the
great progress of the nation in the XIX century...
Literary editor: Licentiate Justus Sierra; artistic
editor: James Ballescá; tr. into English by G.
Sentiñón... Mexico [Barcelona, print.] J. Ballescá
& co., successor, 1900-04.
    2 v. in 3. illus., plates (part col.), ports.
(part col.), fold. maps, plan. facsim. 42 1/2 cm.

8026   Silva, J   Francisco V   , 1893-
        ... El libertador Bolivar y el dean Funes en la
        política argentina (revision de la historia argen-
        tina) Madrid, Editorial-América [1918?]
        421 p.   23 cm.

8027   Silva y la Vanda, Manuel de.
        Defenza juridica por el d.d. Francisco Martines
        Tamayo, colegial de el rèal y mayor de San Phelipe,
        y San Marcos, cathedratico que fuè de digesto-
        viejo en esta reàl universidad, provissor vicario
        generàl, y governador de èl arzobispado de La Plata.
        Por el illustrissimo, y reverendissimo señor, doct.
        don Gregorio Molleda y Clerque, prelado domestico
        de Su Santidad, y assistente al sacro solio ponti-
        ficio, dignissimo arzobispo de la santa iglesia
        metropolitana de la ciudad de La Plata, del consejo
        de Su Magestad. En la causa sobre que el excelen-
        tissimo, sr. vice-patron, declare por nulo, todo lo
        fecho, y actuado, por el venerable dean y Cabildo
        de aquella sta. iglesia, en haver tomado en sì el
        govierno de el arzobispado en lo espiritual, y
        temporal, nombrado vicario general, y economo, y
        removido de el ùso de estos cargos al doct. don
        Francisco, con el pretesto de haver caydo en
        demencia su illustrissima. Escribiala el d.d.
        Manuel de Silva, y la Vanda... Con licencia de los
        superiores. Lima, En la Imprenta que està en la
        plazuela de San Christoval, 1755 [i.e. 1756]
        2 p.l., 48 (i.e. 49) numbered l.   23 cm.

8028   Silva y la Vanda, Manuel de.
        Exmo.s^or. Por parte de don Diego Hidalgo de
        Zisneros, en la causa que sigue con don Francisco
        Vadillo, para que se declare que debe entrar al
        vso, y exercicio de el empleo de corregidor de
        la provincia de Lampa, se proponen los fundamentos
        de justicia que justifican esta pretencion. [Lima,
        1752]
        [45] p.   25 cm.

8029   Silva y la Vanda, Manuel de.
        Por parte de los dueños de navios, en la causa
        que siguen con los abastecedores de pan de esta
        ciudad, para que se declare que los trigos que se

perdieron en las bodegas del Callao, con la in-
undacion del mar la noche del dia 28. de octubre de
746. perecieron à los abastecedores que los havian
comprado, y no à los vendedores, sin embargo de que
no se huviessen medido ni entregado por los
bodegueros, en los casos que separadamente se
pondràn en éste papel, para que sin confussion se
pueda dar una regla general comprehensiva de todos.
[Lima, 1749]
[99] p. 26 cm.

8030   Simpson, Alexander, b. 1811.
The life and travels of Thomas Simpson, the
arctic discoverer. By his brother, Alexander
Simpson ... London, R. Bentley, 1845.
viii, 424 p. front. (port.), fold. map. 21
1/2 cm.

8031   Simpson, Matthew, bp., 1811-1884.
Funeral address delivered at the burial of
President Lincoln, at Springfield, Illinois, May
4, 1865. New York, Carlton & Porter, 1865.
21 p. 18 cm.

8032   Simpson, William S
Report at large of the trial of Charles de
Reinhard for murder (committed in the Indian
territories) at a court of oyer and terminer, held
at Quebec, May 1818. To which is annexed, a
summary of Archibald M'Lellan's, indicted as an
accessary... Montreal, Printed by James Dane,
1819.
340 p. 22 cm.

8033   A sketch of the customs and society of Mexico, in a
series of familiar letters; and a journal of travels
in the interior, during the years 1824, 1825, 1826.
London, Longman and co., 1828.
1 p.l., 242 p. 18 1/2 cm.

8034   Sketches of "Stonewall Jackson," giving the leading
events of his life and military career, his dying
moments, and the obsequies at Richmond and Lexington. English edition. Halifax, N. S., Printed by
James Bowes & sons, 1863.

56 p.   22 cm.

8035   Sketches of the war in northern Mexico. With pictures
of life, manners and scenery. In two parts. New
York, D. Appleton and co., 1848.
75 p.   14 1/2 cm.

8036   Slocum, George Mertz, 1889-
Where Tex meets Mex; a report of recent ramblings
on both sides of the Rio Grande, by George Mertz
Slocum. [Mt. Clemens, Mich.] Rural publishing
company, 1927.
99, [3] p. front., plates. 20 cm.

8037   Small, Samuel.
Genealogical records of George Small, Philip
Albright, Johann Daniel Dunckel (and others)
Philadelphia, Printed for private circulation by
J. B. Lippincott company, 1905.
363 p.   22 cm.

8038   [Smith, Ann Eliza (Brainerd) "Mrs. J. G. Smith"]
1818-1905.
Notes of travel in Mexico and California. By
Mrs. J. Gregory Smith ... St. Albans, Vt., Printed
at the Messenger and advertiser office, 1886.
123 p.   18 cm.

8039   Smith, Arthur G
New Salem, Illinois: a tribute to Ann Rutledge,
whose appearance on this earth brought complete
consummation to the greatness of the life of
Abraham Lincoln. Peoria, Ill., E. J. Jacob, 1946.
[2] p. illus. 22 cm.

8040   Smith, Charles W
... Life and military services of Brevet-Major
General Robert S. Foster... Indianapolis, Edward
J. Heckor, printer, 1915.
523-536 p.   24 cm.

8041   Smith, Francis Hopkinson, 1838-1915.
A white umbrella in Mexico, by F. Hopkinson
Smith ... With illustrations by the author.
Boston and New York, Houghton, Mifflin and company,

1889.
viii, 227 p. illus. 18 1/2 cm.

8042 Smith, Goldwin, 1823-1910.
Canada and the Canadian question, by Goldwin
Smith... London & New York, Macmillan and co.
[etc., etc.] 1891.
x, 325 p. fold. map. 21 cm.

8043 [Smith, Henry Erskine]
On and off the saddle; characteristic sights and
scenes from the great Northwest to the Antilles,
by Lispenard Rutgers [pseud.] ... New York [etc.]
G. P. Putnam's sons, 1894.
viii, 201 p. front., plates. 17 1/2 cm.

8044 Smith, Joseph, 1805-1844.
Joseph Smith tells his own story. [Independence,
Mo., n.d.]
26 p. illus. 19 cm.

8045 Smith, Philip Henry, 1842-
Acadia. A lost chapter in American History,
by Philip H. Smith... Pawling, N. Y., The author,
1884.
1 p.l., [5]-381 p. illus., plates. 21 1/2 cm.

8046 Smith, Truman, 1791-1884.
Considerations on the slavery question, addressed
to the President of the United States. [New York,
1862]
15 p. 22 cm.

8047 Smith, William Benjamin.
A Southern view of the Negro problem. Lexington,
Ky., Erasmus Press, 1973.
[4] p. 22 cm.

8048 Smith, William Henry, of Canada.
Canada: past, present and future. Being a
historical, geological and statistical account of
Canada West... Containing ten county maps, and one
general map of the province, compiled expressly for
the work... Toronto, T. Maclear [1851]
2 v. fold. front., plates, fold. maps. 24

1/2 cm.

8049   Smithsonian institution.
       Catalogue of the Berlandier manuscripts deposited
in the Smithsonian institution. Washington, D. C.
New York, Folger & Turner, printers, 1853.
     8 p.   19 1/2 cm.

8050   Snow, W   Parker.
       Voyage of the Prince Albert in search of Sir
John Franklin: a narrative of every-day life in
the arctic seas... London, Longman, Brown, Green,
and Longman, 1851.
     416 p. illus., map.   23 cm.

8051   Snowden, William H
       Some old historic landmarks of Virginia and
Maryland, described in a hand-book for the tourist
over the Washington-Virginia Railway... 7th ed.
... [Washington? D.C., c1904]
     124 p. illus. (incl. ports.)   23 1/2 cm.

8052   Société des amis des noirs, Paris.
       Adresse à l'Assemblée nationale, pour l'abolition
de la traite des noirs, par la Société des amis
des noirs de Paris. Paris, Imp. de L. Potier de
Lille, 1790.
     1 p.l., 22 p.   19 1/2 cm.

8053   Société des amis des noirs, Paris.
       Réflexions sur le code noir, et dénonciation d'un
crime affreux, commis a Saint-Domingue; adressées à
l'Assemblée nationale, par la Société des amis des
noirs. Paris, Impr. du Patriote françois, 1790.
     15 p.   19 1/2 cm.

8054   Société des amis des noirs, Paris.
       La Société des amis de noirs à Arthur Dillon,
député de la Martinique à l'Assemblée nationale.
[Paris, Impr. du Patriote françois, 1791]
     11 p.   19 1/2 cm.

8055   Society of the Army of the Potomac.
       ... Re-union... 30th, 1899. New York, Macgowan &
Slipper, printers [etc.] 1870-19.

v.   illus., plates, ports., facsim.   23-24 cm.

8056   Solis Vango, Juan Próspero de.
Señor. Haviendo dado cuenta à V. Mag. en 13.
de febrero del año de 1728. con autos, del
estrañamiento del maestro fray Diego Alinas, provincial de san Agustin de esta provincia; de la
causa de esta resolucion... [n.p., 1736]
57 numb. 1.   22 cm.

8057   Solís y Rivadeneyra, Antonio de, 1610-1686.
Historia de la conqvista de Mexico, poblacion,
y progressos de la America Septentrional, conocida
por el nombre de Nueva España, escriviala don
Antonio de Solis... Dedicada al excellentissimo
señor don Joseph de Solis Val-Derrabano Pacheco
Giron Guzman Y Luzon... Con privilegio. Madrid,
En la imprenta de Antonio Gonçalez de Reyes, 1704.
12 p.l., 352, [15] p.   26 cm.

8058   Solís y Rivadeneyra, Antonio de, 1610-1686.
Historia de la conquista de la Mexico, poblacion,
y progressos de la America Septentrional, conocida
por el nombre de Nveva España. Escrivia la don
Antonio de Solis... Dedicase al ilvst. y exc. señor
don Ioseph Francisco Eleasar VVillecardel Marqves de
Trivie, & c. ... Barcelona, por Joseph Llopis, en
la plaça del Angel, 1711.
8 p.l., 473, [14] p.   24 cm.

8059   Solís y Rivadeneyra, Antonio de, 1610-1686.
Historia de la conqvista de Mexico, poblacion, y
progressos de la America Septentrional, conocida por
el nombre de Nveva España. Escriviala d. Antonio
de Solis... Dedicada al muy ilustre señor don Andres
Gonzalez de Barcia, Carballido, Zuñiga, Raudona &
c. ... Con licencia. Madrid, En la Imprenta de
Bernardo Peralta, en la calle de la Paz, 1732.
12 p.l., 349, [15] p.   24 cm.

8060   Solís y Rivadeneyra, Antonio de, 1610-1686.
Historia de la conquista de Mexico, poblacion, y
progressos de la America Septentrional, conocida por
el nombre de Nueva España. Escribiala don Antonio
de Solis... Dedicada a el mvy ilvstra señor don

Andres Gonzalez de Barcia, Carbadillo [!] Zuñiga,
Raudona, &c. ... Sevilla, 1735.
   10 p.l., 349, [15] p.   25 cm.
   Errors in pagination: p. 207, 264 and 332 misnumbered 107, 364 and 323 respectively.

8061   Solís y Rivadeneyra, Antonio de, 1610-1686.
   Historia de la conqvista de Mexico, poblacion,
y progressos de la America Septentrional, conocida
por el nombre de Nueva España. Escribiola don
Antonio de Solis y Ribadeneyra... Barcelona, Impr.
de L. Bejäres y Urrutia, 1756.
   14 p.l., 548, [13] p.   30 cm.

8062   Solís y Rivadeneyra, Antonio de, 1610-1686.
   Historia de la conquista de Mexico, población,
y progressos de la America Septentrional, conocida
por el nombre de Nueva España... Madrid, Imprenta
y libreria de Joseph Garcia Lanza, 1758.
   3 v.   25 cm.

8063   Sölís y Rivadeneyra, Antonio de, 1610-1686.
   Historia de la conquista de Mexico, poblacion,
y progressos de la America Septentrional, conocida
por el nombre de Nueva España... Madrid, Imprenta
de Juan de San Martin, 1763.
   12 p.l., 476 p.   25 cm.

8064   Solís y Rivadeneyra, Antonio de, 1610-1686.
   Historia de la conquista de Mexico, población,
y progressos de la America Septentrional, conocida
por el nombre de Nueva España... Barcelona, Imprent:
de PP. Carmelitas Descalzos, 1766.
   14 p.l., 527 p.   25 cm.

8065   Solís y Rivadeneyra, Antonio de, 1610-1686.
   Historia de la conquista de México, poblacion,
y progressos de la America Septentrional, conocida
por el nombre de Nueva España... Barcelona,
Francisco Oliver, y Marti, 1770.
   3 v.   17 1/2 cm.

8066   Solís y Rivadeneyra, Antonio de, 1610-1686.
   Historia de la conquista de México, población y
progresos de la América Septentrional, conocida por

el nombre de Nueva España.   Madrid, En la imprenta
de Blas, 1776.
549 p.   21 cm.

8067 Solís y Rivadeneyra, Antonio de, 1610-1686.
Historia de la conqvista de Mexico, población y
progresos de la America Septentrional, conocida por
el nombre de Nueva-España...   Madrid, Don Manuel
Martin, 1780.
3 v.   20 cm.

8068 Solís y Rivadeneyra, Antonio de, 1610-1686.
Historia de la conquista de Méjico, población y
progresos de la América Septentrional conocida
por el nombre de Nueva España...   Madrid, Imprenta y
librería de Gaspar y Roig, 1851.
179 p.   illus.   27 cm.

8069 Solorzano Pereira, Juan de, 1575-1655.
D. Ioan de Solorzano Pereyra, Cavallero del
Orden de Santiago, del Consejo de su Magestad...
Obras varias...   Zaragoça, Herederos de Diego
Dormer, [1676]
12 p.l., 712 p.   front. (port.)   29 1/2 cm.

8070 Solórzano Pereira, Juan de, 1575-1655.
Ioannis de Solorzano Pereira... Diligens &
accurata de parricidii crimine disputatio, duobus
libris comprehensa: quorum prior poenas huic sceleri
constitutas exactissimè explicat; posterior, qui eis
subdantur non minori curâ pertractat.   Opus non iuris
tantùm, sed & omnigenâ aliarum litterarum cognitione
conspicuum & vel ipsâ rerum, quae in eo continentur,
varietate, & nouitate censendum, & nulli non vsui,
& voluptati futurum.   Primâ hâc editione curâ quâ
potuit maximâ typis tabernelianis excussum.   Duplici
adiecto indice: vno capitum, & altero rerum
locupletissimo.   Ad illvstriss. et reverendiss.
d.d. Ioannem Baptistam de Azebedo...   Salmanticae,
Excudebat Artvs Taberniel antuerpianus Ioanni
Comanno bibliopolae [n.d.]
12 p.l., 203, [32] p.   27 cm.

8071 Solórzano Pereira, Juan de, 1575-1655.
Memorial o discvrso informativo ivridico, his-

torico, politico, de los derechos, honores, preeminencias, i otras cosas, que se deven dar, i guardar à los consejeros honorarios, i ivbilados. I en particular si se les deve la pitança que llaman de la candelaria. Dirigido al rey nvestro señor, por el doctor d. Ivan de Solorzano Pereira ... Madrid, Por Francisco Martinez, 1642.
    4 p.l., 272, 23 p.   26 cm.

8072 Solórzano Pereira, Juan de, 1575-1655.
Obras varias posthumas del doctor Don Juan de Solorzano Pereyra... Contienen una recopilacion de diversos tratados, memoriales, papeles erudítos, algunos escritos en causas fiscales... Corregidas y enmendadas en esta edicion por el Licenc.do D. Francisco Maria Vallarna... Madrid, Imprenta real de la Gazeta, 1776.
    8 p.l., 354 p.   36 cm.

8073 Solórzano Pereira, Juan de, 1575-1655.
Política indiana, compuesta por el señor don Juan de Solórzano y Pereyra... corrigida, é ilustrada con notas por el licenciado don Francisco Ramiro de Valenzuela... Madrid, Buenos Aires, Compañía iberoamericano de publicaciones [1930?]
    5 v.   25 1/2 cm.

8074 Somerset, Henry Charles Somers Augustus.
The land of the muskeg; with a pref. by A. Hungerford Pollen. With illustrations from sketches by A. H. Pollen and instantaneous photographs and four maps. London, W. Heinemann; Philadelphia, J. B. Lippincott Co., 1895.
    xxxi, 248 p. illus., ports. 4 maps.   23 cm.

8075 Sommer, Johann Gottfried, 1792 or 3-1848.
Beschrijving der nieuwe staten von Amerika; voorafgegaan door een algemeen overzigt der nieuwste en belangrijkste aardrijkskundige nasporingen. Naar het Hoogduitsch van J. G. Sommer ... Amsterdam, Ten Brink & De Vries, 1828.
    2 v. front., plates. 21 cm.

8076 Sons of the American revolution.
A national register of the Society Sons of the

American revolution, comp. and pub... by Leo. H.
Cornish... register list collated and ed. by A.
Howard Clark... [New York, Press of A. H. Kellogg,
1902]
    1035 p. col. front., illus., pl., port.　26 cm.

8077 Sorondo, Xavier, 1883-
    Viñetas. Prólogo de Leopoldo Ramos.　México,
Secretaría de Educación Pública [1949]
    126 p. illus.　19 cm.

8078 Southern Manitoba and Turtle Mountain country.
[n.p., n.d.]
    34 p. fold. map.　23 cm.

8079 Southern Pacific company.
    Vamos á México; pub. and presented by the
Southern Pacific co. [Chicago, Printed by American
tourist association publication bureau] 1896.
    56 p. incl. illus., port.　19 x 15 1/2 cm.

8080 Southesk, James Carnegie, earl of, 1827-1905.
    Saskatchewan and the Rocky Mountains. A diary
and narrative of travel, sport, and adventure,
during a journey through the Hudson's bay company's
territories, in 1859 and 1860... Edinburgh,
Edmonston and Douglas, Toronto, J. Campbell, 1875.
    xxx, 448 p. incl. front., illus. plates, fold.
maps, facsim.　22 cm.

8081 Souvenir book of historic Springfield, Illinois.
Chicago, Curt Teich [c1938]
    28 p. illus.　23 cm.

8082 Spaeth, Adolph, i.e. Philip Friedrich Adolph Theodor,
1839-1910.
    Rede bei der Begräbnissfeier des Präsidenten
Abraham Lincoln... Gehalten in der Evangelisch-
lutherischen Zionskirche zu Philadelphia... 19
April 1865... Philadelphia, C. W. Widmaier, 1865.
    15 p.　22 cm.

8083 Spain. Junta directiva del cuarto centenario del
descubrimiento de America.
    El centenario. Revista ilustrada.　Madrid,

Tipografía de "El Progreso editorial," 1892.
4 v. illus. plates (part fold., part col.),
ports. (part fold., part col.), maps (2 fold.),
fold. plans, facsims.   35 cm.

8084   Spain. Laws, statutes, etc.
Reglamento para el govierno del Monte Pio, de
viudas, y pupilos de Ministros de Audiencias...
de la comprehension del Virreynato de el Perú...
Real Orden de viente de Febrero de 1765... aprobado
en 7. de febrero de 1770. Madrid, Juan de San
Martin [1770]
64 p.   20 cm.

8085   Spain. Laws, statutes, etc.
Svmarios de las cedvlas, ordenes, y provisiones
reales, que se han despachado por Su Magestad,
para la Nueva-España, y otras partes; especialmente
desde el año de mil seiscientos y veinte y ocho, en
que se imprimieron los quatro libros, del primer
tomo de la Recopilacion de leyes de las Indias,
hasta el año de mil seiscientos y setenta y siete.
Con algvnos titvlos de las materias, qve nuevamente
se añaden: y de los autos acordados de su Real
audencia. Y algunas ordenanças del govierno. Qve
jvntò, y dispvso, el doct.^{or} d. Iuan Francisco
Montemayor, y Cordova, de Cuenca ...   Mexico, Impr.
de la viuda de B. Calderon, 1678.
3 pt. in 1 v.   30 1/2 cm.

8086   Spain. Laws, statutes, etc., 1759-1788 (Charles III)
Coleccion general de las providencias hasta
aqui tomadas por el gobierno sobre el estrañamiento
y ocupacion de temporalidades de los regulares de
la Compañia que existian en los dominios de S. M.
de España, Indias, e islas Filipinas, á conseqüencia del real decreto de 27. de febrero, y
pragmática-sancion de 2. de abril de este año.
De orden del consejo, en el extraordinario. En
Madrid en la imprenta real de la Gazeta. Año de
1767. Y por su original en Mexico, En la imprenta
de los herederos de doña Maria Ribera, en la calle
de S. Bernardo. Año de 1768.
2 p.l., 156 p.   27 cm.

8087   Spain. Sovereigns, etc., 1788-1808 (Charles IV)
        Real cedula de S.M. y señores del consejo, en
        que se manda observar y guardar el tratado de
        amistad, límites y navegación concluido y
        ratificado entre su real persona y los Estados
        Unidos de América. Madrid, En la Imprenta real,
        1796.
        31 p.   20 cm.

8088   Spaulding, Elbridge Gerry, 1809-1897.
        The Republican platform: revised speech...
        delivered at Buffalo and Washington, at meetings
        held to ratify the nomination of Abraham Lincoln
        and Hannibal Hamlin... [Washington? 1860]
        8 p.   24 cm.

8089   Spear, Samuel Thayer, 1812-1891.
        Radicalism and the national crisis: a sermon
        preached in the South Presbyterian church of
        Brooklyn... October 19th, 1862... Brooklyn,
        W. W. Rose, 1862.
        23 p.   23 cm.

8090   Speed, James, 1812-1887.
        Address... before the Society of the Loyal
        Legion, at Cincinnati, May 4, 1887, in response to
        the toast, Abraham Lincoln. Louisville, J. P.
        Morton & co., 1888.
        11 p.   22 cm.

8091   Spence, Thomas, b. 1832.
        Manitoba, and the North-west of the dominion,
        its resources and advantages to the emigrant and
        capibalist, as compared with the western states
        of America... [2d rev. ed.] Quebec, S. Marcotte,
        1876.
        36 p. front. (fold. map)   22 cm.

8092   Spence, Thomas, b. 1832.
        The Saskatchewan country of the north-west of the
        dominion of Canada... Montreal, Printed by Lovell
        printing and publishing company, 1879.
        59 p. fold. map.   23 cm.

8093   Sprague, William Buell, 1795-1876.

379

A discourse delivered in the Second Presbyterian church, Albany, April 16, 1865... Albany, Weed, Parsons & co., 1865.
18 p.   19 cm.

8094   Spring, Arthur L
Beyond the Rio Grande. A journey in Mexico.   By Arthur L. Spring. Boston, J. S. Adams, 1886.
70 p.   20 1/2 cm.

8095   Spring, Leverett Wilson, 1840-
... Mark Hopkins, teacher, by Leverett Wilson Spring... New York, Industrial Education Association, 1888.
1 p.l., [99]-128 p.   24 cm.

8096   Squier, Ephraim George, 1821-1888.
Honduras; descriptive, historical, and statistical. By E. G. Squier... Issued by permission of the author, and under the authority of... Carlos Gutierrez... London, Trübner & co., 1870.
viii, 278 p.   front. (fold. map)   19 1/2 cm.

8097   Squier, Ephraim George, 1821-1888.
The states of Central America... New York, Harper & brothers, 1858.
xvi, [17]-782 p.   illus., pl., 4 fold. maps, fold. plan.   23 cm.

8098   Squier, Ephraim George, 1821-1888.
Waikna; adventures on the Mosquito shore, by Saml. A. Bard. With introd. & index by Daniel E. Alleger. A facsimile of the 1855 ed. Gainesville, University of Florida Press, 1965.
xxxvii, ix, 366, 10 p.   illus., map.   21 cm.

8099   Stanwood, Edward, 1841-1923.
A history of presidential elections, by Edward Stanwood. 4th ed. rev. Boston and New York, Houghton, Mifflin and company [1896]
3 p.l., 533 p.   19 cm.

8100   Stapp, William Preston.
The prisoners of Perote: containing a journal kept by the author, who was captured by the Mexicans

at Mier, December 25, 1842, and released from Perote,
May 16, 1844. By William Preston Stapp. Philadelphia,
G. B. Zieber and company, 1845.
    xi, [13]-164 p.   17 1/2 cm.

8101   Star-Hunt, Jack.
    Amcham guide to Mexico, by Jack Star-Hunt.
Mexico, The American chamber of commerce of Mexico,
s.c.l., 1932.
    1 p.l., vi, 178 p.   illus., fold. maps.   17 cm.

8102   Stark, James Henry.
    Stark's illustrated Bermuda guide; containing a
description of everything on or about the Bermuda
islands concerning which the visitor or resident
may desire information... with maps, engravings, and
sixteen photoprints. By James H. Stark.   Boston,
Photo electrotype co. [etc., etc., 1890]
    viii, 157 p.   illus., plates (1 fold.), maps.
(1 fold.)   19 cm.

8103   Starr, Frank Farnsworth.
    The Williamson and Cobb families in the lines
of Caleb and Mary (Cobb) Williamson of Barnstable,
Mass., and Hartford, Conn. Cambridge, Mass., University press, J. Wilson & son, 1896.
    66 p.   22 cm.

8104   Steele, James William, 1840-1905.
    Cuban sketches. New York, G. P. Putnam, 1881.
    220 p.   22 cm.

8105   Steele, James William, 1840-1905.
    To Mexico by palace car. Intended as a guide to
her principal cities and capital, and generally as
a tourist's introduction to her life and people.
By James W. Steele ... Chicago, Jansen, McClurg &
company, 1884.
    95 p.   incl. front., illus.   15 x 12 cm.

8106   Steele, Samuel Benfield, 1849-
    Forty years in Canada: reminiscences of the great
Northwest, with some account of his service in
South Africa, by S. B. Steele. Ed. by Mollie Glen
Niblett, with an introduction by J. G. Colmer.

Toronto, McClelland, Goodchild & Stewart; London,
Herbert Jenkins, 1915.
xvii, 428 p. plates, ports. 22 cm.

8107 Sten, Maria.
Trzy barwy Meksyku. [Tłumacze tekstów peotyckich:
Konstanty Ildefons Gałczyński, Artur Miedzyrzecki,
Maria Sten. Wyd. 1. Warszawa] Arkady [1961]
81 p. (chiefly illus.) 22 cm.

8108 Stephens, Charles Asbury, 1845-1931.
The Knockabout club in the tropics. The adventures of a party of young men in New Mexico, Mexico,
and Central America. By C. A. Stephens ... Boston,
Estes and Lauriat, 1884 [1883]
240 p. incl. front., illus., plates, ports.
21 1/2 cm.

8109 Stephens, John Lloyd, 1805-1852.
Viaje a Yucatán, 1841-1842, por John L. Stephens;
traducción al castellano de Justo Sierra O'Reilly.
2. ed. ... México [Impr. del Museo nacional de
arqueología, historia y etnografía] 1937.
2 v. front. (port.), illus., plates (part
fold.), fold. map, plans. 24 cm.

8110 Stevens, John Austin.
The valley of the Rio Grande; its topography
and resources, by John Austin Stevens, jr. ...
New York, W. C. Bryant & co., printers, 1864.
33 p. 23 1/2 cm.

8111 Stevens, Rayfred Lionel.
La obra de Alexander von Humboldt en México;
fundamento de la geografía moderna. México [1956]
xxi, 269 p. illus., fold. maps. 24 cm.

8112 Stevenson, William Bennet, b. 1787?
... Memorias de William Bennet Stevenson sobre las
campañas de San Martín y Cochrane en el Perú; versión
castellana de Luis de Terán; noticia sobre Stevenson
por Diego Barros Arana. Madrid, Editorial-América
[1917]
300 p. 23 cm.

8113   Stocking, Charles Henry Wright.
       The history and genealogy of the Knowltons of
       England and America. New York, The Knickerbocker
       press, 1897.
       597 p.   22 cm.

8114   Stoddard, John Lawson, 1850-1931.
       John L. Stoddard's lectures; illustrated and
       embellished with views of the world's famous
       places and people ... New Boston, Balch brothers
       co., 1902.
       10 v. fronts. illus., plates, ports.   23 1/2 cm.

8115   Stoddard, Richard Henry, 1825-1903.
       Abraham Lincoln: an Horatian ode. New York,
       Bruce & Huntington [1865]
       12 p.   23 cm.

8116   Stokes, Frances K   Wister.
       My father, Owen Wister, by Frances K. W. Stokes
       and ten letters written by Owen Wister to his
       mother during his first trip to Wyoming in 1885.
       Laramie, Wyo., 1952.
       54 p.   17 cm.

8117   Stone, Andrew Leete, 1815-1892.
       A discourse occasioned by the death of Abraham
       Lincoln... preached in the Park Street church,
       Boston, on the next Lord's day. Boston, J. K.
       Wiggin, 1865.
       21 p.   26 cm.

8118   Storrs, Richard Salter, 1821-1900.
       An oration commemorative of President Abraham
       Lincoln: delivered at Brooklyn, N. Y., June 1,
       1865... Brooklyn, "The Union" steam presses,
       1865.
       65 p.   23 cm.

8119   Story, Joseph, 1779-1845.
       The miscellaneous writings of Joseph Story...
       ed. by his son, William W. Story. Boston, C. C.
       Little and J. Brown, 1852.
       x p., 1 l., 828 p.   23 1/2 cm.

8120 Strachan, John, bp. of Toronto, 1778-1867.
A letter to the Earl of Selkirk on his settlement at the Red River, near Hudson's Bay. London,
Longman, Hurst, Rees, Orme & Brown [etc., etc.]
1816.
76 p.   23 cm.

8121 Strachan, John, bp. of Toronto, 1778-1867.
A visit to the province of Upper Canada in 1819,
by James Strachan. Aberdeen, Printed by D.
Chalmers & co., [etc., etc.]
224 p.   21 cm.

8122 Street, George G
Che! wah! wah! or, The modern Montezumas in
Mexico. By George G. Street ... illustrated with
photographs taken during the trip by R. D. Cleveland, and wood cuts from sketches by the author.
Rochester, N.Y., E. R. Andrews, printer, 1883.
115 p.   col. front., illus., plates, map.
26 cm.

8123 Stuart, John.
The relief of the Franklin expedition: what
has been done and what yet may be done. Edinburgh,
R. Grant & son [etc., etc.] 1852.
67 p.   fold. map.   23 cm.

8124 Stuart-Wortley, Lady Emmeline Charlotte Elizabeth
(Manners) 1806-1855.
Travels in the United States, etc., during 1849
and 1850. London, R. Bentley, 1851.
3 v.   22 cm.

8125 Sturz, Johann Jakob, 1800-1877, ed.
Reden gehalten bei der Berliner Todtenfeier für
den Präsidenten Lincoln von amerikanischen, englischer
und deutschen Geistlichen: Ein Ausspruch der Kirche
über Sklaverei und freie Arbeit. Hrsg. von J. J.
Sturz. Berlin, C. G. Luderitz, 1865.
39, [1] p.   22 cm.

8126 Stutfield, Hugh Edward Millington, 1858-1929.
Climbs & exploration in the Canadian Rockies, by
Hugh E. M. Stutfield... and J. Norman Collie...

London, New York and Bombay, Longmans, Green and co.,
1903.
xii, 342, [1] p. incl. map. front., 51 pl., fold.
map. 23 cm.

8127 Sucre, Antonio José de, pres. Bolivia, 1795-1830.
... Cartas de Sucre al Libertador (1820-1830)
Madrid, Editorial-América, 1919.
2 v. front. (port., v. 2) 23 cm.

8128 Sulte, Benjamin, 1841-1923.
L'expédition militaire de Manitoba 1870.
Montreal, Eusèbe Senécal, 1871.
50 p. 23 cm.

8129 Sulte, Benjamin, 1841-1923.
Histoire des canadiens-français 1608-1880:
origin, histoire, religion, guerres, découvertes,
colonisation, contumes, vie domestique, sociale et
politique, développment, avenir... Montréal,
Wilson & cie., 1882-84.
8 v. fronts., plates, ports., maps, plans,
tables. 33 x 25 cm.

8130 Sumner, Charles, 1811-1874.
The promises of the Declaration of Independence:
eulogy on Abraham Lincoln, delivered before the
municipal authorities of... Boston, June 1, 1865.
Boston, Ticknor & Fields, 1865.
61 p. 22 cm.

8131 Sumner, William Graham, 1840-1910.
... Alexander Hamilton... New York, Dodd, Mead
and company [1890]
2 p.l., [iii]-x, 281 p. 18 cm.

8132 The Sun, New York.
An interview with Osborn H. Oldroyd, in the house
in which Lincoln died. New York, The Sun [n.d.]
11 p. 23 cm.

8133 Surratt, John Harrison, 1844-1916.
The private journal and diary of John H. Surratt,
the conspirator: edited and arranged by Dion
Haco, esq. [pseud.] ... New York, F. A. Brady

[1866]
1 p.l., [11]-104 p.   19 cm.

8134   Sutherland, Peter C
Journal of a voyage in Baffin's Bay and Barrow
Straits 1850-1851... under the command of Wm.
Penny in search of H. M. Ships Erebus and Terror,
London, Longman, Brown, Green, and Longmans, 1852.
2 v.   illus., maps.   23 cm.

8135   Sutphen, Morris Crater, 1837-1875.
Discourse on the occasion of the death of
Abraham Lincoln... preached in the Spring Garden
Presbyterian church, Philadelphia, by the pastor,
Rev. Morris C. Sutphen, April 16th, 1865.   Phil-
adelphia, J. B. Rodgers, printer, 1865.
19 p.   23 cm.

8136   Swan, Lansing B   , 1809-
Journal of a trip to Michigan...   Rochester,
N. Y., 1904.
53 p.   13 cm.

8137   Sweetser, Seth, 1807-1878.
A commemorative discourse on the death of
Abraham Lincoln.   [Boston, J. Wilson] 1865.
29 p.   23 cm.

8138   Swinton, William, 1833-1892.
McClellan's military career reviewed and exposed:
the military policy of the administration set forth
and vindicated.   By William Swinton... Published by
L. Towers, 1864.
32 p.   22 cm.

8139   Sylvester, Nathaniel Bartlett, 1825-1894.
History of Ulster County, New York, with illustrations and biographical sketches of its prominent
men and pioneers.   By Nathaniel Bartlett Sylvester
...   Philadelphia, Everts & Peck, 1880.
311, 339 p.   illus., plates (1 double) ports.,
map.   30 1/2 cm.

8140   Synge, Millington Henry.
The country v. the company; or, Why British North

America may be peopled and how it may be done...
London, Edward Stanford, 6, Charing Cross, 1861.
22 p.   23 cm.

8141   Synge, Millington Henry.
On practical communication with the Red River
district... [London?] Read before the Royal
Colonial Society, 17th January, 1870.
19 p.   23 cm.

8142   Szyszlo, Vitold de.
... Dix mille kilomètres à travers le Mexique,
1909-1910.   Avec 22 gravures hors texte.   Paris,
Plon-Nourrit et c^{ie}, 1913.
2 p.l., iv, 343 p.   plates.   18 1/2 cm.

T

8143   Tabares de Ulloa, Francisco.
Observaciones prácticas sobre el cacahuete, ó
maní de América: su produccion en España, bondad
del fruto, y sus varios usos, particularmente para
la extraccion de aceyte: modo de cultivarle y
beneficiarle para bien de la nacion.   Por d.
Francisco Tabáres de Ulloa...   Valencia, En la
oficina de Joseph de Orga, MDCCC.
31 p.   22 cm.

8144   Tableau de la situation actuelle des colonies, pré-
senté à l'Assemblée nationale [Paris, 28 decembre
1789] [n.p., 1789?]
11 p.   20 cm.

8145   Taboada e Irarrázabal, Manuel Gervasio de.
Se proponen à VS. los fundamentos de derecho, que
favorecen la justicia de d. Juana Gonzales de Argan-
doña, en la causa, que sigue contra los bienes de d.
Martin de Zelayeta, cavallero que fué del Orden de
Santiago, para que la justificacion de esta R^{l}.
audencia, se sirva de pronunciar sentencia difinitiva,
condemnando à los dichos bienes, ò á entregar los
principales, que se demandan con las utilidades de

sus empleos, y las alhajas depositadas; ò á
pagar hasta su muerte la cantidad de 127 816.
ps. en que se comprehenden el valor del vale de
f.2. y sus costos, el de los arrendamientos de la
casa, el del deposito de las alhajas, y los cor-
respondientes intereses, á más de los que huvieren
de correr hasta su efectiva paga. [Lima, 1757?]
    47 p.   24 cm.

8146   Taché, Alexandre Antonin, abp., 1823-1894.
        The amnesty again; or, Charges refuted...
    Winnipeg, Printed at "The Standard" Office, 1875.
        31 p.   23 cm.

8147   Taché, Alexandre Antonin, abp. 1823-1894.
        Archbishop Taché on the amnesty question...
    St. Boniface, Printed by the Canadian Publishing
    Co., 1898.
        60 p.   23 cm.

8148   Taché, Alexandre Antonin, abp., 1823-1894.
        Sketch of the North-West of America. By Mgr.
    Taché... Tr. from the French, by Captain D. R.
    Cameron... Montreal, Printed by J. Lovell, 1870.
        216 p.   22 cm.

8149   Tache, Joseph Charles, 1820-1894.
        Forestiers et voyageurs. Pref. de Luc Lacourcière.
    Montréal, Fides [1946]
        190 p.   22 cm.

8150   [Talbot, John]
        History of North America; comprising a geographical
    and statistical view of the United States, and of
    the British Canadian possessions; including a great
    variety of important information on the subject of
    emigrating to that country. Embellished with
    plates and maps. Leeds, Davies and co., 1820.
        2 v. 4 pl., 3 port., 2 fold. maps. 21 1/2 cm.

8151   Talboys, William P
        West India pickles. Diary of a cruise through the
    West Indies in the yacht Josephine. [New York yacht
    club] By W. P. Talboys. With numerous illustrations
    New York, G. W. Carleton & co.; [etc., etc.] 1876.

209 p. incl. front., illus.   15 cm.

8152 Tamayo, Jorge L   , 1912-
      Geografía general de México. México, Instituto
      Mexicano de Investigaciones Económicas, 1949-62.
      4 v. illus., maps (part fold.), diagrs., profiles,
      tables.   24 cm.

8153 Tanguay, Cyprien, 1819-1902.
      Dictionnaire généalogique des familles canadiennes
      depuis la fondation de la colonie jusqu'à nos
      jours. Montréal, E. Senécal, 1871-90.
      7 v. port., fold. map, 2 geneal. tables.   26 cm.

8154 Tapley, Rufus Preston, 1823-1893.
      Eulogy of Abraham Lincoln, sixteenth president
      of the United States, pronounced by Rufus P.
      Tapley, esq., April 19; 1865, at Saco, Maine,
      including the report of the proceedings of the town
      of Saco consequent upon his death. Biddeford, Printed
      at the Union and journal office, 1865.
      27 p.   22 1/2 cm.

8155 Tasse, Joseph.
      La question Riel... [n.p.] 1886.
      14 p.   20 cm.

8156 Taylor, Bayard, 1825-1878.
      The ballad of Abraham Lincoln; illus. by Sol.
      Eytinge, jr.; engraved and printed in colors by
      Bobbett, Hooper, & co. Boston, Fields, Osgood,
      & co., 1870.
      8 p.   27 cm.

8157 Taylor, Bayard, 1825-1878.
      Eldorado, or, Adventures in the path of empire:
      comprising a voyage to California, via Panama; life
      in San Francisco and Monterey; pictures of the gold
      region, and experiences of Mexican travel. By
      Bayard Taylor... 2d ed. New York, G. P. Putnam;
      London, R. Bentley, 1850.
      2 v. in 1. col. front., col. plates.   19 cm.

8158 Taylor, Bayard, 1825-1878.
      Eldorado; or, Adventures in the path of empire;

comprising a voyage to California, via Panama; life
in San Francisco and Monterey; pictures of the gold
region and experiences of Mexican travel, by Bayard
Taylor. New York, G. P. Putnam and son, 1868.
   xiv, 444 p.   18 1/2 cm.

8159 Taylor, Edward Burnett.
      Anahuac... London, Longman, Green, Longman
      and Roberts 1861.
         xi, [1], 344 p.   front., illus., plate (port.
      col.), fold. map.   22 cm.

8160 Taylor, Isaac, 1759-1829.
      Scenes in America for the amusement and instruc-
      tion of little tarry-at-home travellers... London,
      Printed for Harris and son, 1821.
         122 p.   illus., fold. map.   19 1/2 cm.

8161 Taylor, John Glanville, 1823-1851.
      The United States and Cuba! eight years of change
      and travel. By John Glanville Taylor, London, R.
      Bentley, 1851.
         xii, 328 p.   19 1/2 cm.

8162 Teja Zabre, Alfonso, 1888-
      ... Panorama histórico de la revolución mexicana.
      [México] Ediciones Botas, 1939.
         220 p., 1 l.   incl. plates.   24 cm.

8163 [Temple, Oliver Perry]
      John Sevier, citizen, soldier, legislator,
      governor, statesman. Knoxville, Tenn., The ZI-PO
      press, 1910.
         [32] p.   front. (port.)   15 cm.

8164 Tempsky, Gustav Ferdinand von.
      Mitla. A narrative of incidents and personal
      adventures on a journey in Mexico, Guatemala, and
      Salvador in the years 1853 to 1855. With observa-
      tions on the modes of life in those countries. By
      G. F. von Tempsky. Edited by J. S. Bell ... Lon-
      don, Longman, Brown, Green, Longmans, & Roberts,
      1858.
         xv, [1], 436 p.   col. front., 1 illus., plates
      (part col., 1 fold.), plan. fold. map.   22 cm.

8165   Terasaki, Taro.
       ... William Penn et la paix... Paris, A. Pedone,
       1925.
          3 p.l., 163 p.   23 1/2 cm.

8166   Teresa, Saint, 1518-1582.
       Cartas... con notas del don Iuan de Palafox y
       Mendoza. Madrid, María de Quiñones, 1662.
          20 unnumb. 1., 636 p., 17 unnumb. 1.   26 cm.

8167   [Terhune, Mary Virginia (Hawes)] 1831-1922.
       The story of Mary Washington, by Marion Harland
       [pseud.] ... Boston and New York, Houghton, Mifflin
       and company, 1892.
          2 p.l., [3]-171 p.   front. (port.) 8 pl.   20 cm.

8168   Ternaux-Compans, Henri, 1807-1864, ed.
       Recueil de documents et mémoirs originaux sur
       l'histoire des possessions espagnoles dans l'Améri-
       que, à diverses époques de la conquête, renfermant
       des détails curieux sur les moeurs, les coutumes
       et les usages des Indiens, leurs relations avec
       les Espagnols, et sur la géographie et l'histoire
       naturelle de ces contrées; pub. sur les manuscrits
       anciens et inédits de la bibliothèque de m.
       Ternaux-Compans. Paris, Gide, 1840.
          4 p.l., [5]-297 p.   22 cm.

8169   Ternaux-Compans, Henri, 1807-1864, ed.
       Voyages, relations et mémoires originaux pour
       servir à l'histoire de la découverte de l'Amérique,
       publiés pour la première fois en français... Paris,
       A. Bertrand, 1837-1841.
          20 v.   21 cm.

8170   Terrell, Alexander Watkins, 1827-1912.
       From Texas to Mexico and the court of Maximilian
       in 1865, by Alexander Watkins Terrell ... Dallas,
       The Book club of Texas, 1933.
          xviii, 94 p., 1 l.   front., pl., ports.   24 1/2 cm.

8171   Terrien, Ferdinand.
       ... Douze ans dans l'Amérique latine: voyages,
       souvenirs--travaux apostoliques. 90 gravures et 7
       cartes dans le texte. Paris, Bloud & cie. [1903]

431 p.   incl. illus., ports., maps. front., plates.
25 1/2 cm.

8172 Terry, Thomas Philip, 1864-
Terry's Mexico; handbook for travellers, by T.
Philip Terry; with two maps and twenty-five plans.
City of Mexico, Sonora news company; Boston,
Houghton, Mifflin co., 1909.
2 p.l., [iii]-ccxl, 595, [1] p.   2 maps (incl.
fold. front.), 25 plans (1 fold.)   16 cm.

8173 Terry, Thomas Philip, 1864-
This is the story of Mexico, as it was and as
it is today...   Written, for the most part, by T.
Philip Terry ... The illustrations are by Fred
Ludekens ... [n.p.] Southern Pacific company,
c1935.
[30] p.   incl. illus., plates. fold. col. pl.
30 1/2 cm.

8174 ... Texas o Nuevas Filipinas, 1799; noticias por
S. P. E. P. [i.e. D.P.E.P.] México, Vargas Rea,
1945.
2 p.l., 7-51, [1] p.   24 cm.

8175 [Thayer, James Bradley] 1821-1902.
A western journey with Mr. Emerson.   Boston,
Little, Brown, and company, 1884.
1 p.l., 141 p.   17 x 13 1/2 cm.

8176 Thayer, William Makepeace, 1820-1898.
From boyhood to manhood, the life of Benjamin
Franklin...   Boston, J. H. Earle, 1890.
497 p.   illus.; plates, 2 port. (incl. front.)
facsims.   19 1/2 cm.

8177 Thayer, William Makepeace, 1820-1898.
Turning points in successful careers...   New York,
Boston, T. Y. Crowell & company [1895]
x, 410 p.   front., ports.   18 1/2 cm.

8178 Thielmann, Max Franz Guido, freiherr von, 1846-
... Vier wege durch Amerika.   Mit 18 vollbildern
und 3 karten.   Leipzig, Duncker & Humblot, 1879.
xiv, p., 1., 584 p.   18 pl., 3 fold. maps.   27 cm.

8179　Thirty-six years of a seafaring life.　By an old
　　　　quarter master.　Portsea, Printed and published by
　　　　W. Woodward, and sold by Longman & co., London,
　　　　1839.
　　　　　336 p.　　20 cm.

8180　Thomas, Robert Horatio, 1861-1916, ed.
　　　　Journalists' letters descriptive of Texas and
　　　　Mexico.　Edited by Robert H. Thomas...　Mechanicsburg,
　　　　Pa., Farmers' friend print [1889?]
　　　　　1 p.l., [5]-149 p.　　22 cm.

8181　Thome, James Armstrong.
　　　　Emancipation in the West Indies.　A six months'
　　　　tour in Antigua, Barbadoes, and Jamaica, in the
　　　　year 1837.　By Jas. A. Thome, and J. Horace Kimball.
　　　　New York, Pub. by the American anti-slavery society,
　　　　1838.
　　　　　xi, [12]-489 p.　front. (fold. map)　18 1/2 cm.

8182　Thompson, George Alexander.
　　　　... Narración de una visita oficial a Guatemala
　　　　viniendo de Mexico, por G. A. Thompson, ex
　　　　secretario de la Comisión mexicana de Su Majestad
　　　　británica y comisionado para informar al gobierno
　　　　británico sobre el estado de la república central;
　　　　traduccion de Ricardo Fernandez Guardia ...　Guate-
　　　　mala, C. A. [Impreso en la Tipografía nacional]
　　　　1927.
　　　　　vii, 167 p.　incl. port. pl., fold. map.　26 cm.

8183　Thompson, George Alexander.
　　　　Narrative of an official visit to Guatemala from
　　　　Mexico.　By G. A. Thompson...　London, J. Murray,
　　　　1829.
　　　　　xii, vi, 528 p.　incl. front. (fold. map)　17
　　　　1/2 cm.

8184　Thompson, John Caldwell, 1831-1904.
　　　　In memoriam:　a discourse upon the character and
　　　　death of Abraham Lincoln, preached in Pottstown
　　　　Presbyterian church...　June 1, 1865.　Philadelphia,
　　　　Stein & Jones, 1865.
　　　　　20 p.　　22 cm.

8185   Thompson, John Sparrow David.
       The execution of Louis Riel... Minister of
       Justice, Delivered March 22, 1886. [Ottawa? 1886?]
       31 p.   20 cm.

8186   Thompson, Lawrence Sidney, 1916-
       Books in our time. Washington, D. C., Consortium
       Press [1972]
       356 p.   illus.   23 cm.

8187   Thompson, Lawrence Sidney, 1916-
       Hispanic-American printing. Lexington, Erasmus
       Press, 1973.
       22 p.   facsims.   26 cm.

8188   Thompson, Lawrence Sidney, 1916-
       Kurze Geschichte der Handbuchbinderei in den
       Vereinigten Staaten von Amerika. Stuttgart, Max
       Hettler Verlag, 1955.
       111 p.   illus.

8189   Thompson, Lawrence Sidney, 1916-
       Uncle Remus in Syracuse. Chillicothe, Ohio, 1960.
       6 p.   28 cm.

8190   Thompson, Lawrence Sidney, 1916-
       Victor Hammer in Kentucky. [Vienna, 1954]
       7 p.   21 1/2 cm.

8191   Thompson, Waddy, 1798-1868.
       Recollections of Mexico. By Waddy Thompson...
       New York & London, Wiley and Putnam, 1846.
       x, 304 p.   22 1/2 cm.

8192   Thomson, C   T
       Lindsay Hughes Blanton. An appreciation of his
       life and work... Lexington, Ky., Transylvania
       Press [1907?]
       44 p.   illus.   24 1/2 cm.

8193   [Thomson, Norman]
       El libro rojo del Putumayo, precedido de una
       introducción sobre el verdadero escándalo de las
       atrocidades del Putumayo, ilustrado con tres mapas
       ... Bogotá, Arboleda & Valencia, 1913.

xxiii, 153 p.   incl. 3 maps.   18 1/2 cm.

8194   Thrall, Stephen Chipman, 1825?-1892.
         A sermon delivered in Christ church, New Orleans:
       The President's death: a memorial service, held
       at the request of the officers of the Army and
       Navy. [New Orleans, Rea's Steam Press, 1865]
         12 p.   20 cm.

8195   Through the land of the Aztecs; or, Life and travel
       in Mexico; by a Gringo. London, S. Low, Marston &
       company, 1892.
         x, 236 p.   front., plates.   19 cm.

8196   Thümmel, A   R
         Mexiko und die Mexikaner, in physischer, socialer
       und politischer beziehung; ein vollständiges
       gemälde des alten und neuen Mexiko, mit rücksicht
       auf die neueste geschichte, nach deutschen, fran-
       zösischen, englischen und amerikanischen quellen
       dargestellt von dr. A. R. Thümmel. Erlangen, Palm,
       1848.
         viii, 478 p., 1 l.   21 1/2 cm.

8197   Thwaites, Reuben Gold, 1853-1913.
         ... France in America, 1497-1763, by Reuben Gold
       Thwaites... New York and London, Harper & brothers,
       [1905]
         xxi, 320 p.   incl. front. (port.), 7 maps (1
       double)   21 1/2 cm.

8198   [Tiernan, Mrs. Frances Christine (Fisher)] 1846-1920.
         The land of the sun; vistas mexicanas [a novel] by
       Christian Reid [pseud.]... New York, D. Appleton and
       company, 1894.
         3 p.l, 355 p.   front., plates.   19 1/2 cm.

8199   Tilden, Bryant Parrot, 1817?-1859.
         Notes on the upper Rio Grande, by Bryant P.
       Tilden, jr. Explored in the months of October
       and November, 1846, on board the U. S. steamer
       Major Brown, commanded by Capt. Mark Sterling, of
       Pittsburgh. By order of Major General Patterson
       ... Philadelphia, Lindsay & Blakiston, 1847.
         v, 7-32 p.   9 fold. maps.   23 1/2 cm.

8200 Tilden, Samuel Jones, 1814-1886.
    The union: its dangers!! and how they can be averted; letter from Samuel J. Tilden to Hon. William Kent. [New York, 1860]
    16 p.   22 cm.

8201 Times-review, Port Erie, Ont.
    Tourist and historical supplement, 1937. Port Erie [1937]
    caption title, 18 p. illus.   42 cm.
    "Portage Road... by Louis Blake Duff": p. 10.

8202 Todd, Albert, 1854.
    Daniel Webster. Second annual address before the Webster literary society of the Kansas state agricultural college, June 7th, 1884. [By] Albert Todd, A. M. Manhattan, Kan., Printing dept., Agricultural College, 1884.
    22 p.   22 1/2 cm.

8203 Todd, Lyman Beecher.
    Memoir of Dr. Joseph Smith of Lexington, Ky. ... Louisville, Ky., Printed by John P. Morton and company, 1877.
    10 p.   22 1/2 cm.

8204 Toledano, Francisco de Paula.
    Oracion panegírica, é historial, en justa memoria del excmo. é illmo. señor don Antonio Caballero, y Gongora, del Consejo de S. M. obispo de Chiapa, y de Yucatán, arzobispo de la metropolitana iglesia de Santa Fe de Bogotá...virrey...del Nuevo Reyno de Granada... Por don Francisco de Paula Toledano... Granada, En la imprenta de las herederas de d. Nicolás Moreno, 1798.
    4 p.l., 52 p.   24 cm.

8205 Tolliver, Arthur S
    ... The strange story of Lafcadio Hearn. A brief survey of the life and works of a literary genius who revelled in the weird, gruesome, exotic and unearthly. Girard, Kans., Haldeman-Julius [1944]
    24 p.   21 1/2 cm.

8206 Tolliver, Arthur S

The wild adventures of Davy Crockett, based
mainly on the workings of the hero of the Alamo.
Girard, Kans., Haldeman-Julius, [1944]
23 p.   21 1/2 cm.

8207   Tomes, Robert, 1817-1882.
Panama in 1855.   An account of the Panama railroad, of the cities of Panama and Aspinwall, with
sketches of life and character on the Isthmus.
By Robert Tomes.   New York, Harper & brothers, 1855.
3 p.l., [13]-246 p.   incl. illus., port., map.
front., pl.   17 1/2 cm.

8208   Toor, Frances.
Guide to Mexico...   [2d ed.]   Mexico, D. F.
[n.d.]
xiv, 207 p.   illus.   18 cm.

8209   Tornel, Manuel.
Guía práctica del viajero y del comerciante en
Mexico, escrita para el Centro mercantil, por Manuel
Tornel; editor, Nabor Chavez.   Mexico, Librería de
la Enseñanza, 1876.
8 p.l., 13-128, iv p.   20 1/2 cm.

8210   Toronto.   Public Library.
Map collection of the Public Reference Library
of the city of Toronto, Canada.   Compiled by May
MacLachlan.   Toronto, 1923.
111 p.   26 cm.

8211   Torre, Juan de la.
Historia y descripción del Ferrocarril central
mexicano.   Reseña histórica de esa vía ferrea.-
Noticias sobres sus principales obras de arte.-
Datos históricos, estadísticos, descriptivos,
referentes a los estados, ciudades, pueblos,
estaciones y en general a todos los lugares notables
de la linea.   Noticias semejantes sobre el Ferrocarril internacional mexicano de Torreón a Piedras
Negras, por el Lic. Juan de la Torre...   Llera un
apendice con el reglamento de ferrocarriles en
extracto, itinerarios, tarifas, etc. etc.   Mexico,
Imp. de I. Cumplido, 1888.
1 v, 284 p.   illus.   15 cm.

8212   Torre, Tomás de la, d. 1567.
        ... Desde Salamanca, España, hasta Ciudad Real,
Chiapas; diario de viaje, 1544-1545. Prólogo y
notas por Franz Blom, 1944-1945. México, D. F.,
Editora central [1945?]
        5 p.l., 13-209 p. incl. maps.   23 1/2 cm.

8213   Torrente, Mariano, 1792-1856.
        ... Historia de la independencia de México.
Madrid, Editorial-América, 1918.
        352 p.   22 1/2 cm.

8214   Torres Quintero, Gregorio.
        México hacia el fin del fin del virreinato
español. Antecedentes sociológicos del pueblo
mexicano. Paris, Librería de la Vda. de Ch.
Bouret, México, 45, Av. Cinco de Mayo, 1921.
        156 p. illus.   21 cm.

8215   [Torrie, Hiram D   ]
        The tragedy of Abraham Lincoln; in five acts,
by an American artist. Glasgow, J. Brown & son
[1876]
        57 p.   18 cm.

8216   Tousey, Sinclair, 1818-1887.
        Indices of public opinion: 1860-1870. New
York, Printed for private circulation, 1871.
        128 p.   23 cm.

8217   Towles, Susan Starling.
        John James Audubon in Henderson, Kentucky...
Louisville, Ky., John P. Morton & co., 1925.
        19 p.   22 cm.

8218   Townsend, George Alfred, 1841-1914.
        The life, crime, and capture of John Wilkes Booth;
with a full sketch of the conspiracy... New York,
Dick & Fitzgerald [1865]
        64 p.   21 cm.

8219   Townsend, John Wilson, 1886-1968.
        The address at the unveiling of the Allen Fountain
of Youth in Gratz Park, opposite Transylvania University, Lexington, Kentucky, 15 October 1933...

[Lexington] Transylvania University Press, 1933.
24 p.   28 cm.

8220   Townsend, John Wilson, 1886-1968.
"In Kentucky" and its author, "Jim" Mulligan
... Lexington, Ky., Published for the John
Bradford Club, 1935.
31 p.   23 cm.

8221   Townsend, John Wilson, 1886-1968.
James Lane Allen, still Kentucky's greatest
writer... Lexington, Ky., Bluegrass Bookshop,
1948.
30 p.   23 cm.

8222   Townsend, John Wilson, 1886-1968.
With Mr. Allen in New York... Louisville, Ky.,
1928.
29 p.   23 cm.

8223   Toxar, Francisco de, ed. and tr.
Coleccion de cuentos morales que contiene el
Zimeo, novela americana, las fabulas orientales y
El Abenaki. Los da a luz traducidos del frances d.
Francisco de Toxar. Salamanca: En la imprenta del
editor. Año de 1796. Se hallará en la librería
de d. Joseph Alegría.
viii, 176 p.   24 cm.

8224   Tracy, Frank Basil, 1866-
The tercentenary history of Canada, from Champlain
to Laurier, MDCVIII-MCMVIII, by Frank Basil Tracy;
with many full-page illustrations, portraits and
maps especially made for this work. New York, The
Macmillan company, 1908.
3 v.   fronts., illus., plates, ports., maps.
21 cm.

8225   [Traill, Mrs. Catherine Parr (Strickland)] 1802-1899.
The backwoods of Canada: being letters from
the wife of an emigrant officer, illustrative of the
domestic economy of British America. New ed. London,
C. Knight & co., 1846.
1 p.l., iv, [5]-242 p.   illus.   14 1/2 cm.

8226 [Traill, Mrs. Catharine Parr (Strickland)] 1802-1899.
The young emigrants; or, Pictures of Canada
calculated to amuse and instruct the minds of
youth... London, Printed for Harvey and Darton,
1826.
168 p. 16 cm.

8227 Trautz, Margarete.
Mexiko. Erinnerungen einer Deutschen von
Margarete Trautz... Braunschweig, R. Sattler, 1899.
2 p.l., 45 p. 6 pl. 25 cm.

8228 Travels in North America. Dublin, Printed by Brett
Smith, 1824.
180 p. incl. front., illus. 14 1/2 cm.

8229 Travels in North America. [Illus.] London:
Printed for C. J. G. & F. Rivington, 1831.
2 p.l., 168 p. plates. 14 1/2 cm.

8230 Travels of Anna Bishop in Mexico. 1849. Philadelphia
C. Deal [c1852]
1 p.l., v-xii, [13]-317 p. 19 cm.

8231 Trembley, Ernest.
Riel. Reponse of monsieur J. A. Chapleau...
St. Hyacinthe, 1885.
82 p. 21 cm.

8232 Trent, William Peterfield, 1862-1939.
Southern statesmen of the old regime; Washington,
Jefferson, Randolph, Calhoun, Stephens, Toombs,
and Jefferson Davis, by William P. Trent... New
York, Boston, T. Y. Crowell & company [1897]
xv p., 1 l., 293 p. front., ports. 19 1/2 cm.

8233 Trentini, Francisco.
El florecimiento de México (ed. ilustrada) en
español e ingles, 2 de abril de 1906. Pub. bajo la
autorización del gobierno, por el editor: Francisco
Trentini ... México, Tip. de Bouligny & Schmidt
sucs., 1906.
2 v. in 1. illus., fold. pl., ports. 37 cm.

8234 Trial of Abraham Lincoln by the great statesmen of

the republic: a council of the past on the tyrrany
of the present; the spirit of the Constitution on
the bench -- Abraham Lincoln, prisoner at the bar,
his own counsel... New York, Office of the Metro-
politan Record, 1863.
   29 p.   22 cm.

8235 Trial of the assassins and conspirators for the murder
of Abraham Lincoln, and the attempted assassination
of Vice-President Johnson and the whole cabinet...
Philadelphia, Barclay & co., [1865]
   21-30, 33-102 p. illus.   24 cm.

8236 Trigo, José M
   Recursos y desarrollo de México, por José M.
Trigo. San Francisco, Cal., The History company
[1892-95]
   1 p.l., v-vii, ix-xiii, 604 p. plates, maps
(partly fold.), plan.   30 1/2 cm.

8237 The trip of the steamer Oceanus to Fort Sumter and
Charleston, S. C. ... April 14, 1865, by a committee
appointed by the passengers of the Oceanus.
Brooklyn, "The Union" steam printing house, 1865.
   172, [3] p. illus.   22 cm.

8238 Trollope, Anthony, 1815-1882.
   North America. By Anthony Trollope ... New York,
Harper & brothers, 1862.
   vii, 623 p.   19 1/2 cm.

8239 Trollope, Anthony, 1815-1882.
   The West Indies and the Spanish Main. By
Anthony Trollope... New York, Harper & brothers,
1860.
   iv, 5-385 p.   19 1/2 cm.

8240 Trow, James, 1827-
   Manitoba and Northwest Territories. Letters by
James Trow... Together with information relative
to acquiring Dominion lands; cost of outfit, etc.
Ottawa, The Dept. of Agriculture, 1878.
   100 p. front. (fold. map)   21 1/2 cm.

8241 Trow, James, 1827-

A trip to Manitoba. By James Trow, M. P.
Quebec, S. Marcotte, 1875.
86 p.   16 cm.

8242   Troy, New York. Citizens.
A tribute of respect by the citizens of Troy, to
memory of Abraham Lincoln. Albnay, New York, J.
Munsell, 1865.
xi, 342 p.   31 cm.

8243   Tschiffely, Aimé Felix, 1893–
Zehntausend meilen im sattel vom kreuz des
südens zum polarstern, von A. F. Tschiffely.
Horw (Luzern) und Leipzig, Montana-verlag a.g.
[ᶜ1933]
391, [1] p.   front. (port.), plates, fold. map.
20 cm.

8244   Tuchnin, Ruslan Aleksandrovich.
Мексика без экзотики. Москва, Гос. изд-во полит.
лит-ры, 1963.
125 p.   illus., map.   17 cm.

8245   Tucker, Joshua Thomas, 1812–1897.
A discourse in memory of our late president,
Abraham Lincoln, delivered in the First Parish
Church, Holliston, Mass., Thursday, June 1, 1865...
Holliston, Plimpton and Clark, 1865.
21 p.   23 cm.

8246   Tunis's topographical and pictorial guide to Niagara
Falls, and route book to Montreal, Quebec, Saratoga,
and the White Mountains; also, description of the
St. Lawrence, Ottawa, and Saguenay riverrs [!].
Detroit, W. E. Tunis [1871]
105 p.   incl. advertisements, illus., 1 fold.
map.   17 1/2 cm.

8247   Tuttle, Joseph Farrand, 1818–1901.
Memorial addresses, to Abraham Lincoln and
James A. Garfield, the assassinated presidents.
Crawfordsville, Ind., Review steam book and job
printers, 1881.
18 p.   20 cm.

8248 Tweedie, Ethel Brilliana (Harley) "Mrs. Alec
      Tweedie."
          Mexico as I saw it, by Mrs. Alec Tweedie (née
      Harley)... Illustrated from photographs by the
      author. London, Hurst and Blackett, limited, 1901.
          xii, 472 p. incl. col. front. plates (part col.),
      ports., fold. map. facsims. 23 1/2 cm.

8249 Tyler, Lyon Gardiner, 1853-1935.
          The letters and times of the Tylers. By Lyon
      G. Tyler ... Richmond, Va., Whittet & Shepperson;
      [etc., etc.] 1884-96.
          3 v. fronts., pl., ports., facsims. (part fold.)
      24 1/2 cm.

8250 Tyler, Samuel, 1809-1877.
          Memoir of Roger Brooke Taney, LL.D, chief
      justice of the Supreme court of the United States.
      By Samuel Tyler... Baltimore, J. Murphy & co.,
      1872.
          1 p.l., vii-xv, 17-659 p. front. (port.)
      24 1/2 cm.

8251 Tylor, Sir Edward Burnett, 1832-1917.
          Anahuac: or, Mexico and the Mexicans, ancient
      and modern. By Edward B. Tylor. London, Longman,
      Green, Longman and Roberts, 1861.
          xi, [1], 344 p. front., illus., plates (part
      col.), fold. map. 22 cm.

8252 Tyrrell, James Williams, 1863-
          Across the sub-Arctics of Canada, a journey
      of 3,200 miles by canoe and snow shoe through the
      Hudson Bay region... including a list of plants
      collected on the way, a vocabulary of Eskimo words,
      and a map showing the route of the expedition.
      With new illustrations from photographs taken on
      the journey, and from drawings by Arthur Heming
      and J. S. Gordon. 3d ed., rev. and enl. Toronto,
      William Briggs, 1908.
          vii, 9-280 p. front., illus., plates, ports.,
      fold. maps. 23 cm.

8253   Ubilla y Medina, Antonio Cristobal, marques de
       Rivas, 1645-1726.
           Svccession de el rey D. Phelipe V, nuestro Señor
       en la corona de España; diario de svs viages
       desde Versalles a Madrid; el qve execvto para sv
       feliz casamiento; jornada a Napoles, a Milan, y a
       sv exercito; svccessos de la campaña, y sv bvelta a
       Madrid... Madrid, Juan García Infanzón, 1704.
           672, [38] p. illus.

8254   Ucedo, Sebastian de, 17th cent.
           Indice del mundo conocido diligentemente reducido
       a este solo volumen para facilidad de los aficionados
       a la Cosmografia. Dirigido al excelentissimo señor
       d. Ivan, Thomas, Enrriqvez de Cabrera conde de
       Melgar... Por don Sevastian de Vcedo... segunda im-
       pression. Milan, En el real, y ducal Palacio, por
       Marcos Antonio Pandulfo Malatesta empressor r.c.
       [1672]
           5 p.l., 362, [4] p.   25 cm.

8255   Uhde, Adolf.
           Die länder am untern Rio Bravo del Norte.
       Geschichtliches und erlebtes von Adolph Uhde ...
       Mit einer uebersichtskarte. Heidelberg, In
       commission bei J. C. B. Mohr, 1861.
           viii, 431, [1] p. fold. map.   24 cm.

8256   Umfreville, Edward.
           The present state of Hudson's bay. Containing
       a full description of that settlement, and the
       adjacent country; &c. likewise of the fur trade,
       with hints for its improvement, &c. To which are
       added, remarks and observations made in the inland
       parts, during a residence of near four years; a
       specimen of five Indian languages; and a journal of
       a journey from Montreal to New York. By Edward
       Umfreville... London, Printed for C. Stalker, 1790.

2 p.l., vii, 230 p.   2 fold. tab.   20 1/2 cm.

8257   The Union almanac for 1866.   Philadelphia, King &
       Baird [1865]
           34, [1] p.   illus.   19 x 16 cm.

8258   U. S. Adjutant-general's office.
           List of military posts, etc., established in
       the United States from its earliest settlement
       to the present time [Feb. 1, 1902]... Washington,
       Govt. prtg. office, 1902.
           109 p.   23 cm.

8259   The United States and Canada, as seen by two brothers
       in 1858 and 1861.   London, Edward Stanford, 1862.
           3 p.l., 137 p.   fold. map.   19 cm.

8260   The United States biographical dictionary and portrait
       gallery of eminent and self-made men.   Illinois volume.
       Chicago, New York [etc.] American biographical pub-
       lishing co., 1876.
           798 p.   fronts., ports.   28 1/2 x 23 cm.

8261   U. S. Congress., 1st sess., 1875-1876.   House.
           Mr. Blaine and the "Mulligan" letters.   The whole
       story as told in the House of Representatives, June
       5, 1876.   Reprinted verbatim from the "Congressional
       Record."   With an introduction.   Boston, J. S.
       Cushing & co.
           vi, 54 p.   18 cm.

8262   U. S. Department of justice.
           Opinion on the constitutional power of the
       military to try and execute the assassins of the
       President, by Attorney General Speed.   Washington,
       Govt. prtg. office, 1865.
           16 p.   23 cm.

8263   U. S. Military secretary's dept.
           ... Memorandum relative to the general officers
       in the armies of the United States during the civil
       war, 1861-1865.   (Compiled from official records)
       1906.   [Washington, Govt. print. off., 1906]
           73 p.   23 cm.

8264   U. S. Puerto Rico reconstruction administration.
          Puerto Rico; a guide to the island of Boriquén,
       compiled and written by the Puerto Rico reconstruc-
       tion administration in co-operation with the Writer·
       program of the Work projects administration ...
       Sponsored by the Puerto Rico Department of educatioɪ
       New York, The University society, inc., 1940.
          xii, 400 p.   illus. (maps), plates.   21 cm.

8265   U. S.   Santiago battlefield commission.
          Tablets and monuments marking the battlefields
       of the campaign of Santiago de Cuba...   Santiago
       battlefield commission [n.d.]
          46 p.   22 cm.

8266   Unknown Mexico.   Edinburgh, 1903.
          291-297 p.   19 cm.

8267   Urdaneta, Rafael, 1788-1845.
          ... Memorias del general Rafael Urdaneta (general
       en jefe y encargado del gobierno de la gran
       Colombia) Prólogo de R. Blanco-Fombona.   Madrid,
       Editorial-América [pref. 1916]
          xxxi, 444 p.   23 cm.

8268   Urquinaona y Pardo, Pedro de, fl. 1820.
          ... Memorias de Urquinaona (comisionado de la
       regencia española para la pacificación del Nuevo
       reino de Granada) ...   Madrid, Editorial-América
       [1917]
          383 p.   23 cm.

8269   Urrutia, Francisco José, 1872-
          ... Los Estados Unidos de América y las repúblicas
       hispano-americanas de 1810 à 1830; páginas de histor
       diplomática.   Madrid, Editorial-América, 1918.
          485 p.   23 cm.

8270   Urrutia, Francisco José, 1872-
          ... La evolución del principio de arbitraje en
       America.   La Sociedad de naciones.   Madrid, Editoria
       America, 1920.
          298 p.   23 cm.

8271   Valbuena, Bernardo de, 1560-1627.
       Siglo de oro en las selvas de Erifile... En
       qve se descrive vna agradable y rigurosa imitación
       del estilo pastoril de Teocrito, Virgilio, y
       Sanazaro...   Madrid, Alonso Martin, 1607.
       175 numb. l.   25 cm.

8272   Valcarce Velasco, Manuel Antonio.
       Por el maestro de campo don Toribio de la Torre
       y Caso, don Pedro de Medranda y Vivanco, general
       del Mar del Sur, y consortes.   Con el capitan don
       Diego de Segvra, don Roque de la Barreda, y con-
       sortes.   Sobre los caudales, e interesses que se
       salvaron en la lancha de la fragata S. Juan Bap-
       tista, su capitan d. Francisco Sorarte, y prorrateo
       de ellos.   Y por el mismo maestre de campo d.
       Toribio de la Torre.   Con d. Jacome Francisco
       Andriani, embiado por los Quatro Cantones.   Sobre
       el pago de 575. doblones de à dos escudos de oro
       [Havana? 17--]
       20 numb. l.   23 cm.

8273   [Valdés, Maximino]
       De Mexico a Necaxa, por el conde de Fox [pseud.];
       prólogo del Prof. Jesus Romero Flores ... l. ed.
       Mexico, D. F., Compañía impresora mexicana, 1919.
       xiii p., 1 l., 267 p., 2 l.   ports., plates.
       22 cm.

8274   Valdivieso y Torrejón, Miguel de.
       Exc^{mo}. señor.   Por parte de don Francisco
       Vadillo y Medina en la causa, que sigue con d.
       Diego Hidalgo de Zisneros, para que se declare à
       su favor el proximo ingresso en el oficio de Lampa,
       se proponen los fundamentos de derecho, que in-
       struien su justicia.   [n.p., 1752]
       [39] p.   22 cm.

8275 Valdivieso y Torrejón, Miguel de.
Por parte de don Lorenzo Pheliphe [:] de la
Torre, en la causa executiva que sigue contra los
bienes de d. Ambrosio Boorjes de Orepesa, se ponen
en consideracion de US. los fundamentos de derecho
para que se sentencie de tranze, y remate. [Lima,
1755]
58 numb. l.   24 cm.

8276 Valdivieso y Torrejón, Miguel de.
Por parte de doña Antonia Pacheco, se ponen en
consideracion de V.S. los fundamentos de derecho
que hazen à su favor, para que en justicia se le
absuelva de la demanda puesta por los dueños de
los trigos perdidos en la innundacion del Callao.
[Lima, 1750]
[75] p.   25 cm.

8277 Valdivieso y Torrejón, Miguel de.
Por parte de doña Isabel de la Pressa Carrillo,
tutora y curadora de los menores hijos del conde
de Montemar, su alvazea y thenedora de bienes,
se ponen en consideracion de U.S. los fundamentos,
que le assisten, para que se deniegue el despojo
intentado por el señor marquès de Casa Calderon,
sobre el impedimento de las luzes. [n.p., 1750]
[55] p.   23 cm.

8278 Vallarna, Francisco María de.
Memorial ajustado hecho con citacion y asistencia
de las partes del pleyto que se controvierte en
el consejo, entre don Antonio Estevez y Pombal,
n.12, en representacion de su muger doña Maria
Antonia Vazquez Varela, n.13, vecinos de la villa
de La Guardia, obispado de Tuy, reyno de Galicia:
don Vicente Quiroga Mendez de Sotomayor, n.14, como
marido de doña Teresa Bermudez, n.15, vecinos de la
villa de Vigo en el mismo obispado y reyno: y
don Josef Gonzalez conde de Fuente Gonzalez, n.3,
como albacea de su difunta consorte dona Rosa de
la Fuente, n.2, padre y legítimo adminstrador de
la persona y bienes de don Juan y don Josef Gonzalez,
nn.6 y 7, y à representacion de don Matias Elizalde,
su yerno, y marido de doña Francisca Gonzalez, n. 8,
vecino de la ciudad de Lima: y en el que tambien

se le ha dado vista al señor fiscal, sobre la
subsistencia ó insubsistencia de la real fucultad
[!] obtenida para la fundacion del vinculo, que
del tercio de sus bienes mandó establecer el
difunto don Josef del Villar y Andrade, conde de
Villar de Fuentes, n.l., vecino que fué de dicha
ciudad de Lima; si se deben verificar en el todo
las fundaciones de dos aniversarios que instituyó
el mismo, para cuyos capitales asignó 17 pesos, y
sobre la sucesion à dichos vinculo y aniversarios
y titulo de Castilla de conde de Villar de Fuentes,
segun el órden de los llamamientos hechos por éste en
su última disposicion. Madrid, En la oficina de don
Benito Cano, 1795.
1 p.l., 67 numb. l. 24 cm.

8279 Valle, Juan N   del.
El viajero en México: completa guia de forasteros
para 1864; obra util a toda clase de personas,
formada y arreglada por Juan N. del Valle. México,
Impr. de Andrade y Escalante, 1864.
4 p.l., [5]-764 p. ports., fold. plan. 20
1/2 cm.

8280 Valle, Rafael Heliodoro, 1891-   , ed.
Semblanza de Honduras. Tegucigalpa, D. C., Imp.
Calderón [1947?]
260 p. 22 cm.

8281 Vallejo, Antonio R
Compendio de la historia social y política de
Honduras, aumentada con los principales aconteci-
mientos de Centro America; para uso de los colegios
de 2.ª enseñanza de la República de Honduras, por
Antonio R. Vallejo... 2. ed. Tegucigalpa, Honduras,
Tipografía nacional, 1926-
v. 28 cm.

8282 Valois, Alfred de.
Mexique, Havane et Guatemala; notes de voyage
par Alfred de Valois. Paris, E. Dentu [1861]
2 p.l., 446 p. 18 cm.

8283 Vancouver, George, 1757-1798.
A voyage of discovery to the North Pacific ocean,

and round the world; in which the coast of north-
west America has been carefully examined and
accurately surveyed. Undertaken by His Majesty's
command, principally with a view to ascertain
the existence on any navigable communication between the North Pacific and North Atlantic oceans;
and performed in the years 1790, 1791, 1792, 1793,
1794, and 1795, in the Discovery, sloop of war,
and armed tender Chatham, under the command of
Captain George Vancouver. London, Printed for
G. G. and J. Robinson, 1798.
   3 v. 17 pl., map. 31 x 24 cm.

8284 Vancouver Island. Council.
   ... Minutes of the Council of Vancouver island.
Commencing August 30th, 1851, and terminating
with the prorotation of the House of assembly,
February 6th, 1861... Victoria, B. C., Printed
by William H. Cullin, 1918.
   93 p. 24 1/2 cm.

8285 Vancouver Island. House of Assembly.
   ... House of assembly correspondence book.
August 12th, 1856, to July 6th, 1859... Victoria,
B. C., Printed by William H. Cullin, 1918.
   62 p. 24 1/2 cm.

8286 Vancouver Island. House of Assembly.
   ... Minutes of the House of assembly of Vancouver
island. August 12th, 1856, to September 25th,
1858... Victoria, B. C., Printed by William H.
Cullin, 1918.

8287 Van Horne, John Douglass.
   Jefferson Davis and repudiation in Mississippi.
[Glyndon, Md.? 1915]
   16 p. 22 1/2 cm.

8288 Van Sinderen, Adrian, 1887-
   A journey into neolithic times. [Illus. from
photos by the author. New York, 1947?]
   [80] p. illus. (part col.) 25 cm.

8289 Vaquero, pseud.
   Adventures in search of a living in Spanish-

America, by "Vaquero" [pseud.] London, J. Bale,
sons & Daniels son, ltd., 1911.
    viii, 304 p. front., plates, 3 maps. 25 cm.

8290 Vargas, Elvira.
        ... Por las rutas del sureste ... México, D. F.,
      Editorial "Cima" [1940]
        8 p.l., 11-323 p., 2 l. 19 cm.

8291 Varias relaciones del Perú y Chile y conquista de
      la isla de Santa Catalina. 1535 à 1658. Madrid,
      Imprenta de Miguel Ginesta, 1879.
        361 p. 16 1/2 cm.

8292 Vásquez de Velasco, Pedro.
        Por don Pedro Vazqvez de Velasco, cavallero
      del Orden de Calatrava, provisto fiscal de la
      Real audiencia de las Charcas, en que continua
      la satisfaccion de la querella criminal, que contra
      su persona se diò en el real, y supremo Consejo
      de las Indias por parte de doña Teresa Carreño,
      viuda de don Francisco Ruiz Canduelas, que falleciò
      en la Ciudad de los Reyes el dia. 5. de julio del
      año passado de 1696. Y se haze notoria la inocencia
      de don Pedro, assi por el contexto de los autos,
      declaraciones de las mismas partes, como por la
      notoriedad con que deponen testigos de suma ex-
      cepcion, que se hallaron en la Ciudad de los
      Reyes el dia de la desgracia, y fueron examinados
      en esta corte, y en Cadiz, con citacion de las
      partes, y la del señor fiscal... [n.p., 1709?]
        1 p.l., 20 numb. l. 21 cm.

8293 Vázquez de Coronado, Francisco, 1510-1549.
        ... Coronado's letter to Mendoza, August 3, 1540.
      The relation of Francis Vasquez de Coronado,
      captaine generall of the people which were sent
      in the name of the Emperours Maiestie to the
      countrey of Cibola newly discouered, which he
      sent to don Antonio de Mendoça, viceroy of Mexico, of
      such things as happened in his voyage from the 22.
      of Aprill in the yeere 1540. Which departed from
      Culiacan forward, and of such things as hee found
      in the countrey which he passed. [Boston, Directors
      of the Old South work, 1896]
        16 p. 20 cm. (Old South leaflets. [Gen.

ser., 1] no. 20)

8294 Vázquez de Coronado, Francisco, 1510-1549.
The relation of Francis Vazquez de Coronado
... of such things as happened in his voyage from
the 22. of Aprill in the yeere 1540. which de-
parted from Culiacan forward, and of such things
as hee found in the country which he passed. (In
Kaklyut, Richard. Collection of voyages. London.
1809-12. 31 cm. v. 3 [1810] p. 446-457)

8295 Veere, Theo de.
Mexico: reis-studies van een journalist, door
Theo de Veer. Amsterdam, Scheltema & Holkema
[1910]
3 p.l., [ix]-x p., 1 l., 231 p. illus. 28 cm.

8296 Vega, Alonso de la, 17th cent.
Las religiones del Perv, no estan comprehendidas
en vna real cedvla, despachada en caso particular
para el nvevo reyno de Granada. Alegacion qve haze
a favor de todas, y Agustin, el M^{tro}· fr. Alonso
de la Vega... [n.p.] 1704.
1 p.l., 3-20 numb. l. 21 cm.

8297 Vega y Mendoza, Francisco José de la.
Manual de exercicios, y meditaciones para los
desagravios de Christo Señor Nuestro, reducidos,
o acomodados de los que ha exercitado hasta aora,
la devocion, à el estado de las señoras religiosas,
para que sin embargo de su comunidad, y reglas,
puedan exercitarlos; como para otras personas
seculares, à quienes tambien se han ajustado, para
que sin impedimento del suyo puedan emplearse en
su devocion. Por el lic. Francisco Joseph de la
Vega, y Mendoza ... Con licencia en Mexico: Por
Francisco de Rivera Calderon. Y por su original, en
dicha ciudad, en la imprenta de Joseph Bernardo de
Hogal, en la calle de la Monterilla. Año de 1726.
4 p.l., 136 p. 26 cm.

8298 Vela, David.
Nuestro Belice, por David Vela... Guatemala,
[Tipografía nacional] 1939.
195 p. 26 1/2 cm.

8299 Velasco, Diego del, d. 1648.
Descubrimiento del camino que de la ciudad de
Quito, y su reyno, ha pretendido abrir para el
puerto, y baya de Caracas, en el mar del sur...
[Madrid? 1620?]
[4] p.   20 cm.

8300 Velásquez, César Vicente.
... México en conjunto, un pueblo entre dos
mundos. Quito, Imp. Caja del seguro, 1941.
5 p.l., [9]-97 p., 1 l.   18 1/2 cm.

8301 Verissimo, Erico, 1905-
México; história duma viagem.   Rio de Janeiro,
Editôra Globo [1957]
299 p.   illus.   23 cm.

8302 Verrill, Alpheus Hyatt, 1871-
Cuba past and present, by A. Hyatt Verrill ...
New York, Dodd, Mead & company, 1914.
9 p.l., 257 p.   front., plates, 2 fold. maps.
19 1/2 cm.

8303 Los Viajes de Cockburn y Lièvre por Costa Rica.
San José, Editorial Costa Rica. 1962.
134 p.   illus.   21 cm.

8304 Victor, Orville James, 1827-1910.
The private and public life of Abraham Lincoln
... New York, Beadle & co. [1865]
96 p.   front.   16 cm.

8305 Victoria, Paulo de.
Advertencias en hecho, y en derecho para
accreditar el de los herederos de Diego Sanchez
Pascual, vezino que fue de la Concepcion del
Valle de Iauxa, y sindico del señor San Francisco
que en estos reynos de llamo Antono Lopez Duarte,
y de Geronima de la Parra su muger. [n.p., 1644]
5 l.   22 cm.

8306 Vidal Ladrón de Guevara, Juan José.
Por parte de doña Petronila Ruydiaz, en la
causa que sigue contra don Pedro del Villar y
Zuviaur, caballero del Orden de Santiago, como

albazea thenedor de bienes, y heredero de doña
Juana Villaverde, quien lo fue assimismo de don
Simòn Ruydiaz, del mismo orden; se ponen en consideracion de V.S. los fundamentos de derecho, que
patrocinan su justicia, sobre que se libre mandamiento de mission, en possesion pro indiviso, para
la percepcion de la sexta parte en que fue instituida
por el dicho d. Simòn su padre: declarandose al
mismo tiempo, que esta sexta, se debe deducir con
preferencia à todos los legados. [n.p., 1758]
[56] p.   23 cm.

8307   Vigne, Godfrey Thomas, 1801-1863.
Travels in Mexico, South America, etc. etc.   By
G. T. Vigne ...   London, W. H. Allen & co., 1863.
2 v.   illus., plates, fold. map.   18 1/2 cm.

8308   Vigneaux, Ernest.
Viaje a Méjico.   Introd. de Leopoldo I. Orendáin.
Guadalajara, Banco Industrial de Jalisco, 1950.
xvii, 115 p.   illus.   23 cm.

8309   [Villarreal, Francisco Joaquín de] b. 1691.
Representacion del reyno de Chile sobre la
importancia, y necessidad de sujetar, y reducir
à pueblos los indios araucanos. La impossibilidad
de conseguirlo, perseverando en la conducta passada; y la facilidad, con que puede lograrse,
sin costo alguno del real erario por medio de
las providencias, que se expressan.   [Madrid?
1741?]
127 p.   27 cm.

8310   Villaseñor y Sánchez, José Antonio de.
Theatro americano, descripcion general de los
reynos, y provincias de la Nueva-España, y sus
jurisdicciones: dedicala al rey nuestro señor el
señor d. Phelipe Quinto, monarcha de las Españas.
Su author d. Joseph Antonio de Villa-Señor, y
Sanchez ... Quien la escribió de orden del excelentissimo señor conde de Fuen-Clara, virrey gobernador,
y capitan general de esta Nueva-España, y presidente
de su Real audiencia, &c. México, Impr. de la viuda
de d. J. Bernardo de Hogal, 1746-48.
2 v.   2 pl.   30 cm.

8311 Villegas, Antonio Claudio de, b. 1700.
Tercera iglesia de Terceros dominicos de la
imperial ciudad de Mexico, compuesta de la primitiva
iglesia de los mismos Terceros, y de la parrochial
de indios mistecos peregrinos, y advenedizos de dicha
ciudad. Reducida a una por el prior superior, y
thesorero de la milicia de Christo. y Tercer orden
de n. gran p. santo Domingo, y en su dedicacion
predicada como imagen de la mystica iglesia, el
dia 20 de febrero de 1757, por n.m.r.p.f. Antonio
Clavdio de Villegas... Sacala a luz la v. Tercer
orden de penitencia, quien la dedica a su gloriosis-
simo patriarcha santo Domingo de Guzman. [Mexico]
Con licencia en la imprenta de la Biblioteca
mexicana, dicho año [i.e. 1757]
17 p.l., 19 p.   22 cm.

8312 Villegas, Francisco de.
Reparos qve propone al exc.mo s.or conde de
Alva de Aliste virrey deste reyno, en orden a la
moneda resellada. A pedimiento del prior, y
consules desta Ciudad de los Reyes. Francisco de
Villegas ensayador aprobado, y contraste publico
della. [Lima, 1657]
[15] p.   22 cm.

8313 Vincent, Mrs. Elizabeth Kipp.
In the days of Lincoln: girlhood recollections
and personal reminiscences of life in Washington
during the Civil war... foreword by F. Ray Risdon...
Gardena, Calif., Spanish American institute press,
1924.
35 p.   facsim.   22 cm.

8314 Vincent, Marvin Richardson, 1834-1922.
A sermon on the assassination of Abraham Lincoln
... First Presbyterian church, Troy... April 23,
1865. Troy, N. Y., A. W. Scribner, 1865.
47 p.   23 cm.

8315 Vincent, Ralph Waterman.
Mexico today and tomorrow; an outline of the
present earning power and future possibilities of
her railroad systems. Facts, figures and suggestions
regarding the principal traffic producing centers.

By Ralph Waterman Vincent ... [New York?] 1906.
1 p.l., 5-85 p. incl. illus., port. 19 1/2 cm.

8316 Virginia. Governor.
Governor's letter, transmitting a letter from
the governor of Maryland, containing a report
with sundry resolutions relative to the appropria-
tion of the public land for the purpose of education, adopted by the legislature of Maryland,
February 13, 1821. [Printed by order of the House
of Delegates] Richmond, Printed by Thomas Ritchie,
1821.
28 p. 21 cm.

8317 Voeu patriotique d'un américain, sur la prochaine
assemblée des États-généraux. [n.p., 1788]
15 p. 20 cm.

8318 Voorhees, Luke.
Personal recollections of pioneer life on the
mountains and plains of the great west. [Cheyenne,
Wyo., 1920]
25 p. port. 21 1/2 cm.

8319 [Vowell, Richard Longeville]
... Memorias de un oficial de la legión británica;
campañas y cruceros durante la guerra de emancipa-
ción hispano-americana. Madrid, Editorial-América
[1916]
241 p., 2 l. 23 cm.

8320 The voyages and adventures of the Chevalier Dupont.
Translated from the French. London, Printed for T.
Jones and B. Jones, 1772.
4 v. 17 cm.

8321 Voyages et aventures du chevalier de ***. Contenant
les voyages de l'auteur ... Londres et Paris,
Dessain, jr., 1769.
4 v. in 2. 17 cm.

8322   Wade, Mark Sweeten.
       ... The overlanders of '62... Edited by John
       Hosie... Victoria, B. C., Printed by Charles F.
       Banfield, 1931.
          xiv, 176 p. illus.   24 1/2 cm.

8323   Waerdenburgh, Dirk van.
          Two memorable relations. The one a letter
       vvritten from Colonell Generall VVeerdenbvrk,
       out of the VVest-India from Farnabuck, to the
       Lords the States Generall of the Vnited Provinces,
       touching the surprisall of the towne of Olinda
       in Farnabuck with the forts thereunto belonging.
       Translated out of Dutch into English. The other,
       the coppy of the true relation of all that hath
       passed and beene done at the taking and reducing
       of the citty and cittadell or castle of Pignarolle,
       after a very hot and furious assault was given. To-
       gether with all the passages and occurrences that
       happened at the pillaging of Rivolle. By the Lord
       Marshall De Crequy. Faithfully translated out
       of the French coppy. With priviledge, printed at
       Roane by Tho. Mallard... 1630. London, Printed
       for N. Bourne, 1630.
          12 p.   20 cm.

8324   Wagner, Moritz, 1813-1887.
          ... La república de Costa Rica en Centro América.
       Traducción del alemán por el professor Jorge A.
       Lines, asesorado por el dr. Ernesto J. Wender y
       el prof. José Dávila Solera. San José, Costa Rica
       [Imprenta Lehmann] 1944.
          1 p.l., [v]-x p., [A]-F, 353 p., 1 l. fold. map.
       26 cm.

8325   Wakefield, Mrs. Priscilla (Bell) 1751-1832.
          Excursions in North America, described in letters
       from a gentleman and his young companion, to their
       friends in England. By Priscilla Wakefield ... 2d
       ed. London, Printed and sold by Darton, Harvey,
       and Darton, 1810.
          x (i.e. xi), 420, [4] p. front. (fold. map)

17 1/2 cm.

8326 Walden, Treadwell, 1830–
      The national sacrifice: a sermon preached the
      Sunday before the death of the president, and two
      addresses, on the Sunday and Wednesday following,
      in St. Clement's church, Philadelphia... Phil-
      adelphia, Sherman & co., 1865.
      41 p.   23 cm.

8327 Walker, Edwin C
      A sketch and appreciation of Moncure Daniel Conway,
      freethinker and humanitarian. An address at the
      Paine-Conway memorial meeting of the Manhattan
      Liberal Club, January 31, 1908... New York, Pub-
      lished by Edwin C. Walker, 1908.
      55 p.   20 cm.

8328 Walker, Jeanie Mort.
      Life of Capt. Joseph Fry, the Cuban martyr.
      Being a faithful record of his remarkable career
      from childhood to the time of his heroic death
      at the hands of Spanish executioners; recounting
      his experience as an officer in the U. S. and
      Confederate navies, and revealing much of the
      inner history and secret marine service of the
      late civil war in America. By Jeanie Mort Walker...
      Hartford, The J. B. Burr publishing co., 1875.
      589 p. incl. front., plates, ports.   21 cm.

8329 Walker, Robert James, 1801–1869.
      Letter of Hon. R. J. Walker, in favor of the
      re-election of Abraham Lincoln. London, Sept. 30,
      1864. [New York, 1864]
      20 p.   22 cm.

8330 Walker, Thomas, 1715–1794.
      Doctor Walker diary of exploration with will
      subjoined, arranged by Francis Marion Rust...
      Fifth ed. [Barbourville, Ky., The Advocate pub-
      lishing co.] 1950.
      45 p. illus., map.   17 cm.

8331 Wallace, Daniel, d. 1859.
      Letter of Daniel Wallace, of South Carolina, to

his constituents. [Washington? 1850]
8 p.   23 cm.

8332 Wallace, Dillon, 1863-
Beyond the Mexican Sierras, by Dillon Wallace ...
with 75 illustrations from photographs by the
author, and a map. Chicago, A. C. McClurg & co.,
1910.
xxxv, 301 p. front., illus. (facsim.), plates,
fold. map.   21 cm.

8333 Wallace, William Stewart, 1884-
The family compact; a chronicle of the rebellion
in Upper Canada, by W. Stewart Wallace. Toronto,
Glasgow, Brook & company, 1915.
5 p.l., ix-xii, 172 p. col. front., 10 port.
18 1/2 cm.

8334 Walsh, William Shepard, 1854-1919, ed.
Abraham Lincoln and the London Punch: cartoons,
comments, and poems, published in the London
charivari, during the American civil war (1861-
1865) New York, Moffat, Yard & co., 1909.
113 p. illus.   24 cm.

8335 Walworth, Reuben H
Hyde genealogy; or, The descendants in the female
as well as the male lines from William Hyde of
Norwich. Albany, J. Munsell, 1864.
2 v.   22 cm.

8336 Wappäus, Johann Eduard, 1812-1879.
Geographie und statistik von Mexiko und Central-
amerika. Von dr. J. E. Wappäus ... Leipzig, J.
C. Hinrichs, 1863.
v, [1] p., 368 p.   23 cm.

8337 Warburton, Alexander Bannerman, 1852-1929.
A history of Prince Edward Island from its discovery in 1534 until the departure of Lieutenant-
Governor Ready in A.D. 1831, by A. B. Warburton
... St. John, N. B., Barnes & co., limited,
printers, 1923.
xv, 494 p. front., pl., ports., map, plans.
23 cm.

8338   [Warburton, George Drought] 1816-1857.
            The conquest of Canada. By the author of "Hoche-
        laga". New York, Harper & brothers, 1855.
        2 v.   20 cm.

8339   Ward, [Emily Elizabeth (Swinburne)] lady.
            Six views of the most important towns, and
        mining districts, upon the table land of Mexico.
        Drawn by Mrs. H. G. Ward, and engraved by Mr.
        Pye. With a statistical account of each. London,
        H. Colburn, 1829.
            2 p.l., 6 l. pl.   28 x 26 cm.

8340   Ward, Sir Henry George, 1797-1860.
            Gedrängtes gemälde des zustandes von Mexiko im
        jahre 1827. Von dem englischen geschäftsträger
        H. G. Ward ... Übertragen mit anmerkungen und
        vorwort von F. A. Rüder ... Leipzig, C. H. F.
        Hartmann, 1828.
            xxvi, 158 p.   21 cm.

8341   Ward, Sir Henry George, 1797-1860.
            Mexico im jahre 1827. Nach dem englischen des
        H. G. Ward ... Weimar, Verlag des Gr. H. S. pr.
        Landesindustrie-comptoirs, 1828-29.
            2 v. in 1.   22 1/2 cm.

8342   Ward, Sir Henry George.
            Mexico in 1827. By H. G. Ward, esp. ...
        London, H. Colburn, 1828.
            2 v. fronts., illus., plates (partly fold., 1
        col.) 2 fold. maps.   22 cm.

8343   Warner, Charles Dudley, 1829-1900.
            Baddeck, and that sort of thing. Boston, J. R.
        Osgood, 1874.
            191 p.   15 cm.

8344   Warren, Henry Waterman, 1838-
            Reminiscences of a Mississippi carpet-bagger, by
        Henry W. Warren. Holden, Mass., 1914.
            110 p. front., pl., ports.   23 cm.

8345   Warren, Louis Austin, 1885-
            Lincoln memorial building, Hodgenville, Kentucky

420

... Hodgenville, Ky., Herald news co. [c1921]
[11] p.   18 cm.

8346   Warren, Louis Austin, 1885-
Lincoln on metal, silk, and paper: cultivating
the collective instinct in children. Fort Wayne,
Indiana, Lincoln National Life Insurance Co.,
1929.
[4] p. illus.   20 cm.

8347   Warren, Louis Austin, 1885-
Lincoln sheet music; check list [by] Louis A.
Warren, director, Lincoln national life foundation. Fort Wayne, Ind., Lincolniana publishers,
1940.
[12] p.   16 1/2 cm.

8348   [Warren, Louis Austin] 1885-
Little known Lincoln episodes. [Ft. Wayne, Ind.,
Lincoln National Life Insurance Co. [n.d.]
8 p. illus.   18 cm.

8349   Warren, Louis Austin, 1885-
Louisville Lincoln loop; a day's tour in "old
Kentucky". Louisville, The Standard prtg. co.
[c1922]
43 p. illus.   22 cm.

8350   Warren, Louis Austin, 1885-
The slavery atmosphere of Lincoln's youth...
Fort Wayne, Indiana, Lincolniana publishers,
1933.
[16] p.   23 cm.

8351   Warren, Louis Austin, 1885-
Souvenir of Abraham Lincoln's birthplace, Hodgenville, Kentucky... Morganfield, Ky., Munford
publishing company [n.d.]
[32] p. illus.   24 cm.

8352   Warrick county Lincoln route association.
Brief prepared by the Warrick county Lincoln
route association and presented to and filed with
the Indiana Lincoln memorial highway commission
... to aid... in determining the correct route

over which Abraham Lincoln and his family travelled
when they moved from Indiana to Illinois in 1830
... [Boonville, Indiana, Boonville Standard, 1931]
75 p. illus. maps. 23 cm.

8353 Washburn, Robert Morris.
Calvin Coolidge, his first biography... Boston,
The Roosevelt Club [1924]
47 p. illus. 20 1/2 cm.

8354 Washington, D. C. Daily morning chronicle.
Assassination and death of Abraham Lincoln:
a contemporaneous account of a national tragedy,
as published in the Daily morning chronicle...
introd. by F. Ray Risdon. Gardena, Calif.,
Spanish American Institute press, 1925.
17 p. port. facsim. 20 cm.

8355 Watkins, Floyd C
James Kirke Paulding, humorist and critic of
American life... Nashville, Tenn., 1951.
29 p. 24 cm.

8356 Watson, Edmund Henry Lacon, 1865-
A conversational tour in America... London,
E. Matthews, 1914.
3 p.l., 9-191 p. 20 x 15 cm.

8357 Webb, Edwin Bonaparte, 1820-1901.
Memorial sermons: The capture of Richmond;
some of the results of the war; The assassination
of the president. Boston, G. C. Rand & Avery,
1865.
61 p. 23 cm.

8358 Wehe, Trude (Petersen) 1888-
Schatten über Mexiko. [1. und 2. Aufl.] Berlin,
Junge Generation Verlag [1943]
290 p. 20 cm.

8359 Weld, Isaac, 1774-1856.
Reise durch die Nordamerikanischen Freistaaten
und durch Ober- und Unter-Canada, in den Jahren
1795, 1796 und 1797. Aus dem Englischen frei
übersetzt. Berlin, Haude und Opener, 1800.

410 p.   20 cm.

8360   Weld, Isaac, 1774-1856.
Reisen durch die Staaten von Nordamerica, und
die Provinzen Ober- und Unter-Canada, während
den Jahren 1795, 1796 und 1797. Aus dem Englischen
übersetzt. Berlin und Hamburg 1801.
475 p.   2 fold. maps.   22 cm.

8361   Weld, Isaac, 1774-1856.
Reisen durch die Vereinigten Staaten von Nord-
Amerika und durch die provinzen Ober und Unter-
Canada, in den jahren 1795, 1796 und 1797, von
Isaac Weld. Nach der 2. ausg. aus dem englischen
übersetzt, mit anmerkungen ... Berlin, Oehmigke
dem jüngern, 1800.
2 v.   4 fold. pl.   22 cm.

8362   Weld, Isaac, 1774-1856.
Reizen door de Staaten van Noord-Amerika, en
de provintiën van Opper- en Neder-Canada; in de
jaaren 1795, 1796 en 1797. Ondernomen door Isaäc
Weld, junior. Naar den derden druk. Uit het
Engelsch vertaald door S. van Hoek ... In den
Haage, J. C. Leeuwestijn, 1801-02.
3 v. fold. plates, fold. maps.   24 cm.

8363   Weld, Isaac, 1774-1856.
Travels through the states of North America,
and the provinces of Upper and Lower Canada, during
the years 1795, 1796, and 1797. 2d ed. London,
Printed for J. Stockdale, 1799.
2 v. fold. plates, fold. maps.   22 cm.

8364   Weld, Isaac, 1774-1856.
Travels through the states of North America, and
the provinces of Upper and Lower Canada, during the
years 1795, 1796, and 1797. By Isaac Weld, junior.
4th ed. Illustrated and embellished with eight
plates. London, Printed for John Stockdale, 1800.
viii, 552 p. front., plates, fold. maps.   22 cm.

8365   Welles, Albert.
American family antiquity. New York, Society
Library, 1880.

4 v. pl., ports., photos, col. coats of arms.
24 1/2 cm.

8366 Welles, Alonzo Merritt.
Reminiscent ramblings, by A. M. Welles ...
Illustrations by the author. Denver, Colo., The
W. F. Robinson printing co., 1905.
459 p. illus. 19 1/2 cm.

8367 Wells, David Ames, 1828-1898.
A study of Mexico, by David A. Wells ... New
York, D. Appleton & co., 1887.
261 p. front., illus. 19 cm.

8368 Wharton, Joseph.
Mexico, by Joseph Wharton. [Philadelphia, Press
of J. B. Lippincott company] 1902.
[25] p. incl. illus., pl., port. 24 1/2 cm.

8369 What was thought of Amberglow, the Lincoln-Rutledge
booklet, by Arnold Francis Gates. West Leisenring,
Pa., Griglak printery, 1940.
[6] p. 20 cm.

8370 Whates, Harry Richmond, d. 1923.
Canada, the new nation; a book for the settler,
the emigrant and the politician, by H. R. Whates.
London, J. M. Dent & co.; New York, E. P. Dutton
& co., 1906.
xvii p., 1 l., 284 p. 16 pl. (incl. front.),
map. 19 1/2 cm.

8371 [Wheat, Marvin]
Travels on the western slope of the Mexican
Cordillera, in the form of fifty-one letters,
descriptive of much of this portion of the republic
of Mexico; of some of its chief cities and towns; of
the constitutional aspect and topographical features
of that region; and of its productions and capabilities, embracing its commerce, agriculture,
manufactures, industry, mineral and forest resources; as well as the manners and customs of the
people. By Cincinnatus. San Francisco, Whitton,
Towne & co., 1857.
xvi, [17]-438 p. front., illus. 19 cm.

424

8372 Wheeler, Arthur O
        The Selkirk Range, by A. O. Wheeler... Ottawa,
     Govt. print. bureau, 1905.
        xvii, [1], 459 p. front., plates, ports,
     diagr., profile and atlas of 9 fold. pl., 4 fold
     maps, fold profile. 24 1/2 cm.

8373 Wheeler, Joseph, 1836-1906.
        Fitz-John Porter... Fiat justitia: speech of
     Hon. Joseph Wheeler, of Alabama, in the House of
     representatives, Thursday, February 15, 1883.
     Washington [Govt. print. off.] 1883.
        85 p. 23 cm.

8374 [White, Charles Thomas] 1863-
        Grant's tribute to Lincoln. [Brooklyn, N. Y.,
     1932]
        18 p. facsim. 21 cm.

8375 White, Erskine Norman, 1833-1911.
        The personal influence of Abraham Lincoln; a
     sermon preached... June 1st, 1865... Presbyterian
     church, New Rochelle, N. Y. ... New York, J. A.
     Gray and Green, 1865.
        25 p. 23 cm.

8376 White, Josiah, 1781-1850.
        Josiah White's history, given by himself.
     [Philadelphia, Press of G. H. Buchanan company,
     1909?]
        75 p. 24 1/2 cm.

8377 White, Pliny Holton, 1822-1869.
        A sermon, occasioned by the assassination of
     Abraham Lincoln... preached at Coventry, Vermont,
     April 23, 1865. Brattleboro, Vt., Vermont
     record office, 1865.
        20 p. 22 cm.

8378 [White, Richard Grant] 1821-1885.
        The new gospel of peace, according to St.
     Benjamin. Book second. N. Y., S. Tousey [1863]
        48 p. 19 cm.

8379 White, Samuel, of Adams Co., Pa.

History of the American troops, during the late war, under the command of Cols. Fenton and Campbell. Giving an account of the crossing of the lake from Erie to Long Point; also, the crossing of Niagara ... The taking of Fort Erie, the battle of Chippewa, the imprisonment of Col. Bull, Major Galloway and the author ... together with an historical account of the Canadas. By Samuel White, of Adams County Penn. Baltimore, Published by the author. B. Edes, printer, 1829.
107 p. 18 cm.

8380 White, Stewart Edward, 1873-
The forest. Illustrated by Thomas Fogarty. New York, The Outlook Co., 1903.
276 p. 20 cm.

8381 Wide Awake Central committee.
To Hon. Abraham Lincoln, President elect of the United States... [n.p.] 1861.
[1] p. 21 cm.

8382 Wiesse, María, 1894-
... Croquis de viaje. Maderas originales de José Sabogal. Lima, Librería francesa científica y casa editorial E. Rosay, F. y E. Rosay, 1924.
104 p., 1 l. incl. plates. 17 1/2 cm.

8383 Wilcox, Walter Dwight, 1869-
The Rockies of Canada. A rev. and enl. ed. of "Camping in the Canadian Rockies," with ... illustrations from original photographs by the author ... New York and London, G. P. Putnam's sons, 1900.
ix p., 1 l., 309 p. front., pl., 2 maps in pocket. 25 cm.

8384 Wilkins, James Hepburn.
A glimpse of old Mexico; being the observations and reflections of a tenderfoot editor while on a journey in the land of Montezuma, by Jas. H. Wilkins. San Rafael, Cal., 1901.
115 p. illus. 20 1/2 cm.

8385 Willcox, Giles Buckingham, 1826-1922.

Funeral observances at New London, Connecticut,
in honor of Abraham Lincoln... April 19, 1865;
including the public addresses of Rev. G. B. Willcox and Rev. Thomas P. Field. New London, C.
Prince, 1865.
34 p. 21 cm.

8386 Williams, Cynric R
A tour through the island of Jamaica, from the
western to the eastern end, in the year 1823. By
Cynric R. Williams. 2d ed. London, T. Hurst, E.
Chance & co., 1827.
1 p.l., xviii, 352 p. front. 22 cm.

8387 Williams, W   H
Manitoba and the Northwest... Toronto, Hunter,
Ross & Company, 1882.
258 p. 22 cm.

8388 Williams, Wellington.
Appletons' new and complete United States
guide book for travellers: embracing the northern,
eastern, southern, and western states, Canada
Nova Scotia, New Brunswick, etc. Illustrated
with forty-five engraved maps. Including plans of
the principal cities of the union, and numerous
engravings. By W. Williams. New York, Appleton,
1850.
313, 140 p. illus., maps, plans. 17 cm.

8389 Williams, Wellington.
Appletons' railroad and steamboat companion.
Being a travellers' guide through the United
States of America, Canada, New Brunswick, and
Nova Scotia ... Illustrated by 30 maps, engraved
on steel, including four plans of cities, and
embellished with twenty-six engravings. By W.
Williams. New York, D. Appleton & company; Philadelphia, G. S. Appleton, 1849.
313 p. illus., 30 maps (part fold.; incl. front.)
16 1/2 cm.

8390 Wilson, Charles Henry, of Northallerton.
The wanderer in America, or Truth at home; comprising a statement of observations and facts rela-

tive to the United States & Canada, North America;
the result of an extensive personal tour, and from
sources of information the most authentic; including soil, climate, manners & customs, of its civil-
ized inhabitants & Indians, anecdotes, &c. of distinguished characters. By C. H. Wilson... Thirsk
[Eng.] Printed for the author by Henry Masterman, 182
120 p.   19 1/2 cm.

8391   Wilson, Herbert Michael.
Topography of Mexico. New York, 1897.
249-260 p.   map.
Reprint from the Journal of the American Geographical Society, v. 29, 1897.

8392   Wilson, James A
Bits of old Mexico, by James A. Wilson. San
Francisco, Cal. [c1910]
2 p.l., 156 p.   plates.   20 cm.

8393   Wilson, Lawrence Maurice, 1896-1962.
L'appel du Chibougamou. "L'histoire d'une région
minière du Québec." [Montréal, Thérien frères,
ltd., 1956]
184 p.   19 cm.

8394   Wilson, Robert Anderson, 1812-1872.
Mexico and its religion; with incidents of travel
in that country during parts of the years 1851-52-
53-54, and historical notices of events connected
with places visited. By Robert A. Wilson ... New
York, Harper & brothers, 1855.
1 p.l., xiii, [15]-406 p.   incl. illus., plates,
front. (port.)   20 cm.

8395   Wilson, Robert Anderson, 1812-1872.
Mexico: its peasnats and its priests; or, Adventures and historical researches in Mexico and its
silver mines during parts of the years 1851-52-53-
54, with an exposé of the fabulous character of the
story of the conquest of Mexico by Cortez. By Robert
A. Wilson ... With engravings. A new ed. New York,
Harper & brothers; London, S. Low, son & co., 1856.
1 p.l., xii, [15], 418 p.   incl. illus. (incl.
map), plates. front. (port.)   18 cm.

8396   Wilson, Robert Anderson, 1812-1872.
A new history of the conquest of Mexico. In
which Las Casas' denunciations of the popular
historians of that war are fully vindicated. By
Robert Anderson Wilson ... Philadelphia, J.
Challen & son, 1859.
xx, [21]-539 p. incl. front., illus. 25 cm.

8397   Wilson, Samuel (writer on temperance)
Abraham Lincoln an apostle of temperance and
prohibition: base slanders refuted. [Westerville,
O., American issue pub. co., 191-?]
14 p. illus. 21 cm.

8398   Wilson, William Thomas, 1834-1890.
The death of President Lincoln: a sermon
preached in St. Peter's church, Albany, N. Y. ...
April 19, 1865... Albany, Weed, Parsons & co.,
1865.
25 p. 23 cm.

8399   Wimpffen, François Alexandre Stanislaus, baron de.
... Saint Domingue à la vielle de la révolution
(souvenirs du baron de Wimpffen) Annotés de'après
les documents d'archives et les mémoires. Illustrations documentaires. Paris, L. Michaud [1911]
vi, [7]-190 p. illus. (incl. map, ports.)
19 cm.

8400   Wineburgh, M[ichael]
Where to spend the winter months. A birdseye
view of a trip to Mexico, via Havana. By M.
Wineburgh. New York, M. Wineburgh & co., 1880.
69 p. illus. 22 cm.

8401   Winsor, Justin, 1831-1897.
Cartier to Frontenac... Geographical discovery
in the interior of North America in its historical
relations, 1534-1700; with full cartographical
illustrations from contemporary sources... Boston
and New York, Houghton, Mifflin and company, 1900.
viii, 379 p. incl. illus., ports., maps, plans.
23 cm.

8402   Winter, Nevin Otto, 1869-

Mexico and her people of to-day; an account of the customs, characteristics, amusements, history and advancement of the Mexicans, and the development and resources of their country, by Nevin O. Winter; illustrated from original photographs by the author and C. R. Birt. New rev. ed. Boston, L. C. Page & company [inc.] 1923.
3 p.l., v-xvi, 548 p. front., plates, ports., fold. maps. 21 1/2 cm.

8403 Winthrop, Theodore, 1828-1861.
The canoe and the saddle, adventures among the northwestern rivers and forests, and Isthmiana. By Theodore Winthrop... Boston, Ticknor and Fields, 1863 [c1862]
375 p. 19 cm.

8404 Wirt, William, 1772-1834.
The life and character of Patrick Henry, by William Wirt... Philadelphia, Porter & Coates [188-?]
xvi, 19-443, [447]-468 p. incl. front. (port.) 19 1/2 cm.

8405 Wirth, Conrad Louis, 1899-
... Address... at dedication of Visitor center, Abraham Lincoln National Historical Park, Kentucky ... May 30, 1959.
5 p.

8406 Wise, Henry Augustus, 1819-1869.
Los gringos: or, An inside view of Mexico and California, with wanderings in Peru, Chili, and Polynesia. By Lieut. Wise, U.S.N. New York, Baker and Scribner, 1849.
xvi, 453 p. 19 1/2 cm.

8407 Wise, Henry Augustus, 1819-1869.
Los gringos: or, An inside view of Mexico and California, with wanderings in Peru, Chili, and Polynesia; by Lieut. Wise, U.S.N. New York, Baker and Scribner, 1850.
xvi, 453 p. 18 1/2 cm.

8408 Wislizenus, Adolphus, 1810-1889.

Denkschrift über eine reise nach Nord-Mexiko,
verbunden mit der expedition des obersten Donniphan,
in den jahren 1846 und 1847. Von dr. A. Wislizenus.
Aus dem englischen übertragen von George M. von
Ross. Mit einem wissenschaftlichen anhange und
drei karten. Braunschweig, F. Vieweg und sohn,
1850.
    viii, 211 p. incl. tables. 3 fold. maps.   22 cm.

8409 Witter, Frau Marina (Krebs) 1838-
    Das heutige Mexiko. Land und volk unter
Spaniens herrschaft, sowie nach erlangter selb-
ständigkeit. Unter benutzung der zuverlässigsten
und neusten quellen hrsg. von Th. Armin [pseud.]
Mit 150 in den text gedruckten abbildungen, nebst
sechs tonbildern. Leipzig, O. Spamer, 1865.
    xii, 427, [1] p. incl. front., illus., plates.
20 1/2 cm.

8410 [Wollschläger, Alfred] 1901-
    Pelzjäger, prärien und präsidenten; fahrten und
erlebnisse zwischen New York und Alaska, von A. E.
Johann [pseud.] Mit 3 karten und 45 aufnahmen.
Berlin, Ullstein [ᶜ1937]
    316, [2] p. plates, ports., maps (1 fold.)
22 cm.

8411 Wood, Louis Aubrey, 1883-
    The Red river colony; a chronicle of the begin-
nings of Manitoba, by Louis Aubrey Wood. Toronto,
Glasgow, Brook & company, 1915.
    5 p.l., ix-xi, 152 p. 4 pl., 4 port. (incl.
col. front.), fold. map, plan. 18 1/2 cm.

8412 Wood, William Charles Henry, 1864-
    The fight for Canada; a sketch from the history
of the great imperial war. Definitive ed. Boston,
Little, Brown, 1906.
    xx, [1], 370 p. 2 ports., 2 fold. maps.   23 cm.

8413 Wood, William Charles Henry, 1864-   , ed.
    The logs of the conquest of Canada, ed., with an
introduction, by Lt.-Colonel William Wood...
Toronto, The Champlain society, 1909.
    xxvi, 335 p. 4 fold. maps (in pocket) 25 cm.

8414 Wood, William Charles Henry, 1964-
       The passing of New France; a chronicle of
       Montcalm, by William Wood. Toronto, Glasgow,
       Brook & company, 1914.
       5 p.l., xiii-xv, 149 p. 4 port. (incl. col.
       front.), 2 maps (1 fold.), 3 plans. 18 1/2 cm.

8415 Woodbury, Augustus, 1825-1895.
       A sketch of the character of Abraham Lincoln:
       a discourse preached in the Westminster church,
       Providence, R. I., Thursday, June 1, 1865, by
       Augustus Woodbury. Providence, S. S. Rider and
       brother, 1865.
       28 p.   29 cm.

8416 Woodbury, Augustus, 1825-1895.
       The son of God calleth the dead to life: a
       sermon suggested by the assassination of Abraham
       Lincoln... Westminster church, Providence, R. I.,
       Sunday, April 16, 1865. Providence, S. S. Rider
       & brother, 1865.
       27 p.   19 cm.

8417 Woodley, William J
       The impressions of an Englishman in America, by
       William Woodley ... New York, W. J. Woodley,
       1910.
       6 p.l., 3-180 p. front. (port.)   18 cm.

8418 Woods, Nicholas Augustus.
       The Prince of Wales in Canada and the United
       States. By N. A. Woods ... London, Bradbury &
       Evans, 1861.
       xv, 438 p. fold. map.   19 1/2 cm.

8419 Words in affliction; or, Lays of the spirit land,
       by M. C. L. New York, W. H. Kelley & Bro., 1868.
       49 p.

8420 Work, John.
       ... The journal of John Work, January to October,
       1835. With an introduction and notes by Henry
       Drummond Des. Victoria, B. C., Printed by Charles
       F. Banfield, 1945.
       98 p. illus., facsim.   24 1/2 cm.

8421 Wright, Irene Aloha, 1879-
      Cuba. New York, Macmillan Co., 1910.
      xiv, 512 p. plates, map.   20 cm.

8422 Wright, Mrs. Marie (Robinson) 1866-1914.
      Picturesque Mexico, by Marie Robinson Wright.
      Philadelphia, J. B. Lippincott company [c1897]
      445 p. incl. front., illus., ports.   32 1/2 x
      26 cm.

8423 Wyllie, Robert Crichton, 1798-1865.
      México. Noticia sobre su hacienda pública
      bajo el gobierno español y después de la indepen-
      dencia ... Cálculos sobre la deuda pública interior
      y esterior. Presupuestos aprócsimados de sus
      ingresos y egresos ... tablas ilustrativas sobre
      sistema mercantil, manufacturero y prohibitivo, y
      observaciones sobre la colonizacion ... dirigido al
      caballero George B. Robinson, presidente de la
      comisión de tenadores de bonos españoles y améri-
      canos ... por Roberto Crichton Wyllie ... México,
      Impr. de I. Cumplido, 1845.
      2 p.l., 91, 37, [8] p. fold. tables.   23 cm.

8424 Wyss-Dunant, Édouard.
      ... Sur les hausts-plateaux mexicains; des
      volcans aux forêts vierges; avec 29 illustrations
      hors-tevte [!] Neuchâtel, Paris, V. Attinger [1937]
      3 p.l., [9]-205 p., 1 l. plates.   19 cm.

                            Y

8425 Yardley, Edmund, ed.
      Addresses at the funeral of Henry George.
      Sunday, October 31, 1897 at the Grand Central
      Palace, New York City. Compiled by Edmund Yardley,
      with an introduction by Henry George, Jr. New
      York, Reprinted by the Robert Schalkenbach Founda-
      tion, 1931.
      55 p.   17 cm.

8426 Yeaman, George Helm, 1829-1908.

Abraham Lincoln: an address before the Commandery
of the state of Colorado, Military Order of the
Loyal Legion of the United States, Denver, Feb. 13,
1899. Denver, 1899.
25 p. 22 cm.

8427 [Young, Edward James] 1829-1906.
The lesson of the hour. [Boston? 1865?]
caption title, 9 p. 23 1/2 cm.

8428 Young, Egerton Ryerson, 1840-1909.
By canoe and dog-train among the Cree
and Salteaux Indians... With an introduction by
Mark Guy Pearse... New York, Hunt & Eaton; Cincinnati, Cranston & Stowe, 1891.
xvi, 267 p. front., illus., port. 20 1/2 cm.

8429 Young Men's Christian Association, Chicago.
Eulogistic services, under the auspices of the
Young Men's Christian Association, of Chicago, in
memory of Abraham Lincoln, at Bryan Hall, on
Saturday, April 22d, 1865, at 8 p.m., George W.
Kimbark... presiding. [n.p.] 1865.
[3] p. folder. 20 cm.

8430 Young Men's Republican Union, New York.
For President, Abraham Lincoln, of Illinois; for
Vice-president, Hannibal Hamlin, of Maine... New
York, Young Men's Republican Union, 1860.
4 p. 20 cm.

8431 Yount, Charles Allen.
William Bross, 1813-1890... Foreword by Herbert
McComb Moore. Lake Forest, Ill., Lake Forest
College, 1940.
30 p. front. (port.) illus. 28 cm.

8432 Yourtree, Samuel L   , d. 1880.
A sermon, delivered in the Central Methodist
Episcopal church, Springfield, Ohio, April 19th,
1865, on the occasion of the funeral of Abraham
Lincoln... Springfield, O., News & Republic job
printing rooms, 1865.
16 p. 21 cm.

8433 Yucatan.
Yucatán y Belice. Colección de documentos importantes que se refieren al tratado de 8 de julio de 1893, celebrado entre el Sr. Lic. Ignacio Mariscal en representación de México, y Sir Spencer Saint Jhon en representación de la Gran Bretaña. Mérida, Tip. de G. Canto, 1894.
1 p.l., 172 p. fold. map. 22 1/2 cm.

8434 Yurami, Antonio Miguel.
Oracion panegirica, que en la solemne fiesta celebrada en honor del catolico rey s.^{n} Fernando en su dia 30 de mayo da 1797. por el real Consulado de la m.n.é.ille ciudad de Santandér segun sus estatutos dixo el m.r.p. fr. Antonio Miguel Yurami... Dala a luz don Josef Gutierrez de Palacio... Santander, En la oficina de d. Francisco Xaviér Riesgo, impresor de dicho real Consulado [1797]
1 p.l., 33 p.   22 cm.

Z

8435 Zabriskie, Andrew Christian, 1853-
A descriptive catalog of political and memorial medals struck in honor of Abraham Lincoln..., New York, Printed for the author, 1873.
32 p.   26 cm.

8436 Zamorano, Rodrigo, b. ca. 1542.
Cronologia y reportorio de la razon de las tiempos. El mas copioso que hasta oi se á visto. Compvesto por el licenciado Rodrigo Çamorano ... Dirigido a don Pedro Fernandez de Cordova y Aguilar. marques de Priego ... Emendado y añadido por el autor: con el lunario y fiestas movibles hasta el año 1654. Es obra utilissima para toda la republica. Con privilegio. Tassado a tres maravedis el pliego. En Sevilla, En la imprenta de Rodrigo de Cabrera, 1594.
4 p.l., 380 (i.e. 390) numbered l., [8] p. illus. (incl. port., maps)   24 cm.

8437　Zaremba, Charles W
　　　　The merchants' and tourists' guide to Mexico,
　　　by Chas. W. Zaremba ...　Chicago, The Althrop
　　　publishing house, 1883.
　　　　1 p.l., 182 p.　7 fold. maps (incl. front.)
　　　24 1/2 cm.

8438　Zenkovich, Vsevoled Pavlovich, 1910–
　　　　В дальнем снием море.　Москва, "Мысль," 1969.
　　　　204 p. with illus. and maps., 8 l. of illus.
　　　21 cm.

8439　Zepeda Rincón, Tomás.
　　　　Geografía y atlas de la República mexicana, por
　　　el profesor Tomás Zepeda Rincón ... Revisada y
　　　corregida por el ingeniero José Luis Osorio
　　　Mondragón ...　México, D. F., 1934.
　　　　136 p.　illus. (part col., incl. maps), diagrs.
　　　28 x 23 cm.

8440　Zepeda Rincón, Tomás.
　　　　La República Mexicana, geografía y atlas; con la
　　　"división pentagráfica" de la República Mexicana
　　　según José Luis Osorio Mondragón. 2. ed.　México,
　　　Editorial Progreso, 1941.
　　　　152 p.　col. illus., col. maps.　30 cm.

8441　Zerecero, Anastasio, 1799–1875.
　　　　Memorias para la historia de las revoluciones en
　　　México.　Escritas por el lic. Anastasio Zerecero.
　　　[v. 1]　Mexico, Impr. del gobierno, a cargo de
　　　J. M. Sandoval, 1869.
　　　　1 p.l., ii, 608 p.　3 port.　20 cm.

8442　Zúñiga Montúfar, Tobías.
　　　　... Selecciones de la tribuna y de la prensa.
　　　San José, Costa Rica, Editorial Spolo, 1935.
　　　　222 p.　21 1/2 cm.

8443　Zurita, Fernando.
　　　　Theologicarvm de Indis qvaestionvm, enchiridion
　　　primum.　Auctore licentiato Ferdinãdo Zurita ...
　　　Ad illustriss. & reuerendiss. dominum, d. Gomecium
　　　Zapatam ... Sub correctione sanctae Ecclesio romane.
　　　Madriti, apud Querinum Gerardum, Anno 1586.
　　　　8 p.l., 128 unnumbered l., [8] p.　23 cm.

WITHDRAWAL